COURSE
OUTLINE

First Edition ▸ 1994
Second Printing ▸ 1995

Education Law

Frank D. Aquila, Ph.D., J.D.
Professor of Educational Administration
Cleveland State University

Author of over 100 books, monographs and articles, including:
Race Equity in Education: The History of School Desegregation
School Desegregation: On the Cutting Edge

James J. Petzke, J.D.
Attorney at Law

NORMAN S. GOLDENBERG
Senior Editor

PETER TENEN
Managing Editor

CHERYL STEETS
Editorial Director

casenote EDUCATION SERIES

Published and Distributed by: CASENOTES PUBLISHING CO., INC.
1640 Fifth Street, Suite 208, Santa Monica, CA 90401

ISBN 0-87457-300-9
Second Printing ▸ 1995

With this Course Outline, Casenotes Publishing Co., Inc., introduces a dual-purpose reference work for those who are interested in the impact of the American legal system on public education. *Education Law* is a comprehensive guide to the current state of the law of public education. Teaching professionals, administrators, school board members and other education officials and employees will find this compact reference work a handy, pertinent, and user-friendly guide to questions and issues that may arise regarding the basic framework of education and the continuing impact that courts and state legislatures exert upon it. *Education Law* also provides an overview of an important legal subject area for those who are interested in developing a better understanding of the "bigger picture" of public education.

Furthermore, *Education Law* is an invaluable tool for students of education law, both at the collegiate and graduate (law school, masters and doctoral) levels. To law school students and law professors, Casenotes Publishing Company has long been known for its accurate and insightful *Casenote Legal Briefs* and *Casenote Law Outlines*. In *Education Law,* Casenotes provides the student of education law with in-depth briefs of 118 federal and state court cases. A number of these cases have been decided very recently and thus are at the cutting edge of the development of our American educational system. Briefs of earlier precedent-setting cases are also included since they are of great importance and will likely have an effect on the education system for years to come.

Important cases are discussed or referred to in outline-style text at the beginning of each chapter so that the reader may begin his studies by coming to a general understanding of a particular subject matter area and then expand upon it by referring to the related case briefs which conclude each chapter. Also, for facility of classroom use, the cross-reference chart in the back of the book compares the contents of leading education law textbooks to materials in the outline portion of this work. For similar ease of reference, selections from the U.S. Constitution and various important education law statutes are also provided in the back of the book, as are a glossary, table of cases, table of code sections, and index.

Two features of the book should be mentioned. The word *"See"* is used to refer the reader to a case brief that appears in this book, whereas references to other cases not briefed here appear with a citation but without the word "see." Also, in an attempt to provide gender-neutral text, we have alternated use of masculine and feminine pronouns throughout the book.

This Course Outline reflects the state of the law today; however, we recommend that anyone facing pending legal action always consult an attorney for advice.

We welcome your comments and questions with regard to the outline-style text and case briefs contained in *Education Law*. Please write us at:

> 1640 Fifth Street, Suite 208
> Santa Monica, CA 90401

Sincerely,

CASENOTES PUBLISHING CO., INC.

COURSE OUTLINE – SUPPLEMENT REQUEST FORM

Casenotes Publishing Co., Inc. prides itself on producing the most current study outlines available. Sometimes between major revisions the authors of the outline series will issue supplements to update their respective outlines to reflect any recent changes in the material. Certain subjects change more quickly than others, and thus some outlines may be supplemented, while others may not be supplemented at all.

In order to determine whether you should send us this supplement request form, first check the printing date that appears by the subject name below. If this outline is less than one year old, it is unlikely that there will be a supplement for it. If it is older, you may wish to write, telephone, or fax us for current information. You might also check to see whether a supplement has been included with your *Course Outline* or has been provided to your bookstore. If it is necessary to order the supplement directly from us, it will be supplied without charge, but we do insist that you send a <u>stamped, self-addressed return envelope</u>. If you request a supplement for an outline that does not have one, you will receive the latest *Casenotes* catalogue. If you wish to request a supplement for this outline:

#3000, EDUCATION LAW, FIRST EDITION, SECOND PRINTING ► 1995, by Aquila and Petzke

Please follow the instructions below.

► **TO OBTAIN YOUR COMPLIMENTARY SUPPLEMENT(S), *YOU MUST FOLLOW THESE INSTRUCTIONS PRECISELY IN ORDER FOR YOUR REQUEST TO BE ACKNOWLEDGED.***

1. **REMOVE AND SEND THIS ENTIRE REQUEST FORM:** You *must* send this *original* page, which acts as your proof of purchase and provides the information regarding which supplements, if any, you need. The request form is only valid for any supplement for the outline in which it appears. *No photocopied or written requests will be honored.*

2. **SEND A STAMPED, SELF-ADDRESSED, FULL-SIZE (9" X 12") ENVELOPE:** *Affix enough postage to cover at least 3 oz.* We regret that we absolutely cannot fill and/or acknowledge requests unaccompanied by a stamped, self-addressed envelope.

3. **PLEASE GIVE US THE FOLLOWING INFORMATION:**

   Name: _____ Telephone: (____)_____

   Address: _____ Apt: _____

   City: _____ State: _____ Zip: _____

   Name and location of bookstore where you purchased this *Course Outline:* _____

   _____

   Any comments regarding *Course Outlines?* _____

   _____

CASENOTES PUBLISHING CO., INC., 1640 Fifth Street, Suite 208, Santa Monica, CA 90401
(310) 395-6500 ● FAX (310) 458-2020

TABLE OF CONTENTS

TC

TC

ABBREVIATIONS

A.	Atlantic
A.2d	Atlantic, Second Series
ADA	Americans with Disabilities Act
aff'd	affirmed
BNA	Bureau of National Affairs
Cal.3d	California Reports, Third Series
cert.den.	certiorari denied
CFR	Code of Federal Regulations
Ct. App.	Court of Appeal
EEOC	Equal Employment Opportunity Commission
EHA	Education of the Handicapped Act
EMR	educable mentally retarded
F. Supp.	Federal Supplement
F.	Federal Reporter
F.2d	Federal Reporter, Second Series
FAPE	free, appropriate public education
HEW	Health, Education and Welfare
IDEA	Individuals with Disabilities Education Act
IEP	individualized education program
L. Ed.	Lawyer's Edition Reports

COURSE
OUTLINE

Education Law

by Frank D. Aquila

*To my wife, Margaret, and
our wonderful son Frank*

by James J. Petzke

To Steve and Leigh, fondly

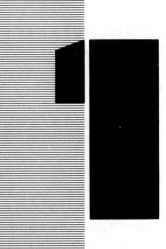

INTRODUCTION TO THE LEGAL SYSTEM AND LEGAL RESEARCH

▶ **CHAPTER SUMMARY**

CHAPTER 1: INTRODUCTION TO THE LEGAL SYSTEM AND LEGAL RESEARCH

Introduction: The material included in this book — case briefs, outlines, and textbook/treatise reference information — provides a summary of the most important aspects of the law regarding education. At the heart of this body of knowledge, commonly identified as education law or school law, is statutory and case law.

Statutory law is made up of civil and criminal laws, or "statutes." Statutes are enacted by a governmental body authorized to pass such laws. For example, Congress enacts federal statutes, state legislatures enact state statutes, and local elected bodies, such as city councils, enact municipal ordinances. *Case law* refers to the body of written decisions that have been rendered at the conclusion of lawsuits, or "cases," that come before various courts.

As to the *types* of courts that the reader will need to be familiar with, there are two: trial courts and the appellate courts. Trial courts render two types of decisions, those based on law and those made with respect to facts. Trial court decisions made on the basis of law are usually made by a judge; those made with respect to facts involve a jury. Appellate courts generally review the decisions of trial courts in order to determine whether proper procedures were followed and whether the correct law was applied. In most cases, only appellate courts render decisions which, when published, become case law.

Another means of categorizing courts is by the nature of the disputes that particular courts consider. In the civil law context, legal disputes arising between two or more parties usually arise within a particular state or are based on state law principles. Such suits are properly filed in state courts. On the other hand, matters that arise in more than one state or that specifically involve the federal government, federal laws, or federal constitutional issues are filed in federal courts.

In the state court system, a case is first heard by a trial court. An appeal "of right" is available to the state appellate level, while the state supreme court has discretion to either grant or deny further review on appeal. This discretionary review is called "certiorari."

The process is similar in the federal court system. A federal case is first filed in a federal district court, the "trial court" of the federal system. On appeal, the case will be heard in the federal court of appeals in the particular circuit where proper jurisdiction is established. The highest federal court, sometimes referred to as the "court of last resort," is the U.S. Supreme Court. Again, an appeal to the Supreme Court is discretionary; the court may either grant or deny certiorari.

Finally, with respect to education law in particular, a little background about the educational system in this country is in order. In the United States, education is the responsibility of state government. Despite the manner in which local school board members are appointed or elected, they are state, not local, officials.

Obviously, state legislatures cannot foresee (and therefore cannot legislate with respect to) every important education-related issue that may arise. For this reason, local school boards have been granted implied authority to set policies and resolve problems as they arise. The exercise of such powers is permitted so long as local school board actions do not conflict with state or federal laws and regulations. This grant of implied authority was actually developed by the courts (and, hence, is a product of case law) as an efficient method of granting stature to local school board actions that appear educationally sound. When school board actions are not sound, litigation between the aggrieved parties and the school board may be — and often is — initiated.

Before a lawsuit is tried, the parties must assess their positions in light of existing statutes and case law — the "building blocks" upon which lawsuits are initiated and defended. We shall now take a closer look at the nature of case law.

I. CASE LAW

CASE LAW

A. **Precedent.** A written court decision in a specific area of law establishes a "precedent." Reliance on precedent is sometimes referred to as the doctrine of "stare decisis." Precedents guide future courts as they decide certain issues and thereafter write their own concise rules of law with respect to the issues before them. The state and federal trial courts will then rely on the appellate decisions rendered in their jurisdiction, unless a "compelling case" indicates that the precedent should not be followed but rather overruled. The only court that can change a precedent is the court that set it or one of higher authority.

B. **Citation.** A citation is how a case is named, located, and referred to. For example, in the desegregation case of *Brown v. Board of Education*, the official citation is:

Brown v. Board of Education, 347 U.S. 483 (1954).

The "U.S." in the citation refers to a collection of bound volumes known as the *United States Reports*, or *U.S. Reports*, the official repository of U.S. Supreme Court decisions. One can find the full text of the *Brown* decision in volume 347 of the *U.S. Reports*, at page 483. The citation also lets us know that the case was decided by the Supreme Court in 1954.

C. **Parallel Citations.** In most cases, a decision may also be referred to by a parallel citation. Each parallel citation leads the reader to the same opinion but in a different set of volumes (i.e., a different reporter system).

1

For example, the full citation for *Brown v. Board of Education* is as follows: *Brown v. Board of Education,* 347 U.S. 483, 74 S.Ct. 686, 98 L.Ed 873 (1954).

"S.Ct." refers to the *Supreme Court Reporter,* an unofficial set of volumes, or reporter series, that parallels the official *U.S. Reports* series. Similarly, "L.Ed." refers to the unofficial reporter series known as the *United States Supreme Court Reports, Lawyers' Edition* (hereinafter, *"Lawyers' Edition"*).

Brown v. Board of Education may now be located in any one of these three publications: the *U.S. Reports,* the *Supreme Court Reporter,* and the *Lawyers' Edition.* As "public documents," official court decisions are not subject to copyright law; private publishing companies may thus copy them and reprint them in any format.

D. Court Reports. Court reports are volumes that contain reported appellate decisions and opinions from various geographical jurisdictions. There are reports for every appellate jurisdiction, including the U.S. Supreme Court, the federal courts of appeals, and state appellate courts. An "official" publication is one that is published by or for a branch of government. For example, the *U.S. Reports* series, the "official" collection of U.S. Supreme Court decisions, is published by the U.S. Government Printing Office. The term "reporter," as in *Supreme Court Reporter,* usually refers to unofficial versions of decisions published by private publishing companies.

DESCRIPTIONS OF PUBLICATIONS

II. DESCRIPTIONS OF PUBLICATIONS

A. United States Reports. As discussed above, the *United States Reports* series (abbreviated "U.S.") is published officially by the U.S. Government Printing Office. The *U.S. Reports* series citation is used when citing U.S. cases in the U.S. Supreme Court and other federal courts. The official citation always precedes a parallel or unofficial citation.

B. Lawyer's Edition. The *Lawyers' Edition* (abbreviated "L.Ed.") is published unofficially by the Lawyers Cooperative Publishing Company. The official texts of cases, as published in the *U.S. Reports,* are published in this series. The L.Ed. (first series) includes volumes 1 through 351 of the *U.S. Reports;* the L.Ed.2d (second series) contains volumes 352 et seq. of the *U.S. Reports. Lawyers' Edition* features parallel citation references to the official *U.S. Reports* printed on the spine of each of its volumes (both editions). Also, within each volume, further parallel citations to the *U.S. Reports* are printed at the beginning of or within each case.

C. Supreme Court Reporter. The *Supreme Court Reporter* (abbreviated "S.Ct.") is unofficially published by West Publishing Company. As with *Lawyers' Edition,* the same cases that are officially published in the *U.S. Reports* are unofficially published in the *Supreme Court Reporter.* This series also has parallel citation references to the official *U.S. Reports.* Such citations appear on the spine of each S.Ct. volume and at the beginning of each case, at the top of the page. For citation accuracy, S.Ct. text pages must correspond to the official *U.S. Reports* pages. Therefore, each S.Ct. page includes a cross-reference to the corresponding page in the official *U.S.* version of the case. Note that the unofficial reporters are published with these pagination features so that citations to the *U.S.* series can be made without actually having to turn to corresponding *U.S.* volumes for specific page cites.

D. United States Law Week. The *United States Law Week* (abbreviated "U.S.L.W.") is an unofficial publication of the Bureau of National Affairs (BNA). It is a loose-leaf, two-volume set that is published annually. The material is sent to the publication's subscribers in loose-leaf form, hole-punched so that it can easily be placed in the volume's three-ring binder. This service affords a subscriber quick access to newly released U.S. Supreme Court opinions. Newly released opinion texts are mailed to subscribers on a weekly basis; other reporter series generally require 6–8 weeks' lead time prior to publication. Citations to this unofficial publication are permitted when U.S., L.Ed.2d, and S.Ct. citations are not yet available.

E. Federal Court Reporters. Federal court cases are published by private publishing companies in the following series:

1. *Federal Reporter.* The *Federal Reporter* (abbreviated "F.") is the only reporter series in which all U.S. Courts of Appeals cases are published. The set contains two series; the first series contains volumes 1–300, with published cases from nine federal circuit courts of appeals and the D.C. circuit. The second series (abbreviated "F.2d") contains all of the published decisions from the same federal circuits as well as several new federal circuits and the U.S. Court of Claims, the Court of Customs and Patent Appeals, and the Temporary Emergency Court of Appeals. When citing a circuit court case, the circuit from which the case originated is always included. *E.g.,* 790 F.2d 345 (9th Cir. 1987).

2. *Federal Supplement.* The *Federal Supplement* (abbreviated "F. Supp.") is published unofficially by West Publishing Company. This set contains cases which are decided in the federal district courts, which are subdivisions of the federal judicial appellate circuits. Every state has at least one federal district court. Depending on the size of the state, there may be more than one. As

with federal courts of appeals decisions, there is no "official" publication for federal district court decisions. The *Federal Supplement* contains only those cases which are selected for publication and is the exception to the rule that only appellate court cases and not trial court cases are published. Federal district court judges have discretion as to whether or not a decision will be published. Usually the cases released for publication are those which the trial court considers unique or which offer guidance on a significant issue that has not previously been litigated. Citations in this set should include the federal district in which the case originated. *E.g.*, 345 F.Supp. 700 (C.D. Calif. 1985).

F. Regional Reporters. The National Reporter System (NRS) is a network of reporters which includes seven regional reporters containing all published state appellate court decisions. For example, the *North Eastern Reporter* (abbreviated "N.E." or "N.E.2d") includes state appellate cases from the states of Illinois, Indiana and Ohio. If a state publishes its own "official" appellate reports, citations should include both the official report citation and the regional reporter citation.

THE COMPONENTS OF OUR CASE BRIEFS

III. THE COMPONENTS OF OUR CASE BRIEFS

Each case brief in this book contains the following parts:

A. Case Caption. This is the official cite, with parallel citations where appropriate. By referring to this cite, the reader may obtain a copy of the full text of the case from any law library.

B. Nature of Case. This is a brief statement of the nature of the case, or of the area of law, involved.

C. General Rule of Law. The general rule of law is the court's legal resolution of the issue. It is the generally accepted rule that arises based on the facts at hand. The rule of law may be derived in whole or in part from previously decided cases in the same or other jurisdictions or higher courts. Please note, however, that in many cases the precedent is sometimes abrogated or changed in order to effect a more judicious decision.

D. Procedural Summary. This section identifies the party who initiated the action (the "plaintiff"); the party who, in response to the plaintiff's lawsuit, has been forced to defend itself (the "defendant"); and all lower court decisions up to but not including the final disposition of the instant case. You must read through to the end of the case to determine the final disposition (in the section entitled **"Holding and Decision"**).

E. **Facts.** This section explains the factual background, including why the case was initiated and/or appealed to a higher court. Prior court dispositions have again been included for a cursory review of lower court decisions prior to the final disposition.

F. **Issue.** The issue is the crux of the case. It is framed in the form of a question to be answered by the the court. Although many issues may be present in any given case, most courts usually narrow in on the one or two that are the most crucial.

G. **Holding and Decision.** The holding is the final disposition of the case by the last or final court that heard it. The judge's name (when available) appears in parentheses at the beginning of this section.

H. **Comment.** This section includes our editorial analysis of the case, where appropriate, and the case's implications for or applicability to your roles as students, educators, and administrators in the field of education.

NOTES:

NOTES

THE CHURCH-STATE DISTINCTION

▶ **CHAPTER SUMMARY**

CHAPTER 2: THE CHURCH-STATE DISTINCTION

QUICK REFERENCE RULES OF LAW

1. **Government neutrality toward religion:** The First Amendment Establishment Clause prohibits government from passing laws that aid a religion or prefer one religion over another. (§ I.A.)

2. **Government noninterference in religious practices:** The First Amendment Free Exercise Clause prohibits government from interfering with legitimate religious practices. (§ I.B.)

3. **Direct government financial aid to students:** Generally, government may provide financial and material assistance directly to parochial school students (as opposed to parochial schools or parents of parochial school students) without running afoul of the Establishment Clause. (§ II.C.)

4. **Direct government financial aid to parochial schools:** Most attempts to provide financial support to parochial schools for the general educational needs of parochial students are unconstitutional because they result in an "excessive entanglement" between church and state in violation of the Establishment Clause. (§ II.C.3.)

5. **Public school on-campus religious instruction:** Public school students may not be released from their regular classes to attend religious classes held in public schools, but they may be released from school to attend such classes if they are held off campus. (§ III.A.)

6. **Prayer in public school:** Bible-reading, prayer, student-led prayer groups, and silent meditation conducted in public schools (in class or at school ceremonies) violate the Establishment Clause. (§ III.B.)

7. **General nonreligious bible study:** The Bible may be studied as part of a general educational program. (§ III.B.2.a)

8. **Religious dress for teachers:** Public school teachers may not wear religious dress or insignia in public schools. (§ III.C.1.)

9. **Distribution/posting of religious literature:** Religious literature may not be distributed, and religious sayings may not be posted, in public schools. (§ III.C.2.)

10. **Flag salute/pledge of allegiance:** Students may not be required to salute the American flag or pledge allegiance if doing so offends their sincerely held religious beliefs. (§ IV.B.)

Introduction: Government must remain *neutral* toward religion, which means that it must not act or must refrain from acting in a manner which advances or inhibits religious expression. This maxim, which is rooted in the First Amendment to the U.S. Constitution, is not easily observed. The obligation to educate a state's school-age children for the most part falls upon state legislators and local school boards. This includes ensuring that parochial school students, like public school students, receive an acceptable degree of general (nonreligious) education in addition to their religious studies.

Sometimes legislators' attempts to assist parochial schools and their students in satisfying state-mandated general educational criteria run the risk of aiding the religious institutions themselves. At other times, actions to accommodate the religious practices and beliefs of students at public schools may in effect "advance" religion in the public school classroom.

The U.S. Supreme Court has developed a three-part test for determining whether governmental support of parochial schools and their students is constitutionally acceptable, *i.e.,* does not improperly advance religion. Similarly, the Supreme Court has developed a balancing test for determining whether it is appropriate for school authorities to limit or restrict the religious practices of students in public schools. What follows is a discussion of various principles that have been developed over the years by the Supreme Court and various federal courts as they have attempted to apply these tests in observance of the church-state distinction.

I. THE OVERRIDING PRINCIPLE — GOVERNMENT MUST REMAIN NEUTRAL TOWARD RELIGION

The issue: The First Amendment to the U.S. Constitution states in part that "Congress shall make no law respecting an *establishment* of religion or prohibiting the *free exercise*" of religion. The Fourteenth Amendment makes this applicable to the states.

A. Establishment of Religion — The Excessive Entanglement Test: U.S. Supreme Court has determined that the *Establishment Clause* prohibits states and the federal government from passing laws that aid a religion or prefer one religion over another. *See Everson v. Board of Education,* 330 U.S. 1, 67 S. Ct. 504 (1947). In other words, government must maintain neutrality toward religion; it *may not advance or hinder any religion.* The Court has devised the excessive entanglement test, a three-part test for determining whether a particular governmental action withstands an Establishment Clause challenge. *See Lemon v. Kurtzman,* 403 U.S. 602, 91 S. Ct. 2105 (1971).

   1. *Secular purpose:* The action must have a nonreligious, or secular, purpose;

   2. *Neither furthers nor impedes:* Viewed in its totality, the action must not further or impede religious practice; and

2

3. *High degree of involvement prohibited:* The action must not result in too high a degree of involvement between government and religion.

B. **Free Exercise of Religion:** The *Free Exercise Clause* prohibits government from interfering with legitimate religious practices. Sometimes, however, an intrusion into the sphere of religious practice is justified by an important governmental interest. In such cases, the U.S. Supreme Court applies a *balancing test* in order to determine if governmental intrusion is lawful:

1. *Impairment of religious practices:* First, practices dictated by sincere religious beliefs must have been impaired by some kind of governmental action.

2. *Compelling interest:* If this is the case, the action will be justified only if it serves a compelling interest (*i.e.,* one that is more critical than the exercise of the religious beliefs in question).

3. *Least burdensome means:* Finally, the action in question must also represent the least burdensome means of achieving the government's objective.

C. **Tension between the Establishment and Free Exercise Clauses:** Complete government neutrality toward religion is not so easily maintained.

1. *Improper advancement:* Sometimes what appears to be a reasonable accommodation of free exercise rights is actually an improper advancement of religion in violation of the Establishment Clause.

2. *Unnecessary limitations:* Conversely, efforts to guard against state sponsorship of religion may result in unnecessary limitations on free exercise rights.

3. *Tension remains:* The Supreme Court has not expressed a preference for the freedoms guaranteed by one clause over those guaranteed by the other.

GOVERNMENTAL SUPPORT AND REGULATION OF PAROCHIAL EDUCATION

II. **GOVERNMENTAL SUPPORT AND REGULATION OF PAROCHIAL EDUCATION**

The issue: Despite the fact that the U.S. Constitution calls for what Thomas Jefferson termed "the separation of church and state," the Supreme Court has permitted state and local governments to provide various forms of assistance to parochial school children. As a general rule, governmental assistance must benefit parochial students directly rather than the religious institutions that educate them. This principle is sometimes referred to as the *child benefit doctrine*. In other cases, government will attempt to provide benefits directly to parochial schools or to parents of parochial school children, also as a means of furthering the general welfare through the creation of an "educated citizenry." With few exceptions, the Court has determined that these forms of aid violate the First Amendment and are therefore impermissible.

A. Child Benefit Doctrine: The child benefit doctrine holds that it is permissible for the State to provide materials to parochial school students if they are the same as those provided to public school students and the materials are necessary for an equal nonsectarian, nonreligious education.

   1. ***Basis of support:*** Support for the doctrine was grounded somewhat generally in the federal Constitution as opposed to specifically in the Establishment or Free Exercise Clauses of the First Amendment. *Cochran v. Louisiana State Bd. of Ed.*, 281 U.S. 370, 50 S. Ct. 335 (1930).

   2. ***Minority view:*** Some state courts have interpreted their state constitutions as prohibiting the child benefit doctrine.

B. Legitimate Public Purpose: Under the Establishment Clause of the First Amendment, a state-provided service which serves a legitimate public purpose will generally be allowed by the courts.

   1. ***Equal access to nonsectarian, nonreligious education:*** A state-provided service serves a legitimate public purpose if it in some way provides for equal access to a nonsectarian, nonreligious education for all students in public and parochial schools. A recent example of "equal access" to public school facilities arose when the U.S. Supreme Court affirmed a local school district's policy of granting student religious groups equal access to premises already used by nonreligious student groups. *See Board of Education of the Westside Community Schools v. Mergens,* 496 U.S. 226 (1990). Thus, once a limited public forum has been created, a student group cannot be denied equal access based on the content (religious or otherwise) of its meetings.

   2. ***Restrictive state constitutions:*** Some state constitutions are more restrictive of church-state relations than is the First Amendment.

      a. *Nonmandatory state services:* For instance, if a state-provided service is permissible but not mandatory, many state courts will not allow the state to continue to provide the service to parochial schools because it amounts to the use of

2

public funds for sectarian purposes, *i.e.,* in support of a religious sect.

b. *Effect of equal protection:* The Equal Protection Clause of the Fourteenth Amendment provides that states must treat all people the same under the law.

c. *Limitations on equal protection:* However, the Equal Protection Clause does not require that all individuals be treated the same in all respects; sometimes the pursuit of a legitimate public goal justifies treating similarly situated individuals differently.

C. **State Financial Aid to Parochial Schools (sometimes referred to as *Parochiaid*)**

The issue: The continuing dilemma facing the courts is determining when the provision of public financial aid to parochial schools violates the Establishment Clause. Typically, government seeks to provide various forms of aid — such as direct financial reimbursements, tax benefits, loans of instructional materials, and services — to parochial schools as a means of carrying out its general educational responsibilities to all of the state's children. *See Everson v. Board of Education of the Township of Ewing, supra.*

1. ***Provision of textbooks to parochial students by state or local governments:*** So long as the textbooks furnished to children in parochial schools are the same as those furnished to children in public schools, and none of the textbooks have been adapted to religious instruction, the Supreme Court has determined that this practice is constitutional. Similarly, the Court has upheld the constitutionality of a state statute which required local school boards to loan textbooks to parochial school children in the interest of quality education for all. *See Board of Ed. of Central School Dist. No. 1 v. Allen,* 392 U.S. 236, 88 S. Ct. 1923 (1968).

2. ***Provision of transportation services:*** In its first consideration of the Establishment Clause in the education context, the Supreme Court gave its approval to the use of public funds to provide bus service to children attending parochial school.

Example: A New Jersey school board's authorization of reimbursements to parents of money spent by them for parochial school bus fares was upheld because it extended a general service to all, not unlike that of police or fire protection. Thus, reimbursing parochial school parents satisfied a *legitimate public purpose:* that of helping all parents get their children to and from school safely, regardless of their religious affiliations. *See Everson v. Board of Ed., supra.*

a. *Equal protection claims:* In the case of transportation services for parochial school students, most state courts have rejected equal protection claims.

b. *Permissible, not mandatory:* In some cases, parents of children who have not been provided publicly funded transportation services have sued local school districts, claiming a violation of their equal protection rights. Because the Supreme Court held that public funding of parochial bus fares is permissible but not mandatory, several state courts have determined that this practice is constitutionally impermissible.

3. ***Purchase of nonreligious educational services from parochial schools and the provision of salary supplements to parochial school teachers for the teaching of nonreligious subjects.***

   The issue: Both types of aid are intended to provide financial support to parochial schools for the general educational needs of their students. In the first instance, the state "purchases" secular (nonreligious) educational services on behalf of parochial students by reimbursing parochial schools for teachers' salaries, textbooks, and instructional materials. In the second instance, the state pays a salary supplement directly to parochial school teachers for teaching secular subjects to parochial students.

   a. *Landmark Opinion:* A state provided money to pay for the services of parochial schools to provide nonsectarian instruction and to supplement the salaries of parochial school teachers. In a landmark decision, the Supreme Court considered the constitutionality of both forms of aid and concluded that neither was permissible under the First Amendment. Both resulted in the expenditure of time and resources on the part of government in order to ensure that the services being purchased from parochial sources satisfied secular requirements. This, in and of itself, promoted an *excessive entanglement* between church and state, regardless of the state's secular motivation for providing the support in the first place. *See Lemon v. Kurtzman, supra,* in which the Supreme Court enunciated a three-part test for determining whether a particular governmental action will withstand an Establishment Clause challenge. *See* § I.A., above. *See also Aguilar v. Felton,* 475 U.S. 402 (1985).

2

b. *Promoting a secular legislative purpose:* A state may provide aid to parochial schools if its provision promotes a secular legislative purpose while not principally or primarily advancing or inhibiting religion or fostering excessive government entanglement with religion. The provision of books, standardized testing and scoring, and diagnostic and therapeutic services is constitutional, while providing instructional materials and transportation has been held to be unconstitutional. *See Wolman v. Walter,* 433 U.S. 299 (1977).

4. ***State-provided parochial school tuition reimbursement:*** In a later case, the Court also disapproved of state-sponsored grants to parents of parochial school students for purposes of reimbursing the cost of tuition for secular courses offered at parochial schools because such grants could be construed as financial support for religious institutions, as they were not restricted in terms of how they were to be applied. *Committee for Public Ed. and Religious Liberty v. Nyquist,* 413 U.S. 756, 93 S. Ct. 2955 (1973).

5. ***Provision of income tax benefits:*** As with tuition reimbursements, above, the Supreme Court held in the same case, *Committee for Public Ed.,* that providing parents with income tax benefits in recognition of the cost of parochial school tuition violated the First Amendment.

a. *Government encouragement prohibited:* The Court reasoned that the tax benefit program rewarded parents for sending their children to parochial school and thus improperly advanced their respective religions.

b. *No analogy to property tax exemptions:* The Court refused to analogize the tuition-related tax benefit scheme to tax exemptions that historically have been provided for church-owned property.

c. *Education tax deductions allowed:* The Court has since determined that a state legislature may provide income tax deductions for the cost of education-related expenses to parents of all schoolchildren, not just to parents with children who attend parochial schools. *See Mueller v. Allen,* 463 U.S. 388, 103 S. Ct. 3062 (1983).

*RELIGIOUS
INFLUENCES IN
PUBLIC SCHOOLS*

III. **RELIGIOUS INFLUENCES IN PUBLIC SCHOOLS**

The issue: How far can public school officials go in accommodating free exercise rights before they run afoul of the Establishment Clause?

A. Religious Instruction of Public School Students: As a rule, public school students may not be excused from their regular instruction to attend religious classes held in public school classrooms. However, local school boards are free to excuse students to attend religious classes that are held off campus.

1. *No religious instruction in public schools:* The Supreme Court is opposed to religious instruction in the public schools for two reasons:

   a. *Dissemination in public setting:* First, such instruction involves the dissemination of religious material in a public setting, a clear violation of the church-state separation principle; and

   b. *Benefit to religious education:* The religious sects that sponsor the instruction benefit from the state's compulsory education requirements insofar as attendance records are kept for all classes, and therefore students who choose to attend must attend. This amounts to an advancement of religion. *See People of State of Illinois ex rel. McCollum v. Board of Ed. of School Dist. No. 71, Champaign County,* 333 U.S. 203, 68 S. Ct. 461 (1948).

2. *Off-campus religious instruction:* On the other hand, a policy which provides for the release of public school students so that they might attend religious instruction *off campus* neither establishes a religion nor denies free exercise rights. Rather, it accommodates freedom to worship without providing tangible support (such as access to public school classrooms or financial aid). *See Zorach v. Clauson,* 343 U.S. 306, 72 S. Ct. 679 (1952).

B. The Bible and Prayer in Public Schools: The Supreme Court has held that Bible-reading and prayer in the public schools violate the Establishment Clause.

1. *Bible-reading in public schools:* In considering the permissibility of Bible-reading in public schools, the Court paraphrased two parts of the three-part test that it had enunciated several years earlier as a means of assessing Establishment Clause violations:

   a. *Purpose:* What is the purpose of the governmental action, and

   b. *Primary effect:* What is the primary effect of the action?

2. *Result of purpose-effect test:* If the purpose is anything other than secular, or if the effect is such that religion is either ad-

vanced or inhibited, then the action is constitutionally impermissible. *See School Dist. of Abington Township, Pennsylvania v. Schempp,* 374 U.S. 203, 83 S. Ct. 1560 (1963). In this case, Bible-reading was viewed as religious in purpose. The fact that it took place on public property under the supervision of public school teachers suggested an effect that advanced religion.

    a. *Ceremonial reading/general study distinguished:* It is important to note, however, that the Court distinguished ceremonial Bible-reading from the study of the Bible (or religion) as a part of a general educational program. The latter would not violate the Establishment Clause.

3. *Ceremonial prayer recitation:* The ceremonial *recitation of prayer* in public schools amounts to state sponsorship of religion, regardless of whether or not participation is compulsory and whether or not it occurs in class or at school ceremonies.

    a. *Voluntary, student-led prayer:* Even voluntary, student-led prayer groups conducted on the public school campus prior to the beginning of or at the end of classes appear to be constitutionally impermissible.

    b. *Silent meditation periods:* Likewise, the Supreme Court has indicated that state laws calling for a daily period of silent meditation violate the Establishment Clause, if they were passed as a means of circumventing school prayer restrictions.

C. Miscellaneous Religious Influences

1. *Wearing religious dress or insignia:* While the Supreme Court has not considered the issue, several state courts have upheld legislation which prohibits public school teachers from wearing religious dress or religious insignia. Such legislation does not violate a teacher's right to the free exercise of her religion because its restrictions are aimed at the *act* of wearing religious dress as opposed to the *underlying belief* that motivates the act.

2. *Distribution of religious literature:* The distribution of religious literature to public school students is generally viewed as unconstitutional because it appears to favor one religion over another. Even if students may only obtain the literature upon submission of a parental permission slip, the fact that all children are provided with blank slips may result in pressure to return them. The effect is thus an advancement of religion.

3. *Display of national motto:* The display of the national motto of the United States, "In God We Trust," is permissible in a public school classroom. The posting of the Ten Commandments is not; the first requirement of the three-part Establishment Clause test is not met in this case since there is no valid secular reason for posting these religious principles.

4. *Observance of religious holidays:* Religious holidays may be observed in public schools so long as they are tied to a secular-oriented instructional program. This is accomplished by stressing the cultural and historical (*i.e.,* secular) significance of the holidays.

5. *No invocations or benedictions by clergy at graduation:* A school may not invite clergy to perform invocations or benedictions at public secondary school graduation ceremonies. Likewise, the state may not compose official prayers, even those purporting not to favor one religion over another. Such actions amount to the creation of a state religion. This is forbidden by the Establishment Clause. *See Lee v. Weisman,* 112 S. Ct. 2649 (1992).

IV. RELIGIOUS OBJECTIONS TO PUBLIC SCHOOL PRACTICES

RELIGIOUS OBJECTIONS TO PUBLIC SCHOOL PRACTICES

The issue: In certain instances, parents of public school children have sought to have their children excused from activities which conflict with their religious beliefs. Here, a *balancing* of competing interests must take place — the parents' interests in guiding the religious upbringing of their offspring versus the state's interest in providing for an educated citizenry.

A. **Saluting the American Flag:** The Supreme Court has determined that students may not be required to salute the American flag if doing so offends their religious beliefs. The Court was guided by evidence which suggested that refusal of students to participate in flag saluting would not interfere with the rights of others to do so and would not disrupt their doing so.

B. **Pledging Allegiance:** Students and teachers have a First Amendment (freedom of speech) right to refuse to pledge allegiance. Put another way, the right to remain silent when called upon to speak is as firm as the right to speak when called upon to remain silent.

C. **Exemptions from Offensive Curricula:** On the one hand, public school officials may not force students to pursue studies which conflict with their sincerely held religious beliefs.

1. ***In-school alternative programs:*** On the other hand, officials may run the risk of impermissibly advancing religion if they accommodate those who object by providing them with alternative programs.

2. ***At-home alternative instruction:*** The solution, according to one federal court, is to permit the children in question to receive instruction at home.

NOTES:

EVERSON v. BOARD OF EDUCATION OF THE TOWNSHIP OF EWING
330 U.S. 1, 67 S. Ct. 504 (1947).

NATURE OF CASE: Appeal of reversal of decision holding unconstitutional a state statute authorizing reimbursement to parents for their children's bus fare to sectarian schools.

GENERAL RULE OF LAW: A state may reimburse the cost of transporting children to sectarian schools where it does not support the schools and such aid is provided without regard to a particular religion.

PROCEDURE SUMMARY:
Plaintiff: Everson (P), a New Jersey taxpayer.
Defendant: Board of Education of the Township of Ewing (D).
New Jersey Supreme Court Decision: Held for Everson (P); the statute was unconstitutional because the state legislature lacked power to authorize reimbursement under the state constitution.
New Jersey Court of Errors and Appeals Decision: Reversed; the statute was constitutional and violated neither the state nor federal constitutions.
U.S. Supreme Court: Affirmed (with respect to validity under the federal Constitution).

FACTS: New Jersey enacted a statute authorizing local school districts to make rules regarding the transportation of children to and from school. Ewing's Board of Education (D), pursuant to the statute, authorized reimbursement to parents of bus fare incurred transporting their children by public transit. Some parents received reimbursement for fares incurred sending their children to parochial schools. Everson (P) filed suit, arguing that reimbursement of parochial school fares violated both the state and federal constitutions. The trial court held the state lacked authority to enact such a statute. The state court of appeals reversed, upholding the statute. The U.S. Supreme Court granted the appeal as to the federal question under the U.S. Constitution.

ISSUE: May a state reimburse the cost of transporting children to parochial schools where it does not support the schools and is provided without regard to a particular religion?

HOLDING AND DECISION: (Black, J.) Yes. A state may reimburse the cost of transporting children to parochial schools where it does not support the schools and provides reimbursement without regard to a particular religion. The Establishment Clause is founded upon the framers' desire to prevent state aggression toward and interference with the free exercise of religion. It at least means that neither a state nor federal government can create a church or pass laws which aid one religion or all religions or prefer one religion over another. Here, the state contributed no money to the parochial schools. It was not supporting them; it merely was assisting parents in providing their children, regardless of their religion, with an education, a legitimate state interest. This does not violate the Establishment Clause. Affirmed.

COMMENT: *Everson* was one of the first cases to address whether public funds could be provided to parochial schools for secular purposes. Though only addressing the issue with respect to transportation reimbursement, it created the basic framework within which the Court later addressed the issue in other contexts. Most importantly, *Everson* made it clear that the Establishment Clause of the First Amendment applied to the states through the Fourteenth Amendment.

NOTES:

LEMON v. KURTZMAN
EARLY v. DICENSO
403 U.S. 602, 91 S. Ct. 2105 (1971).

NATURE OF CASE: This action involved challenges to Rhode Island and Pennsylvania laws that provided assistance to private parochial schools and their students and teachers.

GENERAL RULE OF LAW: A state may not enact a system of assistance to parochial schools.

PROCEDURE SUMMARY:

Plaintiffs: Various individual taxpayers/citizens of Rhode Island and Pennsylvania.

Defendants: Various state officials responsible for executing the educational assistance laws.

U.S. District Court Decision: Action dismissed in Pennsylvania; motion to dismiss denied in Rhode Island.

U.S. Court of Appeals Decision: Certiorari taken directly to Supreme Court; no Court of Appeals decision.

U.S. Supreme Court Decision: Finding both programs unconstitutional, the court held for the plaintiffs.

FACTS: Rhode Island enacted an educational assistance program aimed at aiding private education, including parochial schools. The law provided for supplemental teacher salaries. Pennsylvania enacted a statute with a similar goal. It consisted mainly of aiding schools in the purchasing of supplies and textbooks in secular subjects. In the case of both states, the vast majority of schools and students subject to the programs were religious, with church-affiliated personnel often providing instruction. Several citizens of each state brought actions in U.S. district courts in their respective states, seeking a declaration that the programs violated the First Amendment's separation of church and state. The district court in Pennsylvania dismissed the action filed there; the court in Rhode Island held the law of that state unconstitutional. The U.S. Supreme Court granted a direct petition for certiorari.

ISSUE: May a state enact a system of assistance to parochial schools?

HOLDING AND DECISION: (Burger, C.J.) No. A state may not enact a system of assistance to parochial schools. The First Amendment not only prohibits the passing of a law establishing religion, but it also prohibits the passing of a law even respecting such establishment. Therefore, for a law not to violate the First Amendment, it must (1) have a secular purpose, (2) neither advance nor inhibit religion, and (3) not excessively entangle church and state. Respecting the Rhode Island law, it cannot be disputed that parochial schools constitute an integral part of the church's sweeping mission. A state cannot assume that a church-affiliated teacher will not indoctrinate his or her religious beliefs into pupils, even if the subject matter is secular. To supplement such a teacher's salary constitutes an unacceptable entanglement. As to the Pennsylvania law, the requirement that books and supplies be used for secular subjects necessarily implies surveillance and control. Such surveillance and control is precisely the kind of entanglement the First Amendment prohibits. In view of this, the programs must be held to be violative of the First Amendment. The Rhode Island ruling is affirmed; the Pennsylvania ruling is reversed.

COMMENT: The separation of church and state aspect of the First Amendment has always been one of the more problematic areas of constitutional law. On the one hand, a state cannot establish religion; on the other hand, it cannot abridge the right to worship. These two mandates are often at odds, and the Court has often had difficulty reconciling them. This particular case is one of the more important ones dealing with church and state. The three-part test described above has been the standard for Establishment Clause decisions since 1971.

NOTES:

BOARD OF EDUC. OF THE WESTSIDE COMMUNITY SCHOOLS v. MERGENS
496 U.S. 226, 110 S. Ct. 2356 (1990).

NATURE OF CASE: Review of decision holding that the Equal Access Act does not violate the Establishment Clause and prohibits a limited open forum school from denying a student religious group use of the school premises.

GENERAL RULE OF LAW: The Equal Access Act constitutionally prohibits limited open forum schools from denying student groups use of school premises based on the religious content of the groups' meetings.

PROCEDURE SUMMARY:
Plaintiff: Mergens (P), a Westside High School student.
Defendant: Board of Education of the Westside Community Schools (D) (Westside).
U.S. District Court Decision: Held for Westside (D); the Equal Access Act did not apply to Westside (D), and Westside's (D) denial of Mergens' (P) request to use school premises was constitutional.
U.S. Court of Appeals Decision: Reversed for Mergens (P), holding the Act constitutionally prohibited Westside (D) from denying Mergens' (P) request.
U.S. Supreme Court: Affirmed.

FACTS: Congress enacted the Equal Access Act, which prohibited public secondary schools (which by their nature are limited open forums) from discriminating against students who wish to conduct meetings within the forum on the basis of the religious content of the meetings. Mergens (P) petitioned Westside (D) for permission to conduct a religious meeting on the Westside High School premises. Westside (D) denied the request, contending the meeting would violate the Establishment Clause. Mergens (P) filed suit, alleging that the denial of her request violated the Act. Westside (D) responded that the Act did not apply to the school and was unconstitutional. The district court held for Westside (D) and upheld the denial. The court of appeals reversed, holding that the Act was constitutional and prohibited Westside (D) from denying the request. The U.S. Supreme Court granted review.

ISSUE: Does the Equal Access Act constitutionally prohibit open forum public schools from denying student groups use of school premises based on the religious content of the group's meetings?

HOLDING AND DECISION: (O'Connor, J.) Yes. The Equal Access Act constitutionally prohibits a limited open forum public school from denying a student group's request to use school premises based on the religious content of the group's meetings. The Act grants equal access to both secular and religious speech. The Act also limits school official participation in religious meetings and requires that such meetings occur at noninstructional times. The Act thereby creates little risk of government endorsement of or coercion toward a particular religion. Further, the Act does not create a substantial risk of excessive entanglement of government and religion because it prohibits faculty participation in the meetings. The Act therefore satisfies the three-pronged test established in *Lemon v. Kurtzman, supra,* and is constitutional on its face. Affirmed.

COMMENT: *Widmar v. Vincent,* 454 U.S. 263, 102 S. Ct. 269 (1981), the Court struck down a state university's action denying student groups access to university facilities for purposes of religious worship and teaching. The Equal Access Act, enacted three years later, represented Congress' determination that an equal access policy serves a secular purpose and that high school students are not so immature as to make *Widmar* inapplicable in the high school context.

NOTES:

BOARD OF EDUCATION OF CENTRAL SCHOOL DISTRICT NO. 1 v. ALLEN
392 U.S. 236, 88 S. Ct. 1923 (1968).

2

NATURE OF CASE: Constitutional challenge to a New York state law which required school authorities to loan textbooks to students attending private religious schools.

GENERAL RULE OF LAW: A state may permit school authorities to lend textbooks for use in parochial schools.

PROCEDURE SUMMARY:
Plaintiff: New York Central School District No. 1 Board of Education (P).
Defendant: Allen, New York Commissioner of Education (D).
U.S. District Court Decision: Held for Board of Education (P), finding state law unconstitutional.
U.S. Court of Appeals Decision: Reversed, finding state law constitutional.
U.S. Supreme Court Decision: Affirmed, upholding court of appeals decision.

FACTS: New York enacted a law requiring local school authorities to loan textbooks to students attending private parochial schools. The express purpose of the law was the "furtherance of the educational opportunities available to the young." The New York Board of Education of Central School District No. I (P) brought an action against Allen (D), the New York Commissioner of Education. The Board (P) sought a declaration that the law violated the First Amendment's Establishment Clause separation of church and state. The U.S. District Court held the law to tend to establish religion, in violation of the First Amendment. The court of appeals reversed, holding the law to be neutral with respect to religion, as it benefited public and private school students equally. The U.S. Supreme Court granted the Board's (P) petition for review.

ISSUE: May a state permit school authorities to lend textbooks for use in parochial schools?

HOLDING AND DECISION: (White, J.) Yes. A state may permit school authorities to lend textbooks for use in parochial schools. A law will withstand Establishment Clause attack if it has a secular purpose and tends neither to advance nor hinder religion. The law in question meets this test. The law applies equally to religious and nonreligious school students. The recipient of the public benefits here are the students, not churches or schools. Considering the extent to which sec-

tarian schools provide secular education, this court is not prepared to say that the processes of secular and religious training are so intertwined that benefiting the former at a religious school necessarily advances religion. Confirmed.

DISSENT: (Black, J.) The law here allows tax dollars to be used to advance religious purposes, in clear violation of the First Amendment.

COMMENT: In this case the Court relied on *Everson v. Board of Education, supra,* which held that New Jersey could use tax revenues to pay bus fares to parochial schools as part of a program that also paid fares for students "attending public and other schools." In his dissent, Justice Douglas warned of the possibility that in the future, parochial school authorities might select books that further sectarian/religious teachings. The law providing for the state-subsidized loan of secular textbooks to both public and private school students was held to be constitutional. The rationale was that the books were loaned as part of a general program for furthering the secular education of all students. The books were not, in fact, used to teach religion; therefore, the program did not establish a religion. Furthermore, the state aid goes to parents and students rather than to the religious schools directly, another indication of not establishing a religion.

NOTES:

AGUILAR v. FELTON
473 U.S. 402, 105 S. Ct. 3232 (1985).

NATURE OF CASE: Review of reversal of decision upholding the constitutionality of a program using state funds to pay the salaries of public employees teaching in parochial schools.

GENERAL RULE OF LAW: A state may not fund programs for sectarian schools which require a permanent and pervasive state presence in the funded schools.

PROCEDURE SUMMARY:
Plaintiff: Aguilar (P), a resident taxpayer.
Defendant: Felton (D), Chancellor of the Board of Education.
U.S. District Court Decision: Granted Felton's (D) motion for summary judgment, upholding the program as constitutional.
U.S. Court of Appeals Decision: Reversed, holding program violated the Establishment Clause.
U.S. Supreme Court Decision: Affirmed.

FACTS: New York City administered a program using federal Title I funds to pay the salaries of public employees teaching secular subjects in parochial schools. All materials used were provided by the government and could only be used for the secular purposes of the program. Direct contact between the public employees and parochial school personnel was to be avoided and kept to a minimum. Public employees were to avoid involvement in religious activities, and all religious materials and symbols were to be removed from the classrooms used by public employees. Additionally, the program required that the public employees be supervised by field personnel with at least one unannounced visit per month. Aguilar (P) filed suit against Felton (D), Chancellor of the Board of Education, to enjoin use of state money to fund the program, alleging it violated the Establishment Clause. The district court held the program constitutional. The court of appeals reversed. The U.S. Supreme Court granted review.

ISSUE: May a state fund a program in parochial schools which requires a permanent and pervasive state presence in the funded schools?

HOLDING AND DECISION: (Brennan, J.) No. A program which requires a permanent and pervasive state presence in parochial schools may not be funded by the state. The purpose of the Establishment Clause is to prevent the intrusion of either church or state into the precincts of the other. The funded parochial schools' goal is the advancement of a particular religion. By requiring pervasive monitoring by public authorities, the school must endure the ongoing presence of state personnel whose purpose is to guard against such advancement. Further, in the program at issue, state administrative personnel by necessity were required to work with employees of the funded parochial schools to resolve together scheduling, classroom assignments, information dissemination, and implementation problems. Such interaction impermissibly entangles church and state and increases the danger of political divisiveness and governmental secularization of a creed. Affirmed.

COMMENT: The program in *Aguilar* was unconstitutional because it failed the third prong of the *Lemon* test. According to the majority, the problem was not that the program primarily benefited parochial schools or used public employees but that the monitoring of the public personnel required too much state presence on the parochial school premises. Justice O'Connor, in dissent, however, argued that this third prong should be abandoned as an independent test. In Justice O'Connor's opinion, if the program in question is found to lack a purpose or effect of advancing or endorsing religion (the second prong of the *Lemon* test), it should be upheld even though some ongoing cooperation between church and state is required. A majority of the Court has yet to agree with this view.

NOTES:

WOLMAN v. WALTER
433 U.S. 229, 97 S. Ct. 2593 (1977).

NATURE OF CASE: Appeal of decision holding various provisions of a statute providing assistance to parochial schools unconstitutional under the Establishment Clause.

GENERAL RULE OF LAW: A state may provide aid to parochial schools if its provision promotes a secular legislative purpose while not principally or primarily advancing or inhibiting religion or fostering excessive government entanglement with religion.

PROCEDURE SUMMARY:
Plaintiff: Wolman (P), a resident taxpayer.
Defendant: Walter (D), Ohio State Superintendent.
U.S. District Court Decision: Held for Walter, finding all provisions of the challenged statute constitutional.
U.S. Supreme Court: Reversed in part and affirmed in part.

FACTS: Ohio enacted a statute which authorized the provision of books, instructional materials and equipment, standardized testing and scoring, diagnostic services, therapeutic services, and field trip transportation to private school pupils. An equal amount of funds provided private schools was to be provided public schools, and the amount expended per pupil in private schools could not exceed the amount expended per pupil in public schools. Wolman (P) filed suit contending the provision of such aid violated the Establishment Clause. The district court held all the provisions constitutional, and Wolman (P) appealed.

ISSUE: May a state provide aid to parochial schools if such aid promotes a secular legislative purpose, while not principally or primarily advancing or inhibiting religion, or fostering excessive government entanglement with religion?

HOLDING AND DECISION: (Blackmun, J.) Yes. A state may provide aid to parochial schools if its provision promotes a secular legislative purpose while not principally or primarily advancing or inhibiting religion or fostering excessive government entanglement with religion. The provisions at issue, concerning books, standardized testing and scoring, and diagnostic and therapeutic services, are constitutional. Wolman's (P) argument that the textbook provision was unconstitutional because it allowed for book substitutes lacks merit. The statute's separate provision for instructional material and the stipulated definition of the term "textbook" guard against abuse of this provision. The standardized testing and scoring serve a legitimate state interest by measuring student progress in only secular subjects. No private school personnel are involved in either drafting or scoring the tests, thereby eliminating the need for state supervision and excessive entanglement. Diagnostic services have little educational content and are not a great risk to ideological views. Therapeutic services, provided away from private facilities, do not advance religion or risk excessive entanglement because the services are provided by public employees only. Providing instructional materials, however, has the primary effect of advancing sectarian education and thereby supports the religious goals of the private school. Further, providing transportation is impermissible because the schools, not the children, receive the aid and would require excessive supervision to ensure that the aid is used for secular purposes. Affirmed in part and reversed in part.

COMMENT: The fundamental issue for providing services, whether on or off the parochial school premises, is whether the government can provide the services in a neutral manner. Though the issue can be stated simply, it is clearly not as easily resolved, as evidenced by the approaches espoused by individual justices of the Court. Justice Brennan argued that the amount of state money being provided alone was sufficient to find the program impermissible. Justice Marshall proffered that the provision of therapeutic services was impermissible simply because they improved the performance of the parochial school students. On the other hand, Justice Stevens believed that providing transportation was permissible.

NOTES:

MUELLER v. ALLEN
463 U.S. 388, 103 S. Ct. 3062 (1983).

NATURE OF CASE: Review of decision affirming grant of summary judgment upholding a statute allowing taxpayers to deduct certain expenses incurred to send their children to secondary and elementary schools.

GENERAL RULE OF LAW: A state may provide aid to parochial schools if provision promotes a secular legislative purpose, does not principally or primarily advance or inhibit religion, and does not foster excessive government entanglement with religion.

PROCEDURE SUMMARY:
Plaintiff: Mueller (P), a Minnesota taxpayer.
Defendant: Allen (D), Commissioner of the Minnesota Department of Revenue.
U.S. District Court Decision: Granted Allen's (D) motion for summary judgment, holding statute constitutional both facially and as applied.
U.S. Court of Appeals Decision: Affirmed.
U.S. Supreme Court Decision: Affirmed.

FACTS: Minnesota enacted a statute which provided parents a tax deduction for tuition, textbook, and transportation expenses incurred to send their children to elementary and secondary school. Some parents took the deduction for expenses incurred to send their children to parochial schools. Mueller (P) filed suit, alleging the statute violated the Establishment Clause by providing financial assistance to parochial institutions. The district court granted Allen's (D) motion for summary judgment and upheld the statute. The court of appeals affirmed. The U.S. Supreme Court granted review.

ISSUE: Must state aid provided to parochial schools promote a secular legislative purpose, not principally or primarily advance or inhibit religion, and not foster excessive government entanglement with religion to be valid?

HOLDING AND DECISION: (Renquist, J.) Yes. State aid provided to parochial schools must serve a secular legislative purpose and not principally or primarily advance, inhibit, or foster excessive government entanglement with religion. The state here clearly has a secular purpose. An educated populace is essential to a community. Assisting citizens in defraying the cost of educating that populace serves this purpose. The statute's primary effect is not the advancement of sectarian aims. The deduction is available to all parents

whether their children attend public, private, or sectarian schools, unlike the case of *Committee for Public Ed. v. Nyquist, supra,* where the tax relief was limited to parents of nonpublic school children, upon which Mueller (P) relies. Thus, any effect from the statute is the result of the choices of private individuals and not of the state or parochial schools. Further, any unequal effect of the statute is balanced by the benefit of a reduced burden on the public school system gained by all. Finally, the state's determining which books are or are not secular does not result in excessive entanglement of church and state. Affirmed.

COMMENT: The holding in *Mueller* is narrow. The decision nevertheless shows a greater tolerance by the Court for programs which assist parents of parochial school students than in years past. It seems that as long as the benefits are at least theoretically available to parents of public school children, a tax relief program will be upheld even though the primary beneficiaries are the parents of parochial school children. This theoretical possibility clearly distinguishes the *Mueller* opinion from *Nyquist,* where a program benefiting only parents of nonpublic school children was struck down.

NOTES:

ILLINOIS ex rel. McCOLLUM v. BD. OF ED., S.D. 71, CHAMPAIGN COUNTY, ILL.
333 U.S. 203, 68 S. Ct. 461 (1948).

NATURE OF CASE: Reversal of decision dismissing constitutional challenge to educational program permitting the teaching of religious doctrine on public school premises during school hours.

GENERAL RULE OF LAW: A school may not permit the teaching of religious doctrine on public school premises during school hours.

PROCEDURE SUMMARY:

Plaintiff: McCollum (P), a taxpayer, resident, and parent of a public school student.

Defendant: Board of Education of School District No. 71, Champaign County, Illinois (D).

State Trial Court Decision: Held in favor of Board of Education (D), upholding the state program.

State Supreme Court Decision: Affirmed.

U.S. Supreme Court Decision: Reversed.

FACTS: The Board of Education of School District No. 71, Champaign County, Illinois (D) instituted a program wherein representatives of certain religious groups would be permitted to provide religious instruction, during school hours, on public school campuses. Attendance by students was voluntary. McCollum (P), an Illinois resident and parent of a public school student, brought an action in state court, seeking a declaration that this practice was a violation of the First Amendment's separation of church and state. The state trial court upheld the practice, and the state Supreme Court affirmed. The U.S. Supreme Court granted review.

ISSUE: May a school permit the teaching of religious doctrine on public school premises during school hours?

HOLDING AND DECISION: (Black, J.) No. A school may not permit the teaching of religious doctrine on public school premises during school hours. The First Amendment rests on the premises that both religion and government work best when left free from the other within their respective spheres. The program at issue here is beyond all question an example of the utilization of established and tax-supported public schools to aid religious groups in the spreading of their faith. This falls squarely within the First Amendment's prohibition of the state's using its resources to establish religion. Reversed.

COMMENT: The state's action offered sectarian groups "an invaluable aid in that it helped to provide pupils with their religious classes through use of the state's compulsory public school machinery," thus aiding one or more religions or preferring one over another. Thus, the basis for declaring unconstitutional a program which permitted religious instruction during schooltime and excused public school students from their secular course work in order to attend the religious classes was based on the First Amendment prohibition against the state's establishment of religion. The court found that allowing public school classrooms to be used for religious instruction as well as providing state support of religious class attendance (because of the state compulsory attendance law) was unconstitutional because it violated the Establishment Clause.

NOTES:

ZORACH v. CLAUSON
343 U.S. 306, 72 S. Ct. 679 (1952).

NATURE OF CASE: Review of order sustaining a New York City program permitting schoolchildren to attend off-campus religious instruction during school hours.

GENERAL RULE OF LAW: A city may permit schoolchildren to attend off-campus religious instruction during school hours.

PROCEDURES SUMMARY:
Plaintiff: Zorach (P) and other New York taxpayer-residents.
Defendant: Clauson (D) and other city officials overseeing New York's educational system.
State Trial Court Decision: Held for Clauson (D).
State Court of Appeals Decision: Affirmed.
U.S. Supreme Court Decision: Affirmed.

FACTS: New York City instituted a program wherein schoolchildren within its public school system could, if their parents so chose, attend off-campus religious instruction during school hours. The administrative and financial aspects of the program were borne by the participating religious groups. Zorach (P), a citizen of New York, brought an action in state court against Clauson (D) and other education officials, seeking a declaration that the program violated the First Amendment's separation of church and state. Zorach (P) also argued that a "released time" program "coerces" students to attend the religious instruction because the public school helped monitor students released and because normal classroom activities halted. The trial court sustained the program, and the New York Court of Appeals affirmed. The U.S. Supreme Court granted review.

ISSUE: May a city permit schoolchildren to attend off-campus religious instruction during school hours?

HOLDING AND DECISION: (Douglas, J.) Yes. A city may permit schoolchildren to attend off-campus religious instruction during school hours. In no way can the program at issue be construed to violate the First Amendment's Free Exercise Clause because no compulsion occurs. Students are free to attend or not attend, as they and their parents choose. Neither does the program violate the Establishment Clause because state resources are not utilized. Since neither clause has been violated, the program withstands First Amendment scrutiny. Affirmed.

COMMENT: The court relied heavily on the fact that the record did not contain any evidence of actual coercion on the part of teachers to implement the program. On the other hand, a dissenting justice suggested that operation of the program itself constituted pressure and coercion upon students and parents to persuade attendance. Taxpayers who challenged this released time religious instruction program wherein public school students were permitted (with parental permission) to leave the school building during school hours in order to go to religious centers for instruction claimed that this policy was, in essence, no different than the one declared unconstitutional in *McCollum v. Board of Education*. The court disagreed, given that this program required no state financial support. The released time policy was not counter to First Amendment prohibitions because it did not create or establish a religion, nor did it deny the free exercise of religion.

NOTES:

SCHOOL DIST. OF ABINGTON TOWNSHIP v. SCHEMPP; MURRAY v. CURLETT
374 U.S. 203, 83 S. Ct. 1560 (1963).

2

NATURE OF CASES: Review of actions challenging practices in two different states of beginning each school day with readings from the Bible.

GENERAL RULE OF LAW: A public school may not begin its class day with readings from religious texts.

PROCEDURE SUMMARY:
Plaintiffs: Parents (P) of two children in Pennsylvania; parents and a child (P) in Maryland.
Defendants: School administrators (D) in Pennsylvania and Maryland.
State Trial Court Decision: Judgment for Schempp (P), a parent in Pennsylvania; for Curlett (D), a school official in Maryland.
State Appellate Court Decision: Affirmed in both cases.
U.S. Supreme Court Decision: Affirmed as to the Pennsylvania action; reversed as to the Maryland action.

FACTS: School districts in both Pennsylvania and Maryland had a similar practice of beginning each school day with a recitation of several verses from the Bible. These were read without comment. In Pennsylvania, Schempp (P), a parent of a child enrolled in school, brought an action to stop the practice, contending it violated the First Amendment. In Maryland, Murray (P), another such parent, brought a similar action. The Pennsylvania trial court held the practice unconstitutional; the Maryland trial court held to the contrary. The appellate courts in both states affirmed.

ISSUE: May a public school begin its class day with readings from religious texts?

HOLDING AND DECISION: (Clark, J.) No. A public school may not begin its class day with readings from religious texts. The First Amendment clearly prohibits state authorities from advancing religion. The place of the Bible as an instrument of religion cannot be disputed. Therefore, to read passages from this or any other religious text to a captive audience amounts to the advancement of religion. The government is under a command to be strictly neutral with respect to religion, and the practices at issue here clearly are not. Affirmed as to the Schempp case; reversed as to Murray.

COMMENT: The Court advanced the following test to illustrate the effect of the statute: when the primary effect of an enactment advances or inhibits religion, the legislative enactment exceeds the scope of legislative power under the Constitution. Even when attendance is not compulsory, it is unconstitutional to promote Bible-reading or the recitation of prayers on school grounds. The First Amendment's Establishment Clause (made applicable to the states by the Fourteenth Amendment) requires that the state remain neutral toward religion and forbids the state to "establish" a religion. The Pennsylvania law which required a prayer at the beginning of the school day was held to be impermissible establishment of religion — regardless of whether or not students were required to participate.

NOTES:

2

LEE v. WEISMAN
112 S. Ct. 2649 (1992).

NATURE OF CASE: Review of decision permanently enjoining the inclusion of invocations and benedictions performed by clergy in the graduation ceremonies of public secondary schools.

GENERAL RULE OF LAW: The state may not invite clergy to perform invocation and benediction services at public secondary school graduation ceremonies.

PROCEDURE SUMMARY:
Plaintiff: Weisman (P), father of a public secondary school graduate.
Defendant Lee (D), a secondary school principal.
U.S. District Court Decision: Held for Weisman (P), that the practice violated the Establishment Clause and should be permanently enjoined.
U.S. Court of Appeals Decision: Affirmed.
U.S. Supreme Court: Affirmed.

FACTS: The City of Providence permitted school principals to invite members of the clergy to perform invocations and benedictions at public school graduation ceremonies. Lee (D), a principal, invited a rabbi to perform such services at the graduation of Weisman's (P) daughter. Lee (D) provided the rabbi with a pamphlet of guidelines for composing public prayers prepared by the National Conference of Christians and Jews and advised him that the prayer must be nonsectarian. Weisman (P) brought suit to permanently enjoin the practice, contending it violated the Establishment Clause. The district court held for Weisman (P) and issued a permanent injunction. The Court of Appeals affirmed. The U.S. Supreme Court granted review.

ISSUE: May the state invite clergy to perform invocation and benediction services at public secondary school graduation ceremonies?

HOLDING AND DECISION: (Kennedy, J.) No. Inviting clergy to perform invocation and benediction services at public secondary school graduation ceremonies violates the Establishment Clause. Lee's (D) decision that the service be performed and his choice of the religious participant are both attributable to the state, amounting to a state decree that prayer occur. Lee's (D) choice of a rabbi clearly creates the potential for divisiveness in a school setting where subtle pressure and coercion exist and no real alternative to par-

ticipation or the appearance of participation exists. The state, through Lee's (D) distribution of the pamphlet to the rabbi, also directed and controlled the content of the prayer. This attempt to make the prayer nonsectarian failed. It is well established that the state may not compose official prayers which purport not to prefer one religion over another. Such action essentially amounts to the creation of a state religion, which the Establishment Clause clearly forbids. Affirmed.

COMMENT: The Court places great reliance on the fact that the ceremony takes place in a school setting. It sees the danger of coercion and pressure upon children and adolescents as much greater than such danger with respect to adults. Thus, the Court is less willing to tolerate any state activity which creates such a danger in the school setting. Further compounding the problem for the Court is the fact that in the graduation setting the student is forced to either acquiesce or protest the activity because the option of not attending the ceremony is not a real, viable alternative.

NOTES:

COUNTY OF ALLEGHENY v. ACLU, GREATER PITTSBURGH CHAPTER
492 U.S. 573, 109 S. Ct. 3086 (1989).

NATURE OF CASE: Review of reversal of denial of injunction against display of a creche in a county courthouse and a menorah outside public buildings as not violating the Establishment Clause.

GENERAL RULE OF LAW: A state practice touching upon religion but not advancing or inhibiting religion in its principal or primary effect is permissible.

PROCEDURE SUMMARY:
Plaintiff: American Civil Liberties Union (P) (ACLU).
Defendant: County of Allegheny (D) (County).
U.S. District Court Decision: Held for County (D), finding displays constitutional.
U.S. Court of Appeals Decision: Reversed, holding practices violated the Establishment Clause.
U.S. Supreme Court Decision: Reversed as to the constitutionality of the creche; affirmed as to the menorah.

FACTS: The County (D) set up two displays in or around public property. The first, a creche depicting the Christian nativity scene with a banner reading "Glory to God in the Highest" in Latin, was placed on the main staircase in the County (D) courthouse. The second was an 18-foot-tall menorah, placed outside County (D) buildings next to a 45-foot-tall Christmas tree. The ACLU (D) filed suit to enjoin permanently both displays, contending they violated the Establishment Clause. The district court denied the injunction, holding the displays constitutional. The court of appeals reversed, holding that the displays were impermissible governmental endorsements of Christianity and Judaism. The U.S. Supreme Court granted review.

ISSUE: Is a state practice which touches upon religion and advances or inhibits religion in its principal or primary effect permissible?

HOLDING AND DECISION: (Blackmun, J.) No. Under the Establishment Clause, a state practice which touches upon religion must not in its principal or primary effect advance or inhibit religion. This clause, at the very least, prohibits government from appearing to take a side on a religious question or belief. The words contained in the banner atop the creche display clearly endorsed a patently Christian message. Here, the reasonable observer would believe the County (D) was endorsing a particular message because the display was in the most notable part of the courthouse and not near any other display or symbol. Additionally, nothing in the display itself detracted from the particular message. Though government may recognize Christmas as a cultural phenomenon, it may not observe it as a Christian holy day, as the creche display at issue does. On the other hand, the menorah display was permissible. Displaying it outside public buildings alongside the Christmas tree did not endorse either Christianity or Judaism; it simply recognized cultural diversity and a season which has attained secular status. Reversed and affirmed.

COMMENT: The first nativity scene case before the Court was *Lynch v. Donnelly,* 465 U.S. 668, 104 S. Ct. 1355 (1984). There the Court found the display permissible. In distinguishing *Allegheny* from *Lynch,* the Court placed particular weight on the fact that the display in *Allegheny,* unlike in *Lynch,* was in the most beautiful and prominent location in the courthouse and was not near other displays. Thus, it appears that so long as a religious display is but a part of a larger display celebrating the cultural diversity of a secular holiday season, it will be upheld.

NOTES:

3

EDUCATION OF THE DISABLED

▶ **CHAPTER SUMMARY**

CHAPTER 3: EDUCATION OF THE DISABLED

QUICK REFERENCE RULES OF LAW

1. **Lack of funds not a proper excuse:** A school district may not argue that a lack of funds prevents it from providing for the special needs of disabled students. (§ I.A.3)

2. **"Free" and "appropriate" education:** The Individuals with Disabilities Education Act (IDEA), a primary source of disabilities-oriented legislation, guarantees all disabled children the right to a *free, appropriate* public education. (§ II.B.)

3. **No benefit need be demonstrated:** Accordingly, disabled children are not required to demonstrate that they can or will benefit from special education as a condition precedent to receipt of appropriate services. (§ II.B.2.)

4. **No special treatment beyond duty to ensure equal access:** The IDEA places an affirmative obligation on each state to ensure that equal access to a public education is not an empty guarantee. Beyond this, the legislation requires no special treatment on behalf of students with disabilities. (§ II.)

5. **Severely disabled students may receive priority services:** However, within the spectrum of disabilities, severely disabled children are guaranteed the same rights as those who are less severely disabled. In fact, the IDEA requires that severe cases be given priority. (§ II.B.5)

6. **Multiple disabilities require commensurate services:** In the case of a child who is profoundly mentally retarded as well as multiply disabled, the IDEA requires that educational services must be provided. Such services will not be limited to traditional academic training but must also include training in basic functional living skills. (§ II.D.)

7. **Classroom disruptions:** Under the IDEA, a state may not remove disabled students from their placements in response to disruptive conduct arising out of their disabilities. It may, however, follow normal safety procedures with regard to non-disability-related, immediate dangers. (§ II.G.)

8. **Legally sufficient "notice" required:** Under the IDEA, a school district must provide the parents of a disabled child with sufficient notice of changes it may be contemplating in the child's educational program. Such a notice must contain a description of procedural actions which have been taken; a description of any action the district proposes, or refuses, to take; a listing of the options which will be or have been consid-

ered; the reasons for rejecting any of the options; and a description of each evaluation component included in the student's individualized education program. (§ V.A.1.)

10. **"Disability" defined under ADA:** Under the Americans with Disabilities Act, a disabled person is one who has a physical or mental impairment that substantially limits a major life activity; a person who has a past record of such an impairment; or a person who is regarded by other people as having such an impairment. (§ III.A.1.)

11. **Conditions for qualification under ADA:** An individual with a disability is qualified under the ADA if, *with or without reasonable accommodations,* she can perform the *essential functions* of the employment position that she holds or desires to hold. (§ I.B.)

12. **Protection from disability-based discrimination:** Section 504 of the Rehabilitation Act of 1973 provides that no otherwise qualified disabled person shall, solely by reason of her disability be excluded from participation in any federal program. (§ I.C.1)

13. **Reaches beyond education:** Thus, Section 504 reaches beyond the educational context to protect all disabled persons of all ages from discrimination in a variety of programs and activities that receive federal financial assistance. (§ I.C.2)

14. **No affirmative action required:** Section 504 does not require affirmative action on behalf of disabled persons. It merely requires the *nonexistence* of discrimination. (§ I.C.3.)

NOTES:

3

Introduction: Three major federal statutes protect individuals with disabilities from discrimination and offer them equal access and opportunity with regard to governmental benefits, facility utilization, and employment. In the school setting, these statutes require school agencies to (1) identify children with disabilities; (2) evaluate their respective educational needs; (3) assign them to appropriate schools or classes; and (4) provide them with education-related supportive services.

I. OVERVIEW OF FEDERAL DISABILITIES STATUTES

A. Individuals with Disabilities Education Act of 1990 (IDEA)

1. *Preceded by former Public Law 94-142:* The IDEA is the successor statutory enactment to the Education of the Handicapped Act of 1975, often referred to as "Public Law 94-142."

2. *Limitations on application:* The IDEA basically guarantees a disabled student's right to a free, appropriate *public education.* IDEA is limited, then, to disabled children who seek a public education.

3. *Entails an affirmative obligation:* Under the IDEA, the U.S. Congress specifically imposed an affirmative obligation on each state to ensure that equal access to a public education is not an empty guarantee. Hence, a school district may not argue that a lack of funds prevents it from providing for the special needs of disabled students.

B. Americans with Disabilities Act of 1990 (ADA)

1. *Prohibits discrimination:* The ADA prohibits discrimination against any "qualified individual with a disability" regarding job application, hiring, training, compensation, fringe benefits, advancement, or any other term or condition of work.

2. *Prohibits "adverse impact" discrimination against an individual with a disability:* The ADA forbids "disparate impact" discrimination in accordance with the principles of Title VII of the Civil Rights Act of 1964. Prohibited is the utilization of any standard, criteria, or administrative method that has the effect of discriminating based upon disability or that perpetuates such discrimination.

3. *Requires making reasonable accommodations:* The ADA requires that a school district make reasonable accommodations for the known disabilities of job applicants and employees. Importantly, once necessary and reasonable accommodations

have been provided, the ADA encourages treating the disabled worker just like the nondisabled worker. Thus, affirmative action plans, preferential treatment of disabled applicants and employees, and expensive accommodations or modifications of current workplaces are not mandated.

C. The Rehabilitation Act of 1973, Section 504

1. *No disability-based discrimination:* Section 504 prevents discrimination on the basis of handicap.

2. *Goes beyond the educational setting:* Section 504 reaches beyond the educational context to protect disabled persons of all ages from discrimination in a variety of programs and activities, all of which receive federal financial assistance.

3. *No affirmative action required:* Section 504 does not require affirmative action on behalf of disabled persons. It merely requires the nonexistence of discrimination against handicapped persons. *Southeastern Community College v. Davis,* 442 U.S. 397 (1979).

II. INDIVIDUALS WITH DISABILITIES EDUCATION ACT OF 1990 (IDEA)

INDIVIDUALS WITH DISABILITIES EDUCATION ACT OF 1990 (IDEA)

The issue: The IDEA establishes both substantive and procedural rights. The substantive right is to a "free, appropriate public education"; the law also guarantees certain procedural mechanisms with respect to the manner in which the rights are instituted.

To qualify for federal IDEA funding for the education of the handicapped, a state must have in effect a policy that assures all disabled children certain specified substantive rights. An approved plan detailing the state's goals, timetables, facilities, personnel, and services for educating children with disabilities must be on file. Additionally, the IDEA requires that federal funds must be allocated first to handicapped children who are not receiving an education, then to children with the most severe handicaps within each handicapping category. Further, the IDEA requires that disabled children be educated with children who are not disabled to the maximum extent possible.

A. Law in effect prior to the IDEA

1. *Education for all:* Prior to the IDEA, the pertinent law in effect was the famous Public Law 94-142 (Education for All Handicapped Act).

2. *Codification of right:* Public Law 94-142 codified the right of each child with a disability to a public school education.

B. The IDEA's "free, appropriate public education" requirement.

1. *Prerequisite to receipt of federal funds:* To qualify for federal funds that are disbursed under the IDEA, a state must adopt a policy "that assures all handicapped children the right to a free, appropriate public education."

2. *No disabled child may be excluded:* Essentially, the IDEA has a zero reject philosophy — no disabled child may be excluded from receiving a free, appropriate public education. Furthermore, no disabled child is required to demonstrate that he or she will benefit from special education as a condition precedent to receipt of appropriate services. *See Timothy v. Rochester, New Hampshire School District,* 875 F.2d 954 (1st Cir. 1989).

3. *Tailored to meet individual needs:* A free, appropriate public education must be specifically designed to meet the unique needs of the disabled schoolchild.

4. *No "special" treatment:* The IDEA does not mandate equality of results, i.e., that disabled students receive special services to the degree that their education levels are commensurate with those of nondisabled students. It merely requires that disabled students "benefit" from instruction. *See, e.g., Hendrick Hudson Central School Dist. Bd. of Education v. Rowley,* 458 U.S. 176 (1982).

5. *Priority for the severely disabled:* However, within the spectrum of disabilities, severely disabled children are guaranteed the same rights as those who are less severely disabled. In fact, the IDEA requires that severe cases be given priority.

6. *Responsibility of state government:* The development of specific educational approaches is the responsibility of the state (which, of course, the state may delegate to local school districts within the state).

7. *Nature and extent of judicial branch overview:* Courts are available to determine whether compliance with the IDEA has been achieved. The legal issues which may arise are limited to the following:

    a. *Compliance:* Has the state complied with the procedures set forth in the IDEA? and

b. *Well-tailored plan:* Is the disabled child's individualized educational program reasonably calculated to enable the child to receive educational benefits? *See Rowley, supra.*

C. The IDEA's "Individualized Educational Program" Requirement

1. *Concept defined:* To ensure the provision of a free, appropriate public education, the individual needs of each disabled school-child are guaranteed through an "individualized educational program" (IEP), which is developed in concert with a district representative, the child's teacher, the child's parents, and, if appropriate, the child.

2. *Mandatory requirements:* Each individualized educational program must include the following:

   a. *Performance assessment:* a statement of the child's present educational performance;

   b. *Goals and objectives:* a statement of annual goals and short-term instructional objectives;

   c. *Services and participation:* a statement of specific educational services to be provided and the extent to which the child will be able to participate in regular educational programs;

   d. *Transition services:* a statement of needed transition services, including, when appropriate, a statement of inter-agency responsibilities with regard to services to be rendered at and after the time the student leaves the school setting;

   e. *Time line for services:* a statement of the projected initiation and duration of such services and action;

   f. *Criteria for measuring success:* a statement of appropriate criteria and procedures for determining, at least annually, whether instructional objectives are being or have been achieved.

3. *Program review and changes:* Each individualized educational program must be reviewed — and, if appropriate, revised — at least once a year. Procedural guarantees require that parents be notified of proposed changes in placement. Parents may object to proposed changes at an impartial due process hearing. Beyond that, unhappy parents may appeal to the state agency and even to a court of law.

D. The IDEA's Education-related Services Requirement

1. *Concept defined:* A related service is a service or program which must be provided in order for a disabled student to benefit from special education.

2. *Examples:* Speech pathology and audiology, psychological services, physical and occupational therapy, recreational programs, and certain medical and counseling services qualify as education-related services.

3. *Arguable medical service held to be a related service:* Litigation has arisen over the difference between medical and related services. The U.S. Supreme Court held that the periodic provision of a clean intermittent catheter was a related, as opposed to medical, service because the disabled party could not receive an education without it, and the procedure for its installation was simple. *See Irving Independent School District v. Tatro,* 468 U.S. 883 (1984).

4. *Scope of requirement:* Under the IDEA, children with disabilities are entitled to and therefore must be provided with education- related services.

E. Least restrictive alternative requirement

1. *Concept defined:* The IDEA requires that children with disabilities be placed in the educational environment that has the least amount of restrictions, whenever and to whatever extent appropriate.

2. *Practical effect of requirement:* The "least restrictive alternative" provision in effect mandates the mainstreaming of disabled students into disability-free environments. This statutory preference for mainstreaming creates a tension between the desire for a less restrictive environment and a free appropriate education (which may call for a more restrictive environment). The problem has been exacerbated by the recent emphasis on inclusion (see below).

F. Inclusion

1. *Concept defined:* Inclusion is an expansion of the mainstreaming concept whereby children with disabilities are placed in regular classrooms.

2. *Difference of opinion:* There is a strong difference of opinion regarding the concept of inclusion. Some educators believe that

inclusion provides disabled children with the best educational environment that is available; others believe that it places children who do not function well in an environment which is not supportive and which often detracts from the education process.

3. *Negative effects:* Furthermore, there is a fear that some districts may use inclusion as a budget-cutting device. Disabled children may suffer if the regular classroom teachers with whom they are placed are not trained to handle their special needs. The overly zealous use of inclusion could result in erroneous placements and subsequent litigation. Even more intriguing is the possibility of a lawsuit filed by a nondisabled child who alleges the denial of rights because he or she did not receive a fair share of the teacher's time and attention.

G. Disciplining Children with Disabilities

1. *Non-disability-related discipline is appropriate:* Neither the IDEA nor Section 504, discussed below, preclude the disciplining of students with disabilities for misbehavior that is not caused by their disabilities. *See Goss v. Lopez,* 419 U.S. 565 (1975) (Chapter 12).

2. *Prohibition against disability-related discipline:* However, a state may not remove disabled students from their placements in response to dangerous or disruptive conduct arising out of their disabilities; "stay-put" provision requires that a disabled student remain in his educational placement pending completion of an IEP review proceeding. *See Honig, California Superintendent of Public Instruction v. Doe,* 484 U.S. 305 (1988).

3. *Discipline must not conflict with the IDEA's objectives:* Even where discipline is justified, sanctions that materially interrupt a child's education (e.g., transfers, suspension, or expulsion) may constitute a change of placement, thereby triggering the IDEA's "stay-put" requirement and other due process provisions. *See Honig v. Doe, supra.*

4. *IDEA permits ten-day suspension:* If a student poses an immediate threat to the safety of others, she or he may be temporarily suspended. Many states allow for up to ten days of suspension before a student is considered to be expelled. This type of ten-day suspension practice also applies to disabled students; such a procedure balances school officials' interest in maintaining a safe learning environment with the mandates of the IDEA.

3

III. AMERICANS WITH DISABILITIES ACT (ADA)

A. Disability status

1. ***"Disabled person" defined:*** A disabled person is one who has a physical or mental impairment that substantially limits a major life activity; a person who has a past record of such an impairment; or a person who is regarded by other people as having such an impairment. *See* Americans with Disabilities Act, § 2(2) [42 U.S. Code, § 12101].

2. ***Parallels other federal legislation:*** This ADA definition corresponds to the definition of a disabled person under the Federal Rehabilitation Act of 1973.

B. "Qualification" of individuals with disabilities for purposes of employment

1. ***Ability to perform essential functions:*** An individual with a disability is qualified under the ADA if, *with or without reasonable accommodations* she can perform the *essential functions* of the employment position that she holds or desires to hold.

2. ***"Essential functions" defined:*** The phrase "essential functions" refers to job tasks that are fundamental and not marginal. An individual with a disability may not be denied a job simply because she is unable to meet a physical or mental requirement that is not really necessary to effective performance of the basic tasks of the job.

3. ***"Reasonable accommodations" defined:*** Employers must make reasonable accommodations to the known physical or mental limitations of an otherwise qualified individual with a disability.

   a. *Limitation for hardship:* The only limitation on this requirement is where the employer can clearly demonstrate that reasonable accommodations would impose an undue hardship.

   b. *Example:* In *Wallace v. Veterans Admin.*, 683 F.Supp. 758 (D. Kan., 1988), a hospital refused to hire a registered nurse who was a recovering drug addict, based on the fact that nurses normally handle controlled drugs. The federal district court found, however, that only a small percentage of a nurse's time was actually spent handling drugs. Therefore, the hospital could make a reasonable accommodation by transferring the disabled nurse's drug-handling responsibilities to other nurses, who in turn could transfer some of their non-drug-related job duties to the disabled nurse.

4. ***Parallels other federal and state legislation:*** These definitions closely follow similar concepts that are contained in the Rehabilitation Act of 1973 and various state disabilities laws.

IV. SECTION 504 OF THE REHABILITATION ACT OF 1973

A. Focus on discriminatory acts and practices

1. ***The gist of the provision:*** Section 504 of the Rehabilitation Act of 1973 is a civil rights law that delineates actions that *cannot* be taken with regard to the treatment of disabled individuals.

2. ***Affects receipt of federal funds:*** Section 504 represents a national commitment to end discrimination in the administration of any program that receives federal funds. In practical terms, funds may be withheld if the section's provisions are not complied with.

3. ***Compared with the IDEA:*** In contrast, the IDEA provides a guideline as to what *can* be done to upgrade education opportunities for disabled children.

B. Similarities with ADA provision on employment-based discrimination

1. ***Overview:*** Staff and teachers with disabilities in our public schools are protected by both Section 504 and the ADA with regard to employment concerns. For instance, a school employee with a contagious disease, such as AIDS, may be considered to be a disabled person under Section 504. AIDS, therefore, will constitute a protected disability so long as a person with AIDS has a physical impairment which substantially limits one or more major life activities, has a record of such an impairment, or is regarded as having such an impairment. *See School Board of Nassau County, Florida v. Arline,* 480 U.S. 273 (1987).

2. ***Otherwise qualified:*** Both Section 504 and the ADA prohibit disability-based discrimination against persons who are "otherwise qualified" for government positions or benefits. They allow individuals to bring private suits to secure relief from disability discrimination that arises in any phase of employment.

3. ***Alcohol and drug exclusion:*** Both Section 504 and the ADA exclude from their purview actions taken in response to current

drug and alcohol use but do protect former addicts and alcoholics who have successfully completed rehabilitation programs.

V. DUE PROCESS ISSUES AND CONCERNS

A. School district procedural concerns

1. *Sufficient notice:* Often there is a need for a school district to provide specific information to the parent or parents of a disabled student. In providing such information, the district meets its "notice" requirements. Under the IDEA, a legally sufficient notice must contain:

   a. *Proper safeguards:* a complete description of procedural actions and safeguards which have been taken;

   b. *Action to be taken:* a description and explanation of any action the district proposes, or refuses, to take;

   c. *Various options:* a listing of the options which will be or have been considered;

   d. *Rejection of options:* the reasons for rejecting any of the options; and

   e. *Method of evaluation:* a description of each evaluation component included in the IEP.

   Code of Federal Regulations, Title 34 ("34 CFR"), § 3000.505.

2. *Failure to obtain consent:* Consent is required in at least two circumstances: prior to conducting a preplacement evaluation of a disabled student and prior to the initial placement of such a student into a special education program. Additionally, school districts have an obligation to provide special education to students who need such programs even if parents refuse to give their consent. 34 CFR, § 300.505b.

3. *Denial of independent education evaluation:* A parent has a right to an independent educational evaluation, at public expense, if he or she disagrees with a school district's evaluation. 34 CFR, § 300.503.

4. *Poorly worded and incomplete evaluations:* Each independent educational evaluation must be complete and must address the unique needs of the student. It must contain, at a minimum: (1) present levels of performance; (2) annual goals and short-

term objectives; (3) a statement of related services and special education opportunities to be provided; (4) least restrictive environment considerations; and (5) duration of services. 34 CFR, § 300.346.

5. *Improper or insufficient evaluations:* The evaluation must be timely, performed by qualified persons, and assess each area of suspected disability. 34 CFR, §§ 300.530–300.534.

6. *Improper independent educational program meeting:* Annual (or more frequent) meetings held for purposes of determining a disabled child's independent educational program must be attended by the following "team": the disabled child's teacher, a representative of the school district who is empowered to commit district resources, and the child's parents. 34 CFR, § 300.344.

7. *Changing a disabled student's program without team participation:* Any significant change in a disabled student's program requires team approval. A change of placement, such as a suspension from school of ten or more days, is significant. 34 CFR, § 300.504.

NOTES:

TIMOTHY v. ROCHESTER, NEW HAMPSHIRE SCHOOL DISTRICT
875 F.2d 954 (1st Cir. 1989).

NATURE OF CASE: Appeal of decision holding that under the Education for All Handicapped Children Act a school district was not obligated to provide special education because the child was not capable of benefiting from special education.

GENERAL RULE OF LAW: A handicapped child is not required to show that he could benefit from special education in order to be eligible for such education.

PROCEDURE SUMMARY:
Plaintiff: Timothy (P), a handicapped child.
Defendant: Rochester, New Hampshire School District (D) (Rochester).
U.S. District Court Decision: Held for Rochester (D), that it did not have to provide special education to a child who could not benefit from same.
U.S. Court of Appeals Decision: Reversed.

FACTS: In 1975, Congress passed the Education for All Handicapped Children Act to ensure that handicapped children received an education appropriate to their unique needs. In 1980, Rochester (D) commenced meetings to determine whether Timothy (P) was educationally handicapped for purposes of the Act and thereby entitled to special education. Timothy (P) had been born two months' premature in 1975 and suffered from severe respiratory problems as a result. He later suffered hemorrhaging and seizures which rendered him multiply handicapped and profoundly mentally retarded. Upon the evidence presented at the meetings, Rochester (D) concluded that Timothy (P) did not fall within the Act because he could not benefit from special education. Subsequently, Timothy (P) filed suit, alleging that the denial of special education violated his rights under the Act. The district court disagreed, holding that Rochester's (D) basis for denial was proper. Timothy (P) appealed.

ISSUE: Must a handicapped child demonstrate that he can benefit from special education to be entitled to such education under the Act?

HOLDING AND DECISION: (Bownes, J.) No. The Act does not require a handicapped child to demonstrate that he can benefit from special education to be entitled to such education. The language of the Act clearly guarantees all handicapped children the right to a free appropriate education. There is no exception for severely handicapped children. In fact, the Act requires that the most severe cases be given priority; it does not make ability to benefit a prerequisite to receiving special education. There is no question that Timothy (P), being multiply handicapped and profoundly mentally retarded, qualified under the Act's definition of handicapped child. Reversed.

COMMENT: The opinion repudiates the views of some educators who wish to limit special education for handicapped children. It greatly confirms Congress' judgment as to the need to provide for such children through national legislation rather than relying on state or local initiative. Further, the court makes clear that the Act is not limited to traditional academic training but must be broadly read to include basic functional living skills as well.

NOTES:

HENDRICK HUDSON CENTRAL SCHOOL DIST. BD. OF EDUCATION v. ROWLEY
458 U.S. 176 (1982).

NATURE OF CASE: Review of order mandating special education program under the Education of the Handicapped Act.

GENERAL RULE OF LAW: The Education of the Handicapped Act does not require special services sufficient to maximize a handicapped child's education to a level commensurate with nonhandicapped children.

PROCEDURE SUMMARY:
Plaintiff: Rowley (P), a handicapped student.
Defendant: Hendrick Hudson Central School District Board of Education (D) .
U.S. District Trial Court Decision: Held for Rowley (P).
U.S. Court of Appeals Decision: Affirmed.
U.S. Supreme Court Decision: Reversed.

FACTS: The Education of the Handicapped Act provided that handicapped children attending public schools should be given special educational programs to meet their particular needs. Rowley (P), who was almost completely deaf, was admitted to kindergarten. She was given a hearing aid, with which she achieved a measure of academic success. However, the School Board (D) turned down a request made on her behalf that a sign-language interpreter be provided. A suit was brought in U.S. district court, contending that Rowley's (P) educational opportunities could not be maximized without the interpreter. The district court held that the Act mandated services which would maximize a handicapped child's educational opportunities and mandated a sign-language interpreter. The court of appeals affirmed, and the Supreme Court granted review.

ISSUE: Does the Education of the Handicapped Act require special services sufficient to maximize a handicapped child's education to a level commensurate with nonhandicapped children?

HOLDING AND DECISION: (Rehnquist, J.) No. The Education of the Handicapped Act does not require special services sufficient to maximize a handicapped child's education to a level commensurate with nonhandicapped children. In deciding whether such a requirement exists, the first place a court must look is in the Act's language. The Act provides that special services are to be provided as are necessary to permit the child "to benefit" from instruction. There is no language to the effect that the benefits are to be maximized to the greatest extent possible. While Rowley (P) may be correct in her argument that the Act was passed with a desire to promote equal educational opportunity, the position asserted on her behalf would tend to indicate an effort to achieve equality of result, an impossible goal not likely contemplated by the Act. In short, it appears that all the Act requires is that special services be provided to handicapped students that would allow them to benefit from education. In view of the relative success that Rowley (P) so far experienced, it would seem that the Board (D) discharged its duty under the Act. Reversed.

COMMENT: It is well recognized that education is a matter traditionally left to the states and their political subdivisions. The Act in question recognized this, leaving much of its execution up to the states themselves. The Court noted that it would be inconsistent with this approach for the federal judiciary to regulate from the bench how the Act would be put into force. Rowley (P) argued that to receive a "free appropriate education," she should have the opportunity to achieve her full potential commensurate with the opportunity provided to other children. This issue of "maximizing" one's opportunities is a critical one. If this decision had not been reversed, the potential cost would have been extensive, seemingly prohibitive.

NOTES:

IRVING INDEPENDENT SCHOOL DISTRICT v. TATRO

468 U.S. 883, 104 S. Ct. 3371 (1984)

3

NATURE OF CASE: Review of order mandating the provision of medical services to a student by a school.

GENERAL RULE OF LAW: The Education of the Handicapped Act mandates that school authorities provide clean intermittent catheterization to students requiring the procedure.

PROCEDURE SUMMARY:
Plaintiff: Tatro (P), a student with a congenital bladder defect.
Defendant: The Irving School Board (D) administering the school attended by Tatro (P).
U.S. District Court Decision: Held for Tatro (P).
U.S. Court of Appeals Decision: Affirmed.
U.S. Supreme Court Decision: Affirmed.

FACTS: Tatro (P) was born with spina bifida. Unable to urinate normally because of a defective bladder, she required clean intermittent catheterization (CIC) every three to four hours to evacuate her bladder. The process was relatively simple, requiring no special medical knowledge, apart from about one hour of training. When Tatro (P) reached school age, her parents requested that the school authorities perform the procedure upon her as needed during the day. The Irving School Board (D) refused. The School Board (D) argued that CIC was a "medical service" which could not qualify as a "related service" because it did not serve the purpose of a diagnosis and evaluation. A suit was brought on Tatro's (P) behalf to compel the Board (D) to administer the procedure. The district court held that the Education of the Handicapped Act and the Rehabilitation Act required that such services be provided. The court of appeals affirmed, and the Supreme Court granted review.

ISSUE: Does the Education of the Handicapped Act mandate that school authorities provide clean intermittent catheterization to students requiring the procedure?

HOLDING AND DECISION: (Burger, C.J.) Yes. The Education of the Handicapped Act mandates that school authorities provide clean intermittent catheterization to students requiring the procedure. The Act mandates that states supply programs providing a public education to handicapped children. This includes special education and related services necessary to achieve this goal. There can be no question but that CIC is a "related service" necessary to promote educational access. It is true that the Act textually excludes "medical services" from the Act's reach. However, this Court believes that this phrase refers to complicated procedures not within the competence of school personnel. CIC is a simple procedure, capable of being performed by a nurse or even a layman. Therefore, the Court holds that CIC is a procedure that must be offered by public schools to children so needing. Affirmed.

COMMENT: The lower courts based their decision on both the Education of the Handicapped Act and the Rehabilitation Act. The Court held, in an opinion released the same day, that the latter Act did not apply when the former was available and partially reversed the lower courts. The main result of this was that Tatro (P) ended up bearing the costs of her attorney fees, as the EHA, unlike the RA, did not provide for attorney fees. Regarding the provision of related services such as CIC, school personnel were very concerned because of their own fears and apprehensions. In the ten years since this ruling, school personnel now handle classroom situations for more extensive procedures without difficulty.

NOTES:

HONIG, CALIFORNIA SUPERINTENDENT OF PUBLIC INSTRUCTION v. DOE
484 U.S. 305, 108 S. Ct. 592 (1988).

NATURE OF CASE: Review of permanent injunction against the suspension and proposed expulsion of a disabled student for conduct arising out of his disability as a violation of the Education of the Handicapped Act.

GENERAL RULE OF LAW: The Education of the Handicapped Act prohibits states from removing disabled children from their placements for dangerous or disruptive conduct arising out of their disabilities.

PROCEDURE SUMMARY:
Plaintiff: Smith (P), a suspended disabled student.
Defendant: Honig (D), California Superintendent of Public Instruction.
U.S. District Court Decision: Held for Smith (P), granting summary judgment and issuing a permanent injunction against Smith's (P) suspension and proposed expulsion.
U.S. Court of Appeals Decision: Affirmed, with the addition that a suspension exceeding ten school days was not a prohibited change in placement.
U.S. Supreme Court Decision: Affirmed, except as to the Court of Appeals' modification.

FACTS: In 1975, Congress enacted the Education of the Handicapped Act (Act) to assure that states provided all disabled children a free appropriate public education. Section 1415 of the Act, called the "stay put" provision, required that a disabled child remain in his educational placement pending completion of any review proceedings. Smith (P) and Doe (P), both emotionally disturbed students, were suspended indefinitely for violent conduct related to their disabilities pending the outcome of expulsion proceedings. Doe (P), who had a history of reacting aggressively to peer ridicule, responded to the taunts of a fellow student by choking him with sufficient force to leave neck abrasions, and he also kicked out a school window while being escorted to the principal's office. Doe (P) filed suit, seeking to enjoin his suspension and the expulsion proceedings. Smith (P) experienced academic and social difficulties as a result of hyperactivity and low self-esteem. Smith (P) had a propensity for verbal hostility, and his disruptive behavior consisted of stealing, extorting money from fellow students, and making sexual comments to female students. Smith (P) intervened, contending the suspension and proposed expulsion violated the "stay put" provision of the Act. The district court agreed and enjoined the action. The court of appeals affirmed. The U.S. Supreme Court granted review.

ISSUE: Does the "stay put" provision of the Act prohibit states from removing disabled children from classrooms for violent or disruptive conduct arising out of their disability?

HOLDING AND DECISION: (Brennan, J.) Yes. States may not remove disabled children from classrooms for violent or disruptive conduct related to their disability under the Act. The language of § 1415 unequivocally prohibits removing the child while any proceedings are pending. The Court cannot read a "dangerousness" exception into the provision, as Honig (D) suggested. Congress clearly intended to strip schools of the unilateral authority they traditionally had to exclude disabled students. However, schools may still use their normal procedures for dealing with children who endanger themselves or others. Students who pose an immediate threat to the safety of others may be temporarily suspended for up to ten school days. This provides schools with an adequate means of ensuring the safety of others. Thus, the lower courts properly balanced the schools' interest in maintaining a safe learning environment and the mandates of the Act. Affirmed, except as to the court of appeals' addition that a temporary suspension could exceed ten days.

COMMENT: The Act was passed after Congress found that school systems across the country excluded one out of eight disabled children from the classroom. It was based on Congress' judgment that not enough was being done on state and local levels to find suitable or appropriate ways of dealing with the problem. The Act demonstrates that Congress will take significant action in the fields of public elementary and secondary education even though these areas traditionally are left to state and local government. This case has caused more consternation among school administrators than any other recent Court decision, and they often feel that their hands are tied when dealing with disruptive behavior by handicapped students. Of course, when disruptive behavior is serious, school authorities may contact local authorities to remove the disruptive student.

SCHOOL BOARD OF NASSAU COUNTY, FLORIDA v. ARLINE

480 U.S. 273, 107 S. Ct. 1123 (1987).

NATURE OF CASE: Review of award of reinstatement upon reversal of decision holding that a fired schoolteacher with tuberculosis was not handicapped for purposes of the Rehabilitation Act and, even if handicapped, not qualified to teach elementary school.

GENERAL RULE OF LAW: A person with a contagious disease may be a handicapped person for purposes of § 504 of the Rehabilitation Act.

PROCEDURE SUMMARY:
Plaintiff: Arline (P), a fired elementary school teacher with tuberculosis.
Defendant: School Board of Nassau County, Florida (D) (Board).
U.S. District Court Decision: Held for the Board (D), finding that Arline (P) was not handicapped for purposes of § 504 of the Act.
U.S. Court of Appeal Decision: Reversed, holding for Arline (P) that persons with contagious diseases come within § 504.
U.S. Supreme Court Decision: Affirmed.

FACTS: Section 504 of the Rehabilitation Act provides that no otherwise-qualified handicapped individual shall, solely by reason of his handicap, be excluded from participation in any program receiving federal assistance. Arline (P) had been hospitalized for tuberculosis. The disease then went into remission for 20 years, during which time she taught elementary school. In 1977 and 1978, she had a relapse. The Board (D) suspended Arline (P) for the remainder of the school year and then discharged her, citing continued recurrence of the disease. Arline (P) filed suit, alleging that the discharge was a violation of § 504 of the Rehabilitation Act. The district court held that the Act did not apply because Arline (P) was not a "handicapped person" for purposes of the Act. The court of appeals reversed, and the U.S. Supreme Court granted review.

ISSUE: Is a person with a contagious disease a handicapped person for purposes of § 504 of the Act?

HOLDING AND DECISION: (Brennan, J.) Yes. A person with a contagious disease may be considered a handicapped person under § 504 of the Act. Section 706 of the Act defines handicapped individuals as any person who has a physical impairment which substantially limits one or more of his major life activities, has a record of such an impairment, or is regarded as having such an impairment. Further, Department of Health and Human Services regulations define "physical impairment" as any physiological disorder affecting the respiratory system and "major life activities," including working. The facts that Arline (P) was hospitalized in 1957 for tuberculosis, which then and now substantially limited her ability to work, clearly places her within § 504. That the disease happens to be contagious does not remove her from § 504's coverage. [The Court cannot determine whether Arline (P) was otherwise qualified to work because the district court failed to properly inquire into the nature of the risk, the duration of the risk, the severity of the risk, and the probability that the disease would be transmitted and cause harm.] Affirmed and remanded.

COMMENT: The case demonstrates just how broadly the term "handicapped" will be interpreted under § 504 of the Act. One can be handicapped, for example, if one has tested positive for HIV, the virus that causes AIDS, without yet exhibiting any symptoms of AIDS itself. Of greater controversy is the question of when one should come under the scope of § 504 if the handicapped is "perceived" rather than actual.

NOTES:

MILLS v. BOARD OF EDUCATION OF THE DISTRICT OF COLUMBIA
348 F. Supp. 866 (D.C. 1972).

NATURE OF CASE: Action seeking order admitting certain children to school.

GENERAL RULE OF LAW: A school district must provide facilities for attendance by behaviorally retarded children.

PROCEDURE SUMMARY:
Plaintiffs: Mills (P), representing a class of behaviorally and developmentally retarded children.
Defendant: Board of Education (D) of the District of Columbia School District.
U.S. District Trial Court Decision: Held for Mills (P).

FACTS: A class action involving approximately 22,000 handicapped students was brought in U.S. district court on behalf of a class of seven children, represented by Mills (P), who had been denied enrollment in public school. Each child had some sort of developmental disorder. The local Board of Education (D), not providing any special programs or facilities, had considered Mills (P) not capable of attending classes. The Board (D) also argued that the lack of funds was sufficient reason to exclude the handicapped students from school. Mills (P) brought suit to compel the Board (D) to admit the seven children.

ISSUE: Must a school district provide facilities for attendance by behaviorally retarded children?

HOLDING AND DECISION: (Waddy, J.) Yes. A school district must provide facilities for attendance by behaviorally retarded children. The district code mandates that children shall attend school and further mandates that if an exceptional child would benefit from special instruction, he shall receive same. To deny poor public school children educational opportunities equal to those available to more affluent public school children violates due process. Consequently, it is no answer that the Board (D) has no funds to pay for programs for the poor students represented in this case; the funds will have to be taken from less essential programs benefiting more affluent students. [The court then fashioned a lengthy order mandating the provision of special education programs.]

COMMENT: Generally speaking, lack of funds is not an excuse that courts look upon with favor in dealing with constitutional rights. In *Goldberg v. Kelly,* 397 U.S. 254, 90 S. Ct. 1011 (1970), the Supreme Court held that a state's interest in streamlining a public assistance program was outweighed by its interest in preserving due process. It should be noted, however, that the Supreme Court has never ruled on the issue involved in the present action. One concern that was addressed was the lack of a procedure to determine the placement of a handicapped child. Courts have held that any placement must follow a due process procedure, which includes the writing of an individualized educational plan. Additionally, parents must be allowed to participate as monitors in the placement decision.

NOTES:

S-1 v. TURLINGTON
635 F.2d 342, 347 (5th Cir. 1981).

NATURE OF CASE: Appeal of preliminary injunction mandating readmission of students previously expelled.

GENERAL RULE OF LAW: An intellectually retarded child may not be expelled without a hearing as to whether the basis for expulsion is related to the disability.

PROCEDURE SUMMARY:
Plaintiffs: S-1 (P) and eight other anonymous high school students.
Defendants: Turlington (D) and various other school officials.
U.S. District Trial Court Decision: Held for the students (P).
U.S. Court of Appeals Decision: Affirmed.

FACTS: Nine students at a high school in Hendry, Florida suffered from moderate to mild mental retardation. In separate actions, these students were expelled for various acts of misbehavior. Only one student, S-1 (P), was afforded a hearing as to whether his handicap had been related to his offense; the others made no such request. In S-1's (P) case, Turlington (D) had determined that since he was not seriously disturbed, his handicap could not be related to his conduct. A suit was brought in district court, contending that S-1 (P) had been denied his rights under the Education of the Handicapped Act (EHA) and seeking an injunction mandating readmission. The district court issued such an injunction, and Turlington (D) appealed.

ISSUE: May an intellectually retarded child be expelled without a hearing as to whether the basis for expulsion is related to the disability?

HOLDING AND DECISION: (Hatchett, J.) No. An intellectually retarded child may not be expelled without a hearing as to whether the basis for expulsion is related to the disability. Under the EHA, a handicapped student may not be expelled from school for conduct which results from the handicap itself. This is true whether the handicap is physical, emotional, or mental. From this it follows that any expulsion of a handicapped student must be accompanied by a hearing to determine this issue. It is no defense that a hearing was not requested; the EHA and its implementing regulations place an independent obligation upon school authorities to make this determination, whether or not a hearing is requested. Handi-capped students and their parents will often not have sufficient sophistication to understand their right to a hearing. In this instance, eight of the nine students involved had no hearing, so their EHA rights were violated. With respect to S-1 (P), the authorities (D) apparently assumed that only a serious emotional handicap would invoke the EHA. This was an incorrect reading of the Act; any handicap, if it relates to the misconduct at issue, prevents expulsion. Consequently, a rehearing would be necessary before S-1 (P) could be legitimately expelled. Affirmed.

COMMENT: The EHA provides that certain procedural protections shall accompany any change in educational placement. Consequently, the district court and the court of appeals had to decide as a threshold matter whether expulsion was a change in placement for purposes of the Act, which was silent on the issue. Both courts decided this in the affirmative, noting that a school could circumvent a handicapped child's right to an education in the least restrictive environment if the Act were otherwise construed. The guarantees recognized in this circuit court decision were later established by the Supreme Court in *Honig v. Doe*, 484 U.S. 305, 108 S. Ct. 592 (1988). The key in any disciplinary action involving the expulsion of a handicapped student is that the hearing be conducted by the individualized educational plan (IEP) team. The IEP team must make the determination as to the relationship between the misconduct and the handicap.

NOTES:

DELLMUTH, ACTING SECRETARY OF EDUCATION OF PENNSYLVANIA v. MUTH
491 U.S. 223, 109 S. Ct. 2397 (1989).

NATURE OF CASE: Appeal from award of damages for tuition paid by the parent of a handicapped child who was placed in a private school when administration proceedings were delayed.

GENERAL RULE OF LAW: The states' Eleventh Amendment immunity from suit in federal court may be abrogated by Congress only when the intention to do so is made unmistakably clear in a particular act.

PROCEDURE SUMMARY:
Plaintiff: Muth (P), the parent of a disabled child.
Defendant: Dellmuth (D), Acting Secretary of Education of Pennsylvania.
U.S. District Court Decision: Held for Muth (P), awarding damages for Dellmuth's (D) violation of the Act.
U.S. Court of Appeals Decision: Affirmed.
U.S. Supreme Court Decision: Reversed and remanded.

FACTS: Congress passed the Education of the Handicapped Act to ensure that handicapped children received a free public education appropriate to their needs. It provided that parents of such children could challenge the appropriateness of their child's individualized education program (IEP) in an administrative hearing followed by judicial review. Muth (P) challenged his child's IEP. While the proceedings were pending, Muth (P) placed the child in private school. The IEP was then revised and found appropriate in the administrative proceedings. Muth (P) filed suit, challenging both the appropriateness of the IEP and the validity of the administrative proceedings and seeking reimbursement for the child's private school tuition and attorney fees. The district court found that the states' Eleventh Amendment immunity was abrogated by the Act and entitled Muth (P) to damages because of the delay caused by the flaws in the administrative proceedings. The court of appeals affirmed, and Dellmuth (D) appealed.

ISSUE: May the states' Eleventh Amendment immunity from suit in federal court be abrogated by Congress only when its intention to do so is made unmistakably clear in a particular act?

HOLDING AND DECISION: (Kennedy, J.) Yes.

Congress may abrogate the states' immunity only by making its intention unmistakably clear in the language of the statute. The Education of the Handicapped Act does not abrogate the states' Eleventh Amendment immunity from suit in federal court. The Act's preamble and judicial review provision and the 1986 amendment to the Rehabilitation Act evidence no such intention here. The Act makes no reference to the Eleventh Amendment or the states' sovereign immunity. The preamble has nothing to do with states' immunity. The 1986 amendment to the Rehabilitation Act did not clearly indicate whether Congress intended to abrogate states' immunity in 1975 when the Education of the Handicapped Act was adopted. The judicial review provision makes no mention of state immunity or abrogation, and abrogation is not "necessary" to achieve the Act's goals. The statutory language of the Act does not evince an unmistakably clear intention to abrogate the states' immunity from suit. Thus, Muth's (P) attempt to collect tuition is barred by the Eleventh Amendment. Reversed and remanded.

COMMENT: Dellmuth followed *Atascadero State Hospital v. Scanlon*, 473 U.S. 234, 105 S. Ct. 3142 (1985), where the Court established that the states' immunity could only be abrogated by congressional intent made unmistakably clear by the language of a statute. However, four dissenting justices were of the opinion that the majority was improperly applying the unmistakably clear test and that the history and language of the Act satisfied the test if properly applied, and, thus, state immunity was abrogated. For the dissenting justices, the 1986 amendment to the Rehabilitation Act providing that a state shall not be immune under the Eleventh Amendment for violations of that Act or any other federal statute prohibiting discrimination by recipients of federal assistance made clear once and for all the requisite congressional intent.

NOTES:

CHALK v. U.S. DISTRICT COURT, CENTRAL DISTRICT OF CALIFORNIA

840 F.2d 701 (9th Cir. 1988).

NATURE OF CASE: Appeal from denial of motions for preliminary and permanent injunctions filed under § 504 of the Rehabilitation Act of 1973 by a teacher, diagnosed with AIDS, who sought to prevent reassignment from the classroom to an administrative position.

GENERAL RULE OF LAW: A person with AIDS is considered "otherwise qualified" under § 504 of the Rehabilitation Act of 1973 and is therefore afforded full protection under the Act.

PROCEDURE SUMMARY:

Plaintiff: Vincent L. Chalk (P), a teacher of hearing-impaired pupils.

Defendant: U.S. District Court, Central District of California (D).

U.S. District Court Decision: Chalk's (P) motions for preliminary and permanent injunctions denied.

U.S. Court of Appeals Decision: Reversed and remanded.

FACTS: Chalk (P), a certified teacher of hearing-impaired pupils in Orange County Schools, taught in that district for approximately six years. While hospitalized for pneumonia in February of 1987, Chalk (P) learned he had contracted Acquired Immune Deficiency Syndrome (AIDS). Chalk's (P) physician, Dr. Siskind, declared Chalk (P) fit to return to work April 20, after nearly eight weeks of treatment and recuperation. However, after learning of the diagnosis, the Orange County Department of Education barred Chalk (P) from teaching in the classroom and reassigned him to an administrative position. Chalk (P) agreed to remain at the administrative position until an opinion could be submitted by Dr. Prendergast, the Director of Epidemiology and Disease Control for the Orange County Health Care Agency, regarding the degree of risk Chalk (P) posed to his students. On May 22, Dr. Prendergast reported to the Department that Chalk (P) did not present any risk of transmitting HIV, the virus believed to cause AIDS, to students or to anyone else at the school. Chalk (P) then agreed to stay at his administrative post for the remaining weeks of the school year. Chalk (P) met with Department representatives on August 5 to discuss his returning to his teaching position. Chalk (P) refused the Department's offer of another administrative posi-

tion with the option of working at home or in the office, at his present salary and with the same benefits he was currently entitled to. The Department informed him it would file an action for declaratory relief if he demanded to be returned to the classroom. The Department filed the action on August 6 in state court. Meanwhile, Chalk (P) filed in federal district court (D), requesting a preliminary and permanent injunction to prevent the Department from excluding him from classroom duties. Chalk (P) claimed that the Department's action violated the Rehabilitation Act of 1973, which prohibits recipients of federal funds from discriminating against otherwise qualified handicapped persons. Chalk (P) contended that he was "otherwise qualified" under the Act, and could not be transferred because he posed no risk to the health of persons around him. After some discussion, the Department dropped its state court action and filed a counterclaim in district court (D). The district court (D) denied Chalk's (P) motion for a preliminary and permanent injunction, finding that he had not shown sufficient monetary loss and therefore had not proven irreparable injury, one of the prerequisites for an injunction. As a result, the Department reassigned Chalk (P) to an administrative position. Chalk (P) filed a writ of mandamus and a motion for an expedited appeal with the court of appeals, which granted the latter. Pending the appeal, Chalk (P) filed an emergency motion for an injunction. On November 18, the court of appeals reversed, remanding the case to the district court (D). [Procedurally, the district court (D) was the named defendant for purposes of this case in the motion for an emergency injunction to order the district court (D) to act.]

ISSUE: Is a person with AIDS considered to be "otherwise qualified" under § 504 of the Rehabilitation Act of 1973 and therefore entitled to full protection under the Act?

HOLDING AND DECISION: (Poole, C.J.) Yes. Section 504 of the Rehabilitation Act of 1973 is applicable to a person with AIDS. This conclusion is compelled by application of the standard formulated in *School Board of Nassau County v. Arline*, 480 U.S. 273, 107 S. Ct. 1123 (1987). In the Arline decision, the Supreme Court held that a person with a contagious disease could be excluded from the "otherwise qualified" provision of § 504 of the Act only if reasonable accommodation by an employer could not eliminate the transmission risk presented by the contagious person. To determine this, the Supreme Court required that four specific fact findings be made based on reasonable medical judgments with deference to public health officials' judgments. The fact findings included determining how the disease was transmitted (nature of the risk), the length of time the individual was infectious (duration of the risk), the potential harm the person presented (severity of the risk), and the probability of transmission. In this case, the district court (D) neglected to follow the legal standards in Arline by improperly relying on unsupported scientific speculation instead of deferring to the public health officials' reasonable medical judgments entered into evidence. In addition, Chalk (P) had met the burden of proving one of the elements necessary for granting a preliminary injunction. The two elements were: (a) showing that the motion would probably succeed on the merits of the case and that a denial of the motion had the possibility of inflicting irreparable injury to him or (b) showing that the motion raised serious questions which tipped the balance of hardships sharply in Chalk's (P) favor. In assessing the possibility of irreparable injury, both monetary loss and nonmonetary deprivation must be taken into account. Chalk (P) successfully demonstrated that the motion would probably succeed on the merits of the case. Thus, the district court (D) erred in focusing solely on monetary loss when making its determination. Accordingly, the district court (D) erred when it denied Chalk's (P) motion for a preliminary injunction. Reversed and remanded.

COMMENT: The court noted that a person with AIDS could be reevaluated under the "otherwise qualified" clause contained in § 504 of the Rehabilitation Act if the person developed a contagious disease. Administrators must balance the rights of an employee with AIDS against the risk presented to other employees and to students who come within the infected employee's presence; however, the balancing test must rest on the best medical knowledge and not on irrational fear and prejudice. As HIV cannot be transmitted casually, mere infection with the virus is not enough to justify reevaluation. Moreover, development of symptoms of AIDS, i.e., specific secondary infections which are typical of the disease, will not necessarily justify reevaluation. For example, Karposi's sarcoma, a rare cancer, poses no risk of casual transmission, whereas tuberculosis, an air-

borne lung infection, does. The former would not justify reevaluation but the latter probably would. School administrators, when transferring a teacher with a contagious disease such as AIDS, are best protected against suit by obtaining the written permission of the employee to be transferred. This case is a warning to school administrators that they cannot operate in the personnel area without exercising caution. Great care must be taken when transferring a teacher with a contagious disease such as AIDS. Regardless of the community pressure which may be generated for an administrative transfer, unless permission is secured from the person, an arbitrary transfer could result in a tortious situation.

NOTES:

NOTES

LOCAL SCHOOL BOARDS

▶ CHAPTER SUMMARY

CHAPTER 4: LOCAL SCHOOL BOARDS

QUICK REFERENCE RULES OF LAW

4

1. **Legislature-delegated authority:** Local school boards are delegated the authority with which to govern their respective districts by state legislatures. (§ I.A.)

2. **Board jurisdiction:** Local boards are generally empowered to take action with respect to local curricula, revenue generation, personnel issues, among other functions. (§ I.B.)

3. **Distinct entities:** Local school boards and local government are separate, distinct entities. (§ I.E.)

4. **Nature of authority:** Authority delegated to local boards may be express or implied and discretionary or ministerial. Implied authority is commonly upheld by courts as a necessary and practical means of effectuating express authority. Discretionary authority, which involves judgment, generally cannot be delegated to subordinate personnel. (§ I.C.D.)

5. **State officers:** Local school board members are state, not local, officers (§ II.A.)

6. **Member selection and limitations:** Generally speaking, board members are elected or appointed, may not use their sovereign positions for their private gain, and may be removed only for cause. (§ II.B.)

7. **Board elections:** School board elections are set by statute; the "one person, one vote" principle predominates, and members may be elected from subdistricts or "at large." (§ II.B.)

8. **Invalid election standard:** A school board election will not be declared invalid unless the disputed conduct of the election renders the results uncertain. (§ II.B.3.)

9. **Collective board action:** School board members must act collectively; individual members may not act on behalf of the entire board. (§ II.B.2.)

10. **Board rules and regulations:** Local boards are generally free to set their own procedural rules and regulations in connection with board meetings. (§ III.A.)

11. **Board meeting requirements:** Board meetings must be held within school district territory, must be open to the public, and must be recorded in official minutes. (§ III.)

Introduction: The local school board is a creature of state government, and, as such, its members are considered state, not local, officers. A state legislature typically enacts legislation providing for the creation of local boards and the selection and retention of board members. The authority delegated to local board members is *sovereign* in nature and is broadly interpreted by the courts. As with most elected or appointed officials, board members are forbidden from delegating their discretionary (as opposed to ministerial) authority to other entities or parties.

I. AUTHORITY OF THE LOCAL SCHOOL BOARD

4

The issue: While education in this country is the responsibility of the states, portions of it must necessarily be administered at the local level. State legislatures generally delegate the responsibility of administering local school districts to local school boards. Note, however, that in some cases, a state board of education, itself a creature of legislative delegation, may oversee various functions or aspects of local school districts. As a rule, a local school board is empowered to make a wide range of operational decisions affecting its district.

A. The Local School Board — An Arm of State Government: Because education is a unique state function, a state government may delegate but not distribute its authority to govern the state school system to local school boards. Authority is commonly delegated by way of legislative enactments or regulations.

B. State-Delegated Authority of Local Boards: State legislatures frequently empower local boards to do part or all of each of the following specific functions:

1. *Establish curriculum:* Oversee and respond to specific curriculum-related needs of the local district.

   a. *Effect of federal law:* Federal law may be controlling with regard to the curriculum-setting practices of the local board.

   Example: A group of Chinese-speaking students challenged the San Francisco school board's refusal to provide them either with instruction in the English language or with classes in their native language. The U.S. Supreme Court held that the local board's inaction in this regard was a violation of the federal Civil Rights Act of 1964. *See Lau v. Nichols,* 414 U.S. 563, 94 S. Ct. 786 (1974).

   b. *Effect of federal Constitution:* The U.S. Constitution is also controlling. Therefore, when there is a conflict between the U.S. Constitution and a local school board action, the school board's preference must give way to the Constitution.

4

Example: An Arkansas school board prohibited the teaching of Darwin's theory of evolution in schools. This was held to be unconstitutional: neither a state nor a local school board may forbid the teaching of evolution because doing so promotes a religion (as embodied in the board-approved Genesis creation theory) in violation of the First Amendment to the federal Constitution. *See Epperson v. Arkansas,* 393 U.S. 97, 89 S. Ct. 266 (1968).

Example: A Nebraska statute prohibited the teaching of a foreign language to a child before the eighth grade. This was held to be a violation of the Fourteenth Amendment's liberty guarantees. Among these guarantees are the rights of teachers to teach and students to acquire knowledge. *See Meyer v. Nebraska,* 262 U.S. 390 (1923).

Example: Florida state courts would not entertain § 1983 claims against school boards on the ground that doing so would violate sovereign immunity. Such an interpretation would lead to a rule that state agencies are not subject to liability under § 1983. This state court failure to enforce a federal law is a violation of the Supremacy Clause. *See Howlett v. Rose,* 496 U.S. 356 (1990).

2. *Raise school revenues:* Raise revenues for school construction and maintenance.

3. *Employ and discharge personnel:* Hire and fire personnel, such as teachers and administrators.

4. *Establish policy:* Set and implement other policies necessary to the operation of the school district, such as rules and regulations pertaining to student conduct, athletic activities, and competitive examinations.

   a. *Pledge of Allegiance:* A student's First Amendment right to refrain from reciting the pledge of allegiance was upheld by a federal court of appeals in *Goetz v. Ansell,* 477 F.2d 636 (2nd Cir. 1973). Specifically, a local school board's rule requiring that all students who chose not to pledge must leave the classroom or stand in silence during the recitation was declared unconstitutional.

   b. *Access to school athletics:* A student's constitutional right to a public education does *not* prohibit a state (and by delegation a local school board or state athletic association) from restricting access to athletic activities. In *Albach v. Odle,* 531 F.2d 983 (10th Cir. 1976), a rule barring newly transferred students from participating in athletics was upheld in light of the court's ruling that athletic participation was not a protected part of the broader right to a public education.

c. *Pregraduation competency exams:* A federal court of appeals held that a challenge to a state law requiring passage of a competency exam prior to high school graduation would not lie where the students challenging the exam requirement had received sufficient instruction in the skills tested and where the exam helped remedy rather than perpetuate past discrimination. *See Debra P. v. Turlington,* 564 F. Supp. 177, aff'd. 730 F.2d 1405 (11th Cir. 1984).

d. *Management of school affairs:* Local school boards have wide discretion in the management of school affairs. Nevertheless, this discretion is not unlimited. For example, a local school board may not remove selected books from the library simply because it dislikes the ideas conveyed in the books. *See Board of Ed. of Island Trees Union Free School District #26 v. Pico,* 457 U.S. 853 (1982).

C. Express or Implied Local Board Authority

1. **Express power:** An express power is one that is specified in state laws or administrative regulations.

2. **Implied power:** An implied power generally flows from an express power, *i.e.,* it is "implied" in the grant of an express power such that if it was not assumed, the express power could not be exercised.

   a. *Court reluctance to recognize:* Generally, courts are not disposed toward recognizing implied powers.

   b. *Broadly construed:* However, with regard to local school boards, most courts construe implied powers broadly, perhaps in recognition of the practical need for them.

D. "Discretionary" or "Ministerial" Authority: Authority delegated to local boards is either "discretionary" or "ministerial" in nature.

1. **Discretionary powers:** Powers are referred to as "discretionary" when they call for an exercise of judgment or discretion on the part of the person to whom they have been delegated.

   a. *Generally nondelegable:* Such powers generally cannot be delegated by local board members to subordinate employees, such as superintendents and other administrators.

b. *Typical nondelegable discretionary powers:* Typical nondelegable discretionary powers include the powers to transfer or reassign teachers, close schools, and raise revenues.

2. *Ministerial powers:* Powers are referred to as "ministerial" if they are more or less perfunctory or administrative in nature, *i.e.,* involve little or no discretion and are a necessary means of carrying out a particular policy, *e.g.,* the development (as opposed to the adoption) of a district budget.

a. *Generally delegable:* Such powers can be and are often delegated by local board members to district employees.

b. *Court noninterference:* As a rule, courts will not interfere with a local school board's exercise of its discretionary authority unless in doing so the board violates the law or in some manner abuses its authority. Soundness of judgment is not a criterion considered by a reviewing court.

E. **Separate and Distinct Nature of Local School District and Local Government:** The local school district and local government are separate, distinct entities. Local school districts and municipal government functions are rarely, if ever, merged.

SCHOOL BOARD OFFICERS AND ELECTIONS

II. **SCHOOL BOARD OFFICERS AND ELECTIONS**

A. **State Officer Status of Board Members:** School board members are state officers — as opposed to employees.

1. *Sovereign functions:* One who holds an office carries out a sovereign function on behalf of the general public.

2. *Appointment or election:* An officer acquires her sovereign position by appointment or election.

3. *Private gain prohibited:* As a rule, an officer may not exercise her public position in a manner which leads to her private gain.

4. *Acceptance of resignation:* In some cases, an officer may not resign without the approval of the sovereign (in the case of a school board member, this means the state legislature).

5. *Removal for cause:* An officer may be removed for cause only unless the law provides otherwise. Notice and some sort of a fair hearing are generally required.

B. **School Board Election Requirements:** School board elections are set by statute.

1. *"One person, one vote":* School board members are generally elected according to the "one person, one vote" principle.

   a. *Election by geographical districts:* Board members may be elected from geographical subdistricts of the entire school district by the voters of their respective districts.

   b. *Election "at large":* As an alternative to district elections, board members may be elected "at large," *i.e.,* by the voters of the entire school district. In such cases, the candidates with the highest number of votes become school board members.

2. *Collective board action:* Once elected, the board must act collectively. Individual board members may not set policies on behalf of the entire board, nor may they alone represent the interests of the full board.

3. *Standard for invalidation of irregular election:* Irregularities in the conduct of a school board election will not result in the invalidation of the election so long as the results are reasonably certain.

III. SCHOOL BOARD MEETINGS

SCHOOL BOARD MEETINGS

A. **Procedural Rules and Regulations:** Generally speaking, each local school board is free to set its own procedural rules and regulations.

   1. *Statutory rules and regulations:* In some cases, state legislatures prescribe by statute pertinent rules and regulations.

   2. *Use of parliamentary procedure:* In other cases, where no statutory requirements exist and the local board has not adopted its own rules, common parliamentary procedure will control.

B. **Meeting Location:** All meetings must be conducted within the territorial jurisdiction of the local school board.

C. **Open and Public Deliberations:** Most courts and a large number of state statutes require that local school board meetings be conducted in a manner that is open to the public, *i.e.,* deliberations must be conducted and official actions must be taken in public.

D. **Executive Session:** Board members sometimes adjourn public meetings in order to consider sensitive matters in private (or in executive session, as this type of meeting is commonly termed).

1. *Sensitive matters:* Sensitive matters include those that would adversely affect the public interest if presented at an open meeting, such as the board's intended posture in connection with specific ongoing litigation.

2. *Formal action prohibited:* However, no formal actions may be taken in executive session; such meetings are for purposes of discussion only. If a local board wishes to take action based on executive session discussions, it must readjourn in open session and thereafter make its action official.

E. **Proper Notice of Meetings:** Proper notice as to the time and place of each scheduled board meeting must be provided to each board member. Notice is proper if it is likely to be considered reasonable by a court of law.

F. **Voting Procedures:** Local school boards are free to establish their own voting procedures, if they have not been preempted in this area by state law. A quorum, usually defined as a majority of board members, is required for action to be taken.

G. **Minutes:** The official, *i.e.,* legal, record of the local school board is contained in the minutes of its meetings, to which the public must be allowed access once they have been transcribed.

NOTES:

LAU v. NICHOLS
414 U.S. 563, 94 S. Ct. 786 (1974).

NATURE OF CASE: Class action by Chinese students challenging San Francisco school district's curricula.

GENERAL RULE OF LAW: Federally funded schools violate the 1964 Civil Rights Act if they do not provide their non-English-speaking students with either instruction in how to speak English or with classes in their native language.

PROCEDURE SUMMARY:
Plaintiffs: Lau (P) and other non-English-speaking Chinese students.
Defendant: San Francisco Unified School District (D).
U.S. District Court Decision: Held for San Francisco Unified School District (D).
U.S. Court of Appeals Decision: Affirmed.
U.S. Supreme Court Decision: Reversed.

FACTS: California law required English to be the language of instruction in its schools and required graduating students to pass standard proficiency examinations given in English. However, the San Francisco Unified School District (D) did not provide its non-English-speaking students of Chinese descent either course instruction in Chinese or separate classes on the English language. Lau (P) and other Chinese students filed a class-action lawsuit against the school district in order to break down this language barrier, which effectively prevented them from getting an education equivalent to that received by English-speaking students. As federally funded institutions, the San Francisco schools were subject to the 1964 Civil Rights Act as well as (the then) Department of Health, Education, and Welfare (HEW) regulations which assured equal access to education for students of all races and which mandated correction of language deficiencies which made access unequal. The U.S. district court and the court of appeals both denied the students' (P) claim, in part on the ground that all students, regardless of race, enter school with unique disadvantages which the school itself had not caused and had no responsibility for correcting.

ISSUE: Do federally funded schools violate the 1964 Civil Rights Act if they do not provide their non-English-speaking students with either instruction in how to speak English or with classes in their native language?

HOLDING AND DECISION: (Douglas, J.) Yes. Federally funded schools violate the 1964 Civil Rights Act if they do not provide their non-English-speaking students with either instruction in the English language or with classes in their native language. The Civil Rights Act bans discrimination based on race, color, or national origin in any program which receives federal financial assistance. The San Francisco Unified School District (D) is federally funded. Even though it provides its students of Chinese ancestry the same facilities, textbooks, teachers, and curricula as its non-Chinese students, it has denied them meaningful access to education because these students cannot understand English, the language used in all classes. They are not provided instruction in the English language. This practice also violates HEW regulations, which require federally funded schools to correct language deficiencies which prevent non-English-speaking students from effectively obtaining the same education as English-speaking ones. Reversed.

COMMENT: This case left many questions unanswered. First, the exact threshold number of non-English-speaking students of a particular ancestry which would trigger the need for special instruction was not specified. Justice Blackmun, in a concurring opinion, said that he had voted with the majority in this case principally because San Francisco had such a large number (1,800) of non-English-speaking students but that his decision would have been different if only one or a few students had been involved. Although smaller school districts were thus given little guidance, an informal standard of 20 or more students with the same language difficulty (perhaps the size of the average classroom) appeared to develop soon after this decision was handed down. Second, because the Court based its decision on the Civil Rights Act and HEW regulations, it did not rule whether the failure to offer remedial English instruction violated the Equal Protection Clause of the Fourteenth Amendment. Finally, no specific remedy was mandated by the Court, perhaps because the remedies were rather limited in number (*e.g.*, English language classes or course instruction in the students' native language) and obvious and because the Court wished to leave the choice of remedy to the local school districts themselves. Bilingual education was not required in order to correct such a language inequity. Any remedy which corrects the constitutional inequity will suffice.

EPPERSON v. STATE OF ARKANSAS
393 U.S. 97, 89 S. Ct. 266 (1968).

NATURE OF CASE: Constitutional review of Arkansas law forbidding school instruction about the theory of evolution.

GENERAL RULE OF LAW: States may not forbid the teaching in public schools of theories, such as Darwinian evolution, which conflict with certain religions.

PROCEDURE SUMMARY:
Plaintiff: Epperson (P), a high school teacher.
Defendants: State of Arkansas (D); Little Rock, Arkansas School District (D).
State Trial Court Decision: Held for Epperson (P), finding state law unconstitutional.
State Supreme Court Decision: Reversed.
U.S. Supreme Court Decision: Reversed (trial court decision reinstated).

FACTS: In 1928, Arkansas enacted an "anti-evolution" law which prohibited the teaching in its public schools and universities of Darwin's theory of evolution. Teachers who taught evolution could be convicted of a misdemeanor. There was no record of a prosecution in Arkansas under the statute. Despite the law, a high school in Little Rock, Arkansas adopted a textbook that described Darwin's theory, upon the advice of its biology faculty. Susan Epperson (P) was then hired to teach biology. She wanted to use the textbook but was worried about being fired for using it, so she brought a constitutional challenge in court to the Arkansas "monkey law." The trial court held that the law interfered with the First Amendment right to freedom of speech, which included the freedoms to learn and to teach. The Arkansas Supreme Court, however, reversed and ruled that the law was constitutional, without deciding whether the word "teaching" as used in the law meant only explaining the theory of evolution as opposed to actually arguing that evolution was the only valid theory of man's creation.

ISSUE: May states forbid the teaching in public schools of theories, such as Darwinian evolution, which conflict with certain religions?

HOLDING AND DECISION: (Fortas, J.) No. States may not forbid the teaching in public schools of theories, such as Darwinian evolution, which conflict with certain religions. The First Amendment protects freedom of speech and inquiry and prohibits states from promoting specific religions. Thus, states may not require that teaching and learning be tailored to the principles of any particular religious sect or dogma. Arkansas' "monkey law" exists solely because the theory of evolution contradicts the ideas of creation as set forth in the Bible's Book of Genesis. But Arkansas cannot demand that Genesis be the exclusive source of doctrine as to the origin of man; to do so violates the First Amendment. To limit science instruction to only an antievolution theory "hinders the quest for knowledge, restrict[s] the freedom to learn, and restrain[s] the freedom to teach." Therefore, Arkansas' antievolution statute is unconstitutional. Reversed.

COMMENT: The U.S. Supreme Court based its decision here on the First Amendment prohibition of the state establishment of religion. Technically, the First Amendment alone does not directly apply to actions taken by the states, so the court also had to base its decision on the Fourteenth Amendment's Due Process Clause so that it would be applicable to state law, here, that of Arkansas. Here, the Establishment Clause was offended because the Arkansas antievolution statute was not neutral toward religion; it in fact aided religions (such as Christianity) which accept the Bible as a guide to church doctrine and which believe that Genesis provides the only acceptable explanation for man's creation.

NOTES:

MEYER v. NEBRASKA
262 U.S. 390, 43 S. Ct. 625 (1923).

NATURE OF CASE: Review of decision affirming criminal conviction for violation of a state law prohibiting the teaching of a foreign language to children before the eighth grade.

GENERAL RULE OF LAW: A law prohibiting the teaching of a foreign language to children before the eighth grade violates the Fourteenth Amendment.

PROCEDURE SUMMARY:
Plaintiff: Meyer (D), parochial school teacher convicted for violating the law.
Defendant: The State of Nebraska (P).
State Trial Court Decision: Convicted Meyer (D).
State Supreme Court Decision: Affirmed.
U.S. Supreme Court Decision: Reversed.

FACTS: Nebraska (P) enacted a statute forbidding the teaching of a foreign language to children before the eighth grade. Meyer (D) taught German to a 10-year-old parochial school student and was convicted for violating the law. The state supreme court upheld the conviction and the law, stating that it was a valid exercise of the police power. Meyer (D) was granted review by the Supreme Court, where it was contended the law violated the Fourteenth Amendment.

ISSUE: Does a law prohibiting the teaching of a foreign language to children before the eighth grade violate the Fourteenth Amendment?

HOLDING AND DECISION: (McReynolds, J.) Yes. A law prohibiting the teaching of a foreign language to children before the eighth grade violates the Fourteenth Amendment. The law unreasonably infringes upon the liberty rights guaranteed by the Fourteenth Amendment. Among these rights are the right of teachers to teach and students to acquire knowledge. Though the state's goal of ensuring that students learn English and American ideals is worthy, the law at issue is an impermissible means of accomplishing it. There is no national emergency justifying the complete ban, and it has not been shown that mere knowledge of a foreign language is harmful. Further, there is no support for the suggestion that the law's purpose was to protect children's health by limiting their mental activities. Thus, there is no rational basis for the law. Reversed.

COMMENT: It is significant that the case arose shortly after World War I. The law was clearly a response to the fear that immigrants coming to the United States would rear their children in something other than American democratic ideals. Also, the case is one of those rare situations where a law or statute failed the highly deferential "rational basis" test applied by the Court. This case has renewed interest in light of contemporary events which have given rise to a movement promoting English as the official language of individual states and the nation as a whole.

NOTES:

4

HOWLETT v. ROSE
496 U.S. 356, 110 S. Ct. 2430 (1990).

4

NATURE OF CASE: Review of dismissal of a § 1983 civil rights claim alleging the search of a student's car by a school official and subsequent suspension of the student violated the Fourth and Fourteenth Amendments of the Constitution.

GENERAL RULE OF LAW: A state court's refusal to entertain a § 1983 claim against a school board on sovereign immunity grounds violates the Supremacy Clause.

PROCEDURE SUMMARY:
Plaintiff: Howlett (P), a former high school student.
Defendant: Rose (D), Superintendent of Schools for Pinellas County.
State Circuit Court Decision: Held for Rose (D), dismissing on grounds the state court lacked jurisdiction over the § 1983 claim.
State Court of Appeal Decision: Affirmed.
U.S. Supreme Court Decision: Reversed.

FACTS: An assistant principal searched Howlett's (P) car while it was parked on school premises. Based on the search, Howlett (P), then a student, was suspended for five days. Howlett (P) filed suit in state court under § 1983 of the Civil Rights Act of 1871, arguing that the search and suspension violated his rights under the Fourth and Fourteenth Amendments of the U.S. Constitution. Rose (D), the school's superintendent, moved to dismiss the action, arguing the state court lacked jurisdiction to hear the § 1983 claim because the state waiver of immunity statute did not apply to federal claims. The circuit court agreed and granted Rose's (D) motion. The state court of appeal affirmed. The U.S. Supreme Court granted review.

ISSUE: May a state court refuse to entertain a § 1983 claim against a school board on grounds that to do so would violate soveriegn immunity?

HOLDING AND DECISION: (Stevens, J.) No. A state court may not refuse to entertain a § 1983 claim on grounds that to do so would violate sovereign immunity where the court otherwise has jurisdiction and the defense could not be raised had the claim been brought in federal court. Absent a valid excuse, a state court's failure to enforce federal law according to the court's normal procedures is a violation of the Supremacy Clause. The refusal to entertain a § 1983 claim against the school board directly violates federal law if the refusal amounts to a rule that state agencies are not subject to liability under § 1983. The lower courts' interpretation of *Hill v. Department of Corrections,* 513 So.2d 129 (1987), as extending immunity to school districts indicates the adoption of an erroneous rule. Reversed.

COMMENT: *Howlett* was a unanimous decision clearly indicating that state infringement upon the supremacy concept of federalism would not be tolerated. State courts may not deny a right guaranteed by the U.S. Constitution based upon a state law or practice that is in conflict with the federal right. Specifically, however, the case may have a chilling effect on school boards and officials. The decision makes clear that their actions must pass federal civil rights protection even when federal law is more stringent than any similar state protections.

NOTES:

GOETZ v. ANSELL
477 F.2d 636 (2d Cir. 1973).

NATURE OF CASE: Appeal from denial of a student's challenge to constitutionality of his suspension for refusal to participate in the pledge of allegiance.

GENERAL RULE OF LAW: The state may not compel students to participate in the pledge of allegiance by requiring them either to say it or to stand while it is being said.

PROCEDURE SUMMARY:
Plaintiff: Goetz (P), a senior high school honor student and class president.
Defendant: Ansell (D), president of North Colonie School District Board of Education.
U.S. District Court Decision: Held for Ansell (D).
U.S. Court of Appeals Decision: Reversed.

FACTS: Goetz (P), a senior high school honor student and president of his class, refused to participate in the pledge of allegiance. The President of the Board of Education, Ansell (D), gave Goetz (P) the option of either leaving the classroom or standing silently during the recitation of the pledge. Goetz (P), contending that he had a First Amendment right to stay quietly seated, sued Ansell (D) in federal district court, alleging that Ansell (D) was violating his right of free speech under the First Amendment. The district court did not reach the merits of Goetz's (P) case, preferring to dismiss it because Goetz (P) had not gone first to the Board of Education for a hearing or to the New York Commissioner of Education. Goetz (P) appealed this dismissal to the Second Circuit Court of Appeals.

ISSUE: May the state compel students to participate in the pledge of allegiance by requiring them either to say it or to stand while it is being said?

HOLDING AND DECISION: (Feinberg, J.) No. A state may not, consistent with the First Amendment of the Constitution, compel a student to stand during recitation of the pledge of allegiance or make the student utter its words. Standing is part of the pledge as much as saying it and is a gesture of acceptance and respect. Thus, boards of education must allow silent, nondisruptive expressions of belief, such as sitting down. Nor can boards of education compel students to leave the classroom while the pledge is being said, as this could be interpreted by other students as punishment for nonparticipation and could subject the student to reproach and contempt among his classmates. Goetz (P), by sitting silently during the pledge, was legitimately asserting his First Amendment rights, and Ansell (D) had no basis for asking him to leave the room or stand during its recitation. Reversed.

COMMENT: In reaching this decision, the Second Circuit heavily emphasized that Goetz's (P) refusal to stand did not disrupt or interfere with the rights of other students to say the pledge. Obviously, if Goetz (P) had been disruptive, Ansell's (D) command to leave the room would have rested on stronger ground because Goetz (P) would then be interfering with the First Amendment freedoms of others. Although not addressed in this decision, Goetz's (P) claim had a legitimate basis in another aspect of the First Amendment: the right to free exercise of religion. Because the pledge explicitly refers to "one nation under God," Ansell's (D) directive that Goetz (P) stand could have also signaled acquiescence in belief in a deity or supernatural being.

NOTES:

ALBACH v. ODLE
531 F.2d 983 (10th Cir. 1976).

4

NATURE OF CASE: Appeal from unsuccessful constitutional challenge to an interscholastic activities association's rule barring transfer students from participating in interscholastic athletic competition.

GENERAL RULE OF LAW: A student's constitutional right to a public education does not prevent appropriate state boards from regulating access to interscholastic athletics.

PROCEDURE SUMMARY:
Plaintiff: Albach (P), a high school transfer student.
Defendant: Odle (D), Executive Secretary of New Mexico Activities Association.
U.S. District Court Trial Decision: Held for Odle (D).
U.S. Court of Appeals Decision: Affirmed.

FACTS: The New Mexico Activities Association, of which Odle (D) was Executive Secretary, barred students from interscholastic high school competition for one year if they had recently transferred between a boarding school and a home district school. Albach (P) was a student covered by the rule, but he wanted to participate in school athletics. Therefore, he sued Odle (D), claiming that the rule barring him from participation was unconstitutional because he had a protected property right in a public education. The district court found for Odle (D), and Albach (P) appealed to the Tenth Circuit Court of Appeals.

ISSUE: Does a student's constitutional right to a public education prevent a state from regulating or restricting access to interscholastic athletics?

HOLDING AND DECISION: (Per curiam) No. A student's constitutional right to a public education does not prevent a state from regulating or restricting access to interscholastic athletics. Appropriate state boards have the discretion to supervise and regulate high school athletic programs, and their rules governing access will not be invalidated unless constitutionally protected "suspect classes," such as aliens or members of certain races, are excluded as a result. Although the right to a public education is constitutionally protected, its many components, including participation in athletic activity, are not individually or separately protected. Affirmed.

COMMENT: The court's decision here appears to be based on the fact that Albach's (P) exclusion from school was not complete and did not last for an unreasonable period of time. Albach (P) had based his claim on the U.S. Supreme Court decision of *Goss v. Lopez,* 419 U.S. 565, 95 S. Ct. 729 (1975), which recognized a student's property interest in public education. The student in the *Goss* case had been suspended for 10 days without a hearing and thus had been denied any and all access to public education for a defined period of time. The Supreme Court in *Goss* held that this deprived him of property without due process. It also held that this right of public education is not limited to classroom attendance but includes all activities, such as athletics and school clubs and social groups, which combined to provide an atmosphere of intellectual and moral advancement.

NOTES:

DEBRA P. v. TURLINGTON
564 F. Supp. 177;
aff'd, 730 F.2d 1405 (11th Cir. 1984).

NATURE OF CASE: Challenge to constitutionality of Florida's literacy test, passage of which is required for graduation from high school, on grounds that it did not test what was taught and that it had a racially discriminatory impact on blacks.

GENERAL RULE OF LAW: Students may be required to pass a competency examination in order to receive a high school diploma if the student has received sufficient instruction in the skills tested and if the test remedies rather than perpetuates the effects of past segregation in the high school district.

PROCEDURE SUMMARY:
Plaintiffs: Debra P. (P) and other Florida high school students.
Defendant: Turlington (D), Florida Commissioner of Education.
First U.S. District Court Decision: Held for Debra P. (P), enjoining use of test until 1982–1983 school year; held for Turlington (D), finding test valid.
First U.S. Court of Appeals Decision: Affirmed as to injunction; reversed as to holding that test was valid and remanded to determine if test covered materials actually taught and if test intentionally discriminated against blacks.
Second U.S. District Court Decision: Held for Turlington (D) on remand questions.
Second U.S. Court of Appeals Decision: Affirmed.

FACTS: In 1978, Florida began to require that public high school students pass a functional competency exam, the SSAT-II, in order to receive a diploma. The test covered both communications skills and math skills. The failure rate was 10 times higher for blacks than for whites in the test's first administration in 1979, but by 1983, 99% of blacks passed the communications part and 91% passed the math part. High school students (P) challenged the constitutionality of the examination, alleging that it denied them due process in requiring them to demonstrate competency in skills they had not been taught and that it violated the Civil Rights Act because it discriminated against blacks. During a first trial in the U.S. district court, surveys were introduced which showed that most students believed Florida taught what it tested; expert witnesses also testified that each student received an average of 2.7 opportunities to

learn skills tested. Further, the schools made extensive remedial efforts to help students who initially failed the test pass it before graduation. The district court held that the SSAT-II's content was valid but also held the test violated the Equal Protection Clause and the Civil Rights Act by perpetuating past discrimination against blacks who had attended segregated schools for the first four years of their education; because only students in the high school class of 1983 would be the first to have attended physically integrated schools for all of their 12 years of education, the test could not be administered until 1983. The U.S. Court of Appeals upheld the injunction but reversed and remanded. It instructed the district court to determine whether the exam was a "fair test of that which is taught" and whether the test reflected present effects of past discrimination or actually helped remedy past discrimination. On remand, the district court held that the test was "instructionally valid" and that although it had a racially discriminatory impact, the disproportionate rate of failure among blacks was not caused by past segregation. The students (P) appealed.

ISSUE: May students be required to pass a competency examination in order to graduate from high school?

HOLDING AND DECISION: (Anderson III, C.J.) Yes. Students may be required to pass a competency examination in order to receive a diploma from high school, if sufficient instruction has been provided for a student to master the skills tested and if the examination helps remedy rather than perpetuate any past history of segregation in the school district. Here, most of the Florida students surveyed (90–99%) believed they had been taught the skills tested, and evidence showed they had 2.7 opportunities to learn the material and were provided many chances for help if they failed it. Further, although proportionately more blacks fail the test than whites, this failure rate is probably caused mostly by other factors, including remaining biases among teachers that black students do not learn as well as whites. In fact, the black passage rate had improved dramatically between 1979 and 1983, indicating that the test helped blacks overcome the effects of past segregation. Affirmed.

COMMENT: The court here was most concerned

4 ▶

with whether "vestiges" of past discrimination against blacks caused poor performance on the SSAT-II, and it concluded that they had not. It emphasized the district court's finding of other facts that contributed to the higher black failure rate, such as frequent suspensions of black students, teacher stereotyping and bias, absence of black administrators, and more frequent assignment to EMR ("educable mentally retarded") classes — practices that were unrelated to the administration of the test. The court found that the use of the test as a "diploma sanction" actually helped motivate black students by creating a "climate of order" (which one expert testified was successful in Catholic schools) and that black improvement in test scores over a four-year period actually reflected progress in battling discrimination. The result has been that competency examinations, which must be instructionally valid, are an accepted educational practice. They are now common as a high school graduation requirement.

NOTES:

4

BOARD OF ED. OF ISLAND TREES UNION FREE SCHOOL DIST., #26 v. PICO
457 U.S. 853 (1982).

NATURE OF CASE: Review of reversal of a grant of a school board's motion for summary judgment in an action brought by students who alleged that the board's order to remove certain books from school libraries violated their rights under the First Amendment.

GENERAL RULE OF LAW: A local school board may not remove certain books from the library simply because it dislikes the ideas conveyed in the books.

PROCEDURE SUMMARY:
Plaintiff: Pico (P), a high school student.
Defendant: Board of Education (D) (Board).
U.S. District Court Decision: Granted summary judgment for Board (D).
U.S. Court of Appeals Decision: Reversed and remanded.
U.S. Supreme Court Decision: Affirmed.

FACTS: Certain members of the Board (D) obtained a listing of books described as "objectionable" for allegedly being anti-American, anti-Christian, and anti-Semitic at a conference sponsored by a politically conservative organization of parents. Subsequently, it was discovered that the local high school library contained nine of the books on the list. Later, the Board (D) appointed a committee, made up of parents and school staff, to read the books and recommend whether they should be removed from the library. The committee recommended that most of the books not be removed. Despite the committee's recommendation, the Board (D) ordered the books removed. Pico (P), a high school student, then filed suit under 42 U.S.C. § 1983, alleging the removal violated his rights under the First Amendment. The Board (D) moved for summary judgment, which the district court granted. Pico (P) appealed, and the court of appeals reversed, holding that a triable issue of fact existed. The Board (D) appealed, and the U.S. Supreme Court granted review.

ISSUE: May a local school board remove certain books from a school library simply because members of the board dislike the ideas conveyed in the books?

HOLDING AND DECISION: (Brennan, J.) No. A local school board may not remove certain books from a school library simply because members of the board dislike the ideas conveyed in the books. To do so would violate students' rights under the First Amendment. Local school boards have wide discretion in the management of school affairs. This discretion, however, is not unlimited. Whether removal of the books denied Pico (P) his First Amendment rights depends upon the Board's (D) motive for doing so. If the motive was to prescribe what is "orthodox in politics, nationalism, religion, or other matters of opinion," the action infringed the students' rights. This is a question of fact to be determined at trial. The court of appeals, therefore, was correct in reversing the district court's grant of summary judgment for the Board (D). Affirmed.

COMMENT: Prior to *Pico*, the courts of appeals were divided on whether and under what circumstances a school board could remove certain books from public school libraries. The Second Circuit, in *President's Council, Dist. 25 v. Community School Board,* 457 F.2d 289, held that a board could remove books that were without artistic or scientific merit. The Sixth Circuit, in *Minarcini v. Strongesville City School District,* 541 F.2d 577, (6 Cir. 1976), held that removal simply because the board found the books objectionable violated the First Amendment. The Court's rule in *Pico* appears to be an adoption of the Sixth Circuit's position, clarified by the observation that the board's motive for removal is the determinative factor. This plurality decision does allow school boards significant discretion in determining content. But this discretion cannot be exercised in a partisan or political manner so as to establish an official orthodoxy. A school board's rights need to be balanced in light of the First Amendment rights of students. Thus, if a board's motivation is to remove educationally unsuitable, vulgar books, this would not constitute an official suppression of ideas. Furthermore, when purchasing materials, school boards have the responsibility and duty to decide and exercise this very discretion. When the materials have been purchased and are in the library, a board's discretion is more limited (although various child-protective actions have been justified). When books are used in the classroom, the board's discretion is even more limited because of a teacher's academic freedoms.

NOTES

FINANCING OF PUBLIC SCHOOLS

CHAPTER SUMMARY

CHAPTER 5: FINANCING OF PUBLIC SCHOOLS

QUICK REFERENCE RULES OF LAW

5

1. **State taxing power:** The power to tax is an inherent power of the state, although it may be delegated to local bodies under certain specified circumstances. (§ I.A.1.)

2. **No local taxing power:** Local school districts have no authority to tax, despite the fact that they are often charged with the responsibility of operating district schools. (§ I.A.2.)

3. **Improper tax levies:** Taxes which have been levied improperly because of the taxing authority's failure to follow formal procedures will be declared invalid if the ignored procedures were mandatory, but if the ignored procedures were merely directory, the taxes will be declared valid. (§ I.A.6.)

4. **No recovery for illegal taxes already paid:** Taxpayers may not recover taxes they have paid pursuant to a tax levy that is subsequently declared illegal if their payments were made voluntarily as opposed to under duress or compulsion. (§ I.B.)

5. **No authority to borrow or issue:** Local school districts have no inherent authority to borrow funds or issue bonds or similar negotiable instruments. (§ I.C.)

6. **Limit on indebtedness:** The amount of debt that a local school district may incur is usually limited by statute or by state constitution. (§ I.D.)

7. **Federal education spending:** Congress may spend on education throughout the various states, so long as the purpose of its expenditures is not to control local education programs. (§ I.E.)

8. **Constitutional mandate:** Many state constitutions set forth specific plans for the distribution of education funds, while others merely set forth an intended purpose or goal of the distributions. (§ II.A.)

9. **Limited to constitutional funds:** Only those funds contemplated within a state's constitution are subject to constitutional mandates concerning their distribution. (§ II.A.3.)

10. **Unequal expenditures of funds:** Numerous lawsuits throughout the nation have challenged state school finance plans that are perceived as permitting uneven per-pupil expenditures of funds across the state's local school districts. (§ II.B.)

11. **Unusual expenditure suits properly brought in state court:** Because the U.S. Supreme Court has ruled that education is not a fundamental interest warranting "strict scrutiny" analysis, the appropriate forum for unequal expenditures suits is state court, not federal court, and the proper basis for unequal expenditures arguments is the state's own constitution and statutes, not federal law. (§ II.B.1.)

12. **Choice plans:** The state may create "choice" plans, permitting the education-consuming public to select from a variety of educational services, in a variety of settings, at public expense. (§ II.C.)

13. **Variations of choice:** Choice plans can be set up to provide various options for students, allowing them to select from any open school in their existing district; to select from any open school in any other district within the state; to receive a voucher redeemable for approved educational services from various sources; and/or to obtain educational service from approved private sector providers. (§ II.C.)

14. **Discretion in making education expenditures:** Local school boards are given considerable discretion in determining what constitutes a "public purpose" in connection with school fund expenditures. (§ III.)

NOTES:

5

Introduction: Most state constitutions empower state legislatures to tax and distribute funds for public schools. Local school districts and other local-level entities may also be authorized to provide funds to their schools. Sometimes, legal challenges are filed in opposition to the methods used by state legislatures to regulate and control revenues and expenditures. Similarly, local districts may be challenged in the courts by those who believe they are operating outside the limits of the powers conferred upon them by state government. Still another area of conflict involves the constitutional rights of students and the resulting impact on state school finance.

*PUBLIC SCHOOL
REVENUES*

I. PUBLIC SCHOOL REVENUES

A. Revenues Raised through Taxation

1. *Inherent power:* The power of taxation is an inherent power of the state which suffers no limitation except that provided by the Fourteenth Amendment to the U.S. Constitution (and by any limitation that may be contained in the state's own constitution).

2. *No inherent power:* Local school districts have no inherent power with respect to the levy of taxes. Such powers must be *specifically* conferred upon a local entity by the state legislature. *See e.g. Marion & McPherson Ry. Co. v. Alexander,* 63 Kan 72 (1901).

    a. *Strict adherence:* School districts must strictly adhere to the express language of their statutory authority.

    b. *Limited by courts:* Most courts are loathe to imply greater taxing authority than is apparent on the face of the conferring statute.

    c. *No powers despite mandate:* Even a statutory mandate to establish and operate a local school system does not give a local school board the authority to tax for funds to accomplish those purposes.

3. *Delegation of taxing authority:* The legislature may delegate its taxing power to subordinate bodies, both as to the form of tax and the rate of taxation.

    a. *Local elected bodies:* The legislature need not set any limits on the delegation of its power if the subordinate body is composed of local elected officials.

    b. *Appointed bodies:* However, if the subordinate body is appointed rather than elected, clear limitations must be placed on the extent of the delegated power, such as specifying the purpose for which the delegated power may be exercised and setting the maximum rates at which taxes may be levied.

4. ***State, not local, taxes:*** Even if the taxing authority is delegated to a local entity, the taxes that are imposed through the exercise of it remain state — not local — in nature.

5. ***Special taxes:*** Funds raised through special purpose taxation may be used only for that purpose. Funds remaining after distribution are to be allocated as the legislature sees fit.

6. ***Improper levies:*** When a school tax has been levied improperly, such as that which occurs as a result of a failure to follow a prescribed statutory procedure, courts will determine whether the statutory provision is mandatory or directory.

   a. *Mandatory provision:* Failure to follow a mandatory provision in levying a tax renders the tax invalid.

   b. *Directory provision:* Failure to follow a directory provision will not result in invalidation.

   c. *No clear guidelines:* Courts have not developed guidelines for determining the difference between mandatory and directory provisions, although they usually construe provisions liberally, *i.e.,* as directory, so as to avoid invalidating taxes and thereby harming educational programs that are dependent on the funds generated by the tax in question.

7. ***Rate of levies:*** Before taxes are levied, the amount of revenue to be generated must be determined. As a rule, a school board may not use its taxing power to over-tax and thereby establish a surplus fund. There is no requirement that the distribution of the funds must benefit all the properties assessed. So long as the tax is assessed equally and for the public welfare, it need not be distributed equally. *See Sawyer v. Gilmore, State Treasurer,* 109 Me. 169 (1912).

B. **Taxpayers' Remedies against Illegal Taxation:** In certain situations, a taxpayer may pay taxes in accordance with a law that is later held invalid for conflicting with the state or federal constitutions or for some other reason. The taxpayer, who will undoubtedly wish to recover the taxes illegally paid, does not necessarily have the right to a refund of such taxes.

   1. ***Taxes paid voluntarily:*** As a general rule, if an illegal tax was paid *voluntarily,* it is presumed that the taxpayer knew the underlying tax law was invalid, and no recovery will be permitted.

2. *Taxes paid under duress or compulsion:* The general rule of nonrecovery does not apply if payment of the tax was made under duress or compulsion.

3. *Taxes paid under protest:* In the case of a payment made following mere *protest*, the general rule of nonrecovery is usually applicable. A protest is usually not enough to make a payment involuntary, except in those jurisdictions that recognize it as such by statute.

4. *Policy considerations affecting recovery:* Whether or not a court rules in favor of a taxpayer may depend upon its characterization of what best serves the public interest. Public hardships may result if local agency funds are depleted by virtue of a court order requiring repayment.

5. *Injunctive relief:* Regardless of the foregoing, the collection of an illegal tax may be enjoined prior to actual collection.

C. **Revenues Raised through Bond Issues**

1. *No authority to borrow funds:* A local school board has no inherent power to borrow funds – despite the fact that it is usually charged with responsibility for the day-to-day management of its school system.

2. *No bond-issuing authority:* No authority to borrow also means no authority to issue bonds or other similar negotiable instruments.

3. *Authority conferred by statute:* The state legislature confers the authority to issue bonds upon the local school board, which usually must follow elaborate procedures.

    a. *Irregularities in issuance:* Failure to follow the required procedures may result in the bond issue being declared invalid.

    b. *View of most courts:* Most courts will likely uphold the validity of the issue if it appears that the irregularity does not deprive taxpayers of significant rights.

4. *Illegal bonds:* A bond issue that falls outside of the law is void. No recovery will be permitted.

    a. *Funds already spent:* A difficult situation arises when the illegality is not discovered until after the school board has spent the funds derived from the issue. There is no hard and fast rule.

b. *Bond holder may recover:* However, some courts will permit the bondholder to recover the value of the benefit conferred upon the school district from the illegal issuance of bonds – so long as the board had the authority to issue valid bonds initially and the issue would have been valid had the district exercised its authority properly.

D. Debt Ceiling Limits: The amount of indebtedness that a local school district may incur is generally limited by statute or by state constitution.

1. *Determination of indebtedness:* When a question arises as to whether the district's debt limit has been exceeded, a net indebtedness figure is determined by subtracting from all outstanding debts those assets which could be used to pay off the debts (such as cash on hand, taxes levied, etc.).

2. *Avoidance of debt:* A school district may resort to long-term leases and installment contracts for materials, services, or use of real estate in order to avoid debt creation, since technically such leases and contracts create a succession of separate obligations in the nature of current expenses (to be paid when due from current revenues).

E. Federal Funds

1. *Constitutional authorization:* Pursuant to the General Welfare Clause of the U.S. Constitution, Congress is authorized to spend money in furtherance of the education of the U.S. citizenry.

2. *Limited purpose:* The purpose of the funds spent, however, may not be that of regulation or control of educational programs within the states.

3. *Conditions may be imposed:* Before Congress offers education dollars to the states, it may attach conditions to such grants, but a state will not be bound to a condition unless it was fully aware of Congress' intent to impose it.

II. ALLOCATION OF STATE FUNDS

ALLOCATION OF STATE FUNDS

A. State Constitutional Mandates

1. *Specific distribution requirements:* In some states, the exact manner in which state school funds are to be distributed is set forth in the state's constitution.

2. *Nonspecific "goal" or "purpose":* In other states, the state constitution merely sets forth a goal or purpose of the intended distribution.

3. *Not all funds covered:* A state constitution's funding distribution requirements establish a mandatory level of education spending. Other funds may be earmarked and distributed by the state legislature, at its discretion, to fund other areas of education so long as such funds do not become a part of the "constitutional fund."

B. **Equalization of Resources:** A matter of continued controversy, over which a good deal of litigation has arisen, is the constitutionality of those state school finance plans that permit uneven per-pupil expenditures of funds among the state's local school districts. Under such plans, school districts with a strong tax base receive more tax dollars than school districts with a weak tax base. The wealthier districts thus receive more money to spend per pupil than the poorer districts, and it is not unusual for neighboring districts to have significantly disproportionate budgets. The obvious consequences include profound differences in facilitates, equipment, programs, and class size, all of which profoundly affect the quality of education provided each district's students.

1. *No fundamental right to education:* The United States Supreme Court held that education was *not* a fundamental interest requiring strict scrutiny of laws that impinge upon it under the Equal Protection Clause. *See San Antonio Indep. School Dist. v. Rodriguez*, 411 U.S. 1 (1973).

   a. *Effect of U.S. Supreme Court view:* The result is that decisions concerning the legality of state school financing plans are left to each state's constitution, its legislature, and its courts for interpretation.

   b. *Unreasonable classifications:* Most state constitutions contain a prohibition against "unreasonable classifications," the state equivalent of the U.S. Constitution's Equal Protection Clause. Those attacking state school finance plans often contend that such plans result in the creation of unreasonable classifications among pupils from different local school systems.

   Landmark: In a landmark state court opinion which preceded the U.S. Supreme Court's decision in the *Rodriguez* case, the California Supreme Court held that a state funding plan which permitted the quality of students' education to vary according to the wealth of their respective school districts discriminated against the poor in violation of the Equal

Protection Clause and a similar provision in the California constitution. The California funding plan had failed to equalize the discrepancies between districts with high property valuations and those with low valuations. *Serrano v. Priest,* 5 Cal.3d 584, 487 P.2d. 1241 (1971).

2. *Post-**Rodriguez** state court decisions:* Because of differences in the various states' constitutions and statutory financing plans, state court opinions pertaining to challenges to state financing plans have not been uniform. Where such courts have struck down financing plans, they have generally done so in response to significant disparity among various local school districts' per-pupil expenditures.

C. **"Choice" Plans:** Choice plans permit the education-consuming public to select from a variety of educational services, in a variety of settings, at public expense. Supporters believe that providing the public with a choice will do away with the education bureaucracy and lead to increased competition among the various educational alternatives, with all of the benefits that can be expected therefrom. Those in opposition argue that choice will destroy the current egalitarian, "melting pot" atmosphere within the public school system.

1. *Choice within and between public school systems:* Students are allowed to attend the school of their choice in their own school district or any other district in their state, so long as there is space for them at the school they desire and their choice does not upset existing desegregation plans.

2. *Choice within a public school system:* Students are allowed to attend a school within their school district other than the one they would normally attend.

3. *Voucher plan:* Parents receive a voucher, redeemable for a specific dollar amount per year per child, which may be spent on approved educational services (such as those provided in public or private schools). Government would ensure that each approved program met certain minimum educational standards.

4. *Services from private firms:* Public school systems contract with outside firms to provide specific educational services. The performance level of the students is the standard by which the outside firm is judged.

5

III. LOCAL SCHOOL DISTRICT BUDGETS AND EXPENDITURES

A. **Public Purpose Rule regarding Expenditures:** Local school boards are given considerable discretion in determining what constitutes a public purpose in connection with school fund expenditures.

1. *Improper purpose:* Courts will not intervene in a school board's exercise of its discretion to spend unless it is apparent that an expenditure has been made for an improper purpose, such as one that is contrary to a state statute or constitutional provision.

2. *Budgets controlled by municipal government:* In the case of a school system that is fiscally dependent upon its local municipal government, the courts construe board powers liberally. The board will not be restricted to the particularities of its budget so long as it does not attempt to spend more than it has been allocated.

B. **Budgetary Itemizations**

1. *Statutory requirement:* Most states require local school boards to prepare budgets of proposed expenditures. State statutes may also regulate the manner in which the budgets are prepared, published, and presented to the public.

2. *Source of litigation:* Occasionally taxpayers bring suit, contending that a local school board has failed to provide a sufficient itemization of expenditures within its budget. Such suits rarely prevail.

NOTES:

MARION & McPHERSON RY. CO. v. ALEXANDER

63 Kan. 72, 64 P. 978 (1901).

NATURE OF CASE: Appeal of decision holding a property tax assessed to fund and support schools constitutional.

GENERAL RULE OF LAW: The authority to assess a tax to fund schools is extraordinary and must be clearly given by the legislature.

PROCEDURE SUMMARY:
Plaintiff: Marion & McPherson Railway Co. (P) (Marion).
Defendant: Alexander (D), County Treasurer.
State District Court Decision: Held for Alexander (D), that tax was authorized by legislature and constitutional.
State Supreme Court Decision: Reversed.

FACTS: Various provisions of a Kansas statute gave counties power to levy a property tax not to exceed 2% annually for school purposes. Alexander (D), the county treasurer, levied a tax of 2% pursuant to these provisions. Marion (P), a property owner, sought to enjoin enforcement of the tax, contending that the assessment caused the total assessment for the district to exceed 2% in violation of the provisions. Alexander (D) countered that the provisions read together allowed the district to levy a 2% tax in addition to and separate from the other levies permitted by the provisions. Finding for Alexander (D), the district court sustained the tax assessment and denied an injunction. Marion (P) appealed.

ISSUE: Is the authority to assess a tax to fund and support schools extraordinary and, thus, must be clearly given by the legislature?

HOLDING AND DECISION: (Cunningham, J.) Yes. The authority to assess a tax to fund and support schools is extraordinary and must be clearly given by the legislature. Such authority can never be found by implication, as Alexander (D) suggests, unless it is a necessary implication. Any other rule would lead to great wrong and oppression. Thus, where there is a reasonable doubt as to the existence of such authority, as here, it must be denied. Reversed.

COMMENT: That school districts have no power to tax absent clearly expressed legislative authority is the rule in most states. State statutes, however, vary as to the extent of board power to raise and collect school taxes. In some states, school boards are fiscally independent, meaning that they have the power to set the tax and distribute the funds collected as they desire. Other boards are fiscally dependent, meaning they only receive a portion of funds collected; some other local entity has the actual power to access the tax and collect and distribute the funds.

NOTES:

SAWYER v. GILMORE, STATE TREASURER
109 Me. 169, 83 A. 673 (1912).

NATURE OF CASE: Action to enjoin a property tax assessment to fund public schools on grounds that unorganized townships would be taxed but would not receive any portion of the funds collected.

GENERAL RULE OF LAW: A tax assessment to fund public schools is not necessarily invalid where the funds are distributed in a manner that does not benefit all the properties assessed.

PROCEDURE SUMMARY:
Plaintiff: Sawyer (P), a taxpayer in an unorganized township.
Defendant: Gilmore (D), state treasurer.
State Supreme Judicial Court Decision: Held for Gilmore (D), finding the tax assessment constitutional.

FACTS: Maine enacted a law assessing a tax on all real property to fund public schools. Real property in unorganized townships was subject to the tax; however, such townships received no portion of the tax benefits. Sawyer (P), a taxpayer who lived in an unorganized township, sought to enjoin Gilmore (D), the state treasurer, from enforcing the tax assessment, contending that it violated the state constitution and the Equal Protection Clause of the U.S. Constitution's Fourteenth Amendment.

ISSUE: Must the funds raised by a tax assessment to fund public schools be distributed in a manner that benefits all the properties assessed?

HOLDING AND DECISION: (Cornish, J.) No. A tax assessment upon all which does not benefit all is not necessarily in violation of the Equal Protection Clause of the Constitution. So long as the tax is assessed equally and is for the public welfare, it need not be distributed equally. The manner in which the funds are distributed is within the legislature's discretion and is valid so long as there is no positive constitutional restriction. Here, the tax is assessed equally and is intended to fund public schools, a purpose clearly in the public welfare. Further, no positive constitutional restriction prohibits the manner in which the legislature has decided to distribute the funds. The assessment is therefore constitutional. Injunction denied; dismissed.

COMMENT: This case is a forerunner of the Su-

preme Court's landmark decision in *San Antonio Independent School District v. Rodriquez,* 411 U.S.1, 93 S. Ct. 1278 (1973). Both *Sawyer* and *Rodriguez* demonstrate the judiciary's unwillingness to hamper the legislature's judgment in dealing with local education funding problems. That the legislature has wide discretion in the manner in which such funds are distributed is rarely disputed nowadays. Today, the claim is that a particular method of distribution is an abuse of that discretion.

NOTES:

SAN ANTONIO INDEPENDENT SCHOOL DISTRICT v. RODRIGUEZ
411 U.S. 1, 93 S. Ct. 1278 (1973).

NATURE OF CASE: Appeal of decision invalidating as unconstitutional a property tax assessment system to fund public schools which gave affluent districts more money per student and poorer districts less money per student.

GENERAL RULE OF LAW: So long as no suspect class or fundamental right is implicated, the state need only show a rational basis for implementing a tax assessment plan to benefit public schools.

PROCEDURE SUMMARY:
Plaintiff: Rodriguez (P), a Mexican-American and parent of students attending public elementary and secondary schools.
Defendant: San Antonio Independent School District (D) (District).
U.S. District Court Decision: Held for Rodriguez (P), finding the assessment system invalid.
U.S. Supreme Court Decision: Reversed.

FACTS: The District (D) supplemented state funds received to support its schools with an ad valorem tax on property within the district. Rodriguez (P), a Mexican-American and parent of children attending District (D) schools, filed suit, alleging that the reliance on the tax base within a district favored the more affluent districts over the poorer districts in violation of the Equal Protection Clause of the Fourteenth Amendment. The district court held "wealth" to be a suspect classification and education a fundamental right requiring the District (D) to demonstrate a compelling state interest for the assessment system. The court held that the District (D) failed to show such a compelling interest or even a rational basis for the system and invalidated it. The District (D) appealed.

ISSUE: Need a state demonstrate only a rational basis for adopting an assessment system if no suspect classification or fundamental right is implicated?

HOLDING AND DECISION: (Powell, J.) Yes. So long as a no suspect classification or fundamental right is implicated, a state need only establish a rational basis for the implementation of a tax assessment system to fund public schools. Though education is one of the most important services

performed by the state, it is not a fundamental right. Furthermore, "wealth" is not a suspect classification. The system has not been shown to discriminate against any definable class of "poor" people. The local taxation, fiscal, and education policy matters at issue caution this Court to take a more restrained review. Therefore, though not perfect, the tax system cannot be said to bear no rational relationship to a legitimate state purpose, which is all the Constitution requires. Reversed.

COMMENT: This is a landmark case in that it establishes that education is not a fundamental right. It also clearly demonstrates the Court's unwillingness to interfere with states' attempts to deal with local fiscal and educational problems. The group alleged to be suspect here did not satisfy any of the traditional indicia of a suspect class. It was large, diverse, amorphous, and not clearly definable. Furthermore, it had not been subjected to a history of purposeful unequal treatment. This decision does not prevent states from determining on the basis of their individual constitutions that the kind of tax system upheld is prescribed. (States can extend rights but not diminish them beyond federal minimum requirements.) In fact, dozens of cases have been initiated in individual state courts challenging the constitutionality of similar "foundation formulas" to finance a state's public schools. State court decisions have been split, some validating the property tax and others holding it to be an unconstitutional violation based on state law. The trend of the last 10-15 cases has been to find unconstitutional those property tax assessment systems which give affluent districts more money per student and poorer districts less money per student.

NOTES:

NOTES

SCHOOL PROPERTY AND FUND USES

▶ **CHAPTER SUMMARY**

6

CHAPTER 6: SCHOOL PROPERTY AND FUND USES

QUICK REFERENCE RULES OF LAW

1. **School property is state, not local, in nature:** School property remains state property. It is merely held in trust by the local school district for the public's benefit. (§ I.A.1.)

2. **Control may be vested in any agency:** The legislature could, conceivably, vest control of local school property in another local agency. (§ I.A.2.)

3. **School property to be used for school-related purposes:** Some courts do not permit the use of school property for nonschool purposes. Where such uses are permissible, they must not interfere with school operations. (§ I.B.)

4. **Discrimination not permissible:** Where nonschool uses of property are permitted, local school boards cannot discriminate between users based on the contents of their expressions. (§ I.B.4.)

5. **Broad authority to acquire property:** Most school board are delegated broad authority to purchase property for school-related purposes. (§ I.C.)

6. **Power to take private property (eminent domain):** The taking of private property for public use is constitutionally permissible so long as it constitutes a necessity and the property owner receives just compensation for her loss. (§ I.C.3.)

7. **Disposition of school property:** Courts may validate unauthorized dispositions of school property if it is determined that they have been made in the public interest. (§ I.D.)

8. **Express authority required to transport students:** A school board must be authorized by statute to expend school funds in order to transport students to and from school. Even when this is the case, such authorizing statutes will be interpreted narrowly by the courts. (§ II.A.)

9. **Implied authority to insure:** Most school boards are impliedly authorized to expend school funds for insurance coverage. (§ II.B.1.)

10. **Short-term medical services permitted:** Most school boards are permitted to expend school funds for short-term, *i.e.,* emergency or first-aid, medical services as opposed to such services of a continuing nature. (§ II.C.1.)

11. **Legal services:** Most local school boards are impliedly authorized to expend school funds in order to pay for legal services provided on behalf of district employees. (§ II.C.2.)

NOTES:

6 ►

Introduction: Taxpayers and citizen groups occasionally challenge the use that a local school board makes of the property that is entrusted to its care by the state. Lawsuits may arise in connection with arguably "nonschool" uses to which school property may be subjected or, more frequently, in connection with the sale or other disposition of such property. Questions about the use of school funds generally arise when it is perceived that funds are not being expended for a school purpose or are being expended in violation of a particular statutory or constitutional provision.

I. SCHOOL PROPERTY

A. Nature of School Property

1. ***Held in trust:*** School property is state property, held in trust by the local school district, as trustee, for the benefit of the public at large.

2. ***Legislature maintains control:*** A state legislature does not relinquish its control over school property when it vests a local district with the power to acquire and hold property.

3. ***Legislature may change trustees:*** A state legislature could conceivably vest control of local school property in an agency other than the local school district. Or, it could reorganize smaller districts into one large district, thereby removing the local districts as trustees in favor of the new, larger district.

B. Permissible Uses of School Property

1. ***School-related uses acceptable:*** The general public may use school buildings for education or school-related purposes. Fees may be charged for usage.

2. ***Nonschool uses questionable:*** The use of school property for nonschool purposes has been forbidden by some courts. In other cases, nonschool uses have been permitted so long as they do not interfere with the school's programs and operations.

3. ***California's "civic center" concept:*** The California legislature has provided for a wide variety of nonschool uses on state school property. By statute, each state school is designated a *civic center* and as such is available for use by local organizations for a variety of community purposes.

4. ***Distinction between property uses and property users:*** When broad nonschool uses of property are permissible, local school boards must be careful not to distinguish between users

of school property based on the content of their respective expressions. *See Board of Education of the Westside Community School v. Mergens,* 496 U.S. 226 (1990) (in Chapter 2); *see also Resnick v. East Brunswick Township Board of Education,* 77 N.J. 88 (1978).

a. *Expression of a religious nature:* In 1981, the U.S. Supreme Court determined that religious groups could not be denied the same opportunities that were provided to nonreligious groups who routinely sought and were given permission to use school property for their own purposes.

b. *Prohibitions against loitering and solicitations:* Loitering on school grounds may be prohibited, provided that the enabling statute or ordinance is not so vague as to make it difficult to determine what type of conduct is proscribed. Blanket prohibitions against solicitations are probably not permissible, given their likely effect on freedom of speech rights.

C. Purchase of Property by Local Districts

1. *Potential for litigation:* Taxpayers sometimes question a local school board's use of tax money for the purchase of property when such a purchase does not appear to satisfy a generally accepted school purpose. Examples of questionable purchases have included acquisitions of property for playgrounds, athletic fields, and recreational centers.

2. *General rule:* Courts interpret the local board's authority *broadly* in this regard. This comports with most courts' expanded definition of the purpose of public education and local districts' authority, where properly delegated, to carry out that purpose.

3. *Taking of private property: Eminent domain* refers to the power of government to take private property for public use.

a. *Local school board use:* When authorized to do so by statute, local school boards may condemn and take for public use property that is needed for public school purposes.

b. *Constitutional requirements:* A taking by eminent domain must satisfy state and federal constitutional requirements of procedural due process, equal protection of the laws, and just compensation. The question of what constitutes "just compensation" has led to a good deal of litigation, although in most cases the fair market value of the property satisfies this requirement.

c. *Necessity requirement:* In taking property for public use, a school board must demonstrate the necessity of its taking, which means that it cannot condemn any more property than that which it actually needs.

d. *Property held by another public agency:* Generally, a school board cannot condemn property that is being held by another public agency. However, if two public agencies seek to condemn the same private property, the agency with the greater need will prevail.

D. Disposal of School Property

1. *Governed by statute:* The disposition of school property is usually governed by statute. Grants of authority to manage and control such property do not imply authority to sell it or give it away.

2. *No statutory authority:* Where no statutory authority exists, courts will review sales of property by local boards in order to determine whether there has been an abuse of discretion, *i.e.,* whether the board has taken an action which is not in the best interest of the school district.

USE OF SCHOOL
FUNDS FOR
PARTICULAR
PURPOSES

II. USE OF SCHOOL FUNDS FOR PARTICULAR PURPOSES

A. Student Transportation Services

1. *No implied authority:* Authority to transport students to and from school must be expressly conferred on local school boards by the state legislature, lest such actions be invalidated by the courts. Even a statute authorizing a local board to take necessary steps to maintain its schools and educate its students does not confer upon it the authority to spend district money on transportation services. Even where a local board has the responsibility to transport, it temporarily may withhold transportation services as a means of controlling improper student bus behavior. However, where such a suspension of services would result in the denial of educational opportunities or bring harm to students' reputations, it will not be permitted because it violates the students' Fourteenth Amendment due process rights. *See Rose v. Nashua Board of Education,* 679 F.2d 279 (1st Cir. 1982).

2. *Position of the courts:* Most courts interpret legislative grants of authority to transport students narrowly, in keeping with their view that transportation of students is the responsibility of parents and not the local school system.

3. *Alternatives to providing transportation:* In some states, school boards are empowered to pay a mileage rate to parents of students who live at considerable distances from public schools as a means of discharging their statutory obligation to provide transportation.

B. Insurance Coverage

1. *Implied power:* The power of a local school board to insure school property is generally implied from the board's mission.

2. *Pooled risk associations:* Occasionally, school boards seek to insure school property by joining associations which do not require premium payments but which do prorate losses among all association members. Because this may subject the district to large, uncertain losses or may amount, in effect, to a loan of public funds to other agencies which sustain losses, litigation has arisen in connection with this alternative. A pooled risk plan which sets no specified limit on the district's liability is probably invalid.

3. *Employee coverage:* Local boards generally may purchase group health, life, and disability insurance for employees, such as teachers and administrators.

C. Professional Services

1. *Medical services*

   a. *Extended services may not be provided:* The implied powers of local school boards usually do not include authority to pay for long-term or extended medical services for students who are injured on school property.

   b. *Limited emergency or first-aid services may be provided:* Implied authority exists to pay for short-term medical services, such as first-aid, in similar circumstances.

2. *Legal services*

   a. *Implied authority to fund:* In most jurisdictions, the authority to pay for legal services is implied.

   b. *Statutory authority under certain circumstances* In some jurisdictions, local school boards are authorized, by statute, to avail themselves of government attorneys when the need for legal services arises.

6

c. *Defense of school officials:* Public school funds may be spent to defend a school official who has been sued in his *individual* capacity so long as the official was fulfilling the duties of his position in good faith. (A suit against an official in his *official* capacity will almost certainly be funded.) Knowing that legal defense costs will be borne by the school district under appropriate circumstances permits school officials to perform their duties freely, without the inhibitions which sometimes result from expectations of lawsuits.

D. **Use of Funds for Other Purposes:** Implied powers may not extend to specialty items: purchases of arguably nonschool items for special segments of the student population may not be upheld by the courts as permissible under local board-implied powers. Examples include, in some instances, athletic gear and supplies and band uniforms. But implied powers have been extended to uphold the use of school funds to pay for a "buyout" of a superintendent's contract where taxpayers challenged this action as an unauthorized gift of public funds. *See Ingram v. Boone,* 91 A.D.2d 1063 (1983).

NOTES:

RESNICK v. EAST BRUNSWICK TOWNSHIP BOARD OF EDUCATION
77 N.J. 88, 389 A.2d 944 (1978).

NATURE OF CASE: Appeal from order prohibiting public school facilities from being made available for use by religious groups during noninstructional hours.

GENERAL RULE OF LAW: A religious group's temporary use of public school facilities at a rental rate reflecting the costs incurred by the school for such use does not violate the Establishment Clause.

PROCEDURE SUMMARY:
Plaintiff: Resnick (P), a high school student.
Defendant: East Brunswick Township Board of Education (D) (Board).
State Superior Court Decision: Held for Resnick (P).
State Court of Appeal Decision: Affirmed.
State Supreme Court Decision: Reversed.

FACTS: The Board (D) allowed a number of local groups, including various religious groups, to use its school facilities during nonschool hours. These groups were charged a rental fee which approximated a portion of the cost of janitorial services for maintenance of the facilities. Resnick (P) filed suit to enjoin use of the facilities by the religious groups, alleging the use of the facilities by religious groups violated the Establishment Clause of both federal and state constitutions. The superior court agreed, holding such use unconstitutional. The state court of appeal affirmed. The Board (D) appealed.

ISSUE: Does a religious group's temporary use of public school facilities at a rental rate reflecting the costs incurred by the school due to such use violate the Establishment Clause?

HOLDING AND DECISION: (Pashman, J.) No. A religious group's temporary use of public school facilities at a rental rate reflecting the costs incurred by the school due to such use does not violate the Establishment Clause. The processing of the applications submitted by religious groups by government employees does not amount to the kind of excessive entanglement of church and state prohibited by the Establishment Clause. Furthermore, where, as here, the Establishment Clause and the Free Exercise Clause of the Constitution confront one another, the Free Exercise Clause must take priority. The First Amendment requires strict neutrality with respect to religion.

The policy at issue, allowing use of public school facilities with reimbursement of cost, does not violate that neutrality. Reversed.

COMMENT: The rationale for the holding is that if one non-curriculum-related group or activity is allowed use of the facilities, it would violate the neutrality requirement not to allow another non-curriculum-related group or activity simply because it has religious affiliations. This rationale is affirmed by recent federal legislation enacted to guarantee equal access to student religious groups. The access issue might be: if co-curricular groups such as the "Key Club" are allowed to use the school facility before and after school hours, then a student religious group (e.g., a prayer group) would have equal access.

NOTES:

6

ROSE v. NASHUA BOARD OF EDUCATION
679 F.2d 279 (1st Cir. 1982).

NATURE OF CASE: Due process challenge to school board policy suspending certain school bus routes because student riders committed vandalism.

GENERAL RULE OF LAW: If school board policy merely inconveniences its students but does not deny them educational opportunity or harm their reputation, it does not violate their due process rights.

PROCEDURE SUMMARY:
Plaintiffs: Rose (P) and other parents of children subject to the suspension rule who had not been identified as "troublemakers."
Defendants: Nashua Board of Education (D) (Board).
U.S. District Court Decision: Held for Board (D), denying claim of civil rights violations.
U.S. Court of Appeals Decision: Affirmed.

FACTS: New Hampshire required its school districts to provide free school bus transportation to pupils under 14. However, vandalism and disruptive conduct, such as slashing seats, making noise, and throwing objects, began to threaten the safety of bus service in Nashua. The bus drivers could not identify which students were responsible because they had to keep their eyes on the road. The Nashua Board of Education (D) met to determine the best policy for preventing such student disruption and after deciding that alternatives such as seat assignments, ID cards, and monitors were too expensive or ineffective, decided to suspend certain routes for up to five days if prior warnings failed. In the policy's first two years of operation, disruptions decreased dramatically, and only 12 suspensions occurred the first year and four the next. The Board (D) also made accommodations for students who could not get to school any other way but left no alternatives for the others, who had to hitch a ride with their parents, walk, or carpool. Rose (P) believed that his child was not one of the "troublemakers," and he and other parents whose children were equally blameless sued the Board (D), claiming that suspending their children without a prior hearing on guilt or innocence deprived them of due process. The U.S. district court held that the policy did not offend the students' due process rights. Rose (P) and the other parents appealed.

ISSUE: If a school board policy does not deny its students educational opportunity or harm their reputation, does it violate their due process rights?

HOLDING AND DECISION: (Breyer, C.J.) No. A school board policy which merely inconveniences students but does not deny them educational opportunity or injure their reputation does not violate their due process rights. Here, Rose (P) and the other parents did not allege sufficient property rights violations to warrant due process scrutiny. A five-day bus suspension is merely an inconvenience, not a deprivation of education, educational opportunity, or reputational injury. A postsuspension hearing, which was provided for students in question, was sufficient protection of their due process rights. Thus, this minimal loss of bus service did not warrant presuspension due process protection, and a hearing to determine student guilt or innocence was not required. Affirmed.

COMMENT: In this case, the court held that the students' property interest in a bus route was not as strong as the state's interest in maintaining safety and discipline. The Board's (D) suspension of service on the bus route had been preceded by sufficient notice regarding the action to be taken to limit student misbehavior and vandalism. This case involved the court in deciding the proper exercise of judgment in a due process case. In *Rose*, the court not only had to decide if due process applied but also how much "process is due."

NOTES:

INGRAM v. BOONE

N.Y. Sup. Ct., 458 N.Y.S. 2d 671, 91 A.D.2d 1063 (1983).

NATURE OF CASE: Action by taxpayers in school district to establish their standing to challenge, on constitutional grounds, their school board's "buyout" of superintendent's contract.

GENERAL RULE OF LAW: Taxpayers in school districts may sue their school boards in order to challenge payments which appear to be unauthorized gifts of public moneys.

PROCEDURE SUMMARY:

Plaintiff: Ingram (P) and other resident taxpayers and parents of children attending public school in Nassau County, New York school district.

Defendant: Boone (D), chairman of Union Free School District, Hempstead, New York.

New York Trial Court Decision: Held for Ingram (P).

New York Court of Appeals Decision: Affirmed.

FACTS: Union Free School District in Nassau County, New York hired a superintendent by written contract for a four-year term. However, after becoming displeased with performance after only a year, the Union Free school board voted to buy out the remaining three years under the contract for a lump-sum payment of $65,000 and the continuation of the superintendent's insurance benefits through the expiration of the contract term. Ingram (P) and other resident taxpayers and parents of children attending school in the district filed suit in New York state court challenging the settlement as an unconstitutional gift of public funds; however, the initial issue decided by the court was whether Ingram (P) and the others had "standing," or the right, to maintain the suit. The trial court answered affirmatively, and Boone (D), chairman of the Union Free school board, appealed.

ISSUE: May taxpayers in school districts sue their school boards in order to challenge payments which appear to be unauthorized gifts of public moneys?

HOLDING AND DECISION: (Memorandum opinion) Yes. Taxpayers residing in school districts may sue their school boards in order to challenge payments which appear to be unauthorized gifts of public moneys. School boards may not merely assert in defense of such payments that

they properly exercised their discretion and judgment; a hearing is required in order to fully flesh out and test the validity of an agreement which appears to make an improper transfer. As residents who directly contributed to the school district's financing through payment of property taxes, and as parents whose children's quality of education may be affected by the decrease in funds attributable to an improper gift, Ingram (P) and the other parents have a direct interest in this constitutional challenge to the school board's settlement with the superintendent. Affirmed.

COMMENT: This case is important in providing precedent for citizen review of decisions of their school boards. Although school boards are endowed by their residents with broad latitude and discretion in making financial decisions, this discretion is not unlimited, and taxpayer "standing to sue" can provide an important "check" upon or disincentive against a school board's playing fast and loose with public moneys. Such school boards act in quasi-fiduciary capacities with regard to such funds paid to them by taxpayers.

NOTES:

REVELL v. MAYOR, ETC., OF ANNAPOLIS
Md. Ct. App., 81 Md. 1, 31 A. 695 (1895).

NATURE OF CASE: Challenge to legislative power authorizing local authorities to issue bonds to construct schools as unconstitutional "taking" of property.

GENERAL RULE OF LAW: States may confer by statute authority in local school districts to issue bonds to finance school construction.

PROCEDURE SUMMARY:
Plaintiff: Revell, school commissioner of Anne Arundel County (P).
Defendant: City of Annapolis, Maryland (D).
Trial Court Decision: Held for Annapolis (D).
Court of Appeals Decision: Reversed.

FACTS: A special act of the 1894 Maryland legislature authorized and directed the school commissioner of Anne Arundel County, Revell (P), to issue bonds to finance the construction of schools. It also directed the City of Annapolis (D) to issue bonds to help finance the schools. The City of Annapolis (D) refused to issue the bonds, and Revell (P) sued to enforce the state act. Revell's (P) lawsuit was dismissed for failure to state a cause of action, and Revell (P) appealed.

ISSUE: May states confer by statute authority in local school districts to issue bonds to finance school construction?

HOLDING AND DECISION: (Robinson, C.J.) Yes. States may confer by statute authority in local school districts to issue bonds to finance school construction. There is no difference between a state's direction that bonds be issued for the support of school districts and the levying of a tax, nor does this direction depend in any way on the consent of the voters of the school district. Providing schools is an ordinary function of municipal government, and the state does not abuse its power by compelling a municipality to levy a tax or incur a debt for the public purpose of constructing schools. Nor does the incurring of debt constitute a taking of property from citizens without due process of law under the Fourteenth Amendment. Here, the State of Maryland acted within its authority by directing Annapolis (D) to issue a bond to finance schools within Anne Arundel County, and Annapolis (D) violated this statute by refusing to issue the bonds. Reversed.

COMMENT: Bonds which a state authorizes to be issued for a specific purpose (as here, the construction of schools) must be used only for that purpose. This requirement has been construed strictly by the courts; for instance, one court held that a bond issued to finance installation of a new roof could not be used to subsidize the purchase of other equipment for the same school. *E.g., School District No. 6., Chase County v. Robb,* 150 Kan. 402, 93 P.2d 905 (1939). Unfortunately, despite the widespread and common use of municipal or county bonds to finance school expenses, if a school district issues bonds in excess of its authority, the innocent purchaser of the bonds has no recourse and suffers the loss of the purchase price. Further, most states constitutionally limit the amount of debt a school district can legally incur, although, as in the corporate world, some school districts have evaded these restrictions through the use of "holding companies" or "local building authorities" in which debt capacity is pooled among several entities.

NOTES:

TORT LIABILITY OF SCHOOL DISTRICTS, OFFICERS, AND EMPLOYEES

▶ **CHAPTER SUMMARY**

CHAPTER 7: TORT LIABILITY OF SCHOOL DISTRICTS, OFFICERS, AND EMPLOYEES

QUICK REFERENCE RULES OF LAW

1. **"Tort" defined:** A tort is a civil wrong, based in law rather than contract, which occurs when a person violates a duty that he owes to another, thereby causing injury. (*See* Introduction)

2. **Tort of negligence:** Negligence, the most common tort, involves the breach of a legal duty to protect another person from the risk of unreasonable harm. (§ I.A.)

3. **Duty to protect:** There can be no liability if the party being sued had no duty to protect the suing party from unreasonable risks. (§ I.B.)

4. **Standard of care:** A party breaches its duty to another when it fails to exercise a proper standard of care with respect to its conduct. (§ I.B.)

5. **Causal connection:** No recovery in negligence will be permitted unless it can be said that the party who is being sued was the legal cause of the injury suffered by the suing party. (§ I.C.)

6. **Injury suffered:** No recovery may be had in negligence unless the suing party has suffered an injury, translatable into an actual loss. (§ I.D.)

7. **Common duties in the school setting:** School personnel are commonly held to duties and appropriate standards of care in connection with the supervision, instruction, and punishment of students and the administration and maintenance of school buildings and grounds. (§ II.A)

8. **Common defenses to liability:** Defenses to liability commonly asserted by school personnel include the contributory negligence of the suing party, the assumption of an unreasonable risk by the suing party, and the failure of the suing party to establish each of the elements of negligence. (§ II.A.6.)

9. **School board members immune from certain suits:** School officers, such as board members, commonly enjoy immunity from lawsuits which charge them with negligence in the exercise of their discretionary, as opposed to ministerial, functions. (§ II.B.)

10. **Vicarious liability of school districts:** School districts are fictional entities and as such can only be assessed liability vicariously, based on the conduct of district employees and officers. (§ II.C.)

11. **Doctrine of governmental immunity (nonliability):** The old common law rule is that governmental agencies, such as school districts, cannot be held liable for the negligent acts of their officers, employees, and agents. (§ II.C.2.)

12. **Exceptions to doctrine:** In recent years, courts and state legislature have waived governmental immunity, thereby permitting recovery against school districts, in connection with suits concerning nuisances, proprietary activities on school property, administrative functions, violations of safety statutes, and injuries to school employees. (§ II.C.2.)

NOTES:

Introduction: A tort is a civil, as opposed to criminal, wrong. The law of torts is based on the theory that people are liable for the consequences of conduct that results in injury to others. Thus, a person commits a tort when he violates a duty, imposed by law rather than contract, that he owes to another. If his breach of duty has caused injury to the other party, he generally will be required to offer compensation in the form of money damages. Negligence, which involves the breach of a legal duty to protect an individual from the risk of unreasonable harm, is by far the most common category of tort in the context of the school system.[1]

When considering liabilities within the school system, one first must ascertain the nature and extent of the duties that the law requires of school district officers and employees and even of the school district itself. If a duty of care has been breached, it must be determined whether an injury has resulted. If such is the case, one next must determine whether the parties or entities that have committed torts may avail themselves of any special *defenses*, *privileges*, or *immunities* from suit.

ELEMENTS OF THE TORT OF NEGLIGENCE

I. **ELEMENTS OF THE TORT OF NEGLIGENCE: A tort action based on negligence may result from an improper act, or a failure to act, which causes injury to another. Before it will permit recovery, a court of law will determine if each of the following elements of this tort is present.**

A. **Duty**

1. ***"Duty" defined:*** The individual or entity that is being sued must have been held to a duty to protect another party from unreasonable risks.

2. ***Examples of "duty":*** In many states, education professionals are under a duty to their students to provide adequate instruction and supervision, to keep school facilities and property in good repair, and to warn of known dangers. *See* Section II., below.

B. **Standard of Care**

1. ***"Standard of care" defined:*** The individual or entity that is being sued must have breached its duty by failing to exercise *that degree of care which a reasonably prudent person would exercise in the same or similar circumstances. See Dailey v. Los Angeles Unified School District*, 470 P.2d 360 (1970). A child need only exercise the degree of care that is appropriate according to the child's age, experience, and mental capacity. *See Viveiros v. Hawaii*, 54 Haw. 611 (1973).

[1]The two other major categories of tort actions, intentional tort and strict liability, rarely surface in this context.

2. **"Reasonableness" is the key:** The standard of care that will be required in the school setting is based on the reasonableness of a person's actions in fulfilling his duty to another. Courts assess the reasonableness of a party's actions by determining whether a prudent person would have acted in the same manner under similar circumstances. *See Titus v. Lindberg,* 49 N.J. 66 (1967).

3. *Factors affecting the standard of care:* The extent or level of care that may be owed another will vary based on factors such as the age of students, the condition of facilities, etc. For example, greater care may be required when instructing the youngest of students (who have limited attention spans), just as greater care may be required when supervising student activities in older school buildings (where harm is more likely to occur).

C. Proximate (Legal) Cause

1. **"Proximate cause" defined:** The individual or entity that is being sued must be the *proximate* or *legal cause* of the conduct which has resulted in injury, which is another way of saying that there must be a legally recognized *causal connection* between the actions of the party being sued and the injury of the party who is suing.

2. **"Foreseeability" of the injury:** Whether or not the injury that has been sustained was a foreseeable consequence of a party's improper conduct is one means of determining if the party proximately caused the injury. An injury may not be foreseeable if an intervening event occurred after the allegedly improper conduct took place but before the injury manifested. *See Lawes v. Board of Education of the City of New York,* 16 N.Y.2d 302 (1965).

D. Injury

1. **"Injury" defined:** The party who is bringing suit must have suffered some kind of *injury,* be it physical or mental, resulting in a measurable *loss.*

2. *Examples of actual injuries:* Physical injuries may be defined by the financial losses that they have occasioned, *e.g.,* medical expenses, lost wages, etc. Mental injuries may be defined by the less easily quantifiable "pain and suffering."

7

II. TORT LIABILITY AND DEFENSES AGAINST LIABILITY IN THE SCHOOL SETTING

A. Liability of School District Personnel: Teachers, administrators, and other employees who make up the school system may be sued for tortious conduct that occurs in that setting. Below are common duties and standards of care that are required of various school personnel, followed by the defenses they commonly assert against liability.

1. *Adequacy of supervision:* The lion's share of negligence claims in the school setting involve allegations of failure to supervise students adequately.

   a. *Proper supervision defined:* One who adequately supervises is aware of the activities to be supervised, the conditions which surround those activities, and the potential dangers that could arise during activity periods.

   b. *General versus specific supervision:* In some cases, mere general supervision is sufficient to protect students from reasonably foreseeable dangers. In other cases, more specific supervision may be warranted, such as that commonly provided by a vocational instructor in a welding class.

   c. *No fixed time or territory:* It is the student activity itself, rather than the time of day or the location of its occurrence, that determines the type of supervision required and of whom it is required.

2. *Instruction:* Teachers may be liable for failing to provide appropriate instruction to students prior to their engaging in activities which may pose risks of harm.

   a. *Inappropriate instruction may be inferred:* Courts may infer a teacher's failure to provide appropriate instruction from the harm suffered by a student after undertaking an unreasonable risk. By way of example, the fact that a student has sustained a broken jaw after engaging in an authorized boxing match in physical education class indicates that the instructor failed to properly instruct the student in the principles of self-defense.

   b. *No liability where students disregard proper instruction:* However, a teacher may not be held liable in negligence if he can establish that he properly instructed his students, but such instructions were later disregarded.

7

3. *Corporal punishment:* The common law rule, which is in effect in most states today, is that educators will not be liable for administering *reasonable* corporal punishment to students.

    a. *School board overview:* School boards generally are empowered to regulate methods and procedures for administering corporal punishment.

    b. *Trend toward greater regulation:* A greater sensitivity to students' rights has led many school districts to require (1) that each school principal, as opposed to a specific teacher, determine where, when, and how such punishment will be administered and (2) that another adult be present at the time of the administration.

4. *Maintenance of property and facilities:* As a rule, those who own or possess property and buildings have a duty to maintain them in a *reasonably safe condition.* Negligence lawsuits frequently arise when unsafe conditions are not corrected, resulting in harm to an unsuspecting user.

    a. *Actual knowledge of dangerous condition not required:* An owner or possessor will be liable for an unsafe condition even if he is unaware that it exists, so long as a proper inspection would have revealed its existence.

    b. *Effect of conduct of injured party:* However, owners or possessors may not be held liable in negligence if it is apparent that the conduct of the injured party, rather than the unsafe condition, was the primary cause of the injury. *See* the defenses to liability discussed in section II.B.6., below.

5. *Administration:* As a rule, administrators are not liable for negligent acts of a staff member so long as:

    a. *Qualifications in order:* the staff member is qualified to perform the function in question, and

    b. *Adequate guidelines in place:* the administrator has developed sufficient guidelines for proper staff conduct.

6. *Common defenses to negligence:* The following defenses are frequently asserted by teachers and other school personnel in an attempt to avoid altogether or reduce their liabilities.

    a. *Establishing lack of essential element of negligence:* A school employee may seek to demonstrate that one or more of the elements that are required in order to establish negligence (breach of duty, etc.) are not present.

b. *Contributory negligence:* A school employee may seek to prove that the injured party's own conduct contributed to the injury. If contributory negligence is found, the injured party will be precluded from recovering.

(1) Note, however, that in assessing whether contributory negligence exists, children are not held to the same standard of care as adults.

(2) In most cases, contributory negligence will prohibit recovery if it can be proven that a student was aware of, or should have been aware of, the consequences of his actions but undertook a dangerous activity anyway.

c. *Assumption of risk:* Like contributory negligence, the assumption of risk defense prohibits recovery if it can be demonstrated that the injured party knowingly assumed a risk of harm. Once again, the age of the injured party will be crucial to the determination of whether voluntary consent to participate in a dangerous activity existed.

d. *Comparative negligence:* This defense, when permitted, apportions fault among the negligent parties, including the injured party. In some states, a negligent injured party may not recover unless the negligence of the party he is suing is greater than his own.

B. **Liability of Officers:** School board members, like their school district employees, may be the subject of lawsuits arising from acts and omissions undertaken in the course of their official duties.

1. *Officers enjoy "official immunity":* Unlike their employees, however, school board members are subject to immunity from suit under certain specified circumstances.

2. *Limitations on official immunity:* Official immunity extends only to *discretionary,* as opposed to *ministerial,* actions of school officers. Also, it is doubtful that an officer will be immune from suit if he has undertaken discretionary duties with malicious or injurious intent.

3. *Trend toward extending immunity:* In recent years, some state legislatures have extended a similar immunity to teachers and administrators for acts and omissions undertaken in the course of their employment.

C. Liability of School Districts

1. ***Subject to "vicarious" liability:*** The liability of school districts is necessarily *vicarious* since a fictional entity can only act through the individuals whose conduct may be imputed to it.

2. ***Governmental tort immunity:*** As a rule, school districts benefit from the common law principle, extended by the courts, that government agencies cannot be held liable for the negligent acts of their officers, agents, or employees. However, in recent years, some state legislatures and courts have eroded the doctrine of governmental immunity under the following circumstances:

   a. *Nuisances:* A school district may be held liable for the creation and maintenance of conditions which unlawfully invade the property rights of others.

   b. *Proprietary functions or activities:* A school district may not be immune from lawsuits in connection with proprietary activities which it permits on school premises. Proprietary activities are more commercial than governmental in nature, such as extracurricular profit-making events.

   c. *Ministerial functions:* Some courts have rejected the proprietary/governmental functions distinction in favor of granting immunity for discretionary (policy-making) functions and waiving immunity for ministerial (administrative) functions.

   d. *Violations of safety statutes:* Most states waive school district immunity in connection with lawsuits arising from defective school buildings and grounds.

   e. *Workers' compensation statutes:* Most legislatures waive school district immunity for employee injuries.

3. ***Defenses to liability:*** When governmental immunity is not applicable, school districts frequently assert the following defenses to liability.

   a. *No tort committed:* The school district may claim that its officer or employee did not commit the tort in question.

   b. *Not committed in scope of employment:* The district may assert that the officer or employee whose conduct is in question acted outside of the scope of his authority or employment. Pursuant to the common law doctrine of *respondeat superior,* a master may be held responsible only for the *authorized* acts of its servants.

c. *Employee himself is immune:* The district may claim that the officer or employee whose conduct is in question is himself immune from liability.

d. *Failure to abide by "notice of claim" statutes:* The district may assert that the party bringing suit has failed to provide it with a timely written notice of the alleged tort claim, as required by law. This is often described as a statute of limitations defense.

FEDERAL TORT LIABILITY

III. FEDERAL TORT LIABILITY

A. Section 1983 Actions:

1. ***Private suits allowed:*** The Civil Rights Act of 1866, codified as Title 42, United States Code, § 1983, provides the broadest avenue for private suits. Over 30,000 cases are filed annually using § 1983 as the avenue into federal court for tort actions where private citizens claim injury involving state actors. Section 1983, unlike other civil rights statutes, creates no substantive rights; it is purely remedial in nature. Section 1983 subjects to liability any person who, while acting under "color of state law," deprives another person of a federal constitutional or statutory right.

2. ***Section 1983 protects federal rights:*** Those federal rights established by federal law are remedied by § 1983. State law violations are not corrected through § 1983 actions. An act of negligence by a public figure will not automatically be converted into a federal tort. *Golden State Transit Corp. v. Los Angeles,* 498 U.S. 103 (1989).

3. ***"Special relationship" test:*** Section 1983 also covers federal rights not created by a specific statute, such as where a state agency has a "special relationship" to an injured party and where there has been a "deliberate indifference" to the injured party's needs exhibited by a state actor. A special relationship creates a duty to protect the victim from third party harm. Absent a special relationship, there is no duty under § 1983 to protect individuals from harm by others. *See DeShaney v. Winnebago County Department of Social Services,* 489 U.S. 189 (1989).

4. ***"Under color of law:"*** A state actor, such as a school employee, must be acting under their legal authority, i.e., "under color of law," for a § 1983 cause of action to be stated. School employees are "persons" under § 1983 and are acting under color of law

even if their conduct is contrary to school policy or unauthorized. *Monroe v. Pape,* 365 U.S. 167 (1981).

5. *"Persons" expanded to include municipality:* Initially, a "person" under § 1983 referred only to the actual tortfeasor; a municipality was never considered a "person" and was therefore immune. *Monroe, supra.* "Person" has now been expanded to include municipalities as well as individuals. Specifically, the Supreme Court has held that a municipality may be liable under § 1983 for the acts of its employees if such acts reflect municipal policy. *See Monell v. Department of Social Services of the City of New York,* 436 U.S. 658 (1978).

6. *Monetary damages are recoverable:* Damages in the form of money may be recovered only for *actual* damages, not for deprivations of federal rights that have no fiscal consequences. *See Carey v. Piphus,* 435 U.S. 247 (1978). Without proof of actual harm, an aggrieved plaintiff will recover only nominal damages, often no more than one dollar. Actual damages include out-of-pocket losses and emotional distress suffered by reason of the deprivation of a federal right. The Supreme Court has allowed exemplary or "punitive" damages under § 1983 for willful or wanton deprivations of civil rights by individuals, but it has disallowed the recovery of such damages from school districts for the wanton or willful misconduct of their employees. *City of Newport v. Fact Concerts, Inc.,* 453 U.S. 247 (1981)

7. *Legal costs are recoverable:* In a § 1983 tort suit, the prevailing party may receive attorney fees. Civic Rights Attorneys Fees Award Statute (42 U.S.C. § 1988). Only the prevailing party may receive attorney fees. A prevailing party is a party that is successful on a significant issue. *See Texas State Teachers Ass'n v. Garland Independent School District,* 777 F.2d 1046 (5th Cir. 1985).

8. *School officials' immunity:* School officials are immune from liability under § 1983 if they neither knew nor had reason to know that their actions amounted to a civil rights violation. *See Wood v. Strickland,* 420 U.S. 308 (1975). This limited immunity is provided to encourage school officials to perform effectively without fear of litigation. Similarly, if the school official knows or should know that an action violates a protected right, that school official is liable in his or her individual (nonofficial) capacity.

B. **Other Tort Concerns**

1. *Monetary recovery for sexual abuse under Title IX:* Title IX prohibits gender-based discrimination in federally supported

7

educational programs. In an important recent decision, the Supreme Court held that Title IX created a private right to recover monetary compensation for intentional violations of Title IX. *Franklin v. Gwinnett County Public Schools,* 112 S.Ct. 1028 (1992). In the *Franklin* case, a high school student proved that her school district had failed to protect her from sexual abuse perpetuated by one of the district's teachers.

2. *Educational malpractice:*

   a. The tort of educational malpractice is a recognizable cause of action, but its application has been very limited. Courts have avoided establishing any liability for failure of school authorities to exercise due care in testing, evaluation and placement, or for failure to bring a student up to satisfactory levels of achievement in basic skills. The reason courts have steered clear of finding liability in this area is because they have been unable to arrive at an objective standard of duty which could be used to measure the liability of educators. *See Donohue v. Copiague Union Free School District,* 47 N.Y.2d 440 (1979).

   b. While cognizable, an educational malpractice action is very difficult to establish. Difficulties in arriving at a standard of care limit recoveries in the areas of classroom methodology and failure to learn to a satisfactory level. Recoveries are also limited by the courts' reluctance to expose already financially strapped schools to excessive liability. When an educational malpractice claim is eventually upheld by the Supreme Court, it will probably be in the area of negligent evaluation and placement. *See Hunter v. Board of Education of Montgomery County,* 292 Md. 481 (1982).

NOTES:

DAILEY v. LOS ANGELES UNIFIED SCHOOL DISTRICT

Cal. Sup. Ct., 2 Cal. 3d 741, 87, 470 P.2d 360 (1970).

NATURE OF CASE: Appeal of directed verdict denying damages for wrongful death when a 16-year-old student died after "slap boxing" with a fellow student in the school gymnasium.

GENERAL RULE OF LAW: School personnel supervising the conduct of students must exercise the degree of care a person of ordinary prudence charged with comparable duties would exercise.

PROCEDURE SUMMARY:
Plaintiff: Dailey (P), parents of a deceased high school student.
Defendant: Los Angeles Unified School District (D) (District).
State Trial Court Decision: Held for the District (D), finding no negligence on its part.
State Supreme Court Decision: Reversed.

FACTS: During recess, Michael Dailey, a 16-year-old student at Gardena High School, was "slap boxing" with another student in the boys' gymnasium. They "boxed" for five to 10 minutes. A crowd of approximately 30 students gathered to watch. Suddenly, after being slapped, Michael fell backward and fractured his skull on the pavement. The Daileys (P), Michael's parents, filed a wrongful death action for damages, alleging that the District's (D) failure to supervise the students caused their son's death. The physical education department was responsible for supervising the gymnasium. The chairman of that department stated that he did not know he was to assign a teacher to supervise on any particular day, that there was no formal schedule of supervision times, and that supervision was left to whomever was in the gym office. At the time of the incident, the chairman was in the office playing bridge. The trial court granted the District's (D) motion for a directed verdict, and Dailey (P) appealed.

ISSUE: Are school personnel supervising the conduct of students required to exercise that degree of care a person of ordinary prudence charged with comparable duties would exercise?

HOLDING AND DECISION: (Sullivan, J.) Yes. School personnel supervising the conduct of students must exercise that degree of care a person of ordinary prudence charged with comparable duties would exercise. There is enough evidence here for a jury to find that the District (D) failed to meet this standard. The responsible department failed to develop a comprehensive schedule of supervising assignments. Those who did supervise were not informed of their specific duties. The person in the gym office at the time of the incident did not attempt to maximize his ability to oversee students' activities. From these facts, a jury could reasonably find that the school personnel failed to satisfy their duty of care, causing Michael's death. The directed verdict was therefore improper. Reversed.

COMMENT: Dailey illustrates one of many contexts in which courts are increasingly willing to impose a duty of care upon defendants to protect those with whom they are in a special relationship from harm from third parties. The duty may be imposed and the defendant found negligent even where, as here, an intervening negligent or intentional act appears to be the traditional "proximate" cause of the injury. Notice that the reversal did not mean that the Daileys (P) automatically won their case — the court, on appeal, simply found that a triable issue of fact existed, and since the jury, not the judge, is the trier of fact, the judge erred by not letting the jury decide whether the District (D) was negligent. Thus, the Daileys (P) won a new trial.

NOTES:

VIVEIROS v. HAWAII
54 Haw. 611, 513 P.2d 487 (1973).

NATURE OF CASE: Appeal of decision of award of damages for negligence reduced by 25% due to the student's being found comparatively negligent to that degree for injuries she sustained at an unsupervised high school show.

GENERAL RULE OF LAW: A child is only required to use that degree of care appropriate to her age, experience, and mental capacity.

PROCEDURE SUMMARY:
Plaintiff: Viveiros (P), a 15-year-old high school student.
Defendant: The State of Hawaii (D).
State Circuit Court Decision: Held for Viveiros (P) 25% negligent.
State Supreme Court Decision: Reversed.

FACTS: Viveiros (P) attended a light show in a lecture hall at Kailua High School. There were no teachers present to supervise the show. The only staff member present, an education assistant, left the hall shortly after the show began. Viveiros (P) could not find a seat and had to stand in an aisle. A few moments later, a group of students about 35 feet from Viveiros (P) became noisy. A student running the show told them to be quiet or the teachers would come in. Shortly thereafter, Viveiros (P) was struck by a metal object apparently thrown by a member of the noisy group. She suffered permanent damage to her left eye. Viveiros (P) filed a negligence suit for damages against Hawaii (D) under the State Tort Liability Act, claiming that Hawaii's (D) failure to supervise the show caused her injuries. The trial court found Hawaii (D) negligent but also found Viveiros (P) to have been comparatively negligent for 25% of her injuries for failing to leave the scene. Viveiros (P) appealed, arguing that the damages should not have been reduced.

ISSUE: Is a child only required to use that degree of care appropriate for her age, experience, and mental capacity?

HOLDING AND DECISION: (Richardson, C.J.) Yes. A child need only use that degree of care appropriate for her age, experience, and mental capacity. The trial court's finding that Viveiros (P) was 25% negligent must therefore be reversed if this Court finds that her conduct conformed to this standard. At the time of the incident, Viveiros (P) was 35 feet from the noisy group of students. Fur-

ther, the group was merely vocal; the record did not reveal that any threats were conveyed or objects thrown prior to the incident. In addition, none of her peers evidenced a fear of danger because none of them left the program out of concern for the noisy group. On these facts, Viveiros (P) could not have reasonably anticipated the danger she was in, and the trial court erred in finding otherwise. Reversed (full award of damages reinstated).

COMMENT: The standard of care applied here is the same as would be applied in any other case where the issue is whether a child was negligent. *Viveiros* represents the majority view. A few courts, however, attempt to establish varying standards depending upon the age of the child. For example, children under seven are sometimes conclusively presumed incapable of negligence, while, as for those between seven and fourteen, this presumption is rebuttable. Some jurisdictions hold children to the adult standard of care where the child has engaged in adult activities, *e.g.*, driving a motor vehicle or piloting a boat.

NOTES:

TITUS v. LINDBERG
49 N.J. 66, 228 A.2d 65 (1967).

NATURE OF CASE: Review of award of damages for personal injuries suffered by a nine-year-old student who was struck by a paper clip shot by another student while on unsupervised school property.

GENERAL RULE OF LAW: School personnel are liable for injuries sustained by students entrusted to their care where such personnel fail to exercise reasonable supervisory care for the safety of the students.

PROCEDURE SUMMARY:
Plaintiff: Titus (P), an injured student represented by his guardian.
Defendants: Smith (D), the Fairview principal; Lindberg (D), the student who shot the paper clip.
State Trial Court Decision: Held for Titus (P), finding Lindberg (D) and Smith (D) negligent.
State Court of Appeal Decision: Affirmed.
State Supreme Court Decision: Affirmed.

FACTS: Titus (P), a nine-year-old student at Fairview School, arrived on the school grounds at 8:05 a.m. As he headed toward the bicycle rack, he was struck by a paper clip shot by Lindberg (D), a student at Thompson School. Five minutes prior, Lindberg (D) had struck another student with a paper clip. Lindberg (D) was at Fairview awaiting a bus to transport him to Thompson. Fairview classes did not begin until 8:15 a.m.; however, Smith (D), the Fairview principal, supervised children who arrived early. Titus (P) filed a personal injury action for damages, alleging Lindberg's (D) negligent shooting and Smith's (D) negligent failure to supervise caused his injuries. The trial court found for Titus (P), awarding him $44,000 in damages. Smith (D) sought review.

ISSUE: Are school personnel liable for injuries sustained by students entrusted to their care where such personnel fail to exercise reasonable supervisory care for the students' safety?

HOLDING AND DECISION: (Jacobs, J.) Yes. School personnel are liable for injuries sustained by students entrusted to their care where such personnel fail to exercise reasonable supervisory care for the students' safety. That school did not officially begin until 8:15 a.m. did not relieve Smith (D) from this duty. It was expected that children would arrive a little early; they customarily did, and Smith (D) was well aware of this. Furthermore, Smith (D) affirmatively assumed re-sponsibility for supervising the school grounds beginning at 8:00 a.m.; however, he did not announce any rules regulating conduct before class, assign any teachers or other personnel to assist him in supervising, or take sufficient measures himself to oversee the students' presence or activities. Thus, the finding that Smith (D) failed to supervise adequately cannot be said to lack reasonable foundation. Affirmed.

COMMENT: *Titus* illustrates the rule followed in most states that imposes a duty of supervision on teachers over students. Under this duty, a teacher must take reasonable steps to protect students. Further, the amount of care required of the teacher increases or decreases with the relative maturity or immaturity of the students. This principle of supervision is one which is often disregarded by school personnel. They incorrectly assume that if they notify parents that they should not send their children to school in the morning before school personnel begin their supervision, they are released from liability. This practice is clearly wrong and exposes the school district and school personnel should an injury occur as a result of the negligent supervision.

NOTES:

LAWES v. BOARD OF EDUCATION OF THE CITY OF NEW YORK
16 N.Y.2d 302, 266 N.Y.S.2d 364, 213 N.E.2d 667 (1965).

NATURE OF CASE: Appeal of award of damages for injuries sustained by a student struck by a snowball when proceeding to class after having returned to school from lunch.

GENERAL RULE OF LAW: A school is not liable for injuries suffered by a student on school property as a result of the activity of other students where there is no notice of the special danger or previous occasions of dangerous activity.

PROCEDURE SUMMARY:
Plaintiff: Lawes (P), an injured student.
Defendant: Board of Education of the City of New York (D) (Board).
State Court Trial Division Decision: Held for Lawes (P), awarding $45,000 in damages.
State Court Appellate Division Decision: Affirmed.
State Court of Appeal (New York's highest court) Decision: Reversed.

FACTS: Lawes (P), an eleven-year-old student returning to school after having lunch at home, was struck by a snowball thrown by another student as she proceeded to her classroom. She suffered a serious eye injury as a result. The school had prohibited snowball throwing, and Lawes' (P) teacher had warned her students not to throw them. Lawes (P) filed a personal injury action for damages, alleging the Board (D) failed to supervise adequately the students' activities. The trial court held for Lawes (P), awarding her $45,000 in damages. The Board (D) appealed, contending that it could not be responsible for an unforeseeable injury.

ISSUE: Is a school liable for injuries sustained by a student on school premises from student activity where there is no notice of a special danger or previous dangerous activity?

HOLDING AND DECISION: (Bergan, J.) No. A school is not liable for injuries sustained by a student on school premises from student activity where there is no notice of the special danger or previous dangerous activity. In supervising students, school personnel must act as a parent of ordinary prudence would in comparable circumstances. Such a parent would not invariably prohibit her child from throwing snowballs; she would simply prohibit dangerous throwing if she was aware of conditions making the activity so. Similarly, the school need only prohibit play when it is on notice that such play is dangerous. There is no evidence of such notice here. The record did not reveal that teachers knew of any other snowball throwing on the day of the incident, nor was there sufficient evidence of other occasions of snowball throwing to show the requisite notice. Accordingly, the threat of injury by snowball throwing was not reasonably foreseeable, and, thus, no duty of care was owed Lawes (P) to protect her from such injury. Reversed.

COMMENT: *Lawes* clarifies the standard of care to which school officials will be held when supervising students. It was long believed that school officials owed some type of special duty, with the scope and degree of that duty not being clear. The standard of care in this type of situation is that of a parent of ordinary prudence. Nevertheless, the standard adopted not only subjects schools for omission but places upon them a duty to take affirmative actions to protect students in some instances.

NOTES:

DeSHANEY v. WINNEBAGO COUNTY DEPARTMENT OF SOCIAL SERVICES
489 U.S. 189 (1989).

NATURE OF CASE: Review of grant of summary judgment denying damages in a civil rights action alleging deprivation of a child's liberty interest in bodily integrity by the state's failure to remove him from the custody of his abusive father.

GENERAL RULE OF LAW: A state's failure to protect a child from a parent's abusive behavior is not a violation of the child's rights under the Due Process Clause of the Fourteenth Amendment.

PROCEDURE SUMMARY:
Plaintiff: DeShaney (P), an abused child.
Defendant: Winnebago County Department of Social Services (D) (WCDSS).
U.S. District Court Decision: Held for WCDSS (D), granting summary judgment.
U.S. Court of Appeals Decision: Affirmed.
U.S. Supreme Court Decision: Affirmed.

FACTS: DeShaney (P), a one-year-old baby, was placed in his father's custody when his parents divorced in 1980. From complaints made by the father's second wife, WCDSS (D) first learned in 1982 that DeShaney (P) was possibly a victim of abuse. The father denied any abuse, and WCDSS (D) did not pursue the matter. In January 1983, Deshaney (P) was admitted to the hospital with multiple bruises and abrasions. The treating physician, suspecting child abuse, notified WCDSS (D). DeShaney (P) was placed in the protective custody of the hospital, a "Child Protection Team" was formed, and treatment for both DeShaney (P) and his father was arranged. DeShaney (P) was then placed back into his father's custody. One month later the hospital notified WCDSS (D) that DeShaney (P) again had suspicious injuries. WCDSS (D) found no reason for action. On multiple occasions, a WCDSS (D) caseworker noticed suspicious injuries but took no action. Finally, in March 1984, the father beat DeShaney (P) into a coma. DeShaney (P), by his appointed guardian, filed suit, alleging WCDSS (D) deprived him of his right to bodily integrity under the Due Process Clause by failing to protect him from danger about which WCDSS (D) knew or should have known. The district court and court of appeals found that the Clause did not require WCDSS (D) to protect citizens from private violence. The Supreme Court granted review.

ISSUE: Is a state's failure to protect a child from the abusive behavior of a parent a violation of the child's right to bodily integrity under the Due Process Clause of the Fourteenth Amendment?

HOLDING AND DECISION: (Rehnquist, C.J.) No. A state's failure to protect a child from the abusive behavior of a parent is not a violation of the child's right to bodily integrity under the Due Process Clause. That Clause imposes no affirmative duty on a state to provide its citizenry with adequate protective services. Textually, the Clause is only a limitation on a state's power to act, not a mandate to act in a particular manner. Nor does the state's knowledge of a particular danger to an individual establish a special relationship between the state and that individual, creating a constitutional duty to protect. Such a duty arises from state-imposed limitations on the individual's ability to protect himself, not merely from knowledge of a particular danger. Here, state action played no part in creating the danger, nor was the father a state actor. Thus, no duty arose. Affirmed.

COMMENT: The issues raised by this can easily be extended to the school board or district context. They are clearly state agencies like the defendant in *DeShaney.* Thus, it would clearly follow that the Due Process Clause places no affirmative duty to act on them as well. Three dissenting justices, Brennan, Marshall, and White, however, strongly disagreed, arguing that the Due Process Clause required a more active role of the state. The argument has both moral and emotional appeal, especially given the egregious facts of *DeShaney,* but is unlikely to succeed in the near future given that the three dissenting justices are no longer on the Court. Note that the reference to the father as not being a "state actor" concerns the role of the father as not being an agent of the state. Thus, no special duty arises in this situation or in a traditional school setting. A special duty would arise for a prisoner in a state penal institution as affirmative duty of care and protection. The special duty or "special relationship" test is the key in determining whether the state would be liable under § 1983. Here the mere notice of severe child abuse by the custodial father did not trigger this special relationship. Such a special relationship is present when the state renders the person incapable of acting in their own defense, e.g., inmates of mental hospitals or prisons.

MONELL v. DEPARTMENT OF SOCIAL SERVICES OF THE CITY OF NEW YORK

436 U.S. 658, 98 S. Ct. 2018 (1978).

NATURE OF CASE: Review of order dismissing action seeking damages under 42 U.S.C. § 1983.

GENERAL RULE OF LAW: A municipality may be liable under § 1983 for the acts of its employees if such acts are reflective of municipal policy.

PROCEDURE SUMMARY:
Plaintiff: Monell, a private citizen (P).
Defendants: The City of New York (D) and various agencies thereof.
U.S. District Court Decision: Dismissed.
U.S. Court of Appeals Decision: Affirmed.
U.S. Supreme Court Decision: Reversed and remanded.

FACTS: Monell (P) brought a § 1983 action against the City of New York (D) and various agencies, based on acts of City (D) employees. Although the case turned on the issue of municipal liability under § 1983, the facts of the case were as follows. Female employees (P) of the Department of Social Services and the Board of Education of the City of New York brought suit against the Department and Board (D) challenging the policies of those bodies in requiring pregnant employees to take unpaid leaves of absence before those leaves were required for medical reasons. The petitioners brought this class action against the department and its commissioner, the board and its chancellor, and the City of New York and its mayor, seeking injunctive relief and back pay under § 1983 of the Civil Rights Act of 1871. Section 1983 provides that every "person" who, under color of a statute, ordinance, regulation, custom, or usage of any state, subjects or "causes to be subjected" any person to deprivation of any federally protected rights, privileges, or immunities shall be civilly liable to the injured party. The individual defendants were sued solely in their official capacities. The district court dismissed, holding that a municipality was immune from liability under § 1983 for acts of employees. The court of appeals affirmed, and the Supreme Court granted certiorari.

ISSUE: May a municipality be liable under § 1983 for the acts of its employees if such acts are reflective of municipal policy?

HOLDING AND DECISION: (Brennan, J.) Yes. A municipality may be liable under § 1983 if such acts are reflective of municipal policy. An earlier case, *Monroe v. Pape*, 365 U.S. 167, 172 (1981), held that municipalities were absolutely immune from liability under § 1983. This case was inconsistent with the legislative intent of Congress as evidenced by the legislative history, and the Court now overrules it. Nonetheless, the Court declines to adopt a rule of respondeat superior/automatic liability on the part of a municipality for the misdeeds of its employees. Section 1983 speaks of damages being awardable against one "causing" a civil rights violation. "Cause" implies some affirmative act in bringing the violation about. An automatic liability rule would contravene this. Therefore, the better rule is that only a violation caused by either official or unofficial policy may result in municipal liability. Here, the district court must determine this issue on remand. Reversed and remanded.

COMMENT: The Court took some pains to include unofficial as well as official policy. Seldom will a municipality have an official policy of committing civil rights violations. Unofficial policy may be demonstrated by a pattern of violations occurring without reprimand. In addition to expanding the interpretation of who may be included as a "person" subject to suit under § 1983, this case makes school officials liable for their actions. They must be concerned about the rights of individuals. As with other professionals, educators must be concerned with the potential liability attached to their professional acts and policies.

NOTES:

CAREY v. PIPHUS
435 U.S. 247, 98 S. Ct. 1042 (1978).

NATURE OF CASE: Review of order holding that substantial nonpunitive damages could be recovered in a § 1983 action based on violation of procedural due process, absent proof of actual damages.

GENERAL RULE OF LAW: In the absence of proof of actual injury, a violation of procedural due process entitles a plaintiff to nominal damages only.

PROCEDURE SUMMARY:
Plaintiff: Piphus (P) and several other school students.
Defendant: Carey (D) and various other Chicago school officials.
U.S. District Court Decision: Held for plaintiffs, but no damages were awarded.
U.S. Court of Appeals Decision: Plaintiffs were entitled to recover substantial compensatory damages, absent proof of actual injury.
U.S. Supreme Court Decision: Reversed.

FACTS: In a pair of consolidated, unrelated cases, certain Chicago school district students were suspended. Piphus (P) was suspended for 20 days for smoking an "irregularly shaped cigarette." The principal smelled the odor of burning marijuana. Brisco (P) was suspended for 20 days for violating a school rule prohibiting male students from wearing earrings. The earring rule was based on its being a gang emblem. The plaintiff refused to remove the earring, stating that it was a symbol of black pride. In both cases, the Chicago Board of Education policy limited a suspended student's appeal to issues *not* related to guilt or innocence. The students filed actions under 42 U.S.C. § 1983, contending that they had been denied procedural due process. The Seventh Circuit Court of Appeals held that the students (P) were entitled to substantial compensatory damages, even if they were unable to show actual damages. The Supreme Court granted review.

ISSUE: Does a violation of procedural due process entitle a plaintiff to substantial compensatory damages absent proof of actual injury?

HOLDING AND DECISION: (Powell, J.) No. In the absence of proof of actual injury, a violation of procedural due process entitles a plaintiff to nominal damages only. Section 1983 creates an action "at law." From this it can be concluded that the section incorporated common law rules regarding damages. One such rule is that for more than nominal damages to be awarded, proof of actual injury must be demonstrated; damages are not presumed. For this reason, damages may not be presumed for violations of procedural due process. Absent such proof, only nominal damages may be awarded. Reversed.

COMMENT: The common law does provide one exception to the general rule against damages absent actual injury, this being defamation per se. This exception is based on the notion that such defamation almost certainly leads to actual damages while at the same time presenting serious proof problems. The Court declined to find the present situation analogous to defamation per se, which can be defined as defamation likely to endure, such as writing, which harms a person's business reputation. Therefore, a plaintiff whose constitutional rights have been violated must prove any damage claim. A victim is compensated for actual, proven detriment and denial caused by a denial of due process. The burden is on the shoulders of a plaintiff.

NOTES:

TEXAS STATE TEACHERS ASS'N v. GARLAND INDEPENDENT SCHOOL DIST.
777 F. 2d 1046 (5th Cir. 1985)

NATURE OF CASE: Review of denial of award of attorney fees to teachers union on grounds that union was not a prevailing party within the meaning of 42 U.S.C. § 1988 and, thus, not entitled to fees.

GENERAL RULE OF LAW: A party prevailing on a significant issue in an action is a prevailing party under 42 U.S.C. § 1988 and, thus, is entitled to attorney fees.

PROCEDURE SUMMARY:
Plaintiff: Texas State Teachers Association (P) (Union).
Defendant: Garland Independent School District (D) (District).
U.S. District Court Decision: Held Union (P) did not prevail on the central issue of the action and, thus, were not prevailing parties entitled to attorney fees under 42 U.S.C. § 1988.
U.S. Court of Appeals Decision: Affirmed.
U.S. Supreme Court Decision: Reversed and remanded.

FACTS: The Union (P) filed suit challenging several District (D) policies and one in particular which limited the ability of the Union (P) to communicate with teachers concerning employee organization. The District (D) moved for summary judgment, which the court granted on most of the claims. The court of appeals reversed as to the limiting communications claim and affirmed as to the rest. The Union (P) then sought attorney fees under 42 U.S.C. § 1988, arguing that they were due based on the Union's (P) having prevailed on this issue. The district court held that the Union (P) was not a prevailing party under § 1988 because it had not prevailed on the central issue of the action. The court of appeals affirmed, indicating that the Union (P) had been successful only on significant secondary issues, not on the central issue. The U.S. Supreme Court granted review.

ISSUE: Is a party who prevails on a significant issue in an action a prevailing party under § 1988 for purposes of qualifying to recover attorney fees?

HOLDING AND DECISION: (O'Connor, J.) Yes. A party who prevails on a significant issue in an action is a prevailing party under § 1988 for purposes of qualifying to recover attorney fees. Under this standard, a party must show, at a minimum, a resolution of the action which materially altered the parties' legal relationship in a manner intended by Congress. The lower courts' "central issues" test is directly contrary to *Hensley v. Eckerhart,* 461 U.S. 424 (1983), in which the Court did not establish a particular standard but indicated that the degree of a party's success is a critical factor in determining a reasonable fee. That the prevailing party is entitled to recover attorney fees is a given; there is no question as to whether the party is entitled to a fee at all. The "central issues" test is also contrary to the clear legislative intent that fee awards be available to parties who only partially prevail in civil rights actions. Further, such a test too heavily relies on the subjective intent of the parties. Reversed and remanded.

COMMENT: This case is a substantial victory for plaintiffs in civil rights actions. Requiring success on significant issues, as opposed to success on the central issue, clearly gives greater incentive for plaintiffs to bring and attorneys to accept civil rights actions. Though this plaintiff was a teachers union, the rule established applies to other potential plaintiffs against school boards and districts, such as student groups or individual students. However, the rule of this case is not limited to cases involving suits brought against educational institutions. It should be noted that attorney fees are only recoverable where provided by law; attorney fees are otherwise not compensable, no matter how malicious the losing party's conduct may have been.

NOTES:

WOOD v. STRICKLAND
420 U.S. 308, 95 S. Ct. 992 (1975).

NATURE OF CASE: Review of order reversing dismissal of action for damages for civil rights violation under 42 U.S.C. § 1983.

GENERAL RULE OF LAW: A school official is immune from liability under 42 U.S.C. § 1983 if he neither knew nor had reason to know that his actions amounted to a civil rights violation.

PROCEDURE SUMMARY:
Plaintiffs: Strickland and Crain, high school students (P).
Defendants: Wood and other school board officials (D).
U.S. District Court Decision: Dismissed.
U.S. Court of Appeals Decision: Reversed.
U.S. Supreme Court Decision: Reversed and remanded for additional factual development.

FACTS: Strickland (P) and Crain (P) were high school students who were found by the local school board (D) to have "spiked" the punch at a school function, in contravention of school rules. After a hearing in which they essentially admitted to the scheme, they were suspended for the rest of the year. The students (P) appealed to the school board. The board (D) upheld the administrative action suspending the students for the year, but it did not provide an adequate hearing. The lack of an adequate hearing was contrary to "settle" law, *Goss v. Lopez*, 419 U.S. 565, 95 S. Ct. 729 (1975), having been announced by the Court. The students (P) filed an action under 42 U.S.C. § 1983, the federal law allowing a suit for violation of constitutional rights while acting pursuant to state law. They contended that the punishment was unconstitutionally excessive and, thus, in violation of due process. After trial, the federal district court dismissed, holding the school officials (D) immune from § 1983 for acts not amounting to subjective (willful) violations of constitutional rights. The court of appeals reversed, holding that the standard of liability was to be objective, which is to say, not dependant on the officials' state of mind. The Supreme Court granted review.

ISSUE: Is a school official immune from liability under § 1983 if he neither knew nor should have known that his actions amounted to a civil rights violation?

HOLDING AND DECISION: (White, J.) Yes. A school official is immune from liability under § 1983 if he neither knew nor should have known that his actions amounted to a civil rights violation. School officials, in exercising their duties, often have to make judgment calls based on information supplied by others. This being so, it is proper that they enjoy limited immunity from § 1983 liability, as to hold otherwise would chill their ability to properly fulfill their duties. The district court imposed a subjective actual malice standard; the court of appeals thought an objective implied malice standard was more appropriate. In fact, the proper standard is both objective and subjective — it is a "knew or should have known" type of standard. Since insufficient facts were adduced at trial to decide the issue, the matter must be decided on remand. Reversed.

COMMENT: The school officials (D) argued in favor of an absolute immunity. The Court rejected this. First, no lower court has ever deemed it proper to grant such immunity, and this was persuasive of the inappropriateness of such action. More importantly, to do so might leave legitimately aggrieved students with no avenue of redress. At first this case caused great consternation among school board members because it exposed them to a monetary damage recovery if they acted improperly when they either "knew or reasonably should have known" that their action was improper. One result of this decision was the provision of additional insurance coverage for situations where they are exposed because of the more limited interpretation of a "qualified good faith immunity." Another interesting result of this case is that school boards now rely more heavily on a legal opinion of their school lawyer prior to taking action.

NOTES:

DONOHUE v. COPIAGUE UNION FREE SCHOOL DISTRICT

47 N.Y.2d 440, 418 N.Y.S.2d 375, 391 N.E. 2d 1352 (1979).

NATURE OF CASE: Appeal of dismissal of action for damages, alleging a school district's failure to educate a high school student constituted educational malpractice and negligent breach of a constitutionally imposed duty to educate.

GENERAL RULE OF LAW: Causes of action against a school district for educational malpractice and negligent failure to educate are not cognizable.

PROCEDURE HISTORY:
Plaintiff: Donohue (P), a District (D) high school graduate.
Defendant: Copiague Union Free School District (D) (District).
State Trial Court Decision: Held for the District (D), dismissing Donohue's (P) complaint for failure to state a cognizable claim.
State Appellate Court Decision: Affirmed.
State Court of Appeals (New York's highest court) Decision: Affirmed.

FACTS: Donohue (P) attended Copiague High School from 1972 until his graduation in 1976. After graduation, he filed an action for damages against the District (D), contending it failed to educate him as it was required. Donohue (P) claimed that, notwithstanding a certificate of graduation, he was functionally illiterate. The complaint alleged that because of the District's (D) failure to properly teach him and evaluate his mental abilities, he was unable to even complete applications for employment. The District (D) filed a motion to dismiss the action for failure to state a claim. The trial court granted the motion, and the appellate court affirmed. Donohue (P) appealed.

ISSUE: Are causes of action for educational malpractice and negligent failure to educate cognizable against a school district?

HOLDING AND DECISION: (Jasen, J.) No. Causes of action for educational malpractice and negligent failure to educate are not cognizable against a school district. Though traditional notions of tort law may allow for an educational malpractice action against a school district, public policy cautions against it. To entertain such a claim would require the court to judge the validity of broad educational policies and review their day-to-day implementation. Such judgment and review would overly infringe upon duties clearly granted to the legislature and district in the Constitution. In addition, the legislature, through the education law, has provided aggrieved persons, such as Donohue (P), other means of redress. The claim negligent failure to educate fails because, though the state constitution mandates the legislature to maintain and support public schools, it does not require that each student receive a minimum level of education. Affirmed.

COMMENT: This case illustrates the courts' long-held "hands off" policy toward educational policy issues. Only in cases of gross violations of public policy or deprivation of rights are courts usually compelled to intervene. Today, however, there are increasing efforts to hold schools to providing a minimum level of education. Acceptance of such a standard could compel future courts to sustain an educational malpractice action where plaintiff shows the school failed to provide the minimum level of education. But whether mere negligence will sustain such a claim, even where a minimum education standard is recognized, is not yet settled. This case established that while educational malpractice can be pleaded (thus, it is a cognizable cause of action), it will not be sustained based on public policy. Should educational malpractice be recognized, it will probably occur in an area like handicapped education, where accountability, testing, and placement are mandated. The general failure to educate argued in this case will not be the breakthrough area for an educational malpractice claim.

NOTES:

HUNTER v. BOARD OF EDUCATION
OF MONTGOMERY COUNTY
292 Md. 481, 439 A.2d 582 (1982).

NATURE OF CASE: Appeal of order sustaining a demurrer without leave to amend an action for damages, alleging a school negligently evaluated a child's learning abilities and intentionally and maliciously covered up its negligence.

GENERAL RULE OF LAW: School personnel entrusted with a child's care can be held liable for intentionally injurious conduct in evaluating, placing, and teaching the child but not merely negligent conduct.

PROCEDURE SUMMARY:
Plaintiff: Hunter (P), an elementary school student.
Defendant: Board of Education of Montgomery County (D) (Board).
State Circuit Court Decision: Held for the Board (D), sustaining its demurrer to Hunter's (P) complaint without leave to amend.
State Court of Special Appeals Decision: Affirmed.
State Court of Appeals (Maryland's highest court) Decision: Affirmed in part; reversed in part.

FACTS: When Hunter (P) was in elementary school, he was forced to repeat first-grade material though physically placed in the second grade. The plaintiff alleged that this misplacement, which continued through grade school, caused the student embarrassment and led him to develop learning deficiencies and to experience depletion of ego strength. Hunter (P) filed suit, alleging two causes of action: first, that his being forced to repeat first-grade material was a result of the Board's (D) negligence in evaluating his learning abilities and, second, that the Board (D) intentionally and maliciously furnished false information to his parents concerning his learning abilities to cover up the Board's (D) negligence. The Board (D) demurred to Hunter's (P) complaint. The circuit court sustained the demurrer without leave to amend, both holding that neither the negligent nor intentional conduct actions could be maintained. The Court of Special Appeals affirmed, and Hunter (P) appealed.

ISSUE: May school personnel entrusted with a student's care be held liable for intentionally injurious conduct in the evaluating, placing, and teaching of the student?

HOLDING AND DECISION: (Digges, J.) Yes. School personnel entrusted with a student's care may be held liable for intentionally injurious conduct in evaluating, placing, and teaching the student. Mere negligence is not enough. This court adopts the rule of many other jurisdictions that an action for "educational malpractice," which is in essence Hunter's (P) claim, does not lie for merely negligent conduct in the evaluating, placing, and teaching of a child. To allow such a claim would contravene public policy by exposing already financially burdened schools to incalculable liability. This, however, by no means shields school officials from intentionally injurious conduct. Such conduct greatly outweighs the policy considerations precluding liability in the negligence context. Thus, Hunter (P) should be allowed the opportunity to proceed on the intentional conduct claim. Reversed in part and remanded.

COMMENT: Even if cognizable, an educational malpractice action would be difficult to establish. Classroom methodology affords no readily acceptable standard of care, as there are often conflicting theories of how and what students should be taught. These problems combined with the courts' concern for exposing already financially strapped schools to excessive liability also underlie the rejection of the education malpractice cause of action. A demurrer is the equivalent of a motion to dismiss filed with the court after the pleadings have been served but before trial has commenced. The court can sustain a demurrer only when the plaintiff has failed to state a cause of action, i.e., has failed to allege (or have the ability to prove) the required elements of the particular cause of action. The result is no triable issues of fact, which enables the court to enter judgment (on behalf of the defendant) based solely on the law. This area of negligent evaluation and placement is the one which will first be sustained for educational malpractice.

NOTES:

TANARI v. SCHOOL DIRECTORS OF DISTRICT NO. 502

69 Ill.2d 630, 14 Ill. Dec. 874, 373 N.E. 2d 5 (1977).

NATURE OF CASE: Review of order dismissing an action brought by a school district employee for damages resulting from a student-caused injury.

GENERAL RULE OF LAW: A school employee injured during a school function need not show willful misconduct to maintain an action thereon.

PROCEDURE SUMMARY:
Plaintiff: Tanari, a school bus driver (P).
Defendant: Local school authorities (D).
Trial Court Decision: Case dismissed.
State Appeals Court Decision: Affirmed.
State Supreme Court Decision: Reversed.

FACTS: Tanari (P) had been a school bus driver for many years. For as long as she had been employed, she had been given free passes to attend local football games; this was not a part of her official compensation. During one game, she was injured by some students who were engaged in horseplay. She sued the school District (D), contending negligent supervision. The trial court dismissed, holding that Tanari (P) could not show willful misconduct, a requisite for liability on the part of the District (D). The state appellate court affirmed, and the state supreme court accepted review.

ISSUE: Must a school employee injured during a school function show willful misconduct to maintain an action thereon?

HOLDING AND DECISION: (Underwood, J.) No. A school employee injured during a school function need not show willful misconduct to maintain an action thereon. Willful misconduct must be shown for a student to prevail against a school district. This is so because this standard exists for children to recover against parents, and a school district stands in the shoes of parents with respect to its students. However, this "in loco parentis" relationship does not exist with respect to school employees. As to them, regular rules of negligence apply. This being so, whether or not the District (D) was negligent was a question of fact for the jury. Reversed.

COMMENT: The court spent some time ascertaining the status of Tanari's (P) presence on school grounds. The District (D) contended that she was a licensee; the court concluded she was an invitee. At common law, these distinctions made a difference as to the level of care owed to another on one's property. An invitee was one who was invited onto land for a particular purpose, usually to the economic advantage of the possessor of the land. A licensee was one who was permitted to enter but whose entry provided no economic benefit to the possessor. At common law, a possessor of land owed a greater duty of care to an invitee. In most states, the emerging tort standard of recovery in a negligence case depends upon whether the tortfeasor acted "reasonably" under the circumstances.

NOTES:

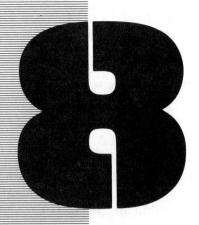

CONTRACTUAL LIABILITY OF LOCAL SCHOOL BOARDS

▶ ## CHAPTER SUMMARY

CHAPTER 8: CONTRACTUAL LIABILITY OF LOCAL SCHOOL BOARDS

QUICK REFERENCE RULES OF LAW

1. **State grant of authority:** Each local school board receives its authority to contract from the state legislature. (§ I.A.)

2. **Competitive bidding:** A competitive bidding selection process is generally required by statute in order to ensure that local school boards make efficient expenditures of public funds. (§ II.)

3. **Lowest responsible bidder:** Most competitive bidding statutes provide that contracts must be awarded to the "lowest responsible bidder." However, school boards that are required by law to award contracts to the "lowest responsible bidder" must conduct thorough investigations into the financial standing, reputation, experience, resources, facilities, efficiency, and judgment of a lowest bidder before accepting a bid. (§ II.A.)

4. **Statutory bidding requirements:** Many states require that school districts enter into contracts whenever the total cost of needed goods or services exceeds a set dollar amount. When the amount is less than the statutorily set amount, a school district may still enter into any contract if doing so leads to a more "efficient and economical" system. (§ II.B.)

5. **Performance by mistaken bidder:** A bidder who discovers a mistake in the bid after it has been accepted may nonetheless be required to perform under the terms of the contract that has been created unless it can be shown that the school board reasonably should have suspected bidding error and investigated prior to accepting the bid. (§ II.C.)

6. **Contract amendments and modifications:** Generally speaking, the parties to a contract may amend or modify it unless doing so contravenes statutory guidelines. (§ II.D.)

7. **Recovery for part performance under a voided contract:** When a contract is declared void, the contracting party who has performed in part may be able to recover the reasonable value of services rendered if the underlying contract was initially a proper subject of the school board's contracting authority. (§ III.A.)

8. **Invalid contracts entered into by school board's agent:** While a school board will not be bound by an invalid contract entered into on its behalf by its agent, it may, however, choose to ratify such a contract by accepting the benefits of the contract. (§ III.C.)

9. **Conflicts of interest:** A school board member may not maintain a personal financial interest in a contract that comes before the board. (§ IV.)

Introduction: Local school boards frequently enter into contracts for a wide range of services which are necessary for the planning and operation of a regional school system. However, there is no inherent authority on the part of the local board to enter into contracts. Rather, such authority exists only insofar as it has been expressly or implicitly granted by the state legislature. Questions often arise as to the nature and extent of the authority that has been granted.

8

I. **GENERAL PRINCIPLES OF STATUTORY CONTRACT LIABILITY**

    A. **Contracting Authority Is Statutory in Origin:** A local school board's authority to contract is granted to it by the state legislature.

    B. **Determining Nature and Extent of Statutory Authority:** Generally accepted principles of statutory construction provide a method for defining the nature and extent of the authority granted local school boards by way of statute.

        1. *Effect of specific authority:* Where the legislature has been specific in its delineation of the authority granted to a local school board, additional authority not granted in the same manner may not be assumed by the board. This principle will be upheld even where a local board in good faith enters into a contract which later is deemed invalid by reason of the board's failure to follow explicit statutory guidelines.

        2. *Effect of nonspecific authority:* Where the legislature has not been specific in its statutory grant of authority, the local board has some latitude in interpreting the nature and extent of its contractual authority.

        Example: Where the manner in which a local board is to execute a particular function is not expressly or implicitly provided for by statute, a board may choose to "contract out" a particular service, *i.e.,* enter into a contract with a private company to provide a particular service for the school district that might otherwise be provided by the district's own personnel.

II. **THE COMPETITIVE BIDDING PROCESS: Most states, by statute, require that local boards entertain competing bids from would-be contractors prior to selecting the best and most economical contract. Such contracts generally involve more than a certain minimum dollar amount.**

A. Lowest Responsible Bidder: As a rule, the "lowest responsible bidder" is chosen from among those who compete for the contract award. *See Hibbs v. Arensberg,* 276 Pa. 24 (1923).

1. *Rationale:* This process is designed to prevent favoritism and influence-peddling from entering into the contractor selection process.

2. *Goal:* The goal is the most cost-efficient expenditure of public funds possible.

3. *Determining who is "responsible":* It is not always easy to determine which bidder is the lowest *responsible* bidder; the bidder who submits the lowest bid may not be as "responsible" as other bidders or sufficiently responsible to be worthy of a particular contract award.

4. *Judicial hesitance to intervene:* Generally, courts will not intervene in the bid selection process unless the selecting entity has acted wholly arbitrarily. Responsible bidder statutes are designed to protect taxpayers, not grant rights to bidders.

B. Miscellaneous Considerations regarding the Submission and Acceptance of Bids

1. *Financial statements:* School boards often require that bidders submit financial statements with their bids; failure to do so is grounds for rejection of a bid.

2. *Right to reject all bids:* School boards often reserve the right to reject all bids if none is considered suitable.

3. *Statutory minimum for competitive bidding:* In most states, competitive bidding is not required if the dollar amount of a contract is below a certain statutory minimum. Courts will not permit school boards to circumvent the bidding process by breaking a contract up into smaller subcontracts, each below the minimum bidding dollar amount. *See Utah Plumb./Heat. Contractor Ass'n v. Bd. of Ed. Weiser Cnty. Sch. Dist.,* 19 Utah 2d. 203 (1967).

C. Withdrawn and Mistaken Bids

1. *Before acceptance:* Before a bid has been accepted, the bidder may wish to withdraw it for various reasons, such as the discovery of an error in the calculation of the bid amount.

   a. *State procedures for bid withdrawal:* Many states have set procedures that allow for the withdrawal of bids in legitimate circumstances (such as those involving error) but prevent withdrawal when it is sought as a means of manipulating the bidding process.

b. *Effect of unilateral withdrawal:* Generally speaking, the benefit of the bidding process would be circumvented if bidders could unilaterally withdraw their bids prior to their acceptance/rejection but after all bids have been opened and made public.

2. ***Postacceptance discovery of bid amount error:*** The discovery of an error in the calculation of a bid amount after it has been accepted presents a different problem. Under the principles of contract law, the acceptance of the bid has created an obligation to perform on the part of the bidder (as well as on the entity accepting the bid).

   a. *Holding bidder to performance:* On the one hand, it may be argued that the bidder should be required to perform since she alone was in the best position to control for error.

   b. *Excusing bidder from performance:* However, if it can be demonstrated that the entity accepting the bid *knew* of the error, most courts will not permit it to benefit thereby. In some such cases, knowledge will be attributed to the acceptor if it is determined that a reasonable person would have suspected the bid error and investigated it prior to accepting the bid.

D. Modified or Amended Bids

1. ***Postacceptance modification/amendment:*** Ordinarily, the parties to a contract are free to modify or amend its terms.

2. ***Public interest requirement for modification of competitively bid contract:*** Since competitive bidding laws exist to benefit the public, the parties to a competitively bid agreement may not be permitted to modify or amend the agreement unless doing so is clearly in the public interest.

   a. *Prohibition against re-creating contract:* As a rule, modifications or amendments that alter a contract to the point of abandoning it in favor of creating a new one are not permissible.

   b. *Unexpected circumstances:* Changes aimed at updating the contract in light of new and unexpected circumstances will generally be permitted by the courts.

III. RECOVERY UNDER THE VARIOUS FORMS OF CONTRACT: It is not always clear what a contractor will be permitted to recover under a contract that has subsequently been declared void, assuming the contractor has performed all or a portion of his obligations. Recovery depends upon various factors, including the type of contract, the nature of the parties' obligations under the contract, when the contract was breached, and who was responsible for the breach.

A. **Types of Contracts**

1. *Express contracts:* Express contracts are characterized by a precise declaration of the rights and duties of the parties, either orally or in writing.

2. *Implied-in-fact contracts:* Implied-in-fact contracts are suggested by the *conduct* of the parties, *i.e.,* the parties' actions clearly indicate that they intended a contract to exist, even though they did not enter into an express contract.

   a. *Based on express contract authority:* Note that an implied-in-fact contract can only be created in those instances in which the school district possessed the authority to enter into an express contract with regard to the subject matter in the first place.

   b. *Enforced like express contracts:* If an implied-in-fact contract is found to exist, its terms will be no less binding than those of an express contract.

3. *Implied-in-law contracts (or quasi-contracts):* Implied-in-law contracts are created by courts in order to promote equity and remedy injustice. A party will be bound by an implied-in-law contract if failing to create such a contract would result in his "unjust enrichment" at the expense of another. *See Oracle Sch. Dist.#2 v. Mammoth High School,* No. 88, 130 Ariz. App. 41 (1981).

B. **Measures of Recovery:** When a plaintiff brings an action for damages for breach of contract, the method the court will use to "measure" or determine the amount of damages to be awarded will depend on the type of contract breached.

1. *Express contracts:* Recovery under an express contract depends on:

   a. *the provisions of the contract,* regardless of whether the recovery is viewed as equitable or just, and

b. *the nature of the breach, e.g.,* failure to deliver goods, failure to deliver goods of contracted-for quality, failure to perform services, or failure to complete partially performed services.

2. *Implied-in-fact contracts:* Recovery under an implied-in-fact contract is based upon the *reasonable value* of goods or services rendered, which may not be the same as the actual price of the goods or services rendered.

3. *Implied-in-law contracts:* Recovery under an implied-in-law contract is based upon the value of the *benefit conferred* upon the party to whom the goods or services have been rendered. Under the theory of "quantum meruit," the benefiting party is required to pay an amount equal to the benefit it has received from the goods or services. *See Responsive Environments Corp. v. Pulaski Cnty. Special School Dist.,* 366 F.Supp 241 (E.D. Ark 1973).

   Note: The "reasonable value" and "benefit conferred" tests are separate and distinct, yet many courts confuse them by using them interchangeably.

C. **Recovery under Invalid or Unauthorized School Contracts:** A contract can be declared invalid when school officials have entered into it without following statutory guidelines. A contract that a school board is unauthorized by law to enter into is said to be *ultra vires,* or "beyond the powers" granted the board. Complicating matters is the fact that it is not always easy to determine which contractual actions or subject matters are within the power of the school board. Statutory authority will govern in most instances, but statutes are sometimes quite difficult to construe.

   1. *Express contracts:* A contractor whose express contract with a school board has been declared invalid will be able to recover the value of the obligations performed, in whole or in part, to the benefit of the school board as of the date of invalidation.

   2. *Implied-in-fact contracts:* In most cases, the courts will hold the school district liable under an implied-in-fact contract for the reasonable value of the goods or services it received so long as the contract does not in some other way violate public policy.

      a. *Express contract basis:* Because an implied-in-fact contract can only be found in situations where a school board could have entered into an express contract with the aggrieved party, recovery for breach of an implied-in-fact contract is treated similarly to breach of an express contract.

      b. *Denial of recovery:* An aggrieved party will be denied recovery when the school district would have been unable for lack

8

of authority to enter into an express contract for the same obligation but mistakenly has done so anyway. *See Juneau Academy v. Chicago Board of Education*, 122 Ill. App.3d 553 (1984).

Example: A contract which runs afoul of competitive bidding requirements will probably be deemed *ultra vires* insofar as school boards generally have no authority to enter into agreements circumventing such statutory procedures.

(1) This harsh consequence results from a court's ability to find an implied-in-fact contract only under circumstances where an express contract could have been entered into by the school board.

(2) The hardships to the aggrieved party who is denied recovery on an *ultra vires* contract are no different than if the underlying contract had merely been invalid but within the contracting authority of the school district.

D. **Recovery under Invalid Contracts Entered into by Agents of the School Board:** School boards can authorize one or more people, such as a school superintendent, to enter into contracts on behalf of the board. A person who has been granted such authority acts as an agent of the board, and the board will be bound by its agent's agreements made within the scope of the agent's authority. However, a board is not bound to a contract when its agent has entered into it without authority (*i.e.*, the agent acts in excess of the scope of her authority), and the contract is invalid.

1. *Ratification:* Although a board will ordinarily not be bound to a contract entered into by its agent without authority, it may choose to be bound after the fact by ratifying the agreement.

   a. *Means of ratification:* The board may ratify an unauthorized contract either by voting to approve it or by signaling its approval through its acceptance of the benefits of the contract with knowledge of the circumstances under which it was formed. Note, however, that if it is impossible for the board to reject the benefits flowing from the contract, retention of the benefits will not signal ratification.

   b. *Validity of ratified contracts:* Ratification renders the contract as valid as if it had been entered into with the proper authority in the first place.

   c. *Postcontract authorization of agent:* In effect, ratification is a retroactive authorization of its agent to have entered into the contract in question as if the agent originally had been granted such authority.

2. ***Ratification of* ultra vires *contracts:*** Note, though, that an *ultra vires* contract cannot be ratified because the school board itself lacks the authority to commit to such an agreement.

IV. **CONFLICTS OF INTEREST: Occasionally a school board member will find herself with the following conflicting interests: that of sitting on the school board as a representative of the people of the school district and that of private party with a stake in a contract to which the board is also a party.**

A. **Statutory Prohibitions:** Most state statutes provide that a person may not officially represent two or more competing interests. In the schools context, a school board member (a public officer) may not maintain a financial interest in a contract on which she may be required to vote as a board member, lest the contract be declared void.

B. **Nature of Conflicting Interests:** As to what constitutes a sufficient financial interest, certainly a board member's direct private participation in a contract with the board presents a conflict. Some courts go even further: a school board contract entered into by a corporation, of which a board member is a stockholder, may be declared void in light of the potential, though less probable, conflict.

NOTES:

8

CONFLICTS OF INTEREST

HIBBS v. ARENSBERG
276 Pa. 24, 119 A. 727 (1923).

8

NATURE OF CASE: Appeal by unsuccessful bidders on a construction contract for a school from a ruling upholding a school board's decision to award the contract to the fourth-lowest bidder without investigating, as required by state law, whether any lower bidders were "responsible."

GENERAL RULE OF LAW: School boards required by law to award construction contracts to the lowest "responsible" bidder must conduct a thorough investigation into the financial condition and practical experience of the lowest bidders before making the award.

PROCEDURE SUMMARY:

Plaintiff: Hibbs (P), an unsuccessful bidder for a construction contract.

Defendants: Arensberg (D), the successful bidder; Fayette County School Board (D).

Pennsylvania Trial Court Decision: Held for Arensberg (D) and Fayette County School Board (D).

Pennsylvania Supreme Court Decision: Reversed.

FACTS: The Fayette County School Board (D) began to have a school built. It advertised for bids for component materials, including "vitrified, wire-cut face brick . . . to cost no more than $34 per thousand"; however, the ad did not refer to the deadline for completion of the school. Many bids were received, but all were rejected as "too high" at an initial meeting of the School Board (D). Nonetheless, at a second meeting, the fourth-lowest bid, submitted by Arensberg (D), was accepted during a vote. Although Pennsylvania state law required that school boards award contracts to the lowest "responsible" bidder, the Fayette County School Board (D) did not investigate whether any of the low bidders were financially safe and possessed the experience and technical resources to do the job well. Hibbs (P), a bricklayer and supplier who bid lower than Arensberg (D), challenged the School Board's (D) action in court as an improper exercise of discretion. The Pennsylvania trial court censured the Fayette County School Board (D) for not conducting this investigation, but it found that the Board (D) had enough general knowledge of the quality of Arensberg's (D) work to award the contract to him. Hibbs (P) appealed.

ISSUE: Must school boards which are required by law to award construction contracts to the lowest "responsible" bidder conduct a thorough investigation into the financial condition and practical experience of the lowest bidders before accepting a bid?

HOLDING AND DECISION: (Kephart, J.) Yes. School boards which are required by law to award construction contracts to the lowest "responsible" bidder must conduct a thorough investigation into the financial standing, reputation, experience, resources, facilities, efficiency, and judgment of the lowest bidders before accepting a bid. Although boards may exercise their sound discretion and are not required to accept the lowest bid submitted if their investigation reveals the bidder to be financially irresponsible, it is not enough for boards merely to rely on the bidder's posting of a bond or the bidder's general reputation for good work. Furthermore, boards must include in their ads for bids the deadline for completion of the bid project and must furnish copies of the project specifications to all prospective bidders; not to do so encourages collusion by local bidders and the exclusion of outside bidders. Here, the Fayette County Board (D) did not investigate Arensberg's (D) financial condition, experience, or resources but relied generally on his reputation, nor did it include in its ads completion deadlines or provide specs to all bidders. Therefore, it improperly exercised its discretion in accepting Arensberg's (D) bid. Reversed.

COMMENT: The court here was particularly worried about the school board's obtaining the most information it could take about the low bidders because the appropriation of public funds was at stake. It was also concerned that the school board, in turn, provide enough information to all prospective bidders, through spec sheets, in order to pre-empt two pervasive practices which restrict competition in bidding: first, the "hoarding" of a limited number of spec sheets by one bidder and second, the submission of an inflated bid by a contractor who has agreed in advance with other potential local bidders to "rake off" some of his excess profit to them in exchange for their "holding off" from submitting lower bids.

UTAH PLUMB./HEAT. CONTRACTOR ASS'N v. BD. OF ED. WEISER CNTY. SCH. DIST.

19 Utah 2d 203, 429 P.2d 49 (1967).

NATURE OF CASE: Appeal from denial of application by plumbing contractors to enjoin a local school board from installing a sprinkler system with its regular maintenance personnel rather than advertising for bids for labor as well as materials for the job.

GENERAL RULE OF LAW: A state statute which requires local school boards to advertise for bids "whenever schoolhouses are to be built" does not prevent them from exercising discretion in economizing when making improvements to a school once it is already built.

PROCEDURE SUMMARY:

Plaintiffs: Utah Plumbing and Heating Contractors Association (P).

Defendant: Utah County Board of Education (D).

State Trial Court Decision: Held for Utah County Board of Education (D).

State Supreme Court Decision: Affirmed.

FACTS: The Utah Plumbing Contractors Ass'n (P) sued a local Utah school board (D) to enjoin it from using its regular maintenance personnel to install a football field sprinkler system and from advertising for bids for materials only for the job. In doing so, it relied on a Utah statute which required the local school boards to advertise for both labor and materials for bids "whenever a schoolhouse is to be built." The school board (D) had decided to use its personnel because it was short of funds and had long put off this and other desirable improvements such as tennis courts, etc. The trial court ruled that the Utah statute granted local school boards discretion to economize when construction of the school had already been completed and improvements to an already existing facility were being made; therefore, if a school district was short of funds, it was entitled to determine the least expensive way of acquiring the system, and using its own personnel was one such legitimate way. The Utah Plumbers Association (P) appealed.

ISSUE: If a state statute requires local school boards to advertise for bids "whenever schoolhouses are built," are they thereby prevented from exercising discretion in economizing when making improvements to a school once it is already built?

HOLDING AND DECISION: (Crockett, C.J.)

No. A state statute which requires local school boards to advertise for bids "whenever schoolhouses are to be built" does not deprive them from exercising broad discretion in cutting costs while making improvements to a school once it is already built. Here, the Utah school district (D) was short on funds and had long put off installation of such things as sprinklers and tennis courts; it was entitled under the statute to determine the most efficient and economical way of carrying out its mission of providing a well-equipped facility for its students. The use of regular maintenance personnel during their off-hours promoted these objectives, saved money, and was well within this discretion. Affirmed.

COMMENT: Although the state supreme court noted that the board's action was in line with its efforts in administering the school system in the most "efficient and economical" manner possible, this decision should not be construed to allow a school board to divide a contract into parts in order to avoid statutory bidding requirements. State bid laws usually indicate the maximum amount which may be expended without requiring competitive bidding. Many states also allow for "alternative" bidding on public contracts. This procedure allows for bid submissions on alternative kinds or qualities of work and materials. While the board may select one of the alternatives (even if the bid is higher than another), it is bound to select the lowest responsible bidder in the category selected.

NOTES:

ORACLE SCH. DIST. #2 v. MAMMOTH HIGH SCHOOL DISTRICT NO. 88

130 Ariz. App. 41, 633 P.2d 450 (1981).

NATURE OF CASE: Appeal of dismissal of challenge to a school district agreement to waive tuition for students attending its schools from another district in return for a redistricting agreement which transfers to it much valuable land.

GENERAL RULE OF LAW: States may require school districts to admit students from other districts within the same county which do not have their own school facilities upon the payment in money (not in kind) of fees equal to the average cost of education for each student in the county.

PROCEDURE SUMMARY:
Plaintiff: Oracle School District (P).
Defendant: Mammoth School District (D).
State Trial Court Decision: Held for Mammoth School District (D)
State Appeals Court Decision: Affirmed.

FACTS: Oracle (P) and Mammoth (D) were two school districts located in the same county in Arizona. When redistricting plans were drawn up, Oracle (P), which did not have its own high school, transferred land to Mammoth (D) in the exchange for the right to have students located in its district attend Mammoth's (D) high school free of charge. Oracle (P) nonetheless provided Mammoth (D) with state aid it received for students which attended Mammoth's (D) high school. Although Mammoth (D) honored this agreement for over 20 years, it eventually demanded that Oracle (P) pay tuition for its students attending Mammoth High. Oracle (P) sued Mammoth (D) to enforce the redistricting agreement, but the trial court dismissed Oracle's (P) complaint. Oracle (P) appealed.

ISSUE: May states require school districts to admit students from other districts in the same county which do not have their own school facilities upon the payment in money (not in kind) of fees equal to the average cost of education for each student in the county?

HOLDING AND DECISION: (Birdsall, J.) Yes. States may require school districts to admit students from other districts in the same county which do not have their own school facilities, provided a payment in money (not in kind) of fees equal to the average cost of education for each student in the county is made. School districts may not circumvent the state statutory scheme, the purpose of which is to provide educational access to all students, by waving tuition and then threatening to withdraw waivers. Therefore, Mammoth's (D) agreement with Oracle (P) was unenforceable. Affirmed.

COMMENT: Oracle (P) here argued a "quasi-contract" theory known in the law as "promissory estoppel." Under this theory, Oracle (P) reasonably relied to its detriment on the promise of Mammoth (D) to allow Oracle's (P) students to attend Mammoth's (D) high school without having to pay tuition. Mammoth (D) also knowingly allowed Oracle (P) to rely and benefit from that reliance. However, the rule that estoppel cannot be invoked against a public agency is well established. *Public Improvements, Inc. v. Board of Education of the City of New York,* (P.S. 72, Bronx), 56 N.Y. 2d 850, 453 N.Y.S. 2d 170, 438 N.E. 2d 876 (1982).

NOTEE:

**RESPONSIVE ENVIRONMENTS CORP. v.
PULASKI CNTY. SPECIAL SCHOOL DIST.**

366 F. Supp. 241 (E.D. Ark. 1973).

NATURE OF CASE: Action for breach of contract by book publisher upon school district's refusal to pay for library books it purchased.

GENERAL RULE OF LAW: Under the theory of quantum meruit, a school district may be legally required to pay a reasonable amount for school materials it has ordered and used but refused to pay for, even if it intended to buy them only if federal funding became available.

PROCEDURE SUMMARY:
Plaintiff: Responsive Environments Corp. (P), a schoolbook dealer.
Defendant: Pulaski County, Arkansas, Special School District (D).
U.S. District Court Decision: Held for Responsive Environments Corp. (P).

FACTS: Responsive Environments Corp. (P), a schoolbook publishing company, sold Pulaski Special School District (D) thousands of volumes of books for use in its school libraries. The Responsive Environments (P) agent, eager to make a sale, recommended books which the Pulaski District (D) librarian deemed unsuitable; he also ignored information that federal funds would not be available to pay for the books. The Pulaski District (D) superintendent, in turn, told the sales agent that the district anticipated paying for the books with Title II funds and approved the purchase even though he needed school board approval to do so. The parties signed a "purchase-lease" agreement under which Pulaski (D) would pay for the books in installments. Pulaski (D) took, distributed, and used the books for a year but collected them and held them for Responsive Environments' (P) pickup when it became clear that federal funds were unavailable. Pulaski (D) made no payment for the books, and when it refused Responsive's (P) demand for the full purchase price, Responsive (P) sued for breach of contract.

ISSUE: Under the theory of quantum meruit, may a school district be legally required to pay a reasonable amount for school materials it has ordered and used but refused to pay for, even if it intended to buy them only if federal funding became available?

HOLDING AND DECISION: (Williams, D.J.) Yes. Under the theory of quantum meruit, a

school district may be legally required to pay a reasonable amount for school materials it has ordered and used but refused to pay for, even if it intended to buy them only if federal funding became available. The theory of quantum meruit applies when no real or implied contract exists between the parties but one party has nevertheless received a benefit from the other which is unjust for him to retain without paying for it. Here, despite the "lease-purchase" agreement, there was no contract between Responsive Environments (P) and Pulaski School District (D) because the Pulaski (D) superintendent had not obtained the approval of the school board before agreeing to buy the library books, nor did the Pulaski (D) superintendent intend to pay for them if the district did not receive federal funding. However, Pulaski (D) used the books for a year, and therefore Responsive Environments (P) deserves them back or a payment of $13,000 (somewhat less than their sales price) at its election.

COMMENT: The court here was mindful that neither party was blameless and that both were, in the words of the court, "seeking the pot of gold at the end of the federal rainbow." It points out the dereliction in duty by the school superintendent, whose actions on behalf of the district were not enforceable absent approval of the school board and who carelessly (and somewhat successfully) attempted to spend public funds for books his own librarian deemed unsuitable for adolescent consumption.

NOTES:

JUNEAU ACADEMY v. CHICAGO BOARD OF EDUCATION

122 Ill. App. 3d 553, 78 Ill. Dec. 13, 461 N.E.2d 597 (1984).

NATURE OF CASE: Appeal of denial of damages for breach of implied contract brought by a special educational school for the handicapped to recover tuition for public school students it had accepted without prior state approval.

GENERAL RULE OF LAW: If private special education schools accept transfer students from state facilities without first obtaining required state approval, they will not be reimbursed for tuition on an implied contract theory.

PROCEDURE SUMMARY:

Plaintiff: Juneau Academy (P), a private special education facility for the handicapped located in Wisconsin.

Defendants: Chicago Board of Education (D) and several Illinois school districts.

State Trial Court Decision: Held for Chicago Board of Education (D).

State Court of Appeals Decision: Affirmed.

FACTS: Juneau Academy (P) was a residential facility located in Wisconsin for the treatment of mentally handicapped adolescent boys. Under Illinois law, Juneau Academy's (P) tuition rates had to be approved by the Purchased Care Review Board of the Illinois governor's office prior to placement of transfer students from Illinois public facilities; without such prior approval, Juneau Academy's (P) costs of care and education would not be reimbursed. An official with the Chicago Board of Education (CBE) (D), however, requested that Juneau Academy (P) accept the students even though rate approval was still pending; a representative from Illinois School District 108 (108) (D) also requested placement for one of its students. However, after Juneau Academy's (P) rates were approved, both CBE (D) and 108 (D) refused to reimburse Juneau Academy (P) for rates incurred ($2,000 per month each) for the six students prior to the rate approval. Juneau (P) sued both the state and regional boards of education, alleging that the requests of their agents for placement of special education students from public facilities and Juneau's (P) acceptance of such students amounted to implied contracts under which the boards agreed to reimburse Juneau (P) for tuition for those students. The trial court found, as matters of fact, that CBE's (D) representative had

agreed to pay for tuition incurred prior to rate approval but that 108's (D) representative had not; however, even CBE (D) had no authority from the state to make such a promise. Therefore, no implied contracts for tuition reimbursement ever arose. Juneau (P) appealed.

ISSUE: If private special education schools accept transfer students from state facilities without first obtaining required state approval, will they be reimbursed for tuition on an implied contract theory?

HOLDING AND DECISION: (Stamos, J.) No. If a state requires prior approval by one of its agencies before a student is transferred from a public school to a private special education facility and/or requires approval of the school's rate schedule prior to placement, then the private school will not be reimbursed for tuition costs incurred for students placed before such approval is granted. No contract for reimbursement for costs of education in return for acceptance, care, and schooling of such students will be implied, even if agents of the state or local school boards make such a promise to reimburse. Here, Illinois state approval was required by statute both for Juneau's (P) rate structure and for placement of students. Because the costs for these students were incurred prior to Illinois' approval of Juneau's (P) rates, Juneau (P) is not entitled to tuition reimbursement. Affirmed.

COMMENT: A contract is "implied in fact" by a court if the facts and circumstances surrounding the "negotiations" suggest that even though one party did not say, "I will pay you X amount if you do Z," and the other party agreed to accept "X for Z." In this case, however, the problem for Juneau Academy (P) was that Illinois law expressly deprived state officials of the power to reimburse Juneau (P) for tuition for transfer students prior to the approval of its rates; any such promise to reimburse, as in fact made by the CBE (D) official, would then be *ultra vires, i.e.,* beyond the power, and thus illegal. Obviously, no court will imply a contract which would have one of the parties perform an illegal act; so the court here did not find one.

TEACHERS–CERTIFICATION AND CONTRACTS FOR EMPLOYMENT

▶ ## CHAPTER SUMMARY

CHAPTER 9: TEACHERS — CERTIFICATION AND CONTRACTS FOR EMPLOYMENT

QUICK REFERENCE RULES OF LAW

9

1. **License to teach:** A teaching certificate is a state-approved license to teach which issues as a matter of course once an applicant has satisfied certain minimum requirements. (§ I.)

2. **State responsibility:** The responsibility for certification rests with the state and is often delegated by a state's legislature to a state agency such as a state board of education. (§ I.A.)

3. **No guaranteed employment:** A certificate does not guarantee employment; it merely indicates that the holder is legally fit to teach. (§ I.E.)

4. **Not a contract:** A certificate is not a contract; new conditions may be imposed upon the holder after the certificate is issued and prior to its renewal. (§ I.D.)

5. **Boards given discretionary authority:** Most states give local school boards the discretionary authority to enter into employment agreements with teachers. (§ II.A.)

6. **Rights of teachers:** However, where state law provides teachers with certain rights, local school boards may not alter or deny those rights. (§ II.B.)

7. **Professional standards:** Most local school boards set professional and academic standards higher than those set by the state for purposes of certification. (§ II.C.)

8. **Additional requirements:** Local school boards may require that teachers live within school district boundaries, remain healthy and reasonably fit, and refrain from engaging in outside employment. (§ II.D.)

9. **Contract law applies:** Basic rules of contract law are applicable to teachers' contracts. (§ III.A.)

10. **Statutory provisions predominate:** Where state statutory provisions are in conflict with the terms of a teacher's contract, the statutory provisions will predominate, and the terms may be held unenforceable. (§ III.C.)

11. **Non-classroom-related responsibilities:** Non-classroom-related responsibilities may be implied in the terms of a teacher's contract if they are reasonably related to the teacher's field of expertise or inherent in the duties of teaching. (§ III.D.)

Introduction: For the most part, the law in connection with the certification and employment of teachers is the province of state legislatures. State and local school boards are required to follow state mandates yet are free to impose certain additional requirements as they see fit. However, neither state laws nor agency regulations may unduly infringe on teachers' federal constitutional rights or rights created by federal civil rights laws except in certain cases in which there is a valid reason set forth.

I. **TEACHER CERTIFICATION: Certification is the process by which a state licenses a person to teach. The holder of a teaching certificate is deemed to be legally competent to teach,** *i.e.,* **he or she has fulfilled certain minimum criteria set by the state as a prerequisite to licensure.**

    A. **State Responsibility:** The responsibility for the licensure of teachers rests with each of the fifty states. As a result, statutes governing teacher certification vary from state to state.

    B. **Assistance from State Education Officials and Agencies:** Most state legislatures delegate portions of their functions to state boards of education or similar state agencies.

        1. *Legislators' reliance on educators' expertise:* Understandably, state legislators must rely on the discretion and expertise of state education officials when it comes to the setting of minimum professional qualifications necessary for licensure.

        2. *Minimum state standards:* In some cases, the state legislature may set minimum certification requirements yet also provide certificate-issuing agencies with discretionary authority pursuant to which such agencies may impose *higher* standards for certification than those contained in the minimum state requirements.

    C. **Effect of Meeting Certificate Requirements:** As a rule, if an applicant satisfies all pertinent certification criteria, a certificate will issue *as a matter of course.*

        1. *Arbitrary denial prohibited:* In other words, a certificate cannot be denied arbitrarily or for no reason at all.

        2. *Limited discretionary authority:* As noted above, state agencies that are responsible for issuing certificates may be vested with some *discretionary* (as opposed to the perfunctory, or "ministerial") authority.

9

3. *Abuse of discretion:* In such cases, courts will not question a decision to deny the issuance of a certificate unless it appears that there was absolutely no valid basis for doing so.

D. **"Certificate" and "Contract" Distinguished:** A teacher's certificate is not a contract and thus is not governed by the law of contracts.

1. *Postissuance modifications:* New or modified conditions may be imposed upon the certificate holder after the certificate has issued. Also, a certificate holder may be required to pursue additional academic or continuing education courses if she wishes to renew or upgrade her certificate.

2. *Certificate revocation:* A certificate may be revoked or suspended by the issuer for "good cause," *i.e.,* for a well-recognized and well-supported reason. This reason must not be arbitrary and must withstand a reasonable challenge. *See Amador v. New Mexico State Board of Education,* 80 N.M. 336 (1969).

   Examples: Evidence of immoral activities, breach of the teaching contract, and lack of teaching competency have been found to constitute good cause.

   Note: Because the revocation or suspension of certification is an extreme measure which generally results in loss of employment, courts usually require certificate-revoking agencies to establish and follow certain fairness-minded procedures in making such decisions.

E. **"Certification" and "Employment" Distinguished:** A certificate does not guarantee its holder a specific teaching position. As discussed below, state legislatures generally vest authority for the employment of teachers in local school boards. *See* Section II., below.

F. **Typical Certification Requirements**

1. *Certification by examination:* Although at one time disfavored, examinations are now required by most states for teacher certification. The most common is the National Teacher Examination (NTE). *See United States v. State of South Carolina,* 445 F.Supp. 1094 (1978).

2. *Academic prerequisites:* Such requirements include a college degree or degrees and course work in specified areas of curricula.

3. *Good moral character:* An applicant must possess good moral character at the time she applies for a certificate (and generally

must evidence such character throughout the term of the certificate).

4. ***Signing of a loyalty oath:*** An oath of loyalty is permissible so long as it does not contravene an applicant's federal constitutional right to associate with those of her choice. Some states require an applicant to pledge her loyalty to state and federal constitutions.

5. ***Minimum age:*** An applicant may be required to be of a specified age for certification purposes.

6. ***U.S. citizenship:*** States may require U.S. citizenship as a condition of certification.

   Example: The U.S. Supreme Court has stated that because the function of teaching is so closely tied to the operation of state government, a state may properly exclude from certification those individuals who have not submitted themselves to our "process of self-government." *Ambach v. Norwick,* 441 U.S. 68, 99 S. Ct. 1589 (1979).

7. ***Temporary certification:*** A state may waive its basic certification requirement. This is unusual and usually only happens when there is a specific shortage in a particular teaching area. *See Oklahoma ex rel. Thompson v. Ekberg,* 613 P.2d 466 (1980).

II. **EMPLOYMENT OF TEACHERS: Once an individual has obtained a certificate attesting to his qualifications for a particular type of public school teaching post, he must face a second (and sometimes formidable) hurdle — that of obtaining an actual teaching position within the state in which he is certified. Employment requirements differ from certification requirements, just as the agencies responsible for making employment decisions (local boards) differ from those responsible for certification (state boards).**

EMPLOYMENT OF TEACHERS

A. **Discretion Vested in Local School Boards:** Most states vest the discretionary authority to hire and fire certified teachers, and the rights and responsibilities attendant with that authority, in local or regional school boards. In such cases, the local board *as a whole* — as opposed to the superintendent or individual board members — is responsible for all employment decisions.

B. **Breadth of Authority:** The authority delegated to local boards is *broad.* Courts generally will not review a particular hiring decision unless it appears that the decision was made in an arbitrary or capricious manner or in violation of an applicant's statutory or constitutional rights. As a general rule, hiring decisions must be *neutral* as to race, religion, gender, and national origin.

C. **Standard of Employment:** Consonant with their broad hiring authority, local school boards are often vested with the discretion to set professional and academic standards at a *higher level* than that set by the state in the context of its minimum certification requirements.

D. **Typical Conditions of Employment:** Aside from competency standards, the local school board may require that any of the following conditions be met prior to extending an offer of employment to a certificate holder.

1. *Residency:* Federal courts have held that a local board may require a teacher to live within the boundaries of the school district so long as it can demonstrate a *rational basis* for the requirement. Note, however, that some states prohibit by statute the adoption of such requirements.

2. *Health and physical fitness:* So long as its standards are not applied in an arbitrary manner, a school board may require that teachers meet reasonable health and fitness requirements for the protection of students and other employees. Many school boards once required teachers who were pregnant to take maternity leave based, in part, on a health and fitness argument. Such policies have now been held to violate federal constitutional rights. *See Cleveland Board of Ed. v. LaFleur/Cohen v. Chesterfield Cnty. Sch. Bd.,* 414 U.S. 632 (1974).

3. *Blindness:* As a general rule, blindness is not a proper ground for declining to employ a teacher who is otherwise qualified for a position.

4. *Outside employment:* A school board may prohibit a teacher from accepting outside employment during the school year.

5. *Employment standards:* School boards must utilize employment standards that are job-related. *See Griggs v. Duke Power Co.,* 401 U.S. 424 (1971). Additionally, if a school board's hiring practices result in racial imbalance, such practices may be attacked in the courts. *See Wards Cove Packing Company, Inc. v. Atonio,* 490 U.S. 642 (1989).

E. **General Rule concerning Employment:** Employment practices and procedures must be applied *uniformly*.

III. TEACHERS' CONTRACTS: Local school boards have been delegated the exclusive authority to enter into contracts for employment with prospective teachers. A contract by definition creates various rights and responsibilities in each of its parties. Questions sometimes arise as to whether (1) a contract was properly created, (2) additional rights and responsibilities should be read into the contract in light of preexisting statutory language, collective-bargaining agreements, and the like (none of which were specifically referred to in the contract), and (3) additional rights and responsibilities are "implied" by custom or the terms of the contract themselves.

TEACHERS' CONTRACTS

9

A. Basic Principles of Contract Law Apply: As with all legal contracts, a contract between a local school board and a teacher must contain the following critical elements.

1. *Offer and acceptance:* One party (almost always the board) must make an offer of employment, and the other party (the teacher) must accept it.

2. *Legal capacity:* Both parties must be competent to enter into a contractual relationship.

3. *Consideration:* There must be value or a benefit conferred by one party in return for the other party's performance.

4. *Legality:* The subject of the contract must be within the bounds of the law.

5. *Form:* The contract must be memorialized in a form prescribed by law.

B. Common Types of Employment Contracts

1. *Tenure contracts:* Contracts which provide for a teacher's termination only upon the existence of "cause," *i.e.,* only if a good reason for terminating the contract is apparent after various procedures designed to ensure fairness to the teacher have been followed. *See Harrah Independent School District v. Martin,* 440 U.S. 194 (1979).

2. *Term contracts:* Contracts of limited duration which may (or may not) be renewed at the discretion of the school board. Such contracts are probationary in nature and usually precede tenure contracts.

C. Effect of State Statutory Provisions and Outside Agreements on Employment: Teacher employment may also be governed by various *state education statutes.* In such cases, statutory requirements will be deemed a part of the teacher's contract as if fully spelled out therein. For instance, tenure provisions mandated by state law may be viewed as if they are a part of the local employment contract.

1. ***Preemptive effect of state law:*** Wherever a statutory requirement conflicts with the terms of a contract, the terms will be held unenforceable. In other words, state statutory requirements will preempt local contract terms. The only qualifications to this would be in a state such as Ohio, where O.R.C. 4017 allows for a properly negotiated teacher's contract to prevail over state law (with the exception of selected civil rights protections).

2. ***Collective-bargaining agreements:*** As with rights created by statutory provisions, rights also accrue to teachers under collective-bargaining agreements.

D. Implied Terms of Employment

1. ***Implied teaching requirements:*** Some courts have determined that teachers have an *implied* obligation to assume various responsibilities outside of classroom instruction that are not specifically provided for in their contracts.

   Examples: Male teachers may be expected to supervise the conduct of students in boys' restrooms. English teachers may be required to coach student plays. All teachers may be required to supervise study halls.

2. ***Significant relationship to expertise:*** Generally speaking, an implied obligation may be seen to exist if the nonclassroom assignment relates in a significant way to the teacher's area of instructional expertise or is fundamental to the teaching role.

NOTES:

AMADOR v. NEW MEXICO STATE BOARD OF EDUCATION

80 N.M. 336, 455 P.2d 840 (1969).

NATURE OF CASE: Appeal of injunction prohibiting a state board of education from suspending the teaching certificate, pursuant to a statute allowing suspension for good and just cause, of a teacher elected to the board.

GENERAL RULE OF LAW: Incompatibility of state board of education membership and certification as a teacher is not grounds for suspension of a teaching certificate under a statute permitting suspension for good and just cause.

PROCEDURE SUMMARY:
Plaintiff: Amador (P), Board (D) member and school teacher.
Defendant: New Mexico State Board of Education (D) (Board).
State Trial Court Decision: Injunction issued prohibiting Board (D) from suspending Amador's (P) certificate.
State Supreme Court Decision: Affirmed.

FACTS: In 1962, the New Mexico State Board (D) adopted a resolution requiring the suspension of the teaching certificate of any teacher elected to the Board (D). In November 1966, Amador (P), a certified teacher, was elected to the Board (D) and was subsequently served with an order to show cause why his teaching certificate should not be suspended. Amador (P) sought, and the trial court granted, an injunction prohibiting the Board (D) from suspending his certificate. The Board (D) appealed, contending that the incompatibility of Board (D) membership and certification was grounds for suspending Amador's (P) certification pursuant to a statute permitting suspension for good cause.

ISSUE: Is incompatibility of board membership and teacher certification grounds for suspension of a teaching certificate under a statute permitting suspension for good and just cause?

HOLDING AND DECISION: (Noble, C.J.) No. Incompatibility of board membership and teacher certification is not grounds for suspension of a teaching certificate under a statute permitting suspension for good and just cause. The right to practice a profession or vocation is a property right. Where a statute permits revocation or suspension of such a right, the suspension or revocation may only be for those reasons specifically provided by the statute. The statute that the Board (D) relied upon allows certificate suspension for "good and just" cause for the purpose of insuring high-quality public education. The suspension of Amador's (P) certificate because he became a member of the Board (D) would not promote or serve this purpose. Therefore, no "good and just" cause within the meaning of the statute existed. Affirmed.

COMMENT: In *Amador,* incompatibility of the two positions was not "good and just" cause within the meaning of the statute. It could be argued, however, that the positions were not even incompatible but to some degree complementary; being certified may give a board as a whole greater ability to consider more options and factors before making a decision. Most courts follow the rule of *Amador* and will not intervene in a certification revocation matter unless the revocation is on grounds other than those expressly permitted by statute or certain mandatory procedures were not followed. In addition, the plaintiff is usually required to exhaust all administrative remedies before coming to court. This case needs to be distinguished from cases involving practicing educators serving on state school boards. In the instant case, there was no conflict. Amador (P) would not fill both posts simultaneously. Thus, there was no incompatibility in the holding of two state positions at the same time.

NOTES:

UNITED STATES v. STATE OF SOUTH CAROLINA

445 F. Supp. 1094, aff'd 434 U.S. 1026, 98 S. Ct. 756 (1978).

NATURE OF CASE: Challenge to the use of standard test scores for both the hiring and establishing of pay scales of teachers.

GENERAL RULE OF LAW: A state's use of the National Teacher Examination in the hiring and pay-scale setting of teachers does not violate the Fourteenth Amendment.

PROCEDURE SUMMARY:

Plaintiff: The federal Government (P) and certain individuals.

Defendant: The State of South Carolina (D) and various political subdivisions thereof.

U.S. District Court Decision: Held for South Carolina (D).

FACTS: The Education Testing Service, Inc. offered a national standardized examination called the National Teacher Examination. South Carolina (D) employed a system of hiring and pay scales that took into account a teacher's score on the exam. The federal Government (P) and certain private persons brought a lawsuit, contending that this practice constituted racial discrimination under the Equal Protection Clause of the Fourteenth Amendment because blacks, as a group, scored lower than whites.

ISSUE: Does a state's use of the National Teacher Examination in the hiring and pay-scale setting of teachers violate the Fourteenth Amendment?

HOLDING AND DECISION: (Haynsworth, J.) No. A state's use of the National Teacher Examination in the hiring and pay-scale setting of teachers does not violate the Fourteenth Amendment. To make out a case of racial classification, a plaintiff must show an intent to create and use a racial classification. If a plaintiff cannot do this, the practice challenged will be upheld so long as it is rationally related to its stated goal. Here, no evidence existed that South Carolina (D) intended to create a racial classification in adopting the National Teacher Examination. A review of the record indicated that South Carolina (D) used the test to ensure that qualified teachers would be hired. This appeared to be a rational use of the test, so no equal protection violation occurred. Judgment for South Carolina (D).

COMMENT: The various plaintiffs challenged South Carolina's (D) practice not only under the Fourteenth Amendment but also under the 1964 Civil Rights Act. The issues were largely the same, but proof regarding intent is somewhat more favorable to plaintiffs under the Act, which is more result-oriented. Nevertheless, the Court rejected the Civil Rights Act claims on much the same grounds as the constitutional claims. Without question, this ruling, which has been supported in other jurisdictions, has caused a great deal of concern to practicing administrators and teachers. These educators believe that factors other than a score or a test should control hiring and salary increases. Nevertheless, the use of test scores has increased for teachers and for students. Statewide student proficiency testing for graduation is now a common practice in most states. These programs have always been upheld where it is shown that the test meets validity standards and is a reasonable exercise of state authority.

NOTES:

OKLAHOMA ex rel.
THOMPSON v. EKBERG
613 P.2d 466 (1980).

NATURE OF CASE: Appeal of decision holding that a school board which hired a principal without a master's degree, after being informed that a state provision requiring principals to hold such degrees would be waived, was not liable for damages.

GENERAL RULE OF LAW: School board members are not liable for damages for actions which violate state requirements where they could not have reasonably known the actions violated the requirements.

PROCEDURE SUMMARY:
Plaintiff: State ex rel. Thompson (P) (Thompson), the state for a group of taxpayers.
Defendant: Ekberg (D), a school board member.
State Trial Court Decision: Held for Ekberg (D), finding no liability in damages.
State Supreme Court Decision: Affirmed.

FACTS: A state statute required that principals in the state school system be certified, and, to be certified, they had to hold a master's degree. Ekberg (D), a member of a local school board, along with other board members, was seeking to hire a principal. After being told by state board of education representatives that the master's degree requirement would be waived, the state board hired Moxom (D), who did not hold a master's degree, as a principal for the 1974–75 school term. After the term, Moxom (D) acquired a master's degree. Thompson (P) and other taxpayers filed suit against Ekberg (D) and other board members, seeking damages for the hiring of Moxom (D) in violation of the master's degree requirement. The trial court held for Ekberg (D), finding that he could not have reasonably known that the state board's waiver of the requirement was ineffective. Thompson (P) appealed.

ISSUE: Are school board members liable for actions that violate a state requirement where they could not have reasonably known the action violated the requirement?

HOLDING AND DECISION: (Simms, J.) No. School board members are not liable for actions that violate a state requirement where they could not have reasonably known the action violated the requirement. The state board of education lacked authority to waive the master's degree requirement. Though the statute grants the state board general authority over matters pertaining to the qualification of school officials, the statute's master's degree requirement is a specific exception to this general grant. There was no way the local board or Ekberg (D) could have reasonably known that the state board lacked authority to waive the master's degree requirement and that, consequently, Moxom (D) was uncertified to be a principal. The statute under which Thompson (P) sought damages only allows damages where school board officials "knowingly" hire uncertified officials. This was not the case here. Affirmed.

COMMENT: Generally, school board members will not be held liable for actions which are later found to be unauthorized, if they act in good faith and without fraud. The clear rationale for not holding the board members in *Ekberg* liable is that they were found to be acting in good faith, especially since they had been informed by state officials that the action was proper. Some argue that the adoption of a harsher standard would hurt local school boards by deterring individuals from running for board positions for fear of liability for mistakes in judgment and chilling the decision-making autonomy of those who are serving as board members. It is common practice for state departments to issue temporary teaching certificates. These certificates are issued to teachers at the request of the district administrator based on the inability to find a teacher in a specific shortage area, such as bilingual education or vocational education. The difference in this case is that there was no shortage of certified personnel eligible to serve as principal. Therefore, to waive the master's degree requirement would violate the statute without a justifiable reason.

NOTES:

CLEVELAND BOARD OF ED. V. LaFLEUR/ COHEN v. CHESTERFIELD CNTY. SCH. BD.
414 U.S. 632, 94 S. Ct. 791 (1974).

NATURE OF CASE: Review of reversal of decision upholding the constitutionality of a school board rule mandating that pregnant public school teachers take unpaid maternity leave four to five months before their due dates.

GENERAL RULE OF LAW: Mandatory leave rules that create a conclusive presumption that all pregnant teachers become physically incapable of performing their duties at four to five months violate due process.

PROCEDURE SUMMARY:
Plaintiff: LaFleur (P), a pregnant school teacher.
Defendant: Cleveland Board of Education (D) (Board).
U.S. District Court Decision: Held for the Board (D), finding mandatory leave requirement constitutional.
U.S. Court of Appeals Decision: Reversed, finding the requirement violated the Equal Protection Clause of the Fourteenth Amendment.
U.S. Supreme Court Decision: Affirmed, finding the requirement unconstitutional under the Due Process Clause of the Fourteenth Amendment.

FACTS: The Board (D) enacted a rule requiring pregnant school teachers to take maternity leave without pay five months before their expected due date. LaFleur (P), a junior high school teacher informed the Board (D) that she was pregnant. Pursuant to the mandatory leave requirement, she was forced to stop working, without pay. LaFleur (P) thereafter filed suit under 42 U.S.C. § 1983, arguing that the requirement was unconstitutional. The district court rejected LaFleur's (P) argument and upheld the requirement. The court of appeals reversed, holding that the requirement violated the Equal Protection Clause of the Fourteenth Amendment. The Board (D) sought, and the U.S. Supreme Court granted, review.

ISSUE: Is a mandatory leave rule that creates a conclusive presumption that pregnant teachers become physically incapable of performing their duties at four to five months constitutional?

HOLDING AND DECISION: (Stewart, J.) No. A mandatory leave rule that creates a conclusive presumption that pregnant teachers become physically incapable of performing their duties at four to five months violates the Due Process Clause. This clause protects an individual's freedom of choice in matters of marriage and family life from unwarranted governmental intrusion. Government may not needlessly, arbitrarily, or capriciously infringe upon this freedom. The Board's (D) mandatory leave rule, however, does so. As long as the teacher gives substantial advance notice that she is pregnant, the arbitrary cutoff date of the Board's (D) rule has no valid relationship to the state's interest in preserving continuity of instruction. Such advance notice is already required by the Board (D). Imposing the mandatory leave cutoff date, in addition to this notice, goes too far. Affirmed.

COMMENT: The Court decided *LaFleur* on substantive due process grounds, finding that the requirement was an excessive infringement of a fundamental right. It seems, however, that the case could have easily been affirmed under the equal protection analysis applied by the court of appeals since the requirement was clearly sex-based and subject to intermediate scrutiny. Generally, the Equal Protection Clause guarantees that similarly situated people will be treated similarly. For example, the government must show greater justification for distinguishing between men and women because the sex of an individual is more often than not an irrational basis for distinction. Under substantive due process, the government must show greater justification for imposing burdens on fundamental rights such as interstate travel, procreation, and marriage. Under either analysis, the government would have had a difficult time showing the requisite greater justification. The Court's ruling still provides for the Board's (D) concern for continuity, and the requirement that a doctor assist the pregnant teacher in deciding maternity leave and return-to-work dates deals with the Board's (D) concern for the unborn child and the mother. Continuity is guaranteed by allowing return from maternity leave at specified, prearranged dates, *e.g.*, the beginning of a new grading period. This seems to be entirely reasonable so as to ensure the normal operation of the school. A school board does need some notice in order to make plans and to provide a continuous and adequate education for children. Of course, notice provisions must be rationally related to the school board's needs.

GRIGGS v. DUKE POWER CO.
401 U.S. 424, 91 S. CT. 849 (1971).

NATURE OF CASE: Review of dismissal of action challenging hiring practices.

GENERAL RULE OF LAW: Employment standards which do not significantly relate to job performance violate the Civil Rights Act if they tend to exclude minority applicants.

PROCEDURE SUMMARY:
Plaintiffs: Job applicants at Griggs Power Co. (P).
Defendant: Griggs Power Co., an employer (D).
U.S District Court Decision: [Not stated in casebook excerpt].
U.S. Court of Appeals Decision: Held for Griggs Power Co. (D).
U.S. Supreme Court Decision: Reversed.

FACTS: Griggs Power Co. (D), as part of its hiring process, required a high school diploma and administered an intelligence test if an employee desired a transfer or promotion. No evidence existed that either criterion was indicative of job performance for the employment positions at issue. Black applicants statistically performed worse than whites in both categories. A group of black applicants (P) challenged the standards in district court as violative of the 1964 Civil Rights Act. The court of appeals held the standard valid, and the Supreme Court granted review.

ISSUE: Do employment standards which do not significantly relate to job performance violate the Civil Rights Act if they tend to exclude minority applicants?

HOLDING AND DECISION: (Burger, C.J.) Yes. Employment standards which do not significantly relate to job performance violate the Civil Rights Act if they tend to exclude minority applicants. The Civil Rights Act proscribes employment practices which have the result of excluding minority groups which have been victims of employment discrimination. A practice need not have a discriminatory intent; a discriminatory result is sufficient. If a challenged practice does not have a discriminatory intent and bears a significant relation to job performance, then it will not violate the Act. Here, however, no such showing was made. Therefore, the discriminatory impact was sufficient to implicate the Civil Rights Act. Reversed.

COMMENT: The Civil Rights Act is broader than the Constitution in two significant ways. The Constitution only acts as a restraint on government; the Act regulates private conduct as well. Further, the Act, unlike the Constitution, is not limited to intentional discrimination. Both areas of difference were relevant to this case, for without the protection of the Civil Rights Act, the Constitution alone would probably not have been enough for the job applicants to prevail in this case. The holding in this case was limited significantly by *Wards Cove Packing Company, Inc. v. Atonio,* 490 U.S. 642, 109 S. Ct. 2115 (1989), by shifting the burden of proof from employers to employees. Recent congressional action has reinstated the Title VII protection enunciated in *Griggs.* This case also has significance for the study of teacher and administrator employment practices. It was in *Griggs* that the Court stated that broad and general testing is inadequate and cannot be used as the controlling factor unless it is a reasonable measure of job performance. This finding was used in *United States v. State of South Carolina,* 445 F. Supp. 1094, aff'd 434 U.S. 1026, 98 S. Ct. 756 (D.S.C. 1978), where it was held that the state's use of test scores for certification and salary purposes did not violate Title VII of the Civil Rights Act of 1964. Care must be exercised to distinguish between a court's use of a Title VII Civil Rights Act analysis and a Fourteenth Amendment equal protection analysis. Title VII prohibits the use of tests and diploma requirements by employers when they operate to disqualify a disproportionate number of members of minority groups — unless the test and diploma requirements can be established as being directly indicative of job performance. In *Griggs,* the requirements were not shown to be directly related to job performance and were, therefore, invalid. Thus, an employer must be able to establish a direct correlation between whatever skill is being tested and performance on the job.

NOTES:

WARDS COVE PACKING COMPANY, INC. v. ATONIO
490 U.S. 642, 109 S. Ct. 2115 (1989).

9

NATURE OF CASE: Review of reversal of judgment for nonwhite former salmon cannery workers in their class action alleging racially discriminatory hiring and promotion practices giving white workers better jobs.

GENERAL RULE OF LAW: A comparison of the racial composition of qualified persons in the labor market and persons holding at-issue jobs is the proper inquiry under disparate impact analysis.

PROCEDURE SUMMARY:

Plaintiff: Atonio (P), a nonwhite former cannery worker.
Defendant: Wards Cove Packing Company, Inc. (D), employer.
U.S. District Court Decision: Held for Wards Cove (D), finding no racial discrimination.
U.S. Court of Appeals Decision: Reversed, finding that Atonio (P) had made a prima facie case of disparate impact.
U.S. Supreme Court Decision: Reversed.

FACTS: Certain canneries generally had two job classifications: cannery jobs and noncannery jobs. The cannery jobs were filled primarily by nonwhite workers. The noncannery jobs were predominantly filled with white workers. Atonio (P), a nonwhite former cannery job worker, filed suit against Wards Cove (D), alleging that its racially discriminatory hiring and promotion practices had a disparate impact in violation of Title VII of the Civil Rights Act of 1964. The district court held for Wards Cove (D), finding that the overrepresentation of nonwhite workers in the cannery jobs was because most of the cannery jobs were filled through a contract with a predominantly nonwhite union. The court of appeals reversed, holding that the statistics showing a high percentage of nonwhite workers in cannery jobs and a low percentage of such workers in noncannery jobs made a prima facie case of disparate impact. The U.S. Supreme Court granted review.

ISSUE: Is a comparison of the racial composition of qualified persons in the labor market and persons holding the at-issue jobs the proper inquiry in disparate impact analysis?

HOLDING AND DECISION: (White, J.) Yes.

The comparison of the racial composition of qualified persons in the labor market and persons holding the at-issue jobs is the proper inquiry in disparate impact analysis. The court of appeals erred in holding that a comparison of the percentage of nonwhite cannery workers and the percentage of nonwhite noncannery workers may make out a prima facie disparate impact case. Under the correct rule, Wards Cove's (D) hiring and promotional practices cannot be said to have had a disparate impact on nonwhites if there was not a sufficient population of nonwhites who were qualified to hold noncannery jobs. Under the court of appeals' approach, an employer could be made to defend its hiring and promotion practices any time a segment of its work force was racially imbalanced. Reversed.

COMMENT: *Wards Cove* clarifies what exactly must be shown to establish a disparate impact claim under Title VII. No longer is it appropriate to simply show that the percentage of minorities in a particular job is less than the percentage of minorities in the population of the locality; it must also be demonstrated that there was a sufficient population of qualified minority workers. The Court's definition of the relevant comparison inquiry more narrowly tailors remedial efforts to the actual discriminatory acts or actors which caused the need for the remedial efforts. Portions of this decision, which modified *Griggs,* were reinstated by Congress. As a public policy position, Congress wanted the more traditional Title VII analysis.

NOTES:

HARRAH INDEPENDENT SCHOOL DISTRICT v. MARTIN
440 U.S. 194, 99 S. Ct. 1062 (1979).

NATURE OF CASE: Review of reversal of dismissal of a complaint alleging that a school board's refusal to renew a tenured teacher's employment contract after she refused to comply with the board's continuing education requirement violated her rights under both the Due Process and Equal Protection clauses of the Fourteenth Amendment.

GENERAL RULE OF LAW: A school board may refuse to renew the contract of a tenured teacher who refuses to comply with a continuing education requirement designed to promote a legitimate state interest if nonrenewal follows a hearing.

PROCEDURE SUMMARY:
Plaintiff: Martin (P), a tenured teacher.
Defendant: Harrah Independent School District (D) (District).
U.S. District Court Decision: Dismissed Martin's (P) complaint.
U.S. Court of Appeals Decision: Reversed.
U.S. Supreme Court Decision: Reversed.

FACTS: Martin (P) was a tenured teacher employed by the District (D) since 1969. Martin (P) constantly refused to comply with the District's (D) continuing education requirements, which caused her to forfeit salary increases for the 1972–1974 school years. Sometime after 1973, the state legislature enacted a law mandating certain salary raises for teachers regardless of compliance with the continuing education policy. The District (D), denied its standard means of compelling compliance, notified Martin (P) that her contract for the next school year would not be renewed unless she completed continuing education before the end of the current year. Martin (P), at a hearing on the matter, informed the District (D) that she did not intend to comply. The District (D), after finding her refusal to be a "willful neglect of duty," voted not to renew her contract. Martin (P) filed suit, claiming the District (D) action denied her due process of law and equal protection in violation of the Fourteenth Amendment. The district court dismissed the complaint, and the court of appeals reversed. The U.S. Supreme Court granted review.

ISSUE: May a school board refuse to renew the contract of a tenured teacher who refuses to comply with a continuing education requirement designed to promote a legitimate state interest where nonrenewal follows a hearing?

HOLDING AND DECISION: (Per curiam) Yes. A school board may refuse to renew the contract of a tenured teacher who refuses to comply with a continuing education requirement designed to promote a legitimate state interest where nonrenewal follows a hearing. Martin (P) was informed of the District's (D) decision not to renew her contract unless she complied and was given opportunity to appear before the District (D) to challenge the decision. Further, the District (D) only conditioned renewal of Martin's (P) contract on compliance, not continued employment under the contract already in force. Thus, the District (D) violated neither Martin's (P) procedural nor substantive due process rights. Finally, the prospect of nonrenewal applied uniformly to that class of teachers who refused to comply with a requirement which clearly bears a rational relationship to the District's (D) objective of compelling compliance; therefore, there was no equal protection violation. Reversed.

COMMENT: *Harrah* was a unanimous decision which illustrates that even tenured teachers' rights are subject to regulations and restrictions imposed to promote a legitimate educational interest of the state. The ruling finds support in earlier decisions allowing the dismissal of tenured teachers for insubordination, defined as "a willful disregard of express or implied directions of the employer and a refusal to obey reasonable orders." The District (D) order in *Harrah* was reasonable because it clearly served the legitimate state interest in providing high-quality education. The Court only required a reasonable relationship to a state interest because the continuing education requirement did not infringe a fundamental right.

NOTES:

MARTIN v. WILKS
490 U.S. 755, 109 S. Ct. 2180 (1989).

9

NATURE OF CASE: Review of reversal of dismissal of an action brought by white fire fighters alleging a personnel board's promotion decisions, pursuant to consent decrees requiring the hiring and promotion of black fire fighters, amounted to reverse discrimination.

GENERAL RULE OF LAW: Employees are not precluded from challenging employment decisions made pursuant to consent decrees entered in proceedings to which they were not parties.

PROCEDURE SUMMARY:
Plaintiff: Wilks (P), a white fire fighter.
Defendant: Jefferson County Personnel Board (D) (Board).
U.S. District Court Decision: Held for Board (D), dismissing Martin's (P) action on the ground that he was precluded from challenging the decisions made pursuant to the consent decrees.
U.S. Court of Appeals Decision: Reversed.
U.S. Supreme Court Decision: Affirmed.

FACTS: After black individuals filed suit against the Board (D), whose duties included the hiring of county fire fighters, consent decrees were entered which included goals for hiring and promoting black fire fighters. Thereafter, Martin (P), a white fire fighter, filed suit against the Board (D), alleging that the Board's (D) promotional decisions pursuant to the decrees violated federal law by favoring less qualified blacks and denying him promotion simply because of his race (*i.e.*, "reverse discrimination"). The district court dismissed the action, holding that Wilks (P) was precluded from challenging promotion decisions made pursuant to the consent decrees because he was not a party to the proceedings in which the decrees were entered. The court of appeals reversed, and the U.S. Supreme Court granted review.

ISSUE: Are employees precluded from challenging employment decisions made pursuant to consent decrees entered in proceedings in which they were not parties?

HOLDING AND DECISION: (Rehnquist, C.J.) No. Employees are not precluded from challenging employment decisions made pursuant to consent decrees entered in proceedings in which they were not parties. One is not bound by a judgment in an action in which he is not designated as a party or to which he has not been made a party by service of process. Fed. R. Civ. P. 24, which governs intervention, is clearly permissive in nature. Nor under Fed. R. Civ. P. 19 is a person obligated to intervene in an action, unless a judgment rendered in the absence of that person could subject those who already are parties to a substantial risk of incurring inconsistent obligations. To preclude Wilks (P) now from collaterally attacking the consent decree, when he was neither joined as a party nor required to intervene in the original proceedings, is contrary to federal law. Affirmed.

COMMENT: The ruling is a victory for individuals making reverse discrimination claims like the plaintiff in *Martin*. *Martin* has clear implications in the school context. School desegregation consent degrees or employment plans providing similar hiring and promotion objectives could be challenged under the analysis of *Martin*. It seems likely that *Martin* would be extended even though it was only a 5–4 decision because two of the dissenting justices, Brennan and Marshall, have since left the Court and been replaced by more conservative justices.

NOTES:

CITY OF RICHMOND v. J.A. CROSON CO.
488 U.S. 469, 109 S. Ct. 706 (1989).

NATURE OF CASE: Appeal of judgment reversing a district court decision upholding the constitutionality of a municipal requirement that prime contractors subcontract a set percentage of city contracts to minority subcontractors.

GENERAL RULE OF LAW: A city may not adopt a preferential plan which is not justified by a compelling state interest or narrowly tailored to accomplish a remedial purpose.

PROCEDURE SUMMARY:
Plaintiff: J.A. Croson Co. (P), a prime contractor.
Defendant: City of Richmond (P) (City).
U.S. District Court Decision: Held for City (D), upholding the plan.
U.S. Court of Appeals Decision: Reversed.
U.S. Supreme Court Decision: Affirmed.

FACTS: The City (D) adopted a plan requiring prime contractors awarded municipal contracts to subcontract at least 30% of the dollar amount of the contract to minority business enterprises (MBEs). The plan, however, allowed the requirement to be waived where it was proved that a sufficient number of qualified MBEs were not able or willing to participate. The purpose of the plan was to remedy the effects of widespread racial discrimination in the local, state, and national construction industries. Croson (P), a prime contractor, unsuccessfully requested a waiver of the requirement. It then filed suit under 42 U.S.C. § 1983, alleging that the plan was unconstitutional under the Fourteenth Amendment's Equal Protection Clause. The district court disagreed and upheld the plan. The court of appeals, however, reversed, applying strict scrutiny and finding that the plan was not justified by a compelling state interest or narrowly tailored to accomplish a remedial purpose.

ISSUE: May a city adopt a preferential plan which is not justified by a compelling state interest or narrowly tailored to accomplish a remedial purpose?

HOLDING AND DECISION: (O'Connor, J.) No. A city may not adopt a preferential plan which is not justified by a compelling state interest or narrowly tailored to accomplish a remedial purpose. The general claim that there has been past discrimination, on a national scale, in the construction industry cannot justify the use of a racial quota. The City (D) provided no evidence that there has been discrimination on the part of anyone in its own construction industry. Further, the City's (D) reliance on the disparity between the number of prime contracts awarded to minority businesses and the size of the City's (D) minority population is misplaced. The correct statistical inquiry is a comparison of the percentage of MBEs in the construction industry with the percentage of total City (D) construction dollars presently awarded to minority subcontractors. Affirmed.

COMMENT: *Croson* is another example of the Court's attempt to more closely tie remedial efforts with the actual discriminatory actions creating the need for the remedial efforts. After *Croson*, state and local entities may no longer simply rely on national findings and statistics indicating discrimination in a particular industry or profession. It appears that this reasoning can be extended to schools and education, including the racial makeup of student body populations and the teaching staff. The case could be read to prohibit school boards from relying on national, or maybe even state, statistics in making decisions regarding remedial measures.

NOTES:

UNIV. OF PENNSYLVANIA v. EQUAL EMPLOYMENT OPPORTUNITY COMM'N
493 U.S. 182, 100 S. Ct. 577 (1990).

9

NATURE OF CASE: Review of issuance of an enforcement order requiring disclosure of peer-review information to the Equal Employment Opportunity Commission upon a professor's Title VII action alleging racial discrimination in being denied tenure by a university.

GENERAL RULE OF LAW: Universities do not enjoy a special privilege requiring that peer-review files need only be disclosed after a court finds particularized necessity for access to the files.

PROCEDURE SUMMARY:
Plaintiff: Equal Employment Opportunity Commission (P) (EEOC).
Defendant: University of Pennsylvania (D) (University).
U.S. District Court Decision: Held for the EEOC (P).
U.S. Court of Appeals Decision: Affirmed.
U.S. Supreme Court Decision: Affirmed.

FACTS: An associate professor filed a Title VII claim of racial discrimination with the EEOC (P) against the University (D) after the University (D) denied her tenure. In the course of investigating the claim, the EEOC (P) issued a subpoena to obtain the professor's tenure-review file. The University (D) refused to produce a number of documents from the file and requested that the EEOC (P) modify the subpoena to exclude "confidential peer-review information." The EEOC (P) denied the request and, upon the EEOC's (P) motion in federal district court, was granted an enforcement order, which the court of appeals affirmed. The University (D) sought review in the U.S. Supreme Court, claiming that its peer-review materials enjoyed a special privilege requiring the EEOC (P) to show a particularized need, beyond mere relevance, to obtain the material.

ISSUE: Does university peer-review material enjoy a special privilege requiring that a particularized need, beyond mere relevance, be established to compel release of the material?

HOLDING AND DECISION: (Blackmun, J.) No. University peer-review material does not enjoy a special privilege requiring that a particularized need, beyond mere relevance, be established to compel release of the material. The University's

(D) claim of privilege finds no basis in the common law under Fed. R. Evid. 501. To the contrary, Congress, by expressly extending Title VII's coverage to educational institutions, did not create a privilege for peer-review materials. In fact, Congress afforded the EEOC (P) a broad right of access to any "relevant" evidence in EEOC (P) investigations. To go further than Congress and create such a privilege would place great obstacles before the EEOC (P) in its efforts to litigate these cases, give universities weapons to frustrate the EEOC's (P) efforts, and cause a wave of privilege claims by other employers. Furthermore, the claim finds no grounds in the First Amendment. The EEOC (P) is in no way attempting to control university speech in a content-based manner or mandate any criteria in selecting teachers other than those set forth under Title VII. Affirmed.

COMMENT: This case is likely to have a tremendous impact on the manner in which tenure decisions are made. Universities argue that denying the special privilege and requiring that peer-review files be revealed will have a substantial chilling effect on professors' ability to evaluate honestly tenure candidates. The Court took another view, stating that making the files subject to revelation would, in fact, encourage them to ground their evaluations on relevant criteria, rather than bias or prejudice. Some argue the decision will finally expose the discriminatory practices believed to have long been prevalent in the tenure process.

NOTES:

TEACHER EMPLOYMENT ISSUES

▶ ## CHAPTER SUMMARY

10

CHAPTER 10: TEACHER EMPLOYMENT ISSUES

QUICK REFERENCE RULES OF LAW

1. **Union membership is lawful:** Teachers may legally maintain memberships in associations that are organized with respect to occupational interests. (§ I.A.)

2. **State law genesis:** Collective bargaining is a creature of the state legislature; a majority of the states have granted some form of collective-bargaining rights to their public employees. (§ I.A.3.)

3. **Promotion of better labor-management relations:** Congress first granted private-sector employees the right to bargain collectively in order to promote better labor-management relations. Today, state statutes that provide for public-sector bargaining reflect the experiences of the private sector. (§ I.B.)

4. **Public and private sectors differ:** However, public-sector practices differ from those of the private sector in several respects: public employees have no right to strike and are subject to various public budget-related restrictions; on the other hand, they, unlike their private-sector counterparts, have inherent (constitutional) rights to equal protection and due process in the face of arbitrary governmental action. (§ I.B.6.)

5. **Most issues must be bargained:** A majority of collective-bargaining statutes *mandate* mutual bargaining between school boards and employee organizations, with certain exceptions carved out for those matters that touch upon "exclusive management rights." (§ I.C.2.)

6. **State law governs:** The scope of required bargaining is governed expressly by state legislation or is implied from that legislation. (§ I.C.2.)

7. **Some bargaining is at the will of school board:** Some states permit local school boards to engage in *permissive* bargaining, *i.e.,* selective bargaining by choice, not by mandate. (§ I.C.3.)

8. **Some items cannot be bargained:** Certain matters are nonnegotiable, *i.e.,* not proper subjects of collective bargaining, because they implicate *public policy* or matters concerning which a local board must be available to exercise *instant discretion*. (§ I.C.4.)

9. **A few states permit consultations only:** A minority of states restrict all negotiations to "meet and discuss" consultations only, with ultimate decision-making authority left to local school boards. (§I.C.5.)

10. **Hands-off approach of the courts:** Because the majority of courts view collective bargaining as a province of the state legislature, their

role has been limited to that of interpreting state statutes and constitutional provisions. (§ I.C.6.)

11. **No right to strike:** The constitutional right to form and join labor unions does not supersede the common law barrier (now codified in state statutes) to public employee strikes. (§ I.D.1.)

12. **Use of injunctions to suppress strikes:** Where teacher strikes are prohibited, local school boards may seek to enjoin teachers from striking when presented with a legitimate threat of strike. (§ I.D.1.c.)

13. **May not interrupt school functions:** Job actions, such as picketing, collective submissions of resignations, and collective absences, may be restrained when they impede school functions or cause others to breach their contracts with school officials. (§ I.D.2.)

14. **Inability to compromise:** An impasse in negotiations arises when an agreement cannot be reached and neither party is willing to compromise. (§ I.D.3.)

15. **Dispute resolution tools are available:** Mediation, fact-finding, and, ultimately, binding arbitration are the dispute resolution options that are available to parties that have reached an impasse. (§ I.D.3.)

16. **All covered employees must pay fees or dues:** All employees in a bargaining unit must, as a condition of employment, either pay union dues as union members or pay a nonmember "agency fee" for representation. (§ I.E.1.)

17. **Implied authority to set salaries:** A local school board's authority to set teachers' salaries is implied from its express authority to employ teachers. (§ II.A.1.)

18. **Assignments and transfer within board's discretion:** Teacher assignments are within school board discretion; teachers must accept assignments that they are competent to undertake. Transfers are also within a school board's discretion so long as the motivation behind the transfer is sound. (§ II.B.)

19. **Loyalty oaths permissible so long as narrowly tailored:** Loyalty oaths are a means of safeguarding public service from disloyal conduct; however, in order to pass constitution muster, loyalty measures must objectively define the differences between "loyal" and "disloyal" conduct. (§ II.C.)

20. **"Specific intent" required:** A teacher's loyalty cannot be questioned simply by reason of his membership in a group that may have been organized to further unlawful purposes, unless it can be shown that he joined the group with the *specific intent* of furthering unlawful purposes or that he actually participated in unlawful activities. (§ II.C.3.)

21. **School boards may regulate teacher conduct:** Because the integrity of each school system is reflected in its teaching staff, school boards may *regulate* the conduct of teachers to a *reasonable* extent. (§ II.D.)

22. **"Compelling interest" required:** However, freedom of speech, like other Constitution-based rights, merits so high a degree of protection that local school boards must demonstrate a *compelling* reason for abridging such a right. (§ II.D.2.)

NOTES:

Introduction: Aside from issues pertaining to certification and contractual relations (Chapter 9) and cessation of employment through termination or retirement (Chapter 11), teachers are also concerned with the primary manner in which their contractual rights and responsibilities are determined – a process known as *collective bargaining* – and with the manner in which their salaries, assignments, and leaves are determined. Other important employment-related issues pertain to teachers' rights to freedom of speech and expression and the administration of loyalty oaths.

I. THE COLLECTIVE-BARGAINING PROCESS

THE COLLECTIVE-BARGAINING PROCESS

The issue: Public employers, such as local school boards, engage in collective negotiations with teachers' representatives in order to reach agreement as to the various rights and responsibilities of the parties. Most state legislatures have enacted laws which govern what is commonly referred to as the "collective-bargaining process."

A. Historical Overview

1. *No room for collective action:* Traditionally, local school boards maintained total control over public school operations, including the hiring of personnel. This was in keeping with the notion that government, as sovereign, was immune from or "above" the forces presented by competing interests.

2. *Advent of collective action:* In the 1960s, teachers sought a greater voice in the management and operations of their school systems. They turned to collective group action as a means of asserting their interests.

3. *General rule:* Public employees, such as teachers, may legally maintain memberships in associations that are organized with respect to occupational interests. A majority of states have now granted some form of collective-bargaining rights to their public employees.

B. Public- versus Private-Sector Bargaining

1. *Common law genesis:* Prior to 1932, labor relations in all sectors were governed by the common law. Courts favored management and readily used their injunctive powers to suppress strikes and boycotts.

2. *Oppressive nature of injunctions:* In 1932, Congress passed the Norris-LaGuardia Act for the primary purpose of preventing federal courts from enjoining union activities that arose out of labor disputes.

3. *Private sector employees secure significant rights:* Three years later, Congress passed the National Labor Relations Act of 1935 (NLRA), commonly referred to as the Wagner Act.

   a. *Overall purpose:* The NLRA specifically encouraged collective bargaining as a means of promoting good management-labor relations.

   b. *Establishment of regulatory body:* The NLRA also established the National Labor Relations Board, whose purpose was to remedy unfair labor practices.

   c. *Additional purposes:* Finally, the NLRA also created a procedure for determining the nature and extent of employee representation and placed a *duty* on both parties to bargain *in good faith*.

4. *Private sector rights curtailed:* In 1947, the NLRA was amended by the Labor Management Relations Act, commonly referred to as the Taft-Hartley Act. The Taft-Hartley Act, in turn, was amended by the Labor Management Reporting and Disclosure Act of 1959 (LMRDA).

   a. *Limitations on union activities:* Both sets of laws placed limitations on union practices and activities following the widespread union mismanagement and corruption of the 1950s.

   b. *Delineation of employee rights:* Additionally, the LMRDA expressly provided for various rights of employees in the face of union abuses, established union election procedures, and established penalties for misappropriation of union funds.

5. *Private sector lays groundwork for public-sector activity:* Today, state statutes governing public-sector bargaining reflect the experiences of the private sector, as evidenced in widespread rules pertaining to the scope of bargaining and employee representation procedures.

6. *Major differences between the sectors:* Despite their similarities, public-sector practices differ from those of the private sector in several fundamental respects.

   a. *No right to strike:* With only a few exceptions, U.S. voters, through their legislatures, have rejected the right of public school teachers to strike. Such laws are in conflict with the standard labor maxim that a party cannot fully negotiate unless it has the ability to reject the terms it has been offered.

b. *Subject to other statutory restrictions:* The public-sector bargaining process is also limited by state and local budgets and various tax code restrictions.

c. *Enhanced protections:* However, unlike their private-sector counterparts, public-sector employees have inherent (constitutional) rights to equal protection and due process in the face of arbitrary governmental action. Further, state statutes commonly provide other protections, such as from discriminatory practices.

C. The Scope of Collective Bargaining

1. ***Look to state legislatures:*** State legislatures set the ground rules concerning the scope of the public-sector bargaining process. Look to state statutes for an understanding of these three key issues:

    a. In what areas can (or must) a local board refuse to negotiate?

    b. In what areas must bargaining continue until both sides reach agreement?

    c. In what areas will bargaining be prohibited, *i.e.,* when will "discussions" of issues alone be permitted prior to unilateral board decisions?

    d. Essentially, school boards are required to bargain in good faith with teacher unions on matters relating to teacher employment and the fulfillment of professional duties. *See Kenai Penin. Bor. Sch. Dist. and Kenai Penin. Bor. v. Kenai Penin. Ed. Ass'n,* 572 P.2d 416 (1977).

2. ***Majority of state statutory schemes favor mandatory bargaining:*** In most states, collective-bargaining statutes *mandate* mutual bargaining by local boards, with certain exceptions being carved out for those matters that touch upon "exclusive management rights." The scope of required bargaining is governed expressly by legislation or is implied from that legislation.

3. ***Permissive bargaining:*** In some states, local boards may engage in *permissive* bargaining, *i.e.,* selective bargaining by choice, not by mandate.

    Example: *Class size* is not identified as a mandatory bargaining item in any state's laws. In several states, it is a permissive subject of bargaining. In other states, class size must be "discussed" during negotiations, but there is no requirement that the parties reach a negotiated settlement on the issue. *See* §

I.C.4., below. In at least one state, it is viewed as a nonnegotiable item due to its policy ramifications.

Example: The negotiation of significant aspects of *teacher performance evaluations* is generally a permissible subject of bargaining. However, when performance evaluations are viewed as a condition of teacher performance, they may be held to be a mandatory bargaining subject.

4. *Nonnegotiable items:* Such matters as determinations of the school calendar, reductions in teacher work force, oversight of the teacher assignment and transfer process, and the granting of tenure are not proper subjects of collective bargaining. They are viewed as *nonnegotiable items* because they implicate *public education policy* or touch upon matters with respect to which a local board must be available to exercise *instant discretion.*

5. *A minority of state statutory schemes foster consultation only:* A minority of states restrict all negotiations to "meet and discuss" consultations only, with ultimate decision-making authority left to local school boards.

6. *Role of the courts is limited:* Because the majority of courts view collective bargaining as completely within legislative authority, their role has been limited to that of interpreting state statutes and constitutional provisions.

    a. *No role where no enabling legislation:* When a state chooses not to mandate collective bargaining, courts will not compel school boards to negotiate with employee representatives.

    b. *Judicial oversight:* However, once a school board has extended recognition to qualified bargaining agents and has begun the bargaining process, the board's (and bargaining agents') actions may be subjected to judicial scrutiny.

D. **Teacher Strikes, Job Actions, and Impasses in Negotiations**

    1. *Strikes*

        a. *Common law rule:* The constitutional right to form and join labor unions does not confer a right to strike. There has always been a common law barrier to teacher strikes, based upon the principle that teachers are government employees and that a strike against government cannot be tolerated. In many states, the common law prohibition against teacher strikes is codified in state statutes.

b. *Minority "limited right to strike":* Some states allow for a *limited* right to strike, so long as certain conditions have been met (such as completion of the mediation and fact-finding process, the provision of written notice of an intent to strike, and the proffering of evidence that a strike will not endanger the public health or safety).

c. *Effect of strike attempts:* Where teacher strikes are flat out prohibited, local school boards may seek to *enjoin* teachers from striking when presented with a legitimate threat of strike. Punishments for violations of court orders include the imposition of fines, the imprisonment of labor leaders for contempt, and the dismissal of striking teachers.

2. Job Actions

a. *Picketing:* Picketing, even when peaceful in nature, may be restrained if it impedes school functions or causes others to breach their contracts with school officials.

b. *Submission of resignations:* Concerted submissions of resignations may lead to sanctions if it is determined this action causes an interruption in services and therefore prevents a local board from fulfilling its duty to the public.

c. *Absences:* Teacher absences that are not related to teaching functions may constitute a strike and serve as grounds for teacher dismissal.

3. Impasses in Negotiations

a. *Failure to reach agreement:* An impasse in negotiations arises when an agreement cannot be reached and neither party is willing to compromise.

b. *Dispute resolution options available:* When the parties reach an impasse, the following dispute resolution options are frequently available:

(1) *Mediation* – a neutral person assists the parties in finding their own common basis for an agreement. The mediator is chosen jointly by the negotiating parties.

(2) *Fact-finding* – a neutral third party goes so far as to investigate the causes of the dispute that has arisen between the negotiating parties and then offers solutions. Proposed solutions are not binding on either party. Fact-finding is usually chosen only after mediation has failed.

(3) *Binding arbitration* – similar to fact-finding, with the exception that the decision of the neutral arbitrator is binding on both parties.

E. The Perpetuation of Teacher Unions

1. *Dues and mandatory fees:* Unions depend on membership dues and, additionally, on the mandatory financial support of those nonmembers who benefit from union negotiations to the same extent as union members.

   a. *Everyone contributes:* The practical effect is that *all* employees in the bargaining unit must, as a condition of employment, either pay union dues as union members or pay a nonmember "agency fee" for representation. In 1977, the U.S. Supreme Court upheld the payment of agency fees by nonmembers as a means of promoting labor peace and eliminating so-called free riders. *See Abood v. Detroit Board of Education,* 431 U.S. 209 (1977).

   b. *No excess fees:* Fees assessed to nonmembers must be used to cover the costs of providing representation services only. They may not be used to pay for the costs of promoting political causes that are unrelated to representation. *See Lehnert v. Ferris Faculty Ass'n,* 111 S. Ct. 1950 (1991). *See also Chicago Teachers Union v. Hudson,* 475 U.S. 292 (1986).

2. *Exclusive privileges:* Unions also perpetuate themselves through privileges gained by virtue of being the sole or majority bargaining agents for a group or groups of employees. Such privileges include dues checkoff, exclusive access to school facilities, and exclusive use of the school mail system. The result is that majority unions are strengthened, and minority unions find it more difficult to survive.

OTHER TERMS AND CONDITIONS OF TEACHER EMPLOYMENT

II. OTHER TERMS AND CONDITIONS OF TEACHER EMPLOYMENT

A. Teacher Salaries

1. *Implied authority to set salaries:* The authority to set teachers' salaries is implied from the local board's express authority to employ teachers.

2. *Use of salary schedules permissible:* Most school boards set and raise teachers' salaries according to specific salary sched-

ules. The use of such schedules is not contrary to the law so long as they are reasonable in design and uniformly applied.

3. *Uniform salary reduction:* A school board may reduce employee salaries for all teachers, including tenured teachers. The only requirements are that such a reduction be uniformly applied and must be based on financial exigency. *See Phelps v. Bd. of Education of Town of West New York,* 300 U.S. 319 (1937).

B. Teacher Assignments, Transfers and Leaves

1. *Assignments within board discretion:* Assignments within the purview of a teacher's teaching certificate are made at the discretion of local school boards. Practically speaking, teachers must accept assignments that they are competent to undertake.

2. *Transfers within board discretion so long as motivation not suspect:* Very few state statutes speak to transfer rights; local school boards generally adopt their own regulations in this area. Involuntary transfers – particularly those which involve changes in status – will be subjected to judicial scrutiny if it appears that any such transfer is based, all or in part, on a teacher's prior exercise of his First Amendment (or other constitutional) rights.

3. *Leaves negotiable through collective bargaining:* Teachers are not entitled to leaves as a right but rather as a benefit negotiated through the collective-bargaining process. In addition to standard leaves for sickness, maternity, etc., school boards must also make reasonable leave accommodations for religious reasons.

C. Oaths of Loyalty

1. *Purpose of oaths:* Viewed in a favorable light, loyalty oaths are a means of safeguarding public service from disloyal conduct. Practically speaking, loyalty oaths prohibit certain types of statements and conduct outside of the school setting. In the past, such oaths also required that teachers swear to the fact that they had not engaged in certain prohibited activities prior to employment.

2. *Importance of defining "disloyal conduct":* The U.S. Supreme Court has stated that loyalty measures must objectively define the differences between loyal and disloyal conduct.

3. *Judicial intervention has narrowed the breadth of oaths:* In a series of opinions spanning the 1950s and 1960s, the U.S. Su-

preme Court struck down as unconstitutional a series of loyalty oaths that were vague, overbroad, or otherwise unfocused.

a. *More recent holding requires specific unlawful intent:* A teacher's loyalty cannot be questioned simply by reason of his membership in a group that may have been organized to further unlawful purposes, unless it can be shown that he joined the group with the *specific intent* of furthering an unlawful purpose or that he actually participated in unlawful activities.

b. *Oath found acceptable:* The U.S. Supreme Court has upheld the constitutionality of an oath which requires that the speaker swear to uphold federal and state constitutions and faithfully discharge his position to the best of his ability. *See Knight v. Board of Regents of University of State of New York,* 269 F.Supp. 339 (1967); aff'd 390 U.S. 36 (1968).

D. Freedom of Speech and Expression

1. *Balancing of interests:* Public employees do not give up all of their rights upon accepting positions in the public sector; at present, courts seek to balance a teacher's private interests with that of the integrity of the educational system. Because the integrity of the system is reflected in its teaching staff, school boards have been permitted to *regulate* the conduct of teachers to a *reasonable* extent.

2. *Compelling state interest required:* Freedom of speech, like other Constitution-based rights, merits so high a degree of protection that state representatives, such as local school boards, must demonstrate a *compelling* reason for abridging such a right.

3. *Demonstrated impact on fitness to teach:* Most teachers' rights cases have involved issues of morality and fitness to teach (e.g., engaging in homosexual activities, various sexual activities, and the use of drugs). In order to prevail in a case against a teacher, a school board must demonstrate that the outside activity or conduct has a *detrimental impact* on the teacher's *fitness to teach.*

4. *Collective bargaining may not restrict free speech:* Teachers have the right to comment on matters of public interest about the operation of the schools in which they work. Speaking out at a school board meeting by a union teacher is not a "negotiation" in violation of the collective bargaining agreement. *See City of Madison v. Wisconsin Employment Relations Commission,* 429 U.S. 167 (1976).

10

E. Other Employment-related Concerns

1. *Impact on the classroom and students:* A school district may fire a teacher whose illegal or immoral public conduct poses a substantial risk of coming to the attention of school children. *See Nat'l Gay Task Force v. Bd. of Education of Oklahoma City,* 729 F.2d 1270 (10th cir. 1984).

2. *Religious practices of teachers:* Title VII of the Civil Rights Act of 1964 requires school districts to reasonably accommodate the religious practices of their employees. *See Pinsker v. Joint District No. 28J of Adams and Arapahoe Counties,* 735 F.2d 388 (10th Cir. 1984).

3. *Employee drug testing:* A warrant and reasonable suspicion are not necessarily required to test employees for drug and alcohol use when the compelling public interests served by such tests outweigh the employees' privacy interests. *See Skinner v. Railway Labor Executives Ass'n,* 489 U.S. 602 (1989).

4. *Breast-feeding as a protected right:* Breast-feeding is a fundamental right, like other Fourteenth Amendment–based rights, that cannot be restricted unless there is a compelling state interest and a narrow tailoring of the restriction. *See Dike v. School Board of Orange County, Florida,* 650 F.2d 783 (1981).

5. *Searching a teacher's desk:* There is no case law specifically addressing an administration's right to search a teacher's desk. The issue is whether such a search would violate the teacher's Fourteenth Amendment rights. Does the teacher have an expectation of privacy? In a nonschool case, the Supreme Court held that a government employer had to meet a standard of reasonableness when searching an employee's office. *See O'Connor v. Ortega,* 480 U.S. 709 (1987). It would therefore appear that a teacher has no expectation of privacy regarding items that are not locked away from the general public.

NOTES:

KENAI PENIN. BOR. SCH. DIST. AND KENAI PENIN. BOR. v. KENAI PENIN. ED. ASS'N
572 P.2d 416 (1977).

NATURE OF CASE: Teachers unions sued school districts and boroughs in two separate actions to compel them to bargain collectively in good faith. In a third action, a school board sought a declaratory judgment that certain issues were not negotiable.

GENERAL RULE OF LAW: School districts are required to bargain collectively in good faith with teachers unions on matters pertaining to employment and professional duty.

PROCEDURE SUMMARY:
Plaintiffs: Kenai Peninsula Education Ass'n (P) (Union); Anchorage Borough Education Ass'n (P) (Union), both teachers unions; Matanuska-Susitna School Dist. (Board), a school board.
Defendants: Kenai Peninsula Borough School Dist. (D) (Board); Anchorage Borough School Dist. (D) (Board), both school boards; Matanuska-Susitna Education Ass'n (D) (Union), a teachers union.
Trial Courts: Held for the Union (P) in one action, for the Board in another, and split on various issues in the third.
Alaskan Supreme Court: Affirmed in part, reversed in part.

FACTS: This decision comprises three separate cases involving the same or similar issues. In the first two cases, the Unions (P) sued the Boards (D) to compel collective bargaining in good faith. In the third case, the Board (P) sought a declaratory judgment that certain issues were not negotiable. In all three cases, the Boards contended that submitting educational policies to a good faith collective bargaining requirement would remove the final decisions on such matters from the Boards, contrary to legislative intent. They argued that delegating any decision-making power on educational policy to labor unions would be unconstitutional, since a teachers union is a private organization, and thus unaccountable to the public. The Unions countered that such delegation is perfectly proper, as there is no delegation of decision-making power inherent in a labor negotiations requirement. Furthermore, they claimed to represent professional employees, whose participation in negotiations was sanctioned by the legislature as professional advice to the Boards. Finally, Alaskan statutes on collective bargaining should be interpreted broadly, the Unions argued, because they are more comprehensive than those found elsewhere. The trial courts ruled in the Union's favor in the Kenai case, in the Board's fa-

vor in the Anchorage case, and for the Board on some issues and for the Union on others in the Mat-Su case. The subsequent three appeals were consolidated.

ISSUE: Are school boards required to bargain collectively in good faith with teachers unions on matters pertaining to their employment and the fulfillment of their professional duties?

HOLDING AND DECISION: (Connor, J.) Yes. School boards must bargain collectively in good faith with teachers unions "on matters pertaining to their employment and the fulfillment of their professional duties." By statute, school boards as public sector employers must negotiate with unions; however, the boards need not accept any union proposal. Statutes did not delegate sole decision-making power to either the union or the board. Since the power to delegate depends on the interpretation of statutes, case law from other jurisdictions must be examined as an aid to interpretation. Future enactments by the Alaskan legislature must provide specific guidance by stating which items would and would not be negotiable. In the meantime, however, questions concerning salaries, fringe benefits, work hours, and the amount of leave time are so closely connected with the economic well-being of the individual teacher that they must be held negotiable under Alaskan law. On the other hand, permitting teachers unions to bargain on matters of educational policy could severly erode the autonomy of the school boards. Consequently, the ability of elected officials to perform in the broad public interest would be threatened, since teachers unions might wield too much power over governmental decisions. Therefore, matters affecting educational policy such as planning time, teacher's aides, class size, pupil-teacher ratio, and selection of instructional materials are not negotiable. However, the school boards should continue to meet and confer with the unions regarding these nonnegotiable matters, in order to benefit from their expertise.

COMMENTS: In both the private and public sectors, negotiable issues are broad. Where collective bargaining involves teachers in the public schools, important issues in labor law and constitutional law may be involved. The trend in collective bargaining, in both the private and public sector, has been to require employers to bargain in good faith. To avoid a finding of bad faith, the parties are required by statutory law to make a reasonable effort to resolve their differences.

ABOOD v. DETROIT
BOARD OF EDUCATION
431 U.S. 209, 97 S. Ct. 1782 (1977).

NATURE OF CASE: Detroit teachers challenged the statutory and constitutional validity of a collective agreement "agency shop" clause which required that nonunion employees pay a service charge to the teachers union to be used for purposes they opposed.

GENERAL RULE OF LAW: A union's expenditures for ideological causes not germane to its duties as a collective-bargaining representative must be financed from dues or assessments paid by employees who do not object to advancing such causes and who are not coerced into doing so.

PROCEDURE SUMMARY:
Plaintiff: D. Louis Abood (P) and nonunion teachers.
Defendant: Detroit Board of Education (Board) (D).
Trial Court: Granted Board's (D) motion for summary judgment.
Michigan Court of Appeals: Reversed trial court's retroactive application of 1973 agency shop clause and remanded.
Michigan Supreme Court: Denied review.
U.S. Supreme Court: Vacated and remanded for further review by the trial court.

FACTS: In 1967, the Detroit Federation of Teachers (Union) became "the exclusive representative of teachers employed by the Detroit Board of Education" (Board) (D). A collective-bargaining agreement between the Board (D) and the Union, effective from July 1, 1969 to July 1, 1971, contained an "agency shop" provision. This provision required nonunion employees to pay the Union a service charge equal to a Union member's regular dues. While the agreement did not require teachers to join the Union, a nonunion employee who neglected to pay the service charge was subject to discharge. In an action filed in state court, Abood (P) challenged the constitutionality of the agency shop clause by contending that it violated her rights under the First and Fourteenth Amendments because the Union was engaging in various political and other ideological activities that Abood (P) did not approve and that were not collective-bargaining activities.

ISSUE: Do union expenditures not germane to the union's primary functions necessarily violate the constitutional First and Fourteenth Amendment rights of employees who have contributed to the union treasury and who object to such expenditures?

HOLDING AND DECISION: (Stewart, J.) Yes. In general, agency shop provisions are constitutionally valid. As stated in *Railway Employees' Department v. Hanson,* 351 U.S. 225 and *Machinists v. Street,* 367 U.S. 740, the determination by Congress that unions can require nonunion members to share the costs of benefits afforded by the collective bargaining agency justifies any constitutional infringement on those employees. Even though public employees differ from their private counterparts in regard to "the special character of the employer" and different types of collective bargaining occur in the two spheres, those differences do not necessarily translate into differences in First Amendment rights. Public employees do not incur a greater infringement on their constitutional rights; they are still free to express their opposing viewpoints in public or private, to vote in accordance with their convictions, and to participate in a full range of political activities open to other citizens. In *Hanson,* the court noted, however, that unions could not require payment by nonunion members for expenses outside the scope of collective bargaining, because such expenditures were not recognized by Congress as justifying this type of constitutional infringement. The *Street* court also concluded that money collected by a union could not be used to support political ideologies because Congress did not state that this type of expenditure justified the union shop agreement. A union can use its money for purposes "not germane to its duties as collective-bargaining representative" only if the union uses the dues of employees who do not object to expenditures for those ideological causes or who are not coerced into doing so. Thus, a cause of action under the First and Fourteenth Amendments exists in this case if allegations concerning misuse or extortion can be proven. If so, two possible remedies exist: an injunction preventing expenses from being financed by opposing parties, or restitution.

COMMENT: Although different types of collective bargaining take place in the public and private sectors, the difference does not result in a greater infringement on public employees' constitutional rights. The Court pointed out that the public sector's collective bargaining was inherently political. In a concurring opinion, Justice Rehnquist questioned whether a public employee, as protected here by the First and Fourteenth Amendments, could truly "believe as he will and act and associate according to [personal] beliefs" when affected by an agency shop provision. Justice Stevens pointed out that remedies in these situations were determined on a case-by-case basis. Later cases would seem to support this position. Justice Powell commented that the majority opinion overturned two legal principles. Prior to this decision, Justice Powell argued, the First Amendment protected union members by allowing them to withhold money from public unions if they opposed the ideological causes the money was to be spent on. In this decision, however, the ability to withhold funding depends on whether or not the expenditure is related to collective bargaining. Secondly, Justice Powell pointed out that, prior to this decision, the state had the burden of proving that overriding state interests justified its action. According to Justice Powell, the Court has now reversed this principle. As a result, an employee claiming infringement of his First Amendment rights by a union in its spending practices bears the burden of proof. In other words, the employee must prove the union has spent funds in ways not related to collective bargaining.

NOTES:

LEHNERT v. FERRIS FACULTY ASS'N
111 S. Ct. 1950 (1991).

NATURE OF CASE: Review of a decision denying nonunion public employees' challenge to a union's use of service fees collected from nonmembers of the collective-bargaining unit.

GENERAL RULE OF LAW: A union may only charge nonmembers for services that are germane to collective-bargaining activity and justified by the government's interest in labor peace and avoiding free riders but not for services that place significant, additional burdens on free speech.

PROCEDURE SUMMARY:
Plaintiff: Lehnert (P), nonunion college faculty member.
Defendant: Ferris Faculty Association (D) (Association).
U.S. District Court Decision: Held for the Association (D).
U.S. Court of Appeals Decision: Affirmed.
U.S. Supreme Court Decision: Affirmed.

FACTS: Under Michigan law, one union served as the exclusive collective-bargaining representative of public employees in a particular bargaining unit. The law permitted the creation of an agency shop in which nonmembers were compelled to pay a service fee to the union. The Association (D) was the exclusive union for the faculty at Ferris State College (Ferris) and charged nonmembers a service fee equivalent to the amount of dues required of members. Lehnert (P) was on faculty at Ferris but not a member of the Association (D). Lehnert (P), along with other nonunion faculty members, filed suit alleging that certain uses by the Association (D) of the fees collected from nonmembers violated their rights under the First and Fourteenth Amendments. The district court, finding the Association's (D) use of the fees to be sufficiently related to its duties as the collective-bargaining representative, held that the Association (D) could constitutionally charge Lehnert (P) for lobbying and electoral politics; bargaining, litigation, and other services on behalf of persons not in his bargaining unit; public relations efforts; miscellaneous professional services; meetings and convention of the parent union; and preparations for a strike. The court of appeals affirmed. The U.S. Supreme Court granted review.

ISSUE: May a union charge nonmembers for services that add significant burdens on free speech and are not germane to collective-bargaining activity or justified by the government's interest in labor peace and avoiding free riders?

HOLDING AND DECISION: (Blackmun, J.) No. A union may only charge nonmembers for services that are germane to collective-bargaining activity and justified by the government's interest in labor peace and avoiding free riders but not for services which place significant, additional burdens on free speech. This rule was established in *Abood v. Detroit Board of Education,* 431 U.S. 209, 97 S. Ct. 1782 (1977), where the Court upheld, as facially constitutional, the same Michigan law challenged in this action. Under this rule, the Association's (D) lobbying and electoral politics activities may not be charged to Lehnert (P) because it would compel him to engage in core political speech which significantly burdens his First Amendment rights; the challenged public relations activities also impermissibly burden Lehnert's (P) First Amendment rights. The bargaining, litigation, and other services on behalf of persons not in his bargaining unit may not be charged to Lehnert (P) because they are not germane to the Association's (D) duties as exclusive bargaining representative. The miscellaneous professional services and parent union convention expenditures are constitutional because they do not infringe First Amendment rights but benefit Lehnert's (P) particular bargaining unit and are germane to the Association's (D) bargaining activity. Affirmed in part; reversed in part.

COMMENT: The constitutional dimensions of union-security provisions such as agency-shop agreements were first addressed in *Railway Employees v. Hanson,* 351 U.S. 225 (1956), where "union-shop" agreements were validated as applied to private employees, as authorized by the Railway Labor Act (RLA). Although *Hanson* did not address how union dues could be utilized, *Machinists v. Street,* 367 U.S. 740 (1961), addressed that issue in light of the RLA. Seeking to protect the expressive freedom of dissenting employees while promoting collective representation, the Court decided to "deny unions the authority to expend dissenters' funds in support of political causes to which those employees objected." Two years later, the Court reaffirmed, noting the distinction between union political expenditures and those being "germane to collective bargaining," the latter being properly chargeable. It was not until *Abood* that the Court addressed these issues in the public employment context, determining that, as in the private sector, agency-shop agreements must not burden dissenters' First Amendment rights through compulsory subsidy of certain ideological activities. The Court in *Abood* did not attempt to precisely differentiate between chargeable and nonchargeable activities. *Lehnert* illustrates the tension created by attempting to promote collective representation while protecting the expressive freedom of those employees who do not wish to take part in the particular representative process. *Lehnert* relied on the general rule established in *Abood*, where the Court held that public employees who chose not to join a union serving as the exclusive collective-bargaining representative could be compelled to pay a service fee but had a right not to have the fees used for support of ideological causes of which they disapproved. *Lehnert* is an attempt to more precisely differentiate between those uses which are allowed and those charges which are not.

NOTES:

CHICAGO TEACHERS UNION v. HUDSON
475 U.S. 292, 106 S. Ct. 1066 (1986).

NATURE OF THE CASE: The Supreme Court reviewed the Chicago Teachers Union (Union) and the Chicago Board of Education (Board) procedure by which nonunion employees could object to "proportionate share" deductions from their paychecks by the Board on behalf of the Union.

GENERAL RULE OF LAW: In developing a procedure which ensures that service fees collected from nonunion members are not used for activities unrelated to collective bargaining to which nonmembers object, the court must strike a balance between a union's compulsory subsidization of objectionable ideologies and the union's ability to collect money from all employees for collective bargaining procedures. In other words, the court must balance First Amendment interests against justifiable state limitations while minimizing infringements.

PROCEDURE SUMMARY:
Plaintiff: Annie Lee Hudson (P) and other nonunion employees.
Defendant: Chicago Teachers Union (D) (Union).
U.S. District Court: Held for the Union (D). Any decision should await the findings of the union procedure already invoked by the plaintiffs.
U.S. Court of Appeals: Reversed. Held the Union's objection procedure and escrow option were inadequate.
U.S. Supreme Court: Affirmed.

FACTS: In an effort to solve a "free rider" problem, the Chicago Teachers Union (D) and the Chicago Board of Education entered into an agreement in 1982. The board agreed to deduct a certain fee from nonunion employees' paychecks, while the Union (D) was authorized to determine the fee. The Union (D) calculated the percentage of expenditures unrelated to collective bargaining. It deducted this amount from the fee assessed to members to arrive at the fee to nonunion employees. The Union (D) also developed a procedure to respond to nonunion employees' objections to the fee deduction. Prior to the fee deduction, no objections could be raised. However, after the deduction was made, a nonmember could object by submitting a letter within 30 days to the Union (D) president. The matter objected to was first reviewed by the Union's (D) executive committee, which would notify the objector of its decision within 30 days. An objector could appeal this decision to the Union's (D) executive board within another 30 days. If the objector wished to appeal the executive board's decision, he could contact the Union (D) president, who would appoint an arbitrator to handle the dispute at the Union's (D) expense. The only remedies in the event an objection was sustained were a rebate to the objector and immediate reductions in future fees for all nonunion employees. The board approved the above procedure developed by the Union (D) without analyzing it. In December 1982, deductions from nonunion employee paychecks began. The Union (D) printed a description of the deduction and the grievance procedures in a Union (D) newspaper, but no explanation of the deduction or Union (D) procedures was provided to nonunion employees by the board. Hudson (P) and other nonunion employees wrote objection letters to the Union (D). The Union (D) responded by advising them to follow the Union (D) procedure for objection. Hudson (P) and other nonunion employees filed suit, contending that the Union (D) procedures violated their First and Fourteenth Amendment rights and permitted the Union (D) to use their money for "impermissible purposes." The district court rejected the challenges and upheld the procedure. On appeal, the Union (D) advised the court that it had voluntarily placed all of of the dissenters' agency fees in escrow to avoid any danger that their constitutional rights would be violated. Nevertheless, the court of appeals reversed, holding that the procedure was constitutionally inadequate. The Union (D) appealed, and the Supreme Court granted certiorari.

ISSUE: (1) Does the Union's (D) original grievance procedure infringe on objectors' First and Fourteenth Amendment rights? (2) Does the Union's (D) self-imposed remedy (i.e., the escrow account) infringe on nonunion objectors' First and Fourteenth Amendment rights?

HOLDING AND DECISION: (Stevens, J.) (1) Yes. Under an agency shop agreement, procedural safeguards are necessary to prevent dissenting nonunion employees from being forced to subsidize ideological activities to which they are opposed. At the same time, unions must not be restricted in their ability to require any employee to contribute to the cost of collective-bargaining activities. The government interest in labor peace is strong enough to support an "agency shop" arrangement, whereby a union may charge nonunion members a fee for acting as their bargaining representative, despite the limited infringement on the nonmembers' constitutional rights. However, the fact that those rights are protected by the First Amendment requires that the procedure be carefully tailored to minimize the infringement. Furthermore, the nonunion employee must have a fair opportunity to identify the impact of the governmental action on his interests and to assert a meritorious First Amendment claim. Here, the Union's (D) original procedure was flawed in three ways: (a) the procedure failed to minimize the risk of the Union's (D) improper use of the dissenters' funds, even if only for a short time; (b) the procedure did not provide nonunion employees with an adequate explanation as to how their deductions were calculated; and (c) the procedure did not provide a "reasonably prompt decision by an impartial decisionmaker" if an objection were raised. The nonunion employee, who bears the burden of objecting, is entitled to have his objections addressed in an expeditious, fair, and objective manner. The Union's (D) procedure, which was controlled from start to finish by the Union (D) — an interested party, obviously, since it was the recipient of the agency fees — did not meet these requirements. Affirmed. (2) Yes. While the Union's (D) self-imposed remedy (the escrow) curtailed the first flaw found in the original procedure noted above, it still did not address flaws (b) and (c). As such, the escrow procedure provided insufficient protection for constitutionally mandated rights. Affirmed.

COMMENT: According to two of the concurring justices, a nonunion employee in the situation presented by this case should exhaust union arbitration procedures before resorting to the courts. This is the only way to proceed, at least initially. For a procedure to be deemed adequate by a court, the three flaws listed under the first holding must be remedied. Nevertheless, it would appear that the court infers that there is a right to decide on additional criteria if a situation so requires. Future cases will explore this possibility as nonunion employees continue to challenge their unions regarding constitutional concerns and the very high percentage of expenditures directly related to collective bargaining.

NOTES:

10

PHELPS v. BD. OF EDUCATION OF TOWN OF WEST NEW YORK
300 U.S. 319, 57 S. Ct. 483 (1937).

NATURE OF CASE: Action for breach of contract and infringement of constitutional equal protection rights brought by tenured employees of the New Jersey public school system when the school board reduced their salaries in violation of the state tenure law.

GENERAL RULE OF LAW: State laws which prohibit school boards from discharging tenured employees without good cause or from reducing their salaries do not give tenured personnel contract rights to permanent employment or minimum pay.

PROCEDURE SUMMARY:
Plaintiff: Phelps (P) and other tenured employees (principals, teachers, clerks) of New Jersey public school system.
Defendant: West New York, New Jersey Board of Education (D).
State Trial Court Decision: Held for West New York Board of Education (D).
State Appellate Court Decision: Affirmed.
U.S. Supreme Court Decision: Affirmed.

FACTS: In the early 1900s, New Jersey enacted a tenure law which prohibited school boards from firing school employees who had served for at least three years. It also prohibited reducing the salary of tenured employees. During the Great Depression, however, New Jersey enacted another law which required school boards to redetermine employee salaries and which authorized uniform salary reductions down to a prescribed minimum but which forbade salary increases. The West New York Board of Education (D) reduced the salaries of its tenured principals, teachers, and clerks, uniformly within each class or grade of employee, by up to 15%. Phelps (P) and others sued the Board (D), alleging that it had breached the state's "contract" with them (as established by the tenure law) not to reduce their salaries and that it violated equal protection because the Board's (D) plan had an unequal effect of providing salaries to the highest-paid employee in a "low" bracket which were in some cases greater than those of the lowest-paid employee in a "high" bracket. The case was filed as a petition with the state commissioner of education, who dismissed it. Both the New Jersey trial court and court of appeals affirmed the commissioner's decision. Phelps (P) and the other tenured employees appealed.

ISSUE: Do state laws which prohibit school boards from discharging tenured employees without good cause or from reducing their salaries create contract rights in the tenured personnel to permanent employment and minimum pay?

HOLDING AND DECISION: (Roberts, J.) No. State laws which prohibit school boards from discharging tenured employees without good cause or from reducing their salaries do not create contract rights in the tenured personnel to permanent employment and minimum pay. Such laws are designed merely to regulate conduct of the board and may be rescinded by the legislature without affecting any rights in tenured employees. Here, New Jersey's law did not create contract rights in the West New York school system's tenured employees to not have their salaries reduced. It merely was a regulation of the Board's (D) power to set salaries and therefore did not constitute a binding promise made directly to the tenured employees. Affirmed.

COMMENT: In law, a contract is an agreement between two parties in which one offers to do or not to do something in exchange for the other's performance or nonperformance of something else. In the schoolteacher context, a contract typically consists of educational and administrative services provided by a teacher in exchange for compensation. When the person to whom the offer is made agrees to the deal, there is in the law an acceptance. What the parties agree to exchange of value between each other is termed "consideration." Obviously, the Court here was focusing on the fact that the parties to the contract quite strictly were the school board and the teachers, not the state and the teachers; however, this was largely a fiction created by the Court to reach a practical result, given the fact that the state undoubtedly wished to continue to educate its young residents but due to the Depression was collecting drastically smaller tax revenues. More typically, state statutes that refer to public school teacher contracts will be deemed included in the contract made between the school board and the teacher and thus inviolate. In recent years, school boards in most states have been allowed to reduce salaries "across the board" as part of a planned reduction. This is allowed only when "financial exigency" has been declared because it is such a drastic action.

KNIGHT v. BOARD OF REGENTS OF UNIVERSITY OF STATE OF NEW YORK

269 F. Supp. 339 (1967); aff'd 390 U.S. 36, 88 S. Ct. 816 (1968)

10

NATURE OF CASE: Challenge by teachers at a tax-exempt private school to the constitutionality of New York state's requirement that they take an oath to uphold the federal and state constitutions and to observe professional standards of dedication and competence.

GENERAL RULE OF LAW: Schoolteachers may be required to swear to uphold their state and federal constitutions as well as observe professional standards of dedication and competence.

PROCEDURE SUMMARY:
Plaintiff: Knight (P), a professor at private Adelphi University in New York.
Defendant: Board of Regents of University of State of New York (D).
U.S. District Court Decision: Held for Board of Regents (D).
U.S. Supreme Court Decision: Affirmed.

FACTS: Faculty members, including Knight (P), of Adelphi University, a private, nonprofit, tax-exempt college in New York, sued the Board of Regents of the University of State of New York (D) to enjoin the enforcement of a law which required them to take an oath. Under this oath, the teachers swore to uphold the constitutions of the United States and New York state and to adhere to professional standards of dedication and competence. Although the law had been on the books since 1934, Adelphi had not attempted to enforce it until 1966, at which time Knight (P) and 27 other professors refused to sign it. The U.S. District Court for the Southern District of New York upheld the oath requirements, and Knight (P) and the others appealed to the United States Supreme Court.

ISSUE: May schoolteachers be required to swear to uphold their state and federal constitutions as well as observe professional standards of dedication and competence?

HOLDING AND DECISION: (Tyler, J.) Yes. The First Amendment rights of schoolteachers in public or private tax-exempt schools are not violated by requiring them to swear an oath to uphold state and federal constitutions and to adhere to professional standards of dedication and competence. This case is significantly different from an earlier Supreme Court case, *West Virginia State Board of Education v. Barnette,* 319 U.S. 624, 63 S. Ct. 1178 (1943), which involved a requirement that schoolchildren salute the flag under penalty of suspension; here, there is no statutory penalty for refusing to swear the teacher's oath. Nor does it resemble earlier cases which struck down "negative loyalty oaths" or "non-Communist" oaths, which were vague in their wording; the requirement here that teachers uphold standards of professional dedication as well as the state and federal constitutions is simple and clear. Affirmed.

COMMENT: As a result of this decision, schools can constitutionally require an oath to uphold professional standards as a condition of employment. Conceptually, this oath is not different from that required of legislators, lawyers, or doctors. It differs substantially from oaths which require statements adhering to or reflecting certain political beliefs; these types of oaths are typically held unconstitutional. *E.g., Connell v. Higginbotham,* 403 U.S. 207, 91 S. Ct. 1772 (1971) (state cannot summarily dismiss teachers who refuse to pledge that they do not believe in the overthrow of the government). However, it is important to recognize that the decision here might have been different if the New York legislature had provided a sanction for refusing to sign the oath; the court specifically relied on this absence of a penalty (which had been present in the flag-salutation cases) in reaching its decision.

NOTES:

CITY OF MADISON v. WISCONSIN EMPLOYMENT RELATIONS COMMISSION

429 U.S. 167, 97 S. Ct. 421 (1976).

NATURE OF CASE: Challenge by a teachers union of the First Amendment right of a non-union teacher to speak on a subject concerning pending collective bargaining during an open public school board meeting.

GENERAL RULE OF LAW: Teachers have the First Amendment right to comment on matters of public interest about the operation of the school in which they work.

PROCEDURE SUMMARY:
Plaintiff: Madison Teachers, Inc., a teachers union (P).
Defendant: Wisconsin Employment Relations Commission (D).
State Supreme Court Decision: Held for Madison Teachers (P).
U.S. Supreme Court Decision: Reversed.

FACTS: The Board of Education of Madison, Wisconsin and Madison Teachers, Inc. (MTI) (P), the local teachers union, were negotiating a collective-bargaining agreement. One of MTI's (P) proposals for the agreement was a "fair share" clause, under which nonunion teachers would be required to pay union dues to defray the costs of collective bargaining. At a meeting of the school board open to the general public, a nonunion teacher made a brief statement in which he announced that he had conducted a survey of 80 teachers from 50 schools concerning the "fair share" clause, which he was presenting to the board. He also asked for "communication, not confrontation" on the issue. MTI (P) filed a complaint with the Wisconsin Employment Relations Commission (D) (WERC) which claimed that the board had committed an unfair labor practice by permitting the union teacher to engage in "negotiation" of a matter which was the subject of a pending collective-bargaining agreement. WERC (D) agreed and was affirmed by the Wisconsin Supreme Court, which held that the nonunion teacher's First Amendment rights were properly limited given that his speech constituted negotiation which violated bargaining exclusivity under the state labor laws. MTI (P) appealed to the U.S. Supreme Court.

ISSUE: Do teachers have First Amendment rights to comment on matters of public interest about the operation of the school in which they work?

HOLDING AND DECISION: (Burger, C.J.) Yes. Teachers have the First Amendment right to comment on matters of public interest about the operation of the school in which they work. The nonunion teacher here who spoke up at an open public meeting issued only a terse statement announcing the results of a survey and the need for communication, not confrontation. This hardly amounted to an attempt to bargain or negotiate, which was the exclusive province of union representatives with regard to the collective-bargaining agreement with the school district. Further, a limitation on a teacher's free speech rights to matters not concerning collective bargaining would be unconstitutional because virtually any subject concerning the operation of the school system could be characterized as a potential subject of collective bargaining. Reversed.

COMMENT: Despite this holding, in other cases courts have ruled that teachers have relinquished First Amendment rights by submitting to the "collective contractual protectionism" afforded by membership in a union. For example, in *Cary v. Board of Education of Adams–Araphoe School District,* 427 F. Supp. 945 (D. Colo. 1977), the federal district court in Colorado denied the claim of teachers that the school board denied them freedom of speech by specifically prescribing the books they could use in the classroom. The court noted that the collective-bargaining agreement the union had negotiated on behalf of the plaintiffs explicitly granted the school board the right to assign reading material.

NOTES:

NAT'L GAY TASK FORCE v. BD. OF EDUCATION OF OKLAHOMA CITY
729 F.2d 1270 (10th Cir. 1984).

10

NATURE OF CASE: Challenge under the First Amendment and Equal Protection Clause to school board policy of dismissal or suspension of teachers who engage in, or advocate, homosexual conduct.

GENERAL RULE OF LAW: While a state may constitutionally mandate the firing of a public school teacher who engages in public homosexual conduct which poses a substantial risk of coming to the attention of schoolchildren or employees, it may not require dismissal of a teacher who merely advocates homosexual behavior at some indefinite future time.

PROCEDURE SUMMARY:

Plaintiff: National Gay Task Force (P).
Defendant: Oklahoma City Board of Education (D).
U.S. District Court Decision: Held for Oklahoma City Board of Education (D).
U.S. Court of Appeals Decision: Reversed.

FACTS: An Oklahoma statute provided that its public schools could fire teachers for engaging in public homosexual conduct or activity. Public homosexual conduct was defined as indiscreet same-sex relations not practiced in private. Public homosexual activity was defined as advocating, soliciting, or promoting public or private homosexual activity in a way that created a substantial risk that the conduct would come to the attention of schoolchildren or employees. National Gay Rights Task Force (NGRTF) (P), a national organization promoting homosexual rights whose members included teachers in the Oklahoma public school system, challenged the statute on constitutional grounds, *i.e.*, that the statute violated its members' rights of free speech, privacy, and equal protection. The federal district court held that although the statute did restrict protected speech, it was constitutionally valid given the United States Supreme Court requirement in *Tinker v. Des Moines Independent Community School District*, 393 U.S. 503, 89 S. Ct. 733 (1969), that a teacher be dismissed for personal expression only if it resulted in a "material or substantial interference or disruption in the normal activities of the school." NGRTF (P) appealed.

ISSUE: May a state constitutionally mandate the firing of a public school teacher who engages in public homosexual conduct which poses a substantial risk of coming to the attention of schoolchildren or employees?

HOLDING AND DECISION: (Logan, C.J.) Yes. A state may constitutionally require the firing of a public school teacher who engages in public homosexual activity, such as a public act of oral or anal intercourse, which poses a substantial risk of coming to the attention of schoolchildren or employees. The Equal Protection Clause does not, as presently interpreted by the Supreme Court, view homosexuals as a suspect classification warranting strict scrutiny of laws that treat homosexuals differently from other groups. However, the Oklahoma statute does penalize free speech concerning homosexuality, without limiting the firing sanction to advocacy or inciting of imminent breaking of the law. The First Amendment does not permit someone to be punished for advocating illegal conduct at some indefinite future time. Thus, the part of the statute requiring dismissal or suspension for speech alone is severed as unconstitutional, and the remainder of the law is allowed to stand. Reversed.

COMMENT: A state has interests in regulating the speech of teachers that differs from its interests in regulating the speech of the general population. The state's interests outweigh the teacher's interests when a teacher's speech materially or substantially disrupts the normal school activities, a standard enunciated by the United States Supreme Court in *Tinker*. However, a state may regulate general public speech in much more limited circumstances: when speech incites imminent lawlessness. *Brandenburg v. Ohio*, 395 U.S. 444, 89 S. Ct. 1827 (1969). The majority opinion in this case prompted a vigorous dissent by Circuit Judge Barrett, who noted that the Oklahoma criminal code equated homosexual conduct with "unnatural, perverse, detestable and abominable ... sodomy" and that as a "crime against nature," expression of homosexuality in any form deserved absolutely no constitutional protection. His argument in effect called for the creation of a unique category of forbidden speech, which would have been unlike any other constitutional limitation on speech.

PINSKER v. JOINT DISTRICT NO. 28J OF ADAMS AND ARAPAHOE COUNTIES
735 F.2d 388 (10th Cir. 1984).

NATURE OF CASE: Challenge by a Jewish teacher under Title VII of the 1964 Civil Rights Act of his school district's policy of requiring him to take unpaid "special leave" days in order to observe Yom Kippur and Rosh Hashanah, when Christmas and Easter were treated as school holidays.

GENERAL RULE OF LAW: Title VII of the Civil Rights Act requires school districts to reasonably accommodate the religious practices of their employees but does not require them to provide paid leave for all religious holidays.

PROCEDURE SUMMARY:
Plaintiffs: Pinsker (P), Jewish teacher in Aurora, Colorado; Aurora Teacher's Association.
Defendant: Aurora school district (D).
U.S. District Court Decision: Held for Aurora school district (D).
U.S. Court of Appeals Decision: Affirmed.

FACTS: Teachers in the Aurora School District (D) were allowed 12 paid personal leave days, all of which might be used for sick time and a certain number of which could be used for religious observance. The District (D) also provided two additional paid "special" personal leave days which could be used as well for religious holidays. Christmas and Good Friday, however, were schoolwide holidays. Pinsker (P), a Jewish teacher, challenged the District's (D) policy because on the average he had had to take one day of unpaid leave per year in order to observe Yom Kippur, Rosh Hashanah, and other Jewish holy days. Pinsker (P) alleged in federal court that the District's (D) policy was not a reasonable accommodation under Title VII of the Civil Rights Act of 1964 and that this policy unconstitutionally burdened his right to free exercise of religion under the First Amendment. The district court ruled that the District's (D) leave policy was reasonable and that the economic impact of one day's unpaid leave did not burden Pinsker's (P) right to practice his faith. Pinsker (P) appealed to the Tenth Circuit Court of Appeals.

ISSUE: Does Title VII of the Civil Rights Act require school districts to reasonably accommodate the religious practices of their employees such that they must provide paid leave for all religious holidays?

HOLDING AND DECISION: (Logan, C.J.) No. Title VII of the Civil Rights Act does require school districts to reasonably accommodate the religious practices of their employees but does not require them to accommodate such practices in ways that spare the employee any cost whatsoever. Teachers are likely to have not only different religions but also different degrees of devotion to their religions, and school districts cannot be expected to negotiate leave policies broad enough to suit every employee's religious needs perfectly. Further, under the First Amendment, an employee's freedom to exercise his or her religion would only be jeopardized if the economic impact of the school policy put substantial pressure on him or her to modify religious behavior. Here, Pinsker's (P) loss of one day's wages per year did not constitute "substantial pressure." Affirmed.

COMMENT: The court's opinion also discusses several other interesting facts which weakened Pinsker's (P) case considerably. Although technically Pinsker (P) took one day of unpaid leave per year for religious holidays, the district had an informal policy of not actually docking him for the missed day. Further, the district also had a formal policy of only allowing a maximum of 20 teachers to take "special leave" on any one day but made an informal exception for Pinsker (P). The court also noted, almost as implied advice to the school district, that other districts avoided this problem entirely by simply allowing paid leave for Yom Kippur and Rosh Hoshanah when they fell on school days, by increasing the number of paid days for all employees for religious observance, or, more innovatively, by allowing teachers to make up religious leave by doing extracurricular work.

NOTES:

10

SKINNER v. RAILWAY LABOR EXECUTIVES ASS'N

489 U.S. 602, 109 S. Ct. 1402 (1989).

10

NATURE OF CASE: Review of a decision enjoining enforcement of railway employee drug and alcohol testing regulations.

GENERAL RULE OF LAW: A warrant and reasonable suspicion are not necessarily required to test employees for drug and alcohol use when the compelling public interests outweigh the employees' privacy interest.

PROCEDURE SUMMARY:
Plaintiff: Railway Labor Executives Ass'n (P) (Association), a labor union.
Defendant: Skinner (D), U.S. Secretary of Transportation.
U.S. District Court Decision: Granted summary judgment for Skinner (D).
U.S. Court of Appeals Decision: Reversed.
U.S. Supreme Court Decision: Reversed.

FACTS: Skinner (D) promulgated regulations mandating that blood and urine tests be performed on certain railroad employees after major train accidents. The regulations also permitted breath and urine testing of employees who violated certain safety rules. Association (P), the railroad employees' union, brought suit to enjoin enforcement of the regulations, contending that they violated the Fourth Amendment by not requiring a warrant and reasonable suspicion. The district court disagreed and granted summary judgment for Skinner (D). The court of appeals, finding a particularized suspicion essential to hold such testing reasonable under the Fourth Amendment, reversed and enjoined enforcement of the regulations. The U.S. Supreme Court granted review.

ISSUE: May the Fourth Amendment's warrant and reasonable suspicion requirements be waived to test employees for drug and alcohol use where the compelling state interests served by the test outweigh the employees' privacy interests?

HOLDING AND DECISION: (Kennedy, J.) Yes. The Fourth Amendment's warrant and reasonable suspicion requirements may be waived when testing employees for drug and alcohol use where legitimate state interests served by the test outweigh the employees' Fourth Amendment privacy concerns. The Fourth Amendment only forbids those searches which are unreasonable, and what is unreasonable depends on the circumstances. Though the tests mandated and permitted by the regulations do implicate the Fourth Amendment, which generally requires a warrant and individualized suspicion for searches to be reasonable and valid, the government's compelling interests in the safety of the traveling public and of the employees themselves present a "special need" which makes the tests reasonable without a warrant or probable cause. A warrant serves to protect the public by imposing rules and structure on a search. Here, the regulations which govern the circumstances under which the drug and alcohol tests are permissible serve the same purpose. They limit the intrusion by narrowly and specifically defining when a test is permissible. Further, the covered employees have notice of these circumstances and limits. Not only is the public adequately protected without a warrant, but imposing a warrant requirement would significantly hinder the objectives of the testing program. Individualized suspicion is not required because the regulations pose limited threats to the employees' justifiable privacy expectations. The railroad industry is already subject to heavy safety regulations, and employees already submit to significant restrictions on their freedom; the additional restrictions created by these regulations are minimal. Reversed.

COMMENT: In a companion case, *National Treasury Employees Union v. Von Raab*, 109 S.Ct. 1384 (1989), the Court upheld the warrantless and suspicionless drug testing of government employees involved in the nation's drug enforcement efforts. The common denominator of the Court's opinions in *Skinner* and *Von Raab* is the categorization of employees subject to the testing as being in positions of a degree of sensitivity creating a special need which justified the waiver of the stringent requirements of the Fourth Amendment. Whether this exception will be extended to the school context depends on whether teachers, principals, or other school officials are found to hold similarly sensitive positions. The Court has not yet had opportunity to address the issue. An appropriate case for consideration might involve mandatory drug and alcohol testing of a teacher being considered for tenure. The issue would be whether the board's potential granting of tenure with its lifelong employment guarantee and opportunity to impact on the lives of thousands of children creates a compelling public interest which would outweigh the teacher's Fourth Amendment privacy interest.

DIKE v. SCHOOL BOARD OF ORANGE COUNTY, FLORIDA
650 F.2d 783 (5th Cir. 1981).

NATURE OF CASE: Appeal of dismissal of a complaint alleging a school board's refusal to permit a teacher to breast-feed her child during a lunch period when she had no duties violated her civil rights.

GENERAL RULE OF LAW: Breast-feeding is entitled to constitutional protection against state infringement in some circumstances.

PROCEDURE SUMMARY:
Plaintiff: Dike (P), a school teacher.
Defendant: School Board of Orange County, Florida (D) (Board).
U.S. District Court Decision: Dismissed Dike's (P) complaint as frivolous.
U.S. Court of Appeals Decision: Reversed.

FACTS: Dike (P), an elementary school teacher employed by the Board (D), desired to breast-feed her child at all feedings. One feeding was necessary during the school day. She arranged to have the child brought to school during her lunch period, when she was free from all duties, so she could feed the child in a locked room into which others could not see. After three months, the school principal instructed Dike (P) to cease nursing the child at the school, citing a Board (D) directive prohibiting teachers from bringing their children to work for any reason. Dike (P) stopped nursing the child on campus. After observing the child's allergic reaction to formula and eventual refusal of a bottle, Dike (P) sought permission to nurse off campus. The Board (D) refused. Dike (P) thereafter filed suit under 42 U.S.C. § 1983, challenging the Board's (D) refusal to permit on-campus breast-feeding. The district court dismissed the complaint as frivolous.

ISSUE: Is breast-feeding entitled to constitutional protection from state infringement in some circumstances?

HOLDING AND DECISION: (Godbold, C.J.) Yes. Breast-feeding is entitled to constitutional protection from state infringement in some circumstances. Breast-feeding is one of those fundamental rights, such as marriage, procreation, contraception, and abortion, protected under the Fourteenth Amendment's guarantee of liberty. The district court's dismissal for failure to state a claim was, therefore, clearly erroneous. Because breast-feeding is among those fundamental rights, the Board (D) must show that prohibiting Dike (P) from breast-feeding during her duty-free lunch-time furthers a compelling state interest and is narrowly tailored to promote that interest. Whether the Board's (D) legitimate interest in preventing disruption of the educational process satisfies this standard is a question of fact to be determined at trial. Reversed.

COMMENT: The problem in the *Dike* case is striking a balance between the state's concededly legitimate interest in maintaining an appropriate educational environment and the personal privacy rights of the educators within that environment. Notwithstanding the result in *Dike* on remand, it would seem that a routine such as that performed by Dike (P) when she was allowed to breast-feed her child on campus should win this balance, given the recognized need to accommodate working mothers and the minimal effect the routine seems to have on the school's efforts to provide an appropriate educational environment. While courts have strongly supported teacher claims regarding personal privacy, courts have also recognized the school board's interest in maintaining an appropriate educational environment. This has sometimes constrained the personal freedoms of teachers. Often, the basis for the school's action is that teachers serve as role models and, therefore, need to conform to traditional community standards. Obviously, standards have changed. In the first third of the century, some school districts even prohibited teachers from dating and would remove a teacher who was married.

NOTES:

O'CONNOR v. ORTEGA
480 U.S. 709, 107 S. Ct. 1492 (1987).

NATURE OF CASE: An employee filed an action for compensatory damages against his employer under 42 U.S.C. § 1983, the federal statute designed to remedy violations of guaranteed rights, alleging that a search of his office while he was on leave violated the Fourth Amendment.

GENERAL RULE OF LAW: In order to search an employee's office without invading that employee's privacy in violation of the Fourth Amendment, a government employer must meet a standard of reasonableness.

PROCEDURE SUMMARY:
Plaintiff: Ortega (P), a physician at a state hospital.
Defendant: O'Connor (D), a physician and director of the state hospital.
District Court: Held for O'Connor (D), granting his motion for summary judgment.
U.S. Court of Appeals: Affirmed in part; reversed in part; remanded.
U.S. Supreme Court: Reversed and remanded.

FACTS: Ortega (P) trained physicians in the psychiatric residency program at a state hospital. The hospital, headed by O'Connor (D), placed Ortega (P) on administrative leave while it investigated allegations against him involving program mismanagement, sexual harassment of a female hospital employee, and inappropriate disciplinary action against a resident. O'Connor (D) and other hospital officials, in an effort to secure state property and take inventory, searched Ortega's (P) office. During the search, the officials seized personal items from Ortega's (P) desk and file cabinets. A formal inventory of property found in the office was never made. Ortega (P) filed suit in federal district court under 42 U.S.C. § 1983, alleging that the search violated the Fourth Amendment. The district court granted summary judgment to O'Connor (D), holding the search did not violate the Fourth Amendment and finding a reasonable need to secure state property in Ortega's (P) office. The court of appeals affirmed in part and reversed in part, concluding that the search violated the Fourth Amendment, as Ortega (P) had a reasonable expectation of privacy in his office, and granted partial summary judgment for Ortega (P) on the issue of liability for an unlawful search. The case was then remanded for determination of damages. The Supreme Court granted certiorari.

ISSUE: Must a government employer meet a standard of reasonableness when searching an employee's office?

HOLDING AND DECISION: (O'Connor, J.) Yes. Fourth Amendment rights are implicated only when the search infringes an expectation of privacy that society is prepared to consider reasonable. A government employee does have a reasonable expectation of privacy in his office, even though government offices are frequently open to fellow employees, supervisors, and the general public. However, in the case of searches conducted by a public employer, the invasion of an employee's legitimate expectations of privacy must be balanced against the government's need for supervision, control, and the efficient operation of the workplace. Given the realities of the workplace, a warrant requirement would be unworkable for such searches. Therefore, in order to allow workplaces to operate efficiently, searches of employee offices for work-related, noninvestigatory reasons, or for investigations of work-related misconduct, need not be based on probable cause. Such intrusions by public employers should be judged by a standard of reasonableness in light of the circumstances. In this case, it cannot be determined from the record whether O'Connor (D) satisfied this standard. Therefore, the case must be remanded to determine the justification for the search and seizure and to evaluate the reasonableness of both the inception and the scope of the intrusion. Reversed and remanded.

COMMENT: The real question is whether an employee with an expectation of privacy in his office can ever be fully protected from an employer's search under the Fourth Amendment. Because the analysis is on a case-by-case basis, the employee will never have a sense of security. The reasonableness standard is far too flexible from an employee's perspective. Nevertheless, it clearly follows the line of reasoning established by the *T.L.O.* case as well as those cases which have followed. Education cases such as *Frazier* and *Hazelwood* have also based their holdings on this expanding "reasonableness" analysis. While there is no certainty, a teacher in a public education setting has no protection from a reasonable search by administration. By analyzing the facts in this case, it is possible that the teacher has an expectation of privacy for those items secured in a locked desk, but administration could search the desk top and other areas, looking for information needed to conduct the business of the school.

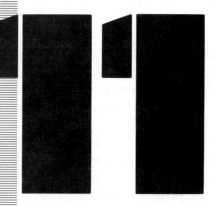

TEACHER DISMISSAL AND RETIREMENT

▶ ## CHAPTER SUMMARY

CHAPTER 11: TEACHER DISMISSAL AND RETIREMENT

QUICK REFERENCE RULES OF LAW

1. **Property interest:** For purposes of due process, a teaching position is a property interest when it is created by contract or under the authority of a tenure statute. (§ I.A.2.)

2. **Protections attach to property interests:** Certain protections automatically attach property interests, such that an owner may not be dispossesed of his property without first being provided such protections. (§ I.A.)

3. **Two common protections:** A teacher is generally entitled to notice of a school board's intention to terminate her and a hearing on the matter. (§ I.A.4.)

4. **Good cause:** A tenured teacher, or one who is on probation but under contract, may not be dismissed unless there is "good cause" for doing so. (§ I.B.1.)

5. **Common grounds for cause:** Common reasons for dismissing a teacher for cause include incompetency, insubordination, unprofessional conduct, immoral conduct, and neglect of duty. (§ I.B.1.)

6. **Invalidation of dismissal:** If required due process protections are not provided and good cause is not found to exist, a dismissal action may be invalidated. (§ I.B.1.)

7. **Nonrenewal versus dismissal:** A school board may choose not to renew a nontenured teacher's contract *without* providing due process or good cause. Some states such as Ohio have provided nontenured teachers an additional right to be informed of the reason for the nonrenewal and to be given timely notification of poor performance and the opportunity to improve. (§ I.B.2.)

8. **No property interest:** A nontenured teacher has no interest in his teaching position but rather merely an *expectation* of reemployment. (§ I.B.2.a.)

9. **Exceptions to the rule:** Despite the fact that no due process or good cause is required for dismissal of a nontenured teacher, dismissal will be unlawful if it (1) contravenes other constitutional rights, (2) occurs in a climate of "de facto" tenure, or (3) damages or impugns the teacher in certain respects. (§ I.B.2.c.)

10. **Legislature-enacted:** Retirement systems are created through state legislation. (§ II.A.)

11. **Main elements:** Most employee retirement plans provide for employee contributions (annuities) and employer contributions (pensions). (§ II.C.)

12. **State law predominates:** Local boards may not supersede statutory retirement provisions with their own regulations. (§ II.E.)

NOTES:

Introduction: In this chapter, we discuss the two principal forms of termination from a teaching position — voluntary termination, such as that which occurs when a teacher retires, and involuntary termination, such as that brought about by a local school board's dismissal of a teacher. The manner in which a teacher may terminate or be terminated is usually governed by the terms of his employment contract, especially when a local school board seeks to dismiss a teacher during the pendency of the contract. (Note, however, that we will also consider the termination that results when a school board decides not to renew a teacher's contract.)

**TERMINATION OF
EMPLOYMENT
THROUGH
DISMISSAL**

I. TERMINATION OF EMPLOYMENT THROUGH DISMISSAL

The issue: Under what circumstances, and according to what procedures, may a local school board dismiss a teacher?

A. Due Process Safeguards

1. *Due process defined:* The due process rights embodied in the Fourteenth Amendment provide for certain protections against arbitrary governmental actions which threaten property interests such as employment.

2. *Property interest:* A teaching position is generally considered a property interest so long as it is the subject of a permanent contract or a statutory tenure provision.

3. *Due process ensures fairness:* The act of terminating a teacher may be viewed as arbitrary if it is not carried out according to a well-defined procedure or plan aimed at ensuring fairness to the teacher. When the appropriate procedures are followed, the teacher's "procedural" due process rights will be protected. *See Knox County Board of Education v. Willis,* 405 S.W.2d 952 (1966); *see also Penasco Independent School District No. 4 v. Lucero,* 86 N.M. 683 (1984).

4. *Common protections:* The most common procedural due process protection requires that a teacher receive notice of a school board's intended termination action, including notification of the charges, and the opportunity for a hearing. *See Vanelli v. Reynolds School Dist. No. 7,* 667 F.2d 773 (9th Cir. 1982). Other protections that may be offered include:

   a. adequate time to prepare for the hearing;

   b. an opportunity to review the employer's evidence;

   c. disclosure of the employer's witnesses;

d.   representation by counsel;

e.   an impartial hearing officer;

f.   an opportunity to present evidence and witnesses, and to cross-examine adverse witnesses;

g.   an official record, *e.g.,* transcript, of the hearing; and

h.   an opportunity to appeal an adverse decision.

B. Dismissal versus Nonrenewal of a Teaching Contract

1. ***"Dismissal" defined:*** Dismissal involves termination of a teacher who is either tenured or probationary (not yet tenured) but under contract.

a.   *Fairness required:* The dismissal of a teacher falling into either of these two categories requires observance of the dictates of procedural due process, discussed *supra.*

b.   *"Good cause" also required:* Aside from affording a teacher the appropriate due process protections, a school board generally must be able to make a showing of good or justifiable *cause* in support of its decision to dismiss.

(1) In some states, the acceptable grounds for cause are identified by statute. Failure to list one of the statutory grounds may lead to the invalidation of a dismissal action.

(2) Common statutory grounds include the following:

(a) insubordination, *i.e.,* a conscious disregard of authority;

(b) incompetency, *i.e.,* lack of ability to perform effectively.

Example: A local school board suspended and attempted to terminate a high school teacher for incompetence after he assigned his senior English class an article which contained a particularly vulgar term. The Court of Appeals sidestepped the issue of the teacher's competency but essentially found in favor of the teacher because censoring the article would have had a chilling effect on his academic freedom. *See Keefe v. Geanakos,* 418 F.2d 359 (1st Cir. 1969).

(c) conduct that is viewed as unprofessional;

11 ▶

Example: A local school board failed to renew the contract of a nontenured teacher because she allowed young men (friends of her son who was in college) to stay in her home with her. The board felt that this conduct was unbecoming of a teacher. The court held for the teacher, stating that this type of dismissal must be based on conduct related either to the education process or to working relationships within the institution. *See Fisher v. Snyder,* 476 F.2d 375 (8th Cir. 1973).

(d) conduct that is viewed as immoral; and

(e) neglect of duty.

c. *Principals also protected:* Under certain conditions protected by state statute, principals have similar tenure and nondismissal protections and guarantees. *See Viemeister v. Board of Education of Borough of Prospect Park,* 5 N.J. Super 215 (1949).

2. **"Nonrenewal of contract" defined:** Nonrenewal may arise when, at the end of the term of a nontenured teacher's contract, the school board elects *not* to renew that contract.

a. *No due process rights:* A probationary teacher is not entitled to procedural due process protections in connection with a school board's nonrenewal decision (although some state statutes require that a teacher be notified of a nonrenewal decision before his contract expires). This is because no liberty interest attaches to a mere expectation of re-employment. *See Board of Regents of State Colleges v. Roth,* 408 U.S. 564 (1972).

b. *No "cause" required either:* A teacher whose contract is about to expire may be terminated for no reason at all — or for any reason whatsoever.

c. *Three exceptions to the rule:* Notwithstanding the above, certain conditions or actions of the school board may entitle a nontenured teacher to the notice and hearing that is generally provided to a tenured teacher prior to dismissal.

(1) When a nonrenewal decision is based on factors which are constitutionally infirm, such as those tied to racial animus or a desire to quell free speech rights.

Example: A nontenured teacher's contract was not renewed after several parents complained about the methods she employed in teaching the history of race relations. The court reasoned that the teacher's methods related to a legitimate educational objective and thus could not serve as grounds for dismissal since such an objective implicated her constitutionally protected freedoms of expression and activity in the classroom. *See Kingsville Independent School District v. Cooper*, 611 F.2d 1109 (5th Cir. 1980).

Example: A school board's nonrenewal of a probationary kindergarten teacher's contract was upheld by the court of appeals. *See Palmer v. Board of Educ. of City of Chicago*, 603 F.2d 1271 (7th Cir. 1979). The teacher refused to teach portions of the school curriculum pertaining to patriotism and the flag because of her belief that doing so would violate her religious principles. The students' right to a balanced education was held to predominate over the teacher's First Amendment right; to hold otherwise would be to permit the teacher to impose her personal beliefs on her students.

(2) When a teacher can demonstrate that various practices and procedures of the school district create a *de facto tenure* system. *See Perry v. Sinderman*, 408 U.S. 593 (1972).

(3) When a teacher can demonstrate that a nonrenewal decision will damage his reputation, impugn his integrity, or foreclose other employment opportunities.

C. *Constitutional Rights Are Protected:*

1. *Free Speech Protection:* A teacher may not be dismissed for the exercise of a constitutional right such as First Amendment protected free speech.

Example: Pickering, a teacher, wrote and published a letter in the local paper criticizing the school administration and the allocation of tax funds raised by the school. Even though the letter contained numerous inaccuracies and contributed to the loss of the school levy, Pickering's dismissal was overturned. A teacher may not be dismissed for public statements without proof that the statements were false and knowingly or recklessly made. *See Pickering v. Board of Education of Township High School District 205*, 391 U.S. 563 (1968).

Qualification: The termination of a nontenured teacher following the exercise of a constitutional right will not be voided if the exercise of the constitutional right was not the principal factor in the termination. *See Mt. Healthy City*

11

School District Board of Education v. Doyle, 429 U.S. 274 (1977). In distinguishing *Pickering,* the court has ensured that nontenured teachers who are not performing satisfactorily and who would *not* be renewed cannot "check themselves with the constitution" to avoid nonrenewal. E.g., a teacher who has been informed of poor performance might engage at divisive speech and/or union activity to create a constitutional protection citing *Pickering.*

*TERMINATION OF
EMPLOYMENT
THROUGH
RETIREMENT*

II. TERMINATION OF EMPLOYMENT THROUGH RETIREMENT

A. Retirement Plans Created by Legislation: The legislatures of the various states created the retirement systems that are in place today.

B. Retirement Plans Consistently Ruled Constitutional: There is no question that retirement plans are constitutional, despite the arguments of opponents who have claimed that retirement benefits are gifts of public funds and serve no public benefit.

C. Two Elements of Most Retirement Plans

1. *Employee contribution:* A portion of retirement benefits are derived from the contributions of the employee who is covered by the plan. This is sometimes referred to as an *annuity.*

2. *Employer contribution:* The remainder of the retirement benefits are derived from the contributions of the employer. This is sometimes referred to as a *pension.*

3. *Typical scenario:* Employee contributions are provided by way of deductions from the employee's salary during the period of his employment; employer contributions come from the state coffers.

D. Common Provisions of Retirement Plans: Most plans contain provisions governing *eligibility,* the *amount of benefits* to be received upon retirement, and the distribution of benefits upon the *death of the retiree.*

E. Conflicts between Local and State Authorities: Local school boards may not supersede state statutory retirement provisions with regulations of their own.

Example: If a compulsory retirement age is set by state statute, a local district may not lower the compulsory age requirement for its employees.

F. Changes in Existing Retirement Plans: Because retirement plans are governed by statute rather than by contract law, a state legislature may make changes to existing plans as it sees fit; such changes, however, may not disadvantage those who are already receiving retirement benefits.

NOTES:

KNOX COUNTY BOARD OF EDUCATION v. WILLIS

405 S.W.2d 952 (1966).

NATURE OF CASE: Appeal of reversal of a board of education's termination of a teacher's employment contract for neglect of duty and incompetence.

GENERAL RULE OF LAW: A board has power to conduct a hearing, without specific rules governing the conduct of the hearing, so long as it is orderly and fundamentally fair.

PROCEDURE SUMMARY:
Plaintiff: Willis (P), a teacher.
Defendant: Knox County Board of Education (D) (Board).
State Circuit Court Decision: Held for Willis (P), reversing the Board's (D) termination of Willis' (P) contract.
State Court of Appeals Decision: Reversed.

FACTS: Willis (P), a teacher employed by the Board (D), was charged with inefficiency, incompetency, and neglect of duty. At the hearing set to determine whether to terminate her contract, the Board (D) voted to terminate Willis' (P) contract, finding, based upon a supervisor's report, that she failed to maintain proper records and lacked control over her class. Willis (P) filed suit, alleging that the Board (D) did not have power to conduct the hearing because it lacked specific rules and regulations governing the conduct of the hearing. The circuit court agreed and reversed the termination. The Board (D) appealed.

ISSUE: Does a board have power to conduct a termination hearing, without specific rules governing the conduct of the hearing, so long as it is orderly and fundamentally fair?

HOLDING AND DECISION: (Clay, Comm'r) Yes. A board has power to conduct a termination hearing, without specific rules governing the conduct of the hearing, so long as the hearing is orderly and fundamentally fair. This allows for procedural flexibility, which is necessary because these hearings are usually conducted by laymen. Further, the statute authorizing the charges brought against Willis (P) adequately outlines the procedure required for a termination hearing. Nothing in the statute required the Board (D) to adopt supplementary rules, though it is permitted to do so under the statute. Reversed.

COMMENT: *Knox* illustrates the court's flexibility in ensuring that an individual has been accorded an opportunity to be heard as required by the Due Process Clause of the Fourteenth Amendment. As a rule, all that is required is "fundamental fairness." What constitutes fundamental fairness is difficult to state. However, it is clear that the more serious the deprivation, the more formal the procedure must be to satisfy the requirement. For instance, a professional license revocation proceeding is usually considered more serious than a proceeding to terminate employment; the former would prevent the subject from practicing his profession for life, while the latter would not prevent the subject from seeking employment in the same field afterward. Thus, the license revocation would require a more formal proceeding than the employment termination proceeding.

NOTES:

PENASCO INDEPENDENT SCHOOL DISTRICT NO. 4 v. LUCERO
86 N.M. 683, 526 P.2d 825 (1974).

NATURE OF CASE: Appeal of a state board's reversal of a local board's finding that no funding was available to provide a teaching position for a tenured teacher and that no other position was available for which the teacher was qualified.

GENERAL RULE OF LAW: Absent grounds personal to a tenured teacher, a board must prove that no other position is available for which the teacher is qualified before it may refuse to reemploy the teacher.

PROCEDURE SUMMARY:
Plaintiff: Penasco Independent School District No. 4 (P), (District).
Defendant: Lucero (D), a tenured teacher.
State Court of Appeal Decision: Held for Lucero (D), affirming state board's reversal of the District's (P) findings.

FACTS: Lucero (D) was a teacher who had been employed by the District (P) for eight years and had attained tenure. The next year, he worked as an elementary school counselor. At a termination hearing, the District (P) found cause to refuse to reemploy Lucero (D) because there was no longer funding to continue his position as elementary school counselor and because there was no other position available for which he was qualified. The state board of education reversed, finding insufficient evidence to support the latter finding. The District (P) appealed the reversal, contending there was sufficient evidence to support both findings.

ISSUE: May a board, absent grounds personal to the teacher, refuse to reemploy a tenured teacher without proof that there is no position available for which the teacher is qualified?

HOLDING AND DECISION: (Hendley, J.) No. Absent grounds personal to the teacher, a board may not refuse to reemploy a tenured teacher without proving that there is no position available for which the teacher is qualified. The District (P) asserted no such grounds and failed to prove that no other position for which Lucero (D) was qualified was available. He was just as qualified to teach a high school special education class as the nontenured instructor the District (P) hired to teach the class. The District's (P) claim that it need not consider Lucero (D) for a high school teaching position because he had been an elementary school counselor the prior year fails for two reasons. First, the laws governing tenure do not distinguish between "teaching" and "counseling" positions and do not require that the teacher remain in one particular school to maintain tenure. Second, the District (P) did not allege that Lucero (D) lost tenure by serving as the elementary school counselor. Affirmed.

COMMENT: The *Penasco* decision illustrates the scope of the tenure right. It does not merely guarantee a teacher employment in a particular position subject to certain competency and performance standards but places an affirmative obligation on the school board or district to find another position for the teacher if his usual or past position is eliminated. It seems that courts will view a board's claim that there was no other position for a tenured teacher with skepticism, especially where, as in *Penasco,* a nontenured teacher, with similar credentials as the tenured teacher, is hired to perform a job that the tenured teacher appears just as qualified to perform. The guarantee of tenure is a right which courts are most hesitant to challenge. A teacher's tenure right will be withdrawn only when specific conditions are met (*e.g.,* a general reduction in force) and then only when specified conditions – usually detailed in the state education code – are satisfied.

NOTES:

VANELLI v. REYNOLDS SCHOOL DIST. NO. 7
667 F.2d 773 (9th Cir. 1982).

11 ▶

NATURE OF CASE: Appeal of decision sustaining a board's midyear termination of a teacher for immoral conduct and assessing damages against the board for failing to hold a pretermination hearing.

GENERAL RULE OF LAW: The midyear termination of a teacher without a pretermination hearing deprives the teacher of property and liberty without due process.

PROCEDURE SUMMARY:
Plaintiff: Vanelli (P), a teacher.
Defendant: Reynolds School Dist. No. 7 (D) (District).
U.S. District Court Decision: Held for the District (D), upholding the termination but assessing damages against District (D) for failure to hold a pretermination hearing.
U.S. Court of Appeals Decision: Affirmed.

FACTS: Vanelli (P), a probationary teacher employed by the District (D), was charged with immoral conduct. Some female students complained that Vanelli (P) stared at their "physical attributes" and made statements with "sexual overtones." He was dismissed by the District (D) without a pretermination hearing at the midpoint of a one-year contract. One month later, the District (D) conducted a full evidentiary hearing and affirmed its earlier dismissal decision. Vanelli ((P) was represented by legal counsel, and four of the five girls who had filed a complaint testified and were cross-examined by Vanelli's (P) counsel. Vanelli (P) brought a civil rights action under 42 U.S.C. § 1983, alleging that the dismissal, without a pretermination hearing, infringed his property and liberty interests, constituting a denial of due process. The district court disagreed, finding that the posttermination evidentiary hearing was sufficient to sustain the termination. Vanelli (P) appealed.

ISSUE: Is the midyear dismissal of a teacher with a one-year contract without a pretermination hearing an impermissible infringement of the teacher's property and liberty interests in violation of due process?

HOLDING AND DECISION: (Kennedy, J.) Yes. The midyear dismissal of a teacher with a one-year contract without a pretermination hearing is an impermissible infringement of the teacher's

property and liberty interests in violation of due process. Public employees are presumptively entitled to some form of notice and opportunity to be heard before being deprived of a liberty or property interest. Vanelli's (P) liberty interest was implicated because the immoral conduct charge might seriously damage his standing in the community; his property interest was implicated because the one-year contract gave him a right under state law. Though, as the district court correctly found, the subsequent evidentiary hearing was sufficient to sustain the dismissal, the failure to hold a pretermination hearing was, nevertheless, a due process violation. Affirmed.

COMMENT: There is a difference between dismissal and nonrenewal in most states. Dismissal involves a teacher who has tenure or a permanent contract. With dismissal the board must show good cause and afford the individual opportunity to refute the reasons for dismissal. Nonrenewal involves a probationary teacher or one with a contract for a specified period. To refuse renewal, a board need only provide the teacher notice of nonrenewal by a specific date. The key in *Vanelli* is that though Vanelli (P) did not have tenure, he had a contract for one full year, which, under state law, created the right protected by the Fourteenth Amendment's Due Process Clause. Termination in the middle of the contract term, if unsupported by due cause and carried out without the required procedural safeguards, is not unlike a simple breach of contract. This general area — where teachers are accused of some variety of sexual misconduct — is a growing area of concern. For example, child abuse charges have been filed against teachers which prove groundless but still result in adverse publicity and great community concern. Often, there are various legal standards involved. For a child abuse complaint, all that is required for a report is merely a suspicion. For the school to report a suspicion of abuse, the level of proof is far less rigorous than for a court conviction for sexual misconduct. The intent is to protect the child from abuse such as that which occurred in *Deshaney v. Winnebago Cnty. Dep. Soc. Serv.*, 489 U.S. 189 (1989). The burden in a criminal case to sustain a guilty verdict would be "beyond a reasonable doubt," while "a preponderance of the evidence" standard would be used if civil charges were filed by a plaintiff.

KEEFE v. GEANAKOS
418 F.2d 359 (1st Cir. 1969).

NATURE OF CASE: Action by a tenured high school teacher to temporarily enjoin a school committee meeting to vote on the teacher's discharge for saying a certain word in class.

GENERAL RULE OF LAW: The propriety of speaking certain words in class by a high school teacher depends on the circumstances of the utterance.

PROCEDURE SUMMARY:
Plaintiff: Keefe (P), a teacher.
Defendant: Geanakos (D), a school committee member.
U.S. District Court Decision: Temporary injunction for Keefe (P) denied.
U.S. Court of Appeals Decision: Reversed.

FACTS: Keefe (P), a tenured teacher, was head of the English department for grades 7 through 12 in the local school system and taught English part-time. On the opening day of school, Keefe (P) assigned an article from the *Atlantic Monthly* magazine to his class. Keefe (P) described the article as a valuable discussion of "dissent, protest, radicalism, and revolt" but not as pornographic. The class discussed the article, including a particularly offensive vulgarity for a son who engages in an incestuous relationship with his mother, which appeared in the article. Keefe (P) was subsequently required to defend his use of the word at a school committee meeting. Keefe (P) gave an explanation and stated that he could not promise not to use the particular vulgarity again. He was thereafter suspended. A proposal that Keefe (P) be discharged was introduced, and a meeting to vote on the proposed dismissal was scheduled. Keefe (P) then sought a preliminary injunction to prevent Geanakos (D) from holding the meeting. The district court denied Keefe's (P) motion, and he appealed to the court of appeals.

ISSUE: Does the propriety of speaking certain words in class by a high school teacher depend on the circumstances in which the words are spoken?

HOLDING AND DECISION: (Aldrich, C.J.) Yes. The propriety of speaking certain words in class by a high school teacher depends on the circumstances in which the words are spoken. While the argument put forth by Geanakos (D), that what is said or read to students is not to be determined by adult obscenity standards, is correct, it does not follow that students must necessarily be protected from offensive language in the classroom. This issue is one of degree and circumstance. However, the evidence demonstrated that the vulgarity was accessible to students elsewhere in the school. No less than five books in the school library contained the word in question. It would be irrational to hold, when students could be exposed to the word by obtaining one of these books from the library, that the students' teacher could not discuss the word in class. Temporary injunction granted; remanded for trial on the merits.

COMMENT: The court of appeals, by simply granting the temporary injunction and remanding for trial on the merits, did not expressly find Keefe's (P) use of the word proper. The tenor of the opinion, however, indicates that the court did at least implicitly approve of it. Thus, the case is a victory for advocates of academic freedom in the sense that an injunction only will be issued when there is a triable issue of fact and it appears that the party seeking the injunction has a highly likely chance of winning the case at trial. Academic freedom, however, like other freedoms, is not absolute. Generally, courts have held that this freedom does not protect conduct which is both offensive and unnecessary to the accomplishment of educational objectives. The inquiry is one of degree, considering the age and sophistication of the students, relevance of the educational purpose, and the context and manner of presentation.

NOTES:

FISHER v. SNYDER
476 F.2d 375 (8th Cir. 1973).

NATURE OF CASE: Appeal of award of order of reinstatement to an untenured schoolteacher who was terminated by the school board for alleged conduct unbecoming a teacher.

11

GENERAL RULE OF LAW: Dismissal of an untenured teacher is arbitrary and capricious where each stated reason for dismissal is unrelated to the education process, unrelated to working relationships within the institution, or wholly without factual support.

PROCEDURE SUMMARY:
Plaintiff: Fisher (P), an untenured teacher.
Defendant: Snyder (D), a school board member.
U.S. District Court Decision: Held for Fisher (P), ordering her reinstatement.
U.S. Court of Appeals Decision: Affirmed.

FACTS: From 1970 to 1972, Fisher (P), a middle-aged divorcee, was employed as a high school teacher in Tyron. Her son lived and taught in a neighboring town. Often, his friends, young ladies and men and married couples, visited Tyron. They often stayed in the one-bedroom apartment in which Fisher (P) lived because hotel and motel accommodations were generally unavailable. One young man, to whom Fisher (P) referred as her second son, visited often. In the spring of 1972, he visited for a week, sitting in on classes per Fisher's (P) arrangements with the school administration. Fisher (P) was thereafter notified that her contract would not be renewed for the next year. At a hearing, the school board stated that the reason for the dismissal was that Fisher's (P) allowing young men, unrelated to her, to stay with her was conduct unbecoming a teacher. In the Board's (D) view, her social behavior suggested a strong potential for sexual misconduct. Fisher (P) filed suit under 42 U.S.C. § 1983, contending this reason was constitutionally impermissible. The district court agreed and ordered her reinstated. The Board (D) appealed.

ISSUE: May an untenured teacher be dismissed for reasons unrelated either to the education process or working relationships within the institutions and wholly without factual support?

HOLDING AND DECISION: (Bright, J.) No. An untenured teacher may not be dismissed for reasons unrelated either to the education process or working relationships within the institutions or wholly without factual support. The school board may legitimately inquire into the character and integrity of its teachers but may not dismiss them based on unsupported conclusions drawn from such inquiries. Simply because Fisher (P) allowed guests to stay in her one-bedroom apartment because other accommodations were sparse or unavailable does not support the Board's (D) conclusions that there was a strong potential for sexual misconduct or social misbehavior unconducive to maintaining the school's integrity. Thus, the district court correctly found the dismissal arbitrary and capricious. Affirmed.

COMMENT: *Fisher* is important in that it illustrates another important area in which the interest of a teacher must be weighed against the interest of the school board. In this case, the teacher's interest in personal privacy was at stake. *Fisher* shows that the state has a legitimate interest supporting an inquiry into a teacher's integrity and character, but that interest is limited. Allowing local school boards any greater discretion in such inquiry would present too great a risk of serious infringement of privacy and personal freedom, especially given the potential, most prevalent in small communities, for community-wide disapproval of certain life-styles or living choices.

NOTES:

VIEMEISTER v. BOARD OF EDUCATION OF BOROUGH OF PROSPECT PARK

5 N.J. Super. 215, 68 A.2d 768 (1949).

NATURE OF CASE: Appeal of a state board of education's direction to a local board of education to reinstate a principal terminated after elimination of his position.

GENERAL RULE OF LAW: A tenured principal may not be replaced by another as principal without charges being brought and a hearing being conducted.

PROCEDURE SUMMARY:
Plaintiff: Viemeister (P), a tenured principal.
Defendant: Board of Education of Borough of Prospect Park (D) (Board).
State Superior Court Appellate Division Decision: Held for Viemeister (P), upholding state board order of reinstatement.

FACTS: Viemester (P) was a tenured principal employed by the Board (D) who performed no teaching duties. For economic reasons, the Board (D) adopted a resolution abolishing the position of principal and creating the position of teaching principal. As a result, Viemester (P) was terminated, without any charges ever being made against him, and a tenured teacher was appointed teaching principal. Viemester (P) appealed his termination to the Commissioner of Education, who directed his reinstatement, which the State Board of Education sustained. The Board (D) appealed.

ISSUE: May a tenured principal be terminated and replaced without charges being brought against him and a hearing being conducted?

HOLDING AND DECISION: (Jacobs, J.) No. A tenured principal may not be terminated and replaced without charges being alleged and a hearing being conducted. School laws expressly state that tenured teachers and principals are only subject to dismissal for cause after charges and a hearing. The Board's (D) argument that this rule has no application here because the Board (D) eliminated the office of principal has no support in law. As the Commissioner of Education correctly found, the office of principal has not been eliminated in fact. Looking to the substance rather than the form of the Board's (D) action, it is evident that the allegedly abolished principal position continued under the guise of the newly created office of teaching principal. To sustain the Board's (D) action would contravene the policy behind the tenure laws of providing principals and teachers with a measure of security in the ranks they hold. Affirmed.

COMMENT: *Viemeister* is unusual because most states do not provide principals with tenure. Courts tend to be skeptical of school board attempts to circumvent state tenure laws. Two questions arise in such situations: has the position been eliminated for a legitimate reason, and has the position actually been eliminated? Here, the court only had to address the latter question. If the position has been eliminated, the court must then determine whether the position was eliminated for a legitimate reason. Most states that do not allow a principal tenure do provide that same principal to be tenured as a teacher. Thus, if the principal qualified for tenure as a teacher, a teaching position would need to be provided if available.

NOTES:

BOARD OF REGENTS OF STATE COLLEGES v. ROTH
408 U.S. 564, 92 S. Ct. 2701 (1972).

NATURE OF CASE: Review of grant of summary judgment for a nontenured professor, with a one-year employment contract, who alleged the college board's decision not to renew his contract violated his Fourteenth Amendment rights.

GENERAL RULE OF LAW: A nontenured teacher has no right to a hearing before his contract is not renewed, unless nonrenewal infringes a liberty or property interest.

PROCEDURE SUMMARY:
Plaintiff: Roth (P), a nontenured teacher.
Defendant: Board of Regents of State Colleges (D) (Board).
U.S. District Court Decision: Held for Roth (P), granting summary judgment.
U.S. Court of Appeals Decision: Affirmed.
U.S. Supreme Court Decision: Reversed and remanded.

FACTS: Roth (P) was hired by the Board (D) as a nontenured professor for a term of one year. At the end of the year, the Board (D) informed Roth (P) that he would not be rehired for the next year. Under a Wisconsin statute, a teacher could not receive tenure until after four years of year-to-year employment; those acquiring tenure were then entitled to employment on condition of efficiency and good behavior. Roth (P) filed suit, alleging the Board (D) violated his Fourteenth Amendment right to free speech by denying renewal of his contract because of his criticism of the school administration and his due process right by failing to inform him of its reason for denial. The district court found for Roth (P) and granted summary judgment, which the court of appeals affirmed. The U.S. Supreme Court granted review.

ISSUE: Does a nontenured teacher have a right to a hearing before a board decides not to renew his contract where nonrenewal infringes no property or liberty interest?

HOLDING AND DECISION: (Stewart, J.) No. A nontenured teacher has no right to a hearing before a board decides not to renew his contract where nonrenewal infringes no property or liberty interest. Due process is only implicated where an action deprives a person of any of those interests encompassed by the Fourteenth Amendment's protection of liberty and property. Under Wisconsin law, only tenured teachers are entitled to continued employment; thus, Roth (P) had no property right to infringe. Further, absent something foreclosing other employment, such as charges against him, stigma, or disability, denial of a hearing is not a violation of due process. The lower court, therefore, should not have granted summary judgment for Roth (P). Reversed and remanded.

COMMENT: The *Roth* opinion represents a retreat by the Court from expansion of "entitlement" theory. Previously, the Court had raised the level of many government benefits from mere privileges to liberty or property interests to which citizens are entitled. One of the benefits elevated to the level of a property interest was government employment in certain instances. The test enunciated by the Court in *Roth* for when an individual has a Fourteenth Amendment property interest in government employment requires that such a property interest must be (1) grounded in state law and (2) presently enjoyed by the individual. As Roth (P) failed the first requirement, there was no need for the Court to consider the second requirement. If the Board (D) had barred Roth (P) from employment at other state universities or imposed a stigma that would hurt Roth's (P) future employment, the Court would have reached a different decision. But this was not the case. Therefore, if a nontenured teacher has a limited contract, this limited, or term, contract provides a guarantee of employment for only the length of the contract term. If a teacher is terminated during the term of the teacher's limited contract, then procedural due process protections attach. Because no life, liberty, or property interest was impaired, the Fourteenth Amendment due process mandate was not implicated. Because Roth (P) was a nontenured teacher, he did not have to be rehired at the end of the academic year. Furthermore, as long as there were no employer statements that would damage his reputation or freedom to seek other employment, there was no protected "liberty" interest. Thus, as long as the employment contract (or state law or university policy) does not contain language which would create an entitlement or an expectation of continuing employment, a teacher would have no protected "property" interest in continued employment.

KINGSVILLE INDEPENDENT SCHOOL DISTRICT v. COOPER
611 F.2d 1109 (5th Cir. 1980).

NATURE OF CASE: Appeal of award of damages to an untenured teacher whose dismissal was precipitated by her use of a disapproved role-playing technique in a post–Civil War Reconstruction period American history class.

GENERAL RULE OF LAW: An untenured teacher may not be discharged for classroom discussion unless the discussion clearly overbalanced the teacher's usefulness as an instructor.

PROCEDURE SUMMARY:
Plaintiff: Kingsville Independent School District (P) (District).
Defendant: Cooper (D), an untenured school teacher.
U.S. District Court Decision: Held for Cooper (D), awarding damages on her counterclaim for unjustified dismissal.
U.S. Court of Appeals Decision: Affirmed.

FACTS: In 1967, Cooper (D) was hired by the District (P) to teach high school without tenure. In 1971, Cooper (D) began using a teaching technique known as "Sunshine simulation," a role play by which students re-created a period, in this case, American history of the post–Civil War Reconstruction period. The technique evoked strong feelings on racial issues. Several complaints were filed by parents, but few were for things other than the use of the Sunshine technique. Cooper (D) subsequently was told not to discuss "blacks in American history" or any controversial issues but never was prohibited from using the technique. The District (P) declined to renew Cooper's (D) contract for the next year, despite the recommendation of both the principal and superintendent that it be renewed. The District (P) thereafter sought declaratory judgment that the decision did not violate Cooper's (D) rights. Cooper (D) counterclaimed for back pay and reinstatement. The district court found for Cooper (D). The District (P) appealed, contending the district court's findings that the classroom discussions were protected and that the District's (P) refusal to renew Cooper's (D) contract was based primarily on these discussions were clearly erroneous.

ISSUE: May a district refuse to renew an untenured teacher's contract based on classroom discussions where the discussions do not clearly overbalance the teacher's usefulness as an instructor?

HOLDING AND DECISION: (Godbold, J.) No. An untenured teacher may not be discharged for classroom discussions unless the discussions clearly overbalance the teacher's usefulness as an instructor. Classroom discussion, which includes the Sunshine project at issue, is protected by the First Amendment. Thus, discussions must overbalance one's effectiveness as an instructor to be sustained. Here, they did not. The record showed that the other complaints filed against Cooper (D) were few and minimal. In fact, the District (P) renewed her contract in prior years, despite these other complaints. And though the lower court's findings of fact did not explicitly show that Cooper (D) would have been rehired despite the Sunshine project complaints, they were sufficient to support such an inference and were not clearly erroneous. Affirmed.

COMMENT: The classroom is viewed as an intellectual marketplace of ideas, where the teacher should be able to investigate and experiment with new ideas. *Kingsville* is clearly a reinforcement of this notion. So long as the teaching method is related to a legitimate educational goal and does not significantly detract from the teacher's effectiveness as an instructor, despite complaints or parental disapproval of the method, the teacher, even untenured, cannot be dismissed simply because of his use of the method. It also illustrates that the right to an education does not necessary guarantee an always "comfortable" education.

NOTES:

PALMER v. BOARD OF EDUCATION OF THE CITY OF CHICAGO
603 F.2d 1271 (7th Cir. 1979).

NATURE OF CASE: Appeal of grant of summary judgment denying damages and reinstatement to an untenured kindergarten teacher who contended that her dismissal for not following the prescribed curriculum violated her religious freedom.

GENERAL RULE OF LAW: An untenured public school teacher is not entitled to disregard a prescribed curriculum that conflicts with her religious principles.

PROCEDURE SUMMARY:
Plaintiff: Palmer (P), an untenured public school kindergarten teacher.
Defendant: Board of Education of the City of Chicago (D) (Board).
U.S. District Court Decision: Held for Board (D), granting its motion for summary judgment.
U.S. Court of Appeals Decision: Affirmed.

FACTS: Palmer (P) was hired by the Board (D) as a probationary public school kindergarten teacher. After hiring but prior to the beginning of classes, Palmer (P) informed the principal that she would be unable to teach subjects related to love of country, the flag, and other patriotic matters, all topics required by the school's curriculum, because of her religious beliefs. The school attempted to accommodate Palmer (P) but could not. She was eventually dismissed without a hearing. Palmer (P) filed suit against the Board (D), seeking damages and reinstatement and alleging that dismissal for failure to follow the prescribed curriculum violated her First Amendment right of religious freedom. The district court disagreed and granted summary judgment for the Board (D). Palmer (P) appealed.

ISSUE: May an untenured teacher be discharged for failing to follow a prescribed curriculum that conflicts with her religious beliefs?

HOLDING AND DECISION: (Wood, J.) Yes. An untenured teacher may be discharged for failing to follow a prescribed curriculum that conflicts with her religious beliefs. The state has a compelling interest in choosing and having public teachers implement a suitable curriculum to benefit citizens and society. Teachers may not disregard this curriculum simply because it may conflict with their religious beliefs. Nor do teachers have any constitutional right to supplant this curriculum with their views. Affirmed.

COMMENT: The key in Palmer is that although the teacher's religious beliefs were clearly protected by the First Amendment, she did not have the right to impose those beliefs on others, which was, in effect, the result of her refusal to teach the subjects. The state's compelling interest in providing a particular education to its citizenry as a whole overrode the teacher's perceived right to "opt out" of teaching those topics which went against individual religious beliefs. The dismissal here was sustained because no means of accommodating all of the competing interests was found. But where there is a feasible way to accommodate the teacher's beliefs while providing the full curriculum, dismissal may be improper, especially under the 1972 Amendment to the 1964 Civil Rights Act, which provides that an employer may not discriminate against an individual because of religion, unless the employer demonstrates that he is unable to reasonably accommodate an employee's religious observance or practice.

NOTES:

PERRY v. SINDERMAN
408 U.S. 593, 92 S. Ct. 2694 (1972).

NATURE OF CASE: Review of order reversing summary judgment dismissing action seeking employment reinstatement.

GENERAL RULE OF LAW: A formal tenure system is not a requisite to a teacher possessing a due process interest in continued employment.

PROCEDURE SUMMARY:
Plaintiff: Sinderman (P), a teacher.
Defendant: Perry (D) and various other officials of the Texas state college system.
U.S. District Court Decision: Dismissed.
U.S. Court of Appeals Decision: Reversed.
U.S. Supreme Court Decision: Affirmed.

FACTS: Sinderman (P) was a teacher in the Texas state college system. The system had no official tenure system, although there allegedly was an informal "understanding" that teachers would be terminated for cause. Sinderman (P) was employed for four successive years by Odessa Junior College, under one-year contracts. During the 1968–69 academic year, he was elected president of the Texas Junior College Teachers Association. In this capacity, he left his teaching duties on several occasions to testify before Texas legislative committees. He also became involved in public disagreements with the policies of Odessa Junior College's Board of Regents. At one point, the state declined without explanation to review Sinderman's (P) contract. Sinderman (P) sued for reinstatement, contending that the termination was in retaliation for certain political stands he had taken. The district court granted summary judgment dismissing the action, holding that since Sinderman (P) did not have tenure, he had no right to a hearing. The court of appeals reversed, and the Supreme Court granted review.

ISSUE: Is a formal tenure system a requisite to a teacher's processing a due process interest in continued employment?

HOLDING AND DECISION: (Stewart, J.) No. A formal system is not a requisite to a teacher's processing a due process with respect to employment. The jurisprudence of due process with respect to employment is not so simple as a "tenured"–"not-tenured" dichotomy. Rather, what gives rise to a due process interest is an interest in continued employment sufficiently concrete as to be considered a property interest. While tenure is a situation that would almost certainly indicate such an interest, it is not exclusive. If an informal understanding regarding continued employment exists, this may also give rise to a property interest. Here, as this was the nature of Sinderman's (P) interest, a hearing on this issue was required. Reversed.

COMMENT: This action involved matters of both procedural and substantive due process. The procedural due process issue was that discussed above. The substantive due process issue related to the First Amendment. A state may not terminate an employee in a manner so as to abridge his right of free speech; Sinderman (P) alleged that Texas had done that very thing. This case, announced at the same time as *Board of Regents of State Colleges v. Roth*, 408 U.S. 564, 92 S. Ct. 2701 (1972), clarified the contract rights of teachers. In *Sinderman*, as in its companion case, plaintiff had no formal tenure or contractual interest in being rehired. Rather, the plaintiff relied on de facto tenure based on administrative policy enunciated in the college's official faculty guide and the guidelines promulgated by state colleges and universities. A teacher's public criticism on matters of public concern is constitutionally protected (*see Roth*). The college's basis for termination of employment could, therefore, not be upheld (regardless of tenure status). The First Amendment prohibited the impairment of the teacher's freedom of speech and expression. Furthermore, the "objective" expectation of tenure required providing the teacher procedural protections prior to termination. Here, the state refused to accord a pretermination hearing.

NOTES:

11

PICKERING v. BOARD OF EDUCATION OF TOWNSHIP HIGH SCHOOL DISTRICT 205

391 U.S. 563, 88 S. Ct. 1731 (1968).

11

NATURE OF CASE: Appeal by a teacher of a decision upholding his dismissal by a board for writing and publishing a letter criticizing the board's allocation of school funds.

GENERAL RULE OF LAW: A teacher may not be dismissed for statements on a matter of public concern without proof that the statements were false and knowingly or recklessly made.

PROCEDURE SUMMARY:

Plaintiff: Pickering (P), a teacher.

Defendant: Board of Education of Township High School District (D) (District).

State Trial Court Decision: Held for District (D), upholding the dismissal.

State Supreme Court Decision: Affirmed.

U.S. Supreme Court Decision: Reversed.

FACTS: Pickering (P), a teacher employed by the District (D), wrote and published a letter in a local paper criticizing the school administration and District's (D) allocation of tax funds raised for schools. The District (D), pursuant to state statute, dismissed Pickering (P) for publishing the letter, finding it detrimental to the efficient operation and administration of the District's (D) schools. Pickering (P) filed suit in state court, contending that the letter was protected by the First and Fourteenth Amendments. The trial court upheld the dismissal, with the state supreme court affirming. The U.S. Supreme Court noted probable jurisdiction of Pickering's (P) constitutional claims.

ISSUE: May a teacher be dismissed for statements on a matter of public concern without proof that the statements were false and knowingly or recklessly made?

HOLDING AND DECISION: (Marshall, J.) No. A teacher may not be dismissed for statements on a matter of public concern without proof that the statements were false and knowingly or recklessly made. The theory that public employment, which may be denied altogether, may be subjected to any conditions, regardless of how unreasonable, has been uniformly rejected. A teacher's interest as a citizen in making public comment must be balanced against the state's interest in promoting the efficiency of its employees' public services.

Pickering's (P) statements were true and false. The true statements regarded matters of public concern and raised no question of faculty discipline or harmony and were, therefore, no reason for dismissal. The false statements were not shown to interfere with his performance of his teaching duties or the school's operations. Absent such a showing, these statements are entitled to the same protection given to members of the general public. Thus, there having been no showing that Pickering (P) knowingly made the false statements or was reckless in making them, dismissal was not justified. Reversed.

COMMENT: Before *Pickering*, the courts followed the "privilege doctrine," which made employment a privilege and not a right, granting school boards unlimited control over the employment and dismissal of teachers. The Court, after years of dissatisfaction with the doctrine, finally disposed of it in *Pickering*. This shifted the focus of the Court's analysis to weighing the effects of a teacher's statement against the teacher's right to make statements criticizing school board policy on matters of public concern under the First Amendment. This was a recognition that the position of teacher is not, in itself, reason to deny an individual the same protection given to the general public. Although the Court upheld a teacher's freedom of speech, this right is not absolute. Individual cases need to be judged in relation to the balance between the employee's right as a citizen and the state's compelling interest to provide the efficient public services it provides through its employees. Essentially, a court must "balance the equities" in such situations. In an interesting dissent, White felt that the court should not have considered harm to the district as being related to First Amendment rights. He felt that this case should have been judged similar to previous Court rulings in defamation cases, *e.g., Times v. Sullivan* and *Garrison v. Louisiana*, 379 U.S. 64, 85 S. Ct. 209 (1964). He felt that deliberate or reckless falsehoods serve no First Amendment ends and deserve no protection under the First Amendment.

MT. HEALTHY CITY SCHOOL DISTRICT BOARD OF EDUCATION v. DOYLE
429 U.S. 274, 97 S. Ct. 568 (1977).

NATURE OF CASE: Review of order mandating reinstatement of fired teacher.

GENERAL RULE OF LAW: The termination of a teacher following his exercise of a constitutional right will be voided only if such exercise was not the principal factor in the termination.

PROCEDURE SUMMARY:
Plaintiff: Doyle, a teacher (P).
Defendant: Mt. Healthy (Ohio) City School District Board of Education (D), Doyle's (P) employer.
U.S. District Court Decision: Held for Doyle (P).
U.S. Court of Appeals Decision: Affirmed.
U.S. Supreme Court Decision: Reversed.

FACTS: Doyle (P) was a nontenured teacher at the Mt. Healthy City School District from 1966 to 1971. During this period of time, he had proven to be somewhat difficult, having been involved in general incidents. One incident included having made insulting comments to two students, while another included having made an obscene gesture to students. He had also gotten into several arguments with other teachers that almost escalated into fistfights. In 1971, he called in and forwarded a memorandum from the school administration to a local radio station, which ran it as a news item. Later that year, the School Board (D) refused to rehire him. Doyle (P) requested, and the School Board (D) provided, the reasons for the dismissal. Among the reasons given was Doyle's (P) contact with the radio station. Doyle (P) sued for reinstatement, contending that he had been terminated for exercising a First Amendment right. The district court ordered him reinstated, and the court of appeals affirmed. The Supreme Court granted review.

ISSUE: Will the termination of a teacher following his exercise of a constitutional right be voided only if such exercise was the principal factor in his termination?

HOLDING AND DECISION: (Rehnquist, J.) Yes. The termination of a teacher following his exercise of a constitutional right will be voided only if such exercise was the principal factor in the termination. A public employee may not be fired for exercising a constitutional right. However, this does not mean that one so doing becomes immune from termination. If a public employer can demonstrate that such exercise was something less than the principal factor, such as only one of numerous factors, then the termination may be valid. Here, there were numerous acts that Doyle (P) had committed that might have influenced the decision to terminate him. However, neither court below appeared to have ruled on whether Doyle's (P) termination was largely due to these incidents, so the matter must be decided on remand. Reversed.

COMMENT: An untenured teacher, unlike a tenured one, has little right to procedural due process. He may be terminated for almost any cause or no cause at all. Nonetheless, one thing an untenured teacher may not be fired for is solely exercising a constitutional right. This case distinguishes *Pickering*, 391 U.S. 563, 88 S. Ct. 1731 (1968), which held that teachers had a constitutional right to speak out freely on matters of public concern. Protected speech may not serve as the basis for the termination of employment. By the same token, a school employee cannot simply cloak himself or herself with the First Amendment by engaging in constitutionally protected conduct. Therefore, a teacher cannot be fired for speaking out on matters of public interest, but a teacher cannot prevent an employer from viewing the employee's total performance record when making a decision on rehiring. After *Doyle*, a school employee must establish that his statements were protected and that protected speech was a motivating, or substantial, factor in the board's termination or nonrenewal action. The school board must establish that it would have taken the termination or nonrenewal action regardless of the employee's protected conduct.

NOTES:

DYKEMAN v. BOARD OF EDUCATION OF SCHOOL DISTRICT OF COLERIDGE

210 Neb. 596, 316 N.W.2d 69 (1982).

NATURE OF CASE: Appeal of dismissal of a petition to review a board's termination of a teacher's contract pursuant to a reduction in force.

GENERAL RULE OF LAW: A school board may consider both education and noneducational factors in determining whether to terminate a teacher pursuant to a reduction-in-force program.

PROCEDURE SUMMARY:

Plaintiff: Dykeman (P), a teacher.

Defendant: Board of Education of School District of Coleridge (D) (Board).

State District Court Decision: Held for the Board (D), dismissing Dykeman's (P) petition for review of the Board's (D) decision to terminate.

State Supreme Court Decision: Affirmed.

FACTS: Dykeman (P) had been employed by the Nebraska Board (D) as a business education teacher for six years. In 1980, the Board (D) determined that it needed to reduce its teaching staff and that one of the two high school business education teachers should be let go. Both teachers were tenured and had identical teaching certificate endorsements. In deciding between the two teachers, the Board (D) considered the contribution each made to the activities program, ultimately deciding to terminate Dykeman (P). Dykeman (P) thereafter petitioned the court for review of the decision, contending that under the statute permitting the reduction, it was improper for the Board (D) to consider the teachers' respective contributions to the activities program. The district court dismissed the petition, finding that the Board's (D) decision was neither arbitrary nor capricious. Dykeman (P) appealed.

ISSUE: May a school board consider noneducational as well as educational factors in determining whether to dismiss a teacher pursuant to a reduction-in-force program?

HOLDING AND DECISION: (Boslaugh, J.) Yes. A school board may consider noneducational as well as educational factors in determining whether to dismiss a teacher pursuant to a reduction-in-force program. Though the statute governing the reduction program did not specifically authorize consideration of a teacher's contribution to an activities program, neither did the statute pro-hibit it. Also, the decision was administrative, not quasi-judicial, and a school board's administrative decisions are only subject to limited review, absent statutory or contractual restrictions upon the decisions. Absent such restrictions, a school board is entitled to broad discretion, and its decisions may not be disturbed unless found to be arbitrary and capricious. The consideration of activities program contributions was not, and Dykeman's (P) petition was properly dismissed. Affirmed.

COMMENT: In arguing that the Board (D) could not consider the contribution teachers made to the activities program, Dykeman (P) relied on *Neal v. School Dist. of York,* 205 Neb. 558, 288 N.W. 2d 725 (1980). In *Neal,* the court held that the provisions of the tenure law did not apply to coaching duties and noted that nothing in the law's language or legislative history indicated that the position of coach was intended to be covered by the law. The *Dykeman* court distinguished *Neal,* rejecting the application of the *Neal* argument by simply stating that nothing in that opinion addressed the question of consideration of activities program contributions. This decision provides the Board (D) with a good deal of discretion in actions such as this. As long as their actions are neither capricious nor wanton, they will usually be upheld as good-faith acts.

NOTES:

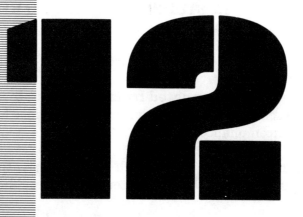

STUDENT RIGHTS AND REGULATIONS

▶ ## CHAPTER SUMMARY

CHAPTER 12: STUDENT RIGHTS AND REGULATIONS

QUICK REFERENCE RULES OF LAW

1. **Attendance mandated by law:** Each state has enacted a compulsory school attendance statute which provides for penalties in the face of noncompliance. (§ I.A.)

2. **Alternatives to public schooling:** Private schooling and home instruction are acceptable alternatives to public education. (§ I.A.3.)

3. **Few exceptions to mandatory attendance:** Exceptions to compulsory school attendance are sometimes granted to married students, working students, and those with certain religious convictions that are opposed to schooling. (§ I.A.4.)

4. **Penalties in the face of noncompliance:** In response to noncompliance with compulsory attendance statutes, parents may be prosecuted and students may be held in contempt, expelled from school, or made wards of the state. (§ I.A.5.)

5. **Obligation to educate resident students:** School districts are obliged to educate school-age children so long as they reside within district boundaries. (§ I.B.1.)

6. **Out-of-district school attendance:** A student who resides in one district has no right to attend school in another but may do so if she obtains the permission of both districts. (§ I.B.3.)

7. **Reasonable health regulations permissible:** Local school boards may be empowered by statute to pass regulations, such as those requiring vaccinations, which are designed to protect the public health. (§ I.C.)

8. **Textbook fees permissible:** No federal laws or constitutional provisions prohibit the states from assessing textbook usage fees. (§ I.D.)

9. **Broad authority to regulate conduct:** School boards are given broad powers to regulate conduct that affects the welfare of the school system. (§ II.A.1.)

10. **Compelling justification must exist:** When a regulation impacts on a student's constitutional rights, school officials must demonstrate a compelling need to regulate student conduct in the manner set forth in the regulation. (§ II.A.2.)

11. **First Amendment rights may be regulated:** While public school students are generally entitled to freedom of speech and of the

press, these rights may be regulated under certain circumstances. (§ II.B.1.)

12. **No right to certain speech:** Defamatory statements, obscenities, and inflammatory statements are among the forms of speech that are not protected by the First Amendment to the U.S. Constitution. (§ II.B.2.)

13. **Prior restraint unacceptable:** Prior administrative reviews of student publications are legally suspect because of the potential they present for infringing students' rights to freedom of the press. (§ II.C.4.)

14. **Freedom of association may be limited:** Public school officials may deny access to student groups whose purposes for meeting are not in line with existing curriculum. (§ II.E.1.)

15. **Establishment of religion prohibited:** Courts frequently invalidate decisions by school officials to provide access to student religious groups on the grounds that such assistance amounts to state sponsorship of religion. (§ II.E.2.)

16. **Common forms of punishment:** When authorized by law and imposed fairly, corporal punishment, suspension from school, expulsion from school, and academic sanctions are all acceptable forms of punishment. (§ III.B.)

NOTES:

12 ▶

Introduction: Every state requires school-age children to obtain some form of education. While attending school, students are subject to a variety of rules and regulations pertaining to the manner in which they conduct themselves and apply themselves to their academic programs. Students are not without certain constitutional and statutory rights, however, and tensions between such rights and the regulations that impact upon them frequently lead to litigation.

I. SCHOOL ATTENDANCE

A. Compulsory Attendance

1. *A creature of state law:* The laws of each state contain a compulsory school attendance statute. Each such statute provides for penalties in the face of noncompliance.

2. *Legal underpinning of the compulsory education requirement:* The legal basis for compulsory education is the common law doctrine of *parens patriae,* which permits government, as guardian of the people, to enact laws for the common good. Education fosters the enlightenment of the citizenry and thus contributes to the well-being of the state.

3. *Alternatives to public school attendance:* In 1925, the U.S. Supreme Court declared that no state could limit the means of satisfying its compulsory education requirement to attendance at public schools. *See Pierce v. Society of the Sisters of the Holy Names of Jesus and Mary,* 268 U.S. 510, 45 S.Ct. 571 (1925). In so holding, the Court balanced the right of parents to supervise the upbringing of their children with the right of the state to establish educational standards. Accordingly, the following alternatives to public school education may be permissible under specified circumstances.

    a. *Private schools:* Students may attend private schools, so long as the private program of instruction meets minimum state standards. *See State of Wisconsin v. Popanz,* 112 Wis.2d 166 (1983).

    b. *Home instruction:* Students may be permitted to receive instruction in the home, so long as a parent or other instructor is competent to teach and the program of instruction is roughly equivalent to that offered in public schools. *See New Jersey v. Massa,* 95 N.J. Super. 382 (1967).

4. *Exceptions to compulsory education:* In some cases, students may be exempted from compulsory attendance requirements. In others, requests for exemptions have been denied.

a. *Statutory exceptions:* In some states, married students are exempt from compulsory school attendance. Also, in a few states, those who have reached a certain minimum age and are certified to work in specific jobs are exempt.

b. *Religious convictions exception:* Amish children who have completed the eighth grade have been exempted from further compulsory education. *See Wisconsin v. Yoder,* 406 U.S. 205, 92 S.Ct. 1526 (1972). However, courts have denied religious conviction exemptions in most other cases seeking removal of children from school.

c. *No exceptions granted:* Courts have denied exemptions which have been sought based on alleged unsafe school conditions or school curricula that failed to instruct students in the tenets of their faith.

5. ***Penalties for noncompliance with compulsory statutes:*** While the consequences of noncompliance with compulsory attendance statutes may vary from state to state, the following "penalties" are most commonly identified:

a. *Prosecution of parents:* The parents of noncomplying students may be prosecuted in criminal or civil court;

b. *Expulsion of students:* Students who are excessively truant may be expelled;

c. *Held in contempt:* Students who are excessively truant may be held in contempt of court if they disobey a court order to return to school; and

d. *Made wards of the state:* In extreme cases, truant students may be made wards of local juvenile courts and supervised by probation officers.

B. **Residency Requirements**

1. ***Overriding principle:*** A public school district is obliged to educate school-age children who reside within district boundaries and intend to remain there.

2. ***Exception to the rule:*** Tuition-free admission to public schools may be denied to minors if their primary reason for maintaining a presence in a particular district is to attend public school. *See Martinez v. Bynum,* 461 U.S. 321, 103 S.Ct. 1838 (1983).

3. ***Enrollment in neighboring districts:*** As a rule, a student who resides in one district has no right to attend school in an-

other but may do so if she obtains the permission of both districts. In most such cases, the student's parents will be required to pay tuition to the neighboring district.

4. *Limited guardianships not permissible:* However, most courts have refused to permit the establishment of limited guardianships in neighboring districts so that student athletes can attend school tuition-free in those districts.

5. *Parents not U.S. citizens:* The U.S. Supreme Court overturned a Texas statute denying a public school education to undocumented school-age children. *Plyler v. Doe,* 457 U.S. 202, 102 S.Ct. 2382 (1982).

C. **Public Health Requirements**

1. *Overriding principle:* Local agencies may be empowered by their respective state legislatures to pass regulations which are designed to protect the public health. Such regulations are important in the context of the schools, where unhealthy students could otherwise endanger the health and well-being of other students.

2. *Most common public health regulation:* States may authorize local school districts to condition a student's attendance in public or private schools on her receipt of a vaccination against communicable diseases.

3. *Exception to vaccination requirement:* Most courts refuse to uphold challenges to mandatory vaccination requirements, including those that are based on religious grounds. However, a few states, by statute, exempt students from such requirements if they practice a religion that prohibits such procedures and their presence in school does not endanger the health of others.

D. **Required Fees**

1. *Validity of textbook fees left to the states:* The U.S. Supreme Court has not ruled on whether the assessment of textbook fees violates the Equal Protection Clause (or any other provision) of the U.S. Constitution. Thus, disputes concerning such fees are resolved by state courts in accordance with each state's constitution and statutes.

2. *Fees waived for those who cannot pay:* When the assessment of textbook fees is permitted by law and upheld by state courts, fees are usually waived for those who can demonstrate that they are unable to pay.

3. *Courts divided regarding other fees:* Assessments of fees for school courses and school supplies have frequently been challenged in court. Fees for academic courses have sometimes been held to violate a student's right to a fair education. In other cases, such fees have been struck down, while fees for elective courses have been permitted.

II. STUDENT CONDUCT

A. Authority to Regulate Student Conduct

1. *Local entities vested with broad powers:* School boards are vested with sufficient authority to regulate conduct that affects the welfare of the school system and its students and personnel.

2. *Burden falls on the party opposing a regulation:* In most cases, the burden of proving that a particular rule or regulation is *unreasonable* falls on the party challenging it. In those cases in which a rule or regulation impacts on a constitutional right, the burden shifts to school officials to demonstrate a *compelling need* to regulate conduct in the manner prescribed.

3. *Regulations must be fair:* In general, a rule or regulation may not be so vague as to permit arbitrary application. In particular, a rule or regulation must provide those students whose conduct will be affected with adequate information as to what is expected of them.

B. Freedom of Speech and Expression

1. *First Amendment protection:* The First Amendment to the U.S. Constitution, applied to the states through the Fourteenth Amendment, limits the government's authority to interfere with citizens' free speech and expression rights. "Expression" may be defined as conduct that communicates an idea. While public school students are generally entitled to freedom of speech and expression, their rights are not coextensive with those of adults in other settings and may be regulated under certain circumstances.

2. *Unprotected speech and expression:* The following forms of speech and conduct are not protected by the First Amendment in the school setting.

   a. *Defamatory statements:* Statements that are false, that are communicated to someone other than the defamed party, and that expose the defamed party to shame or ridicule are defamatory and, as such, are not protected by the First

Amendment. They must contain assertions of fact, not opinion. A public official, such as a school board member, who believes she has been defamed must prove, in addition to the foregoing, that the defaming party acted recklessly and with malice.

b. *Obscenities:* Generally speaking, obscene statements and conduct are not afforded First Amendment protection. The U.S. Supreme Court has specifically held that the prohibition of "vulgar and offensive" language in the schools is an appropriate function of the public educational system. *See Bethel School Dist. No. 403 v. Fraser,* 478 U.S. 675, 106 S.Ct. 3159 (1986).

c. *Inflammatory expression:* Forms of expression which might reasonably be expected to lead to a "substantial disruption of or material interference with school activities" will not be afforded First Amendment protection. *See Tinker v. Des Moines Indep. Comm. School Dist.,* 393 U.S. 503, 89 S.Ct. 733 (1969).

3. ***Protected speech and expression:*** Speech or conduct which expresses a *political or ideological viewpoint* in a manner which is not disruptive is protected by the First Amendment.

a. *Landmark Opinion:* In *Tinker v. Des Moines Indep. Comm. School Dist., supra,* the Supreme Court upheld the rights of students who had been suspended from school for wearing arm bands in protest of the war in Vietnam. Noting that the students' conduct had not led to a disturbance of any kind, the Court warned school officials that "a mere desire to avoid [the] discomfort and unpleasantness that always accompany an unpopular viewpoint" was insufficient to justify the regulation of free expression rights.

b. *Tinker distinguished:* A school may constitutionally adopt a policy which prohibits students from wearing items that bear a message unrelated to school activities but only if that policy applies to all types of non-educational speech without singling out any particular message and if the school can demonstrate a history of disruption caused by the wearing of such items. *See Guzick v. Drebus,* 431 F.2d 594 (6th Cir. 1970). *See also Tate v. Bd. of Ed. of Jonesboro, Ark., Special Education District,* 453 F.2d 975 (8th Cir. 1972).

C. **Freedom of Press**

1. ***First Amendment protection:*** Freedom of the press, like freedom of speech and expression, is guaranteed by the First

Amendment. In the schools, free press issues usually arise in connection with student publications.

2. ***School officials retain editorial control:*** A recent Supreme Court decision has established that official control over the contents of a school-sponsored student newspaper does not violate the First Amendment, so long as the control is reasonably related to legitimate pedagogical concerns. *See Hazelwood School District v. Kuhlmeier*, 484 U.S. 260 (1988). It would appear that the basic tenets of *Tinker* are now open to question.

3. ***School sponsorship versus nonsponsorship:*** The fact that a student publication is school-sponsored or school-affiliated does not mean that it is any less deserving of First Amendment protections than a nonsponsored publication. Moreover, removal of sponsorship may be construed in certain circumstances as an attempt to stifle or curtail free press rights. Nevertheless, after *Hazelwood*, school-sponsored student publications have less First Amendment protections than before.

4. ***"Prior restraint" on publications:*** Most courts are wary of prior administrative reviews of student publications because of the potential for curtailment of free press rights. Prior restraint policies must be narrowly tailored to the achievement of clearly stated goals, must set forth unambiguous restraint criteria, and must provide students with an opportunity to challenge unfavorable decisions. *See Eisner v. Stamford Board of Education*, 440 F.2d 803 (2d Cir. 1971).

D. Dress and Appearance

1. ***Mixed judicial response to lawsuits challenging hairstyle regulations:*** Approximately half of the federal circuit courts of appeals have declared that hairstyle restrictions curtail constitutionally protected expression, while the other half have upheld such restrictions as not affecting constitutional rights or as permissibly infringing on them in order to prevent disruptions in the school setting. *See Massie v. Henry,* 455 F.2d 779 (4th Cir. 1972).

2. ***Mixed judicial response to student dress regulations:*** Regulations of student attire have been invalidated by some courts based on what has been termed the constitutional right to wear clothes of one's own choosing (grounded in the Fourteenth Amendment). However, regulations that merely restrict immodest dress have generally been upheld.

E. Student Organizations

12

1. *"Free association" rights implicated:* The freedom of individuals to associate with others is not specifically enumerated in the First Amendment to the U.S. Constitution, but it is implied. Courts recognize that individuals express their views more effectively when they do so through associations with others. Education-related clubs and societies provide an opportunity for students to associate with fellow students.

2. *Regulation of organizations open to all students:* In the higher education setting, school officials are prohibited from denying recognition to or restricting the activities of student organizations based on the content of their organizational philosophies. *Widmar v. Vincent,* 454 U.S. 263 (1981). At the high school level and below, school officials have more latitude in dealing with student organizations; they can deny access to groups that are not extensions of the existing curriculum.

   a. *Effect of providing access to extracurricular groups:* If, however, non-curriculum-related student organizations are provided access, the school's policy must not discriminate based on the philosophies of the various organizations (see exception, below). *See Board of Education of the Westside Community Schools v. Mergens,* 496 U.S. 226 (1990) (Chapter 2).

   b. *Problems arising from providing access to student religious organizations:* Attempts to regulate religious groups often pit students' free speech and association rights against the Constitution's proscription against the establishment of religion. In the context of the public schools, courts often invalidate decisions by school officials to provide access to student religious groups on the grounds that such assistance amounts to state sponsorship of religion.

3. *Regulation of organizations that are not open to all students:* Courts consistently uphold school officials' decisions to deny recognition to so-called secret societies, such as fraternities and sororities.

STUDENT DISCIPLINE

III. **STUDENT DISCIPLINE**

A. **Regulation of Student Conduct**

1. *Statutory authority:* Most states, through their subordinate agencies, establish codes of conduct within the public schools. Students who are guilty of serious misconduct are subject to disciplinary action.

2. ***Duty to maintain discipline:*** School officials are not only authorized to establish and enforce disciplinary regulations, they are *required* to do so.

3. ***Due process must be afforded:*** Disciplinary actions must be accompanied by some form of procedure designed to ensure that the process whereby discipline is imposed is fundamentally fair. *See Goss v. Lopez,* 419 U.S. 565 (1975). Historically, courts have been as concerned with the due process guarantees afforded disciplined students as they have been with the validity of disciplinary regulations and the severity of punishments imposed.

B. Forms of Punishment

1. ***Corporal punishment:*** In most states, school officials are authorized to inflict reasonable physical punishment on a student's body with the intention of modifying unacceptable behavior. The U.S. Supreme Court has declared that corporal punishment does not violate the Eighth Amendment's proscription against "cruel and unusual punishment" and the Fourteenth Amendment's guarantee of procedural due process. *See Ingraham v. Wright,* 430 U.S. 651, 97 S.Ct. 1401 (1977).

2. ***Suspensions and expulsions:*** The removal of students from school for specified periods of time, or for good, is a common form of punishment for disciplinary infractions of a serious nature. Strict due process guarantees are usually provided to students who face suspension or expulsion actions. *See C.J. v. School Board of Broward County,* 438 So.2d 87 (1983).

3. ***Sanctions for deficient academic performance:*** School officials are authorized to give students failing grades, place them on probation, and remove them from academic programs in response to substandard academic performance. However, the courts are at odds over whether it is permissible to impose such sanctions as punishment for misconduct that is unrelated to academics.

4. ***Searches and seizures:*** The Fourth Amendment to the U.S. Constitution prohibits the government from conducting *unreasonable* searches and seizures of people and their belongings. This principle has been held to apply to school officials. A valid search is one for which there are *reasonable grounds* for believing that the procedure will turn up evidence of an infraction and which is appropriately *limited in scope. See New Jersey v. T.L.O.,* 469 U.S. 325 (1985).

PIERCE v. SOCIETY OF SISTERS
268 U.S. 510, 45 S. Ct. 57 (1925).

NATURE OF CASE: Appeal of preliminary order restraining public school officials from enforcing a law requiring children between the ages of 8 and 16 to attend public schools.

GENERAL RULE OF LAW: A law requiring children to attend public schools unreasonably interferes with parents' liberty interest in directing the upbringing and education of their children.

PROCEDURE SUMMARY:
Plaintiff: Society of Sisters (P) (Sisters), a corporation empowered to establish and maintain private schools.
Defendant: Pierce (D), the Governor of Oregon.
U.S. District Court Decision: Held for Sisters (P), granting a preliminary order restraining Pierce (D) from enforcing the compulsory education law.
U.S. Supreme Court Decision: Affirmed.

FACTS: Oregon enacted the Compulsory Education Act of 1922, which, effective 1926, required every parent, guardian, or other person with custody of a child between 8 and 16 years of age to send the child to public school. Failure to comply was a misdemeanor. Sisters (P), a corporation empowered to establish and maintain private schools, filed suit, alleging the law impermissibly infringed its property interests and the parents' right to choose where their children attend school. The district court agreed, finding that the parents' right to select where their children attend school was a liberty interest protected by the Fourteenth Amendment. It issued a preliminary order restraining Pierce (D), the governor of Oregon, from enforcing the law. Pierce (D) appealed.

ISSUE: May a state require parents to send children between the ages of 8 and 16 to public school?

HOLDING AND DECISION: (McReynolds, J.) No. A law requiring children between the ages of 8 and 16 to attend public schools impermissibly interferes with parents' liberty interest in directing the education of their children. Rights guaranteed by the Constitution may not be abridged by legislation which has no reasonable relation to some legitimate purpose. Compelling attendance at public schools is not such a purpose. The state may lawfully regulate all schools and require that all children of a certain age attend some school meeting certain standards. However, the state may not standardize children by forcing them to attend public schools only. Thus, the district court did not err in ordering Pierce (D) to stop enforcing the compulsory education law. Affirmed.

COMMENT: There appeared to be an insurmountable standing problem in *Pierce* given that the plaintiff was a corporation, which ordinarily could not claim the liberty protections of the Fourteenth Amendment. The Court, however, overcame this problem by recognizing the threat, posed by the law, to plaintiff's business and property interests. Obviously, the parents and/or guardians of private school students would have been the plaintiffs of choice, *i.e.*, the parties with the most direct interest in the issues under consideration. Although the corporation also had a clear interest in the outcome, the Court may have been less stringent in applying standing requirements to the corporation because the constitutional issue before the Court was so substantial.

NOTES:

STATE OF WISCONSIN v. POPANZ
112 Wis.2d 166, 332 N.W.2d 750 (1983).

NATURE OF CASE: Appeal of conviction and sentence for violating a Wisconsin law making it compulsory for parents to send children to school, on procedural due process grounds that the law failed to define "private school."

GENERAL RULE OF LAW: Compulsory education laws must specifically define "private school" in order to meet constitutional standards of procedural due process and to provide notice to parents and school administrators as to which institutions qualify as "private schools."

PROCEDURE SUMMARY:
Plaintiff: Wisconsin state superintendent of the Department of Public Instruction (P).
Defendant: Popanz (D), father of three school-age daughters.
State Court Decision: Held for Wisconsin (P).
State Supreme Court Decision: Reversed.

FACTS: Popanz (D), whose daughters had previously been enrolled in Wisconsin's (P) public schools, joined the Church of the Free Thinker, a not-for-profit corporation organized under Wisconsin (P) law, and attempted to send his girls to a private "school" administered by the Church. Popanz (D) requested his daughters' prior schools to forward to the Free Thinker school their transcripts and recommendations on curriculum in order to ensure that he was complying with Wisconsin's (P) compulsory education law. Under this law, parents with children between the ages of 6 and 18 were required to ensure that their children attend public or private school regularly. The administrator at the public school processing Popanz' (D) requests refused to send on the records because he believed that the Free Thinker school was not a "private school" in compliance with the compulsory education act, since the Free Thinker school was not listed in a state directory of nonpublic schools. However, the compulsory education act did not define "private school" by reference to this publication. Popanz (D) was convicted of violating the act and sentenced to two 90-day jail terms. Popanz (D) appealed to the Wisconsin Supreme Court, arguing that Wisconsin's (P) failure to define "private school" violated his constitutional due process rights.

ISSUE: Must compulsory education laws specifically define "private school" in order to meet constitutional standards of procedural due process?

HOLDING AND DECISION: (Abrahamson, J.) Yes. Compulsory education laws which require persons in control of minor children to ensure that they attend public or private school on a regular basis must specifically define "private school" in order to meet constitutional standards of procedural due process. Procedural due process requires that laws set forth fair notice of prohibited or required conduct and proper standards for enforcement of the law. Here, no definition of "private school" was provided in the statute itself or in any regulations construing the statute. It was left to administrators to improvise on an ad hoc basis as to which institutions met the state requirement. This lack of notice left parents such as Popanz (D) to act at their peril. States such as Wisconsin (P) must provide objective standards as to which institutions are appropriate for minor instruction and not leave definitional decisions to the subjective standards of each person interpreting the law. Reversed.

COMMENT: Typically, private schools are defined in comparison with public schools, that is, as offering academic grades comparable to those established in the public system. Therefore, in this case, the administrator's decision not to provide Popanz (D) with records of his daughters' attendance may have been based as much on inability to confirm a requisite parallel curriculum as on a prejudice against "unorthodox" churches. However, the court expressly noted in reaching its decision that the administrator did not visit the Free Thinker school or ask any questions about its curricula, educational backgrounds of the teachers, types of instructional materials or facilities, or time schedules. This failure made particularly glaring the "subjective" nature of the administrator's decision and the failure of the Wisconsin (P) statute to define "private school." Additionally, the violation of a compulsory education statute is a criminal offence. The proof requirements are more stringent in criminal than in civil law. This is necessary in order to provide a defendant, here Propanz, with more protection when the possibility of incarceration is threatened. The proof standard is "beyond a shadow of a doubt" for more serious criminal offenses and "clear and convincing" for less serious. In contrast, the proof standard for a civil case is the less stringent "preponderance of the evidence" (50.1%) standard.

NEW JERSEY v. MASSA
95 N.J. Super. 382, 231 A.2d 252 (1967).

12

NATURE OF CASE: Challenge to New Jersey's compulsory education law by parents who taught their grade-school child at home rather than sending her to public school.

GENERAL RULE OF LAW: Home instruction of children in subject matter equivalent to that provided in public schools meets the requirements of a state's compulsory education law.

PROCEDURE SUMMARY:
Plaintiff: New Jersey (P).
Defendants: Mr. and Mrs. Massa (D), parents of a child they taught at home.
State Municipal Court Decision: Held for New Jersey (P).
State Superior Court Decision: Reversed.

FACTS: The Massas (D) taught their 12-year-old daughter, Barbara, at home rather than sending her to public elementary school or junior high. Mr. Massa (D) taught Barbara art, which he taught at local schools, and Mrs. Massa (D) prepared special texts which covered all the traditional subjects taught to children of Barbara's age in the public schools. Mrs. Massa (D) supplemented her own prepared texts with numerous maps, textbooks, charts, and outlines and tested Barbara regularly. Neither Mr. nor Mrs. Massa (D) was a certified teacher. On standardized tests taken after home instruction, Barbara scored higher than the national median except in math. The Massas (D) lived in New Jersey (P), which had a compulsory education law requiring parents to send their children to New Jersey (P) public schools or to provide their children with "equivalent instruction elsewhere." Violation of the statute constituted a misdemeanor and subjected the violators to a fine. Mr. and Mrs. Massa (D) were prosecuted in a municipal court by the state of New Jersey (P) and convicted. They appealed to the New Jersey Superior Court.

ISSUE: Does home instruction of children in subject matter equivalent to that provided in public schools meet the requirements of state compulsory education laws?

HOLDING AND DECISION: (Collins, J.) Yes. Home instruction of children in subject matter equivalent to that provided in public schools meets the requirements of a state's compulsory education law. Here, Barbara Massa was taught all subjects covered in local public schools, was tested regularly, and was subject to circumscribed periods of instruction, study, and recreation. New Jersey's (P) requirement that she receive "equivalent" instruction does not require formal enrollment in a private school or group instruction. Reversed.

COMMENT: Some states, such as California, would not necessarily have prohibited home instruction of Barbara by her parents but would have required that they be certified teachers. *E.g., People v. Turner,* 121 Cal. App. Supp.2d 861, 263 P.2d 685 (Cal. Super. Ct. 1953) (instruction by private tutor "equivalent" if the tutor possesses a valid state credential for the grade taught). Here, the New Jersey court did not require a credential because the New Jersey legislature had not inserted such a requirement in the compulsory education statute, reasoning that if the legislature had intended to require credentials it would have explicitly referred to them in the language of the statute. The other principal concern in cases such as this is whether children at home, who are deprived of the social companionship and peer comparison to be had in the typical school setting, grow up ill-equipped to deal with society at large. In other parts of its opinion, the court here discounted such a concern, despite the fact that a teacher in Barbara's new school testified that Barbara was having some difficulty adapting to the group instructional environment.

NOTES:

WISCONSIN v. YODER
406 U.S. 205, 92 S. Ct. 1526 (1972).

NATURE OF CASE: Challenge under the First Amendment to the constitutionality of Wisconsin's requirement that children attend public high school.

GENERAL RULE OF LAW: The First Amendment right to free exercise of religion protects a religious way of life which requires that children past the eighth grade devote themselves to a vocation and overrides a state's compulsory education requirement that all children attend public high school.

PROCEDURE SUMMARY:
Plaintiffs: The State of Wisconsin (P) and the school district administrator for public school system in Green County, Wisconsin.
Defendant: Yoder (D), an Amish parent.
State Trial Court Decision: Held for Wisconsin (P).
State Supreme Court Decision: Reversed.
U.S. Supreme Court Decision: Affirmed.

FACTS: The Amish religion and way of life stresses independence and separateness from society and freedom from the competitiveness that defines much of American life. It is characterized by self-sufficiency and requires that children past the age of 13 devote themselves to a vocation such as farming, building, etc. Many Amish communities build their own schools for children under the age of 13, but some send their children to public schools through the eighth grade. However, all keep their children in the Amish community and away from public high schools. Wisconsin's (P) compulsory education law required that children through the age of 16 attend public school or an "equivalent" private school. The Amish parents in Green County, Wisconsin, including Yoder (D), were prosecuted under this law for refusing to send their children to a traditional school. Yoder (D) was convicted and appealed to the Wisconsin Supreme Court, which held that Yoder (D) and the other Amish parents were merely asserting their First Amendment right to free exercise of their religion because the Amish way of life was inseparable from the Amish religion. It reversed Yoder's (D) conviction, and Wisconsin (P) appealed to the U. S. Supreme Court.

ISSUE: Does the First Amendment right to free exercise of religion protect a religious way of life which, contrary to a state's compulsory education law, requires children past the eighth grade to de-

vote themselves to developing practical skills and a vocation?

HOLDING AND DECISION: Yes. The First Amendment right to free exercise of religion protects a religious way of life which requires that children past the eighth grade devote themselves to a vocation and overrides a state's compulsory education requirement that all children attend public high school. A state's interest in universal education, however important in developing civic integration and political awareness, cannot justify the severe intrusion with the basic religious tenets and practices of a sincerely held religious belief. Here, the Amish religion and culture is based on three centuries of tradition in this country, and the Amish religion and mode of life are inseparable and interdependent. Wisconsin (P) has not made the particularized showing necessary to justify the substantial intrusion on the Amish faith that its compulsory education law requires. Further, the purpose of Wisconsin's (P) law, *i.e.*, to inculcate civic virtues in its young citizens, is largely met through Amish culture, with its emphasis on self-sufficiency, community, and practical vocations. Affirmed.

COMMENT: Although the Supreme Court here appears very respectful of Amish religion, this respect almost certainly arises from the long tradition of self-sufficiency and simple values held up as the American ideal. Indeed, in one part of the opinion, the Court explicitly refers to the Amish as models of Jefferson's "sturdy yeoman" who forms the backbone of American democracy. In another part, it noted that there was in fact only "a minimal difference between what the state would require [in its compulsory education law] and what the Amish already accept." The Court, given this tradition, was ready to accept that the Amish were sincere in their beliefs and were not "creating" a religion in order to evade Wisconsin's laudable aim of universal education. However, the Court in future cases can be expected to give close scrutiny to "ways of life" also claiming to be "religions"; elsewhere it almost facetiously noted: "It cannot be overemphasized that we are not dealing with a way of life and mode of education by a group claiming to have recently discovered some 'progressive' or more enlightened process for rearing children for modern life."

MARTINEZ v. BYNUM
461 U.S. 321, 103 S. Ct. 1838 (1983).

NATURE OF CASE: Challenge under the Equal Protection Clause to the Texas residency requirement for attendance in public school.

GENERAL RULE OF LAW: In order to meet a state's residency requirement for attendance in a district's public school system, a student must physically reside in the district and intend to live there indefinitely.

PROCEDURE SUMMARY:
Plaintiff: Martinez (P), a student; his sister (P), acting as his legal custodian.
Defendant: Bynum (D), superintendent of McAllen, Texas school district.
State Trial Court Decision: Held for Bynum.
State Court of Appeals Decision: Affirmed.
U.S. Supreme Court Decision: Affirmed.

FACTS: Martinez (P) was an American citizen whose parents lived in Mexico but whose sister (P) lived in Texas. Martinez (P) went to live with his sister (P) for the sole reason of attending public school in the district in which she lived, McAllen. Martinez's (P) sister (P) did not become his legal guardian but acted merely as his custodian. Texas law required McAllen to admit Martinez (P) to its school system tuition-free only if his parent or guardian resided in the school district; because his sister (P) was not his guardian, the state attempted to charge him tuition for attendance. Martinez (P) filed suit against the school district, represented by Bynum (D), the superintendent, in Texas state court, alleging that the statute violated the Equal Protection Clause. Both the Texas trial court and court of appeal found against him, and he appealed to the United States Supreme Court.

ISSUE: In order to comply with a state's residency requirement for attendance in a district's public school system, must the student physically reside in the district and intend to live there indefinitely?

HOLDING AND DECISION: (Powell, J.) Yes. In order to meet a state's residency requirement for attendance in a particular district's public school system, a student must physically reside in the district and intend to live there indefinitely. This is called a "bona fide" residence requirement as opposed to a "durational" requirement, which requires a student to have actually resided in a district for a certain period of time before he is allowed to attend school tuition-free. Texas has a substantial state interest in ensuring that services provided for its residents are enjoyed only by its residents. If there were no residency requirements, planning and operation of the schools would suffer significantly. Here, Martinez (P) moved to the district only to attend school there; his parents remained his legal guardians, and he had no other reason for being in Texas other than to go to school. Therefore, he violated the residency statute. Affirmed.

COMMENT: A practical concern influenced the Supreme Court's decision in this case. It was plainly worried that a contrary decision would encourage an influx of illegal aliens who wanted to take advantage of cost-free public education. It served to limit the broad scope of an earlier decision, *Plyler v. Doe*, 457 U.S. 202, 102 S. Ct. 2382 (1982), in which the Supreme Court had held that illegal aliens per se could not be denied access to public education in Texas. State cases have held that school districts may investigate why a child's custodian has changed for the purpose of determining if the child's parent is trying to do an "end run" around a school district's boundary requirements. *Matter of Curry*, 113 Mich. App. 821, 318 N.W.2d 567 (1982). Furthermore, states have held that student athletic associations may deny participation to a student who appears to have changed residence merely to play for a different team. *Pennsylvania Interscholastic Athletic Ass'n v. Greater Johnstown School Dist.*, 76 Pa. Cmwlth. 65, 463 A.2d 1198 (1983).

NOTES:

BETHEL SCHOOL DISTRICT NO. 403 v. FRASER

478 U.S. 675, 106 S. Ct. 3159 (1986).

NATURE OF CASE: Challenge to suspension from school as unconstitutional under the First Amendment by a student who delivered a sexually suggestive speech.

GENERAL RULE OF LAW: A society's interest in teaching students socially acceptable behavior and in protecting minors from exposure to vulgar and offensive spoken language outweighs a student's First Amendment rights to free speech.

PROCEDURE SUMMARY:
Plaintiff: Fraser (P), a high school student.
Defendant: Bethel School District No. 403, Washington (D).
U.S. District Court Decision: Held for Fraser (P).
U.S. Court of Appeals Decision: Affirmed.
U.S. Supreme Court Decision: Reversed.

FACTS: Fraser (P) made a speech during a student assembly in which he nominated a fellow student for student government. During the speech, he made sexually suggestive comments which had the effect of inducing students in the crowd to mimic the sexual acts implied and to laugh, confusing many young students who did not understand the references. Fraser (P) had been warned by teachers who reviewed the speech that it was inappropriate in a high school setting. Fraser (P) was suspended by Bethel School District (D) for three days for giving the speech after five teachers submitted letters to the principal substantiating the event. He was also removed from the list of candidates for graduation speaker. Despite these punishments, Fraser (P) in fact attended school on the third day of his "suspension" and actually spoke at his graduation. Nonetheless, he sued Bethel (D) in federal court, alleging that his suspension had violated his free speech rights. Both the district court and the Ninth Circuit Court of Appeals agreed with him, and Bethel (D) appealed to the U.S. Supreme Court.

ISSUE: Does a society's interest in teaching students socially acceptable behavior and in protecting minors from exposure to vulgar and offensive language outweigh a student's First Amendment rights to free speech?

HOLDING AND DECISION: (Burger, C.J.) Yes. A society's interest in teaching students socially

acceptable behavior and in protecting minors from exposure to vulgar and offensive language outweighs a student's First Amendment rights to free speech. The content of Fraser's (P) speech here was not political; unlike the students in *Tinker v. Des Moines Independent Community School District*, 393 U.S. 503, 89 S. Ct. 733 (1969), who wore black arm bands to protest the Vietnam War, Fraser (P) here merely made a lewd and indecent speech which offended the sensibilities of some fellow students and which confused others too young to understand its implications. Further, Fraser (P) was not deprived of due process because the Bethel School District (D) had issued, prior to his speech, disciplinary rules governing obscene language and behavior; in addition, teachers had specifically warned Fraser (P) against giving the speech in its present form, replete with sexual innuendo. Reversed.

COMMENT: Consistent with the "original intent" trend in constitutional interpretation, Chief Justice Burger in his majority opinion explicitly relied on historical evidence that the founding fathers did not intend free speech protection for language such as that used by Fraser (P). Burger cited, for example, *The Manual of Parliamentary Practice*, drafted by Thomas Jefferson, which prohibits the use of "impertinent language." Burger, however, blithely ignored the patent irrelevance of such a reference, given that specialized and orderly rules of speaking in parliamentary debate are of necessity much more restrictive than those governing speech in the society as a whole on an everyday basis. Justice Marshall issued a stinging dissent, noting that he would have required Bethel School District (D) to actually demonstrate that Fraser's (P) speech was disruptive of the student assembly. Justice Brennan, in a concurrence (he sided with the majority because he found Fraser's (P) conduct to be actually disruptive), quoted Fraser's (P) brief address, which was actually much tamer than the majority (which omitted any quotation from it) implied. It has already been determined that the constitutional rights of students in public schools are not automatically coextensive with the rights of adults in other settings. It is important to realize that what may be a First Amendment violation in one case would not be in another. The time, place, and manner of the speech must also be considered. Note that the

12

Court's decision in *Bethel* turned on the nature of Fraser's (P) speech. Here, the speech was nonpolitical and, thus, not afforded the protections designed to protect political expression in a free society. When viewed in light of previous school cases, such as *New Jersey v. T.L.O.,* 469 U.S. 325, 105 S. Ct. 733 (1985), and later cases, such as *Hazelwood School District v. Kuhlmeier,* 484 U.S. 260, 108 S. Ct. 562 (1988), it is clear that the Court is establishing a "reasonableness" standard when dealing with public education. Part of this lower standard may be due to a concern for the difficult task that schools have in today's educational environment of drugs, violence, and family instability. *Bethel* continues the trend of applying the reasonableness standard.

NOTES:

TINKER v. DES MOINES INDEPENDENT COMMUNITY SCHOOL DISTRICT

393 U.S. 503, 89 S. Ct. 733 (1969).

NATURE OF CASE: Challenge to the constitutionality under the First Amendment of a school rule banning the wearing of black arm bands by students protesting the Vietnam War.

GENERAL RULE OF LAW: Students who engage in silent, passive, symbolic acts of pure speech do not pose a threat to substantial or material interference with school order, and their activities are protected by the First Amendment right of free speech.

PROCEDURE SUMMARY:

Plaintiffs: Tinker (P) and other public school students in Des Moines, Iowa.

Defendant: Des Moines Independent Community School District (D) (School District).

U.S. District Court Decision: Held for School District (D).

U.S. Court of Appeals Decision: Affirmed en banc.

U.S. Supreme Court Decision: Reversed.

FACTS: Tinker (P), a high school student in Des Moines, Iowa, and two other students, protested the Vietnam War by wearing black arm bands to school. The Des Moines principal, forewarned of this silent protest, had adopted a rule banning the wearing of black arm bands under penalty of suspension. Tinker (P) and the others were asked to remove the arm bands or leave school. Tinker (P) and the others decided to continue their protest and did not return to school until after the winter holiday. Tinker (P), through his father, sued the School District (D) in federal district court, alleging that the school's ban on wearing arm bands violated his free speech rights under the First Amendment. The federal court ruled against Tinker (P) on the grounds that the school rule was a reasonable way of preventing disturbance of school discipline. The Eighth Circuit Court of Appeals affirmed, and Tinker (P) appealed to the United States Supreme Court.

ISSUE: Are the activities of students who engage in silent, passive, symbolic acts of pure speech, such as wearing arm bands, protected by the First Amendment right of free speech if they do not pose a threat of substantial or material interference with school order?

HOLDING AND DECISION: (Fortas, J.) Yes.

The rights of students to speak freely are protected by the First Amendment. Speech that is largely symbolic, silent, and passive, such as the wearing of black arm bands to protest a foreign war, constitute pure speech, which is entitled to the greatest form of protection under the Constitution. This speech may only be regulated if it threatens to materially and substantially interfere with school order or discipline. Here, only a few of thousands of students wore the arm bands, and the School District (D) had only an undifferentiated fear or apprehension of disturbance — not enough to overcome the students' freedom of speech. A mere desire to avoid discomfort and unpleasantness associated with the expression of unpopular views does not warrant suppression of this fundamental right. Reversed.

COMMENT: The Court was also swayed by the fact that the school had previously allowed other "symbols" constituting pure speech, such as Iron Crosses (associated with Nazism) and buttons of particular political candidates. The School District (D) had singled out Vietnam War protestors for this one prohibition. However, not all courts have been so protective of symbolic speech when the danger of disruption was greater than here. For example, the Fifth Circuit Court of Appeals has held that symbols indicating a desire to perpetuate segregation, such as the Confederate flag, must be removed from school premises. *Smith v. St. Tammany Parish School Board*, 448 F.2d 414 (5th Cir. 1971). In a closer case, the federal district court in California has held that "vulgar retouchings" of photographs of President Nixon in a school newspaper warranted suspension of high school student editors for 10 days. *Baker v. Downey City Board of Education*, 307 F. Supp. 517 (D.Cal. 1969). Furthermore, *Tinker* has been distinguished by two more recent cases, discussed *infra, Bethel School District No. 403 v. Fraser*, 478 U.S. 675, 106 S. Ct. 3159 (1986), and *Hazelwood School District v. Kuhlmeier*, 484 U.S. 260, 108 S. Ct. 562 (1988).

GUZICK v. DREBUS
431 F.2d 594 (6th Cir. 1970)

NATURE OF CASE: Challenge under the First Amendment to a school rule prohibiting students from wearing any symbol unrelated to education.

GENERAL RULE OF LAW: A school may constitutionally adopt a policy which prohibits students from wearing items that bear a message unrelated to school activities but only if that policy applies to all types of noneducational speech without singling out any particular message and if the school has a history of disruption caused by the wearing of such items.

PROCEDURE SUMMARY:
Plaintiff: Guzick (P), a high school student.
Defendant: Drebus (D), principal of Shaw High in East Cleveland, Ohio.
U.S. District Court Decision: Held for Drebus (D).
U.S. Court of Appeals Decision: Affirmed.

FACTS: Guzick (P), a student at Shaw High School in East Cleveland, Ohio, wore a button which advertised a future demonstration in Chicago against the Vietnam War. Drebus (D), the school principal, called Guzick (P) into his office and requested that he remove the button before returning to class. Drebus (D) cited a long-standing school policy prohibiting the wearing of any items that communicated a message unrelated to school activities such as football games, plays, etc. This rule had its origin in the days when fraternities "rushed" high schools and rivalries caused fights, but during the 1960s, the rule gained new vitality as a way of forbidding "Black Power" or white supremacist messages which — in a school which had been recently integrated — were considered incendiary. Guzick (P) refused to remove his button and was indefinitely suspended. Guzick (P), through his father, filed suit in federal district court against Drebus (D) and Shaw High on First Amendment grounds. The court dismissed Guzick's (P) complaint, and he appealed.

ISSUE: May a school constitutionally adopt a policy which prohibits students from wearing items that bear messages unrelated to school activities?

HOLDING AND DECISION: (O'Sullivan. J.) Yes. A school may, consistent with the First Amendment, adopt a policy which prohibits wearing items that bear messages unrelated to school activities. However, such a policy passes constitutional muster only when it applies to all types of noneducational speech without singling out any particular message and only when the school has suffered a history of disruption caused by the wearing of such items. Here, Shaw High School has had a history of racial conflict, and the policy applies to all types of scarves, buttons, badges, and other apparel which bear any message unrelated to classroom or extracurricular activities at school. Because the button worn by Guzick (P) had no relevance to what was being considered or taught at Shaw High, it had no place in the classroom. Affirmed.

COMMENT: The court here was careful to distinguish this case from the famous case of *Tinker v. Des Moines Independent School District,* 393 U.S. 503, 89 S. Ct. 733 (1969), in which a ban against the wearing of black arm bands in protest of the Vietnam War was held to violate students' First Amendment rights. In *Tinker,* unlike here, the school had previously allowed the wearing of buttons relating to national political campaigns and had even allowed the wearing of Nazi symbols. Thus, it had an implied, if not explicit, policy of allowing clothing with messages unrelated to course content or extracurricular endeavors, and its policy against the black arm bands had a "chilling effect" of singling out a particular political message. It must be noted, however, that the court's position here that buttons such as that worn by Guzick (P) have "no relevance to what is being considered or taught" in the classroom is somewhat illogical, given that school — even at the high school level and particularly in classes such as civics or history — is aimed at promoting and developing critical thinking and discussion.

NOTES:

12

TATE v. BD. OF ED. OF JONESBORO, ARK., SPECIAL EDUCATION DISTRICT
453 F.2d 975 (8th Cir. 1972).

NATURE OF CASE: Challenge on First Amendment grounds of school suspension of students who walked out in protest over the playing of the Civil War song "Dixie" during a school pep rally.

GENERAL RULE OF LAW: School officials may enforce reasonable regulations to prevent disorderly or disruptive conduct during school sessions, even if those regulations infringe First Amendment rights of the students.

PROCEDURE SUMMARY:
Plaintiffs: Tate and others (P), parents of two suspended students.
Defendant: Jonesboro, Arkansas Special School District Board of Education (D).
U.S. District Court Decision: Held for Jonesboro Board of Education (D); dismissed complaint for lack of federal question.
U.S. Court of Appeals Decision: Affirmed.

FACTS: At Jonesboro High in Arkansas, the Civil War song "Dixie" was played during pep rallies. After some students asserted that "Dixie" was racially offensive, school officials took it off the rally program but restored it after other students and parents said they missed it and a school-wide vote came out in favor of hearing it. At the next rally after the vote, Jonesboro High officials warned the dissenting students that "Dixie" would be played and that they could attend a separate function in the school auditorium. Some dissenters elected to do so, but approximately 25 others went to the principal rally and walked out in protest when the band played "Dixie." The school suspended these students for five days but then reduced the suspension to three days and allowed them to make up schoolwork missed so that their grades would not suffer. The students rejected an opportunity to meet with the principal to discuss their conduct. Tate (P) and others, parents of two suspended students, sued the Jonesboro Board of Education (D) in federal court, alleging that their children had a First Amendment right to walk out of a rally in protest of a racially offensive song. The court dismissed the complaint, and Tate (P) appealed to the Eighth Circuit.

ISSUE: May school officials enforce reasonable regulations to prevent disorderly or disruptive conduct during school sessions, even if those regulations infringe the First Amendment rights of the students?

HOLDING AND DECISION: (Mehaffy, C.J.) Yes. School officials may enforce reasonable regulations to prevent disorderly or disruptive conduct during school sessions even if those regulations infringe the First Amendment rights of the students. In order to further the goals of education, school administrators must quell student unrest and have inherent authority to maintain order. Here, the students' walkout during the playing of "Dixie" was not symbolic action protected by the First Amendment; only "pure speech,"—"aggressive action or group demonstrations"—is protected by the First Amendment. Further, there is nothing inherently offensive or racist about the song "Dixie," given its history of use in both the North and South and its having been composed by a Northerner. Finally, Jonesboro (D) school officials accorded their suspended students due process by giving them an opportunity for an informal hearing and to make up missed schoolwork. Affirmed.

COMMENT: Paradoxically, the court here (in other sections of its opinion) praises the Jonesboro School District (D) for previous successes in integration yet ignores the segregational effect of playing "Dixie" at rallies; students who protested the rendition of "Dixie" (who were largely black) were relegated to a separate convocation in the school auditorium. Further, the court slants its lengthy and gratuitous history of the composition and performance of "Dixie" in such a way as to ignore its obvious political symbolism as the military anthem of the Confederate soldiers. The students' walkout, which was done quietly, truly then could be considered a form of political expression and was not designed to be disruptive. Although the school had tried to create other options, these options were largely unpalatable because they were reminiscent of previous "separate but equal" accommodations. Although courts often strain to reach the delicate balance between students' free speech rights and a school's interest in order and discipline, here the court's emphasis on prevention of disruption seems largely a smoke screen for a more insidious rationale.

HAZELWOOD SCHOOL DISTRICT v. KUHLMEIER
484 U.S. 260, 108 S. Ct. 562 (1988).

12

NATURE OF CASE: Review of reversal of decision holding that the deletion of certain articles from a school newspaper by the school principal was not a violation of students' First Amendment rights.

GENERAL RULE OF LAW: Official editorial control over the contents of a school-sponsored student newspaper does not violate the First Amendment, if the control is reasonably related to legitimate pedagogical concerns.

PROCEDURE HISTORY:
Plaintiff: Kuhlmeier (P), former student and student newspaper staff member.
Defendant: Hazelwood School District (D) (Hazelwood).
U.S. District Court Decision: Held for Hazelwood (D), finding no First Amendment violation.
U.S. Court of Appeals Decision: Reversed.
U.S. Supreme Court Decision: Reversed.

FACTS: A high school journalism class wrote and edited a newspaper as part of the school's curriculum. Each issue was reviewed by the school principal before publication. In one issue, the principal deleted two articles. The first article discussed the pregnancy experiences of three of the school's students, and the principal feared that the students could be identified from the article. He believed that this violated their privacy rights. He also believed that the article's references to sexual activity and birth control were inappropriate reading for the school's younger students. The second article discussed divorce and quoted a student complaining about her father's conduct. The principal believed that the article should not be published without first giving the father a chance to respond or consent to publication. Kuhlmeier (P), a student on the paper's staff, filed suit, alleging the deletion violated her First Amendment rights, requesting an injunction against further interference from the school, and for monetary damages. The district court found in favor of Hazelwood (D), holding that no First Amendment violation had occurred and that the principal's actions were reasonable. The court of appeals reversed, and the U.S. Supreme Court granted Hazelwood's (D) request for review.

ISSUE: May school officials exercise editorial control over the contents of a school-sponsored student newspaper where such control is reasonably related to legitimate pedagogical concerns?

HOLDING AND DECISION: (White, J.) Yes. School officials may exercise editorial control over the contents of a school-sponsored student newspaper for legitimate pedagogical concerns without violation of students' First Amendment rights. The First Amendment rights of students are not necessarily the same as those of adults in other settings. The school environment has special circumstances, and a school is not required to tolerate student speech inconsistent with the school's educational mission in school-sponsored activities. The school paper at issue was not a public forum but merely a part of the school curriculum under the teacher's control. There was no intent to open its pages to the indiscriminate ideas of student reporters or editors. Therefore, Hazelwood (D) was entitled to regulate the paper's contents in a reasonable manner, as the district court correctly found. Reversed.

COMMENT: *Hazelwood* gives great latitude to school officials in censoring student expression in school-sponsored activities and events. School assemblies, theatrical events, and sporting events all likely constitute school-sponsored activities within the rule of *Hazelwood*. The dissent, however, argued unsuccessfully that the stricter standard of review applied in *Tinker v. Des Moines Independent Community School District,* 393 U.S. 503, 89 S. Ct. 733 (1969), where the Court struck down a school ban on the wearing of arm bands, should be applied regardless of whether the student speech or expression at issue occurred in a school-sponsored event. Clearly, the issue of the viability of *Tinker* needs to be addressed in a future case. It can be argued that *Hazelwood* is a limited distinguishing of *Tinker,* which would apply in only a specific fact situation. A more accurate position is that *Hazelwood,* (in light of *T.L.O.,* 469 U.S. 325, 105 S. Ct. 733 (1985), and *Fraser,* 478 U.S. 675, 106 S. Ct. 3159 (1986)), has drastically modified the protections which *Tinker* guaranteed children in the school setting. A "reasonableness" standard has been applied by the Court when analyzing student freedoms. Clearly, when considering both *Fraser, supra* and *Hazelwood, supra,* it is clear that the dissent position that the rights of students are coextensive with those of adults is no longer acceptable. School newspapers are no longer "public forums" immune from attempts to regulate the viewpoints which they express. While *Tinker* has not been overturned, its doctrine — that a school should be marketplace of ideas and that the proper socialization for a free people is the early exercise of freedom — has been greatly limited in its implementation. As the dissent feared, school personnel have been less prone to hesitate before prohibiting student expressions that they previously had considered protected under the *Tinker* doctrine. Of course, when a school creates a "public forum" within their school, they still relinquish their discretion to censor student expression. In order to preserve their discretion, school personnel must clearly distinguish curricular activities from activities intended for students' expression of their views. For example, one reason in *Hazelwood* that school authorities prevailed was that the school newspaper was part of the school curriculum for which the school retained ultimate control.

NOTES:

12

EISNER v. STAMFORD BOARD
OF EDUCATION
440 F.2d 803 (2d Cir. 1971).

NATURE OF CASE: Challenge to high school policy requiring prior approval of distribution on school grounds of an independently produced student newspaper.

GENERAL RULE OF LAW: Schools do not violate the First Amendment rights of students by requiring prior approval of distribution of a student publication on school grounds, as long as the period of review is brief and the procedure for approval is clearly specified.

PROCEDURE SUMMARY:
Plaintiffs: Eisner and other Connecticut High School students (P).
Defendants: Stamford, Connecticut Board of Education (D) and Rippowam High School administrators and officials (D).
U.S. District Court Decision: Held for Eisner (P).
U.S. Court of Appeals Decision: Affirmed in part; reversed in part; and remanded.

FACTS: Connecticut high school students, including Eisner (P), mimeographed an independent newspaper which they wanted to distribute on campus. However, the school administration had adopted a policy which required prior approval of distribution, but the policy did not specify the amount of time review would take or to whom the newspaper should be submitted for review. Eisner (P) and the other students sued the Stamford Board of Education (D) and Rippowam High School officials (D) in federal court, alleging that the policy violated their free speech rights. The district court agreed with the students and issued an injunction prohibiting the high school from enforcing the policy. Stamford Board of Education (D) and the Rippowam High officials (D) appealed.

ISSUE: Do schools violate the First Amendment rights of their students by requiring prior approval of distribution of student publications on school grounds, so long as the period of review is brief and the procedure for approval is clearly specified?

HOLDING AND DECISION: (Kaufman, C.J.) No. Schools do not violate the First Amendment rights of their students by requiring prior approval of distribution on school grounds of a student publication, but they must keep the amount of time for review brief and must specify the procedure for submission. Further, schools may constitutionally prohibit distribution of material which in their judgment will interfere with the proper and orderly operation and discipline of the school or will cause violence or disorder or will constitute an invasion of the rights of others. They should, however, specify the types of disruptions and distractions and their degree, which would justify censorship. Here, the Stamford Board of Education (D) policy does not penalize the students for not obtaining prior approval; if it did, its vagueness as to the time for, and process of, review would invalidate it completely. However, it nevertheless should specify the process of submission in detail. Affirmed in part; reversed in part; and remanded.

COMMENT: It is important to distinguish between a school newspaper published as part of the school curriculum, such as a journalism class requirement, and a newspaper published without school support. The first category of publication is subject to the legitimate prior restraint of the teacher's right to set class content, whereas the second category is subject only to the constitutionally permissible restraints outlined in this case. The reason the court here required further specificity in the Stamford Board of Education (D) policy was the potential "chilling effect" an ambiguous policy would have on student speech; if students didn't know how long it would take to get their flier out to fellow students or which teacher would have final say over whether the flier got out at all, they might not exercise the initiative to prepare the flier in the first place.

NOTES:

MASSIE v. HENRY
455 F.2d 779 (4th Cir. 1972).

NATURE OF CASE: Challenge by students to a school personal grooming code.

GENERAL RULE OF LAW: The constitutional right of students under the Due Process Clause "to be secure in one's person" allows students to be free to govern their personal appearance.

PROCEDURE SUMMARY:
Plaintiff: Massie (P), a male high school student with long hair.
Defendant: Henry (D), Chairman of the Tuscola County, North Carolina School Board.
U.S. District Court Decision: Held for Henry (D).
U.S. Court of Appeals Decision: Reversed.

FACTS: A faculty-parent committee of the Tuscola County, North Carolina School Board adopted a "guideline" that students at Tuscola High be required to conform to certain hair and sideburn lengths. This "guideline" was adopted as a rule by the school principal, on grounds of school safety and prevention of disruption. The only reason given for safety was a welding instructor's opinion that sparks might catch the "hippie" students' hair on fire. The only reason given for disruption was that some short-haired students had teased or had a fist-fight with the long-haired students. Massie (P), one such long-haired student, sued Henry (D), the chairman of the school board, for invasion of his constitutional right to govern his personal appearance as guaranteed by the Due Process Clause. The federal district court dismissed Massie's (P) claim, as well as his request for an injunction preventing enforcement of the rule against long hair. Massie (P) appealed to the Fourth Circuit Court of Appeals.

ISSUE: Does the constitutional right of students under the Due Process Clause "to be secure in one's person" allow them to be free to govern their personal appearance?

HOLDING AND DECISION: (Winter, C.J.) Yes. The constitutional right of students under the Due Process Clause "to be secure in one's person" allows them the right to be free to govern their personal appearance. Although such personal freedoms are not absolute and may yield when they intrude on the freedom of others, a school, in defending rules which restrict the way a person may govern his or her appearance, must prove that they are necessary to establish discipline or to assure safety. Here, Massie (P) could have worn a hairnet or protective cap in shop to ward off errant sparks from Bunsen burners. Further, the fact that one or two long-haired students had been beaten up by one or two short-haired students does not prove that the long hair itself was the cause of the disputes. Reversed.

COMMENT: The court here discounted evidence of fights between students with differing hair lengths largely because it is illogical to punish one group of students (those with long hair) for the failure of another group (those with short hair) to exert self-control and to refrain from violence. Although cases in the First, Seventh, and Eighth Courts of Appeal reach the same decision as the Fourth here, the Fifth, Sixth, Ninth, and Tenth Circuit Courts have reached contrary results. These latter courts have focused primarily on the argument that the right to select the length of one's hair is too insubstantial to warrant federal court consideration. *E.g., Ferrell v. Dallas Independent School District,* 392 F.2d 697 (5th Cir. 1968) cert. den. 393 U.S. 856 (male students with "Beatle-type" haircuts excluded from the school). Typically, when there is such a wide gulf between the courts of appeal, the U.S. Supreme Court has granted certiorari to resolve the discrepancy, but such has as yet not been the case in these "hair length" cases.

NOTES:

GOSS v. LOPEZ
419 U.S. 565, 95 S. Ct. 729 (1975).

12

NATURE OF CASE: Challenge to suspensions on constitutional due process grounds by high school students suspended before being given an opportunity to contest their discipline.

GENERAL RULE OF LAW: The Fourteenth Amendment requirement of procedural due process mandates that students threatened with suspension from school for 10 days be given a prior opportunity to contest their suspension.

PROCEDURE SUMMARY:
Plaintiffs: Lopez (P) and eight other public school students in Columbus, Ohio.
Defendant: Goss (D), superintendent of Columbus, Ohio Public School System.
U.S. District Court Decision: Held for Lopez (D).
U.S. Supreme Court Decision: Affirmed.

FACTS: Nine high school students in Columbus, Ohio, including Lopez (P), were involved in demonstrations or lunchroom disturbances which resulted in their suspension from school for 10 days. Lopez (P) and the others were given no opportunity prior to their suspension to challenge the reasons for their discipline. Under Ohio law, principals of public schools were required only to give the parents of a student suspended for 10 days notice within 24 hours of the suspension. Only in the case of expulsion was a student, under Ohio law, given an opportunity to appeal a principal's decision to the Board of Education. Here, the parents of Lopez (P) were orally informed the day after the suspensions that their children had been disciplined. Lopez (P) sued Goss (D) and other administrators of the Columbus Public School System in federal court, alleging that the students' constitutional rights to due process were violated by having been denied an opportunity to refute the charges against them prior to their suspensions. The district court found for Lopez (P), and Goss (D) appealed to the U.S. Supreme Court.

ISSUE: Does the Fourteenth Amendment requirement of procedural due process mandate that students threatened with suspension from school for 10 days be given a prior opportunity to informally contest their suspension?

HOLDING AND DECISION: (White, J.) Yes. The Fourteenth Amendment requirement of proce-

dural due process mandates that students threatened with suspension from school for 10 days be given a prior opportunity to informally contest their suspension. Students have a property right in their education and a liberty interest in their reputation, which may not be taken away without a prior hearing. Ten days is not an insubstantial or trivial period of time to be deprived of an education, and the effect on a suspended student's reputation and chances for future education or employment should not be underestimated. However, in the case of a 10-day suspension, the student need only be given oral or written notice of the charges against him as well as an opportunity to present his side of the story. An informal hearing or give-and-take between student and disciplinarian should precede the suspension, although if a student's presence poses an immediate danger to persons or property or disrupts the academic process, no informal hearing need be held. Further, if the suspension is to exceed 10 days, or if expulsion is threatened, more formal hearings may be required. Here, Lopez (P) and the other plaintiffs were given no opportunity to rebut the charges against them before being suspended. Therefore, they are ordered reinstated, their suspensions reversed, and records of their suspensions expunged. Affirmed.

COMMENT: Education, considered one of the chief obligations a state owes its citizens, cannot be deprived without procedural due process. As this case demonstrates, a student need not be threatened with permanent deprivation of education before he is assured the right to a hearing; however, the type of hearing and its degree of formality will be based on the length of the time the student is required to be absent from school. It is important to note that the Supreme Court here established a "bright line" rule which applies only to 10-day suspensions; suspensions of shorter duration may not require a face-to-face meeting, although good sense as to what constitutes fair treatment would suggest to the principal or administrator to afford the student a talk about the proposed discipline even as to suspensions as short as one day. Each case, with its varying potential impairment, would determine "what process is due." Regardless, some procedural protection would be required unless the state action is de minimis. Many states have overreacted to the *Goss v. Lopez* decision. The Court merely requires an informal notice and hearing to satisfy due process in a short-term suspension. Some school districts have provided far more protection. Of course, as the length of the suspension increases, the more formal protections attach. With an extended suspension or expulsion, more formal legal protections should be provided, including counsel and the right to present and confront witnesses. For student suspensions of up to 10 days, the following should be provided: (1) written or oral notice of the charges; (2) if the student denies the charges, an explanation of the evidentiary basis is necessary; and (3) students must be given the opportunity to present their side of the situation. These procedures should come before the suspension, unless the student's ongoing presence in the school poses a threat. Should the student's removal be required, a notice and hearing must follow in a reasonable time period.

NOTES:

INGRAHAM v. WRIGHT
430 U.S. 651, 97 S. Ct. 1401 (1977).

NATURE OF CASE: Challenge by parents of children subjected to corporal punishment in Florida public schools to its constitutionality under the Eighth Amendment cruel and unusual punishment clause.

GENERAL RULE OF LAW: The disciplinary use of corporal punishment in public schools is not barred by the cruel and unusual punishment clause of the Eighth Amendment.

PROCEDURE SUMMARY:
Plaintiffs: Ingraham (P) and other parents of children in Dade County, Florida public school system.
Defendant: Wright (D), principal of Drew High School, Dade County.
U.S. District Court Decision: Held for Wright (D).
U.S. Court of Appeals Decision: Affirmed.
U.S. Supreme Court Decision: Affirmed.

FACTS: Children enrolled in Drew High School in Dade County, Florida were subjected to paddling or corporal punishment as a means of maintaining student discipline. In a class-action suit filed by Ingraham (P) and other parents on behalf of their children in federal district court, they alleged that the paddling violated the students' Eighth Amendment right to be free from cruel and unusual punishment and violated their due process rights. The district court found that the paddling in Dade County schools was not particularly severe and that Florida's common law actions for battery were sufficient to protect the children against excessive force. Its dismissal of Ingraham's (P) action was affirmed by the court of appeals, and Ingraham (P) appealed to the U.S. Supreme Court.

ISSUE: Is the disciplinary use of corporal punishment in public schools barred by the "cruel and unusual punishment" clause of the Eighth Amendment?

HOLDING AND DECISION: (Powell, J.) No. The Eighth Amendment's prohibition against "cruel and unusual punishment" does not apply to school paddling. The Eighth Amendment, which also prohibits excessive fines and bail, was designed to protect those charged with crimes and was intended to limit the discretion of law enforcement agencies in inflicting bodily injury. Public schools are relatively open and subject to scrutiny, and traditional common law remedies are available to those subjected to excessive force. These afford adequate protection to children who might be disciplined through paddling. Further, the risk of violation of children's substantive rights is low enough that prospective procedural safeguards are unnecessary; thus, paddling does not offend the children's due process rights. Affirmed.

COMMENT: Justice White, in a dissenting opinion, would have extended the Eighth Amendment's ban on inhumane punishment to corporal punishment. He also would have accorded children greater due process rights, such as a discussion in advance, perhaps informally, between the student and disciplinarian concerning the reasons for and against paddling. Justice White noted quite persuasively that corporal punishment, once inflicted, is final and irreparable; precautions such as an informal "hearing" are a small burden given this reality. Some states, such as Pennsylvania, found Justice White's argument convincing and limited or precluded paddling. Today's growing concern with child abuse must also be considered. In a corporal punishment situation, it is entirely likely that a child abuse charge will be filed (in those states where child abuse is not a specific crime, a specific criminal charge would be substituted). Even more likely would be an action through an area human services division which would take prompt investigatory action, regardless of the criminal nature of the activity.

NOTES:

C.J. v. SCHOOL BOARD OF BROWARD COUNTY
Fla. Ct. App., 438 So.2d 87 (1983).

NATURE OF CASE: Challenge on due process grounds by a minor's parents to the expulsion of their daughter from school for a year for bringing to school a commemorative knife given to her by her father.

GENERAL RULE OF LAW: A school rule which requires a student's expulsion must be narrowly construed.

PROCEDURE SUMMARY:
Plaintiff: C.J. (P), a 13-year-old high school student.
Defendant: School Board of Broward County, Florida (D) (School Board).
State Court of Appeals Decision: Held for C.J. (P), on direct appeal to the court.

FACTS: A 13-year-old girl, C.J. (P), received a commemorative pocket knife from her father as a present to give to the child's boyfriend. C.J. (P) had a friend who wanted to see the knife before she moved away from town, so C.J. (P) brought the knife to the bus stop. Unfortunately, the bus came before C.J. (P) could bring the knife back home. Because she did not want to miss school, she brought the knife with her. The knife was still wrapped and enclosed in a gift box. At school, C.J. (P) was then using the girls' lavatory when some of her friends were caught smoking. C.J.'s (P) purse was also checked and the knife found. Broward County's School Board (D) had promulgated a rule requiring automatic expulsion for possession of a weapon on campus. Thus, C.J. (P) was barred from returning to high school for one year. C.J. (P) appealed her expulsion by the School Board (D) directly to the Florida Court of Appeals.

ISSUE: Must a school rule which requires a student's expulsion be narrowly construed?

HOLDING AND DECISION: (Glickenstein, J.) Yes. A school rule which requires a student's expulsion must be narrowly construed. A sentence of banishment from the local educational system is an extreme penalty; therefore, school boards must dot all of their "i's" and cross all of their "t's" in enforcing such a rigid, mandatory rule. Here, the Broward County School Board (D) did not meet this high standard. First, the knife remained wrapped at school and was difficult to open; it was designed as a keepsake, not a weapon. Reversed.

COMMENT: Here, the rule promulgated by the school was not in itself unconstitutional; rather, because the sanction was severe, the court found that the rule had been unconstitutionally applied. In fact, the school board's policy is really not very controversial, given the existence on most states' law books of criminal statutes against possession of weapons. However, it remains an interesting application of the rule that often arises in cases involving searches of student lockers, *i.e.,* that due process requires analyzing both the student's reasonable expectation of "liberty" and his or her property right in a public education. When the penalty is severe, the protection provided a plaintiff/student should be heightened. Expulsion is the most severe penalty that a school board can issue. Therefore, the protection from arbitrary and unfair enforcement must be maximized. In this situation, the school policy is constitutional. The violation is in the rule's application. The narrow construing of the application of an expulsion policy is in line with protecting the rights of students, absent clear and convincing proof of a violation.

NOTES:

12

NEW JERSEY v. T.L.O.
469 U.S. 325, 105 S. Ct. 733 (1985).

NATURE OF CASE: Appeal from determination of juvenile deliquency for marijuana possession and sales by a student who argued that the search of her purse by a school official was prohibited by the Fourth Amendment.

GENERAL RULES OF LAW: (1) Where a school official conducts a search of a student's belongings, the Fourth Amendment requires only reasonable suspicion, not the higher standard of probable cause required for police searches. (2) Evidence found by a school official conducting a search of a student's belongings based on reasonable suspicion cannot be suppressed under the exclusionary rule.

PROCEDURE SUMMARY:
Plaintiff: State of New Jersey (P).
Defendant: T.L.O. (D), a high school student.
New Jersey Juvenile Court: Held for New Jersey (P), denying T.L.O.'s (D) motion to suppress evidence.
Appellate Court: Affirmed.
New Jersey Supreme Court: Reversed, sustaining T.L.O.'s (D) motion and ordering evidence suppressed.
U.S. Supreme Court: Reversed, denying T.L.O.'s (D) motion and allowing evidence admitted.

FACTS: A teacher at a New Jersey (P) high school found two girls smoking in the lavatory in violation of school rules. She brought them to the assistant vice principal's office, where one of the girls admitted to smoking in the lavatory. The other girl, T.L.O. (D), denied she had smoked, claiming that she was not a smoker. The assistant vice principal then asked her to come into his private office, where he opened her purse and found a pack of cigarettes. While reaching for the cigarettes, he noticed a package of rolling papers commonly associated with marijuana usage. He decided to search the entire purse thoroughly. His search uncovered marijuana, a pipe, plastic bags, a large number of dollar bills, and a list of people who owed T.L.O. (D) money. The matter was turned over to police. A juvenile court hearing adjudged T.L.O. (D) delinquent. T.L.O. (D) appealed on the grounds that her constitutional rights had been violated by the search of her purse. Specifically, T.L.O. (D) contended that the vice principal lacked probable cause under the Fourth Amendment to conduct the search of her purse and that the allegedly illegally seized evidence should be suppressed under the exclusionary rule. The juvenile court denied T.L.O.'s (D) motion, and the ap-

pellate division affirmed. The New Jersey Supreme Court, however, reversed and ordered the evidence suppressed. New Jersey (P) appealed, and the U.S. Supreme Court granted review.

ISSUES: (1) Is the standard for Fourth Amendment searches in cases involving school officials searching student belongings the same "probable cause" standard required for police searches? (2) Can evidence found by a school official during a search of a student's belongings based on reasonable suspicion be suppressed?

HOLDING AND DECISION: (White, J.) (1) No. Where a school official conducts a search of a student's belongings, the Fourth Amendment requires only reasonable suspicion, not the higher standard of probable cause required for police searches. The search in this case did not violate the Fourth Amendment prohibition against unreasonable search and seizure. The warrant and probable cause requirements of the Fourth Amendment for police searches would only serve to "unduly interfere with the swift and informal disciplinary procedures needed in schools." As such, a school official's search of a student depends on whether the circumstances dictating the search aroused reasonable suspicion. Reasonable suspicion for such a search can be drawn from the two-pronged inquiry presented in *Terry v. Ohio*, 392 U.S. 20. First, reasonable grounds for the search must exist at the time of the search's inception. Here, a suspicion that the search might produce evidence that T.L.O. (D) violated the law or rules of the school was reasonable under the circumstances in which she was found in the lavatory. Secondly, the scope of the search should be limited to the objectives of the search. Here, reasonable suspicion supported searching the purse for cigarettes. Then, seeing the rolling papers raised reasonable suspicion, which supported searching further for marijuana. Thus, the evidence acquired from the search was properly obtained. (2) No. Evidence found by a school official conducting a search of a student's belongings based on reasonable suspicion cannot be suppressed under the exclusionary rule. Because the search was based on reasonable suspicion, T.L.O. (D) could not obtain suppression of the seized evidence. Reversed.

COMMENT: The concurring and dissenting justices were correct when they forecast that this decision would create an extremely broad reasonableness standard for school officials under the Fourth

Amendment. Clearly, the "rolling" search — i.e., one in which reasonable suspicion arises each time new evidence is found even if unrelated to the reason for the initial search — authorized in this case is now constitutional as long as there is reasonable suspicion for the initial search. Some liberals question whether the Fourth Amendment now provides a student with any protection from an unreasonable search and seizure. At issue is whether a student who is sent to the office for a minor offense can be subjected to an extensive and invasive search based on a reasonableness analysis.

NOTES:

12

TRACHTMAN v. ANKER
563 F.2d 512 (2d Cir. 1977);
cert. denied, 435 U.S. 925, 98 S. Ct. 1491 (1978).

12

NATURE OF CASE: Challenge by a student editor of a school newspaper of the constitutionality of his high school's prohibition of his distribution of a confidential and random questionnaire inquiring into the sexual behavior and attitudes of fellow students.

GENERAL RULE OF LAW: School officials may prohibit student speech without violating the First Amendment if they have reasonable cause to believe the speech will result in significant psychological harm to some of the school's students.

PROCEDURE SUMMARY:
Plaintiffs: Trachtman (P), a high school senior and editor of the school newspaper, and his father (P), a child psychologist.
Defendant: Anker (D), chancellor of New York City Public Schools.
U.S. District Court Decision: Held for Trachtman (P).
U.S. Court of Appeals Decision: Reversed.

FACTS: Trachtman (P) was a senior at Stuyvesant High in Manhattan and editor of the Stuyvesant High school newspaper. His father was a child psychologist at New York University. Together they prepared a questionnaire to be distributed randomly among Stuyvesant students and to be answered confidentially. This questionnaire delved into the sexual knowledge, behavior, and attitudes of Stuyvesant students and addressed such issues as premarital sex, masturbation, and homosexuality. The results would be published in the school newspaper. Stuyvesant's principal prohibited distribution of the questionnaire because he reasonably believed some students would suffer psychological harm from filling it out. The Trachtmans (P) sued the school and school district, represented by Anker (D), the chancellor, in federal court, alleging that the ban infringed Trachtman's (P) First Amendment rights. The district court held that distribution could constitutionally be denied only if the school could prove a strong possibility of psychological harm; it further held that such harm had been proved with regard to 13- and 14-year-olds, but not with regard to older children. Therefore, the questionnaire could be distributed to juniors and seniors, as long as support counseling was available. Both Trachtman (P) and Anker (D) appealed.

ISSUE: May school officials prohibit student speech without violating the First Amendment if they have reasonable cause to believe the speech will result in significant psychological harm to some of the school's students?

HOLDING AND DECISION: (Lumbard, C.J.) Yes. School officials may prohibit student speech without violating the First Amendment if they have reasonable cause to believe that the speech will result in significant psychological harm to some of the school's students. Such authorities are sufficiently experienced and knowledgeable about these matters, which have been entrusted to them by the community, and although they bear the burden for showing a rational basis for decisions to prohibit otherwise protected speech, they do not have to wait until actual harm occurs before prohibiting potentially harmful speech. Here, students in all grades might be psychologically unprepared for the sensitive issues Trachtman's (P) questionnaire raises, and Stuyvesant officials acted reasonably in preventing its distribution. Reversed.

COMMENT: Some schools have addressed the problem raised in this case by establishing Human Subjects Review committees. Outside (or internal) researchers who desire to test, evaluate, or question students must clear their research proposals with the committee, which consists of a panel of educators and psychologists who have studied the effects of particular types of information on adolescents. However, it should be noted that this case promoted a strong dissent from Circuit Judge Mansfield, who noted that the questionnaire had not been shown to raise a danger of disruption — the traditional type of "substantive evil" which had justified a prior restraint on speech. He also persuasively observed that students at Stuyvesant were just as likely to be disturbed by the publication of sexually oriented surveys in newspapers of wide circulation, such as the *New York Times*, the distribution of which Stuyvesant High officials had no control over. It should also be noted that at trial in the federal district court, even Trachtman's (P) father, the child psychologist at NYU who was also a coplaintiff with his son, conceded that there was some possibility of psychological harm to Stuyvesant students from distribution of the survey.

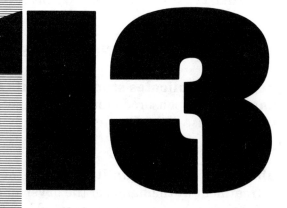

SCHOOL DESEGREGATION

▶ **CHAPTER SUMMARY**

CHAPTER 13: SCHOOL DESEGREGATION

QUICK REFERENCE RULES OF LAW

13

1. **Segregation implicates students' rights to equal protection of the laws:** State-sponsored group discrimination implicates the Equal Protection Clause of the Fourteenth Amendment to the U.S. Constitution. (§ I.A.)

2. **No absolute right to equality:** There is no absolute right to equality of treatment at the hands of the government. In most cases, only classifications which are not supported by sound governmental purposes are forbidden. (§ I.A.2.)

3. **Laws affecting race are strictly scrutinized:** However, under the "strict scrutiny" test, courts will invalidate all race-based classifications unless they support a compelling governmental interest and are instituted in the least restrictive manner possible. (§ I.A.3.)

4. **"De jure" defined:** Segregation that results from classifications that have been instituted or permitted by state law is termed *de jure* segregation. (§ II.A.)

5. **Races treated separately but equally:** At one time, state-sponsored racial segregation was permissible under the "separate but equal" doctrine. (§ II.B.)

6. **U.S. Supreme Court strikes down segregation:** In the landmark *Brown v. Board of Education,* 347 U.S. 483, 74 S. Ct. 686 (1954), decision, the U.S. Supreme Court declared that racially segregated school were "inherently unequal" and therefore unconstitutional. (§ II.C.)

7. **Role of the courts in implementing desegregation:** After the *Brown* decision and its progeny, federal courts were faced with the twofold task of (1) determining whether official action or inaction had created segregated schools and (2) fashioning an appropriate remedy that would lead to a unitary school system. (§ II.C.4.)

8. **Criteria for identifying unlawful desegregation:** The existence of state-imposed segregation can be determined by looking to the quality of buildings and equipment, construction or abandonment of buildings, the racial composition of teachers and staff, the quality and extent of activities offered. (§ II.C.4.c.)

9. **Court-imposed remedies for segregation:** Acceptable remedies for state-imposed segregation include the redrawing of attendance zones, the reassignment of teachers, use of racial quotas, and busing. (§ II.C.4.c.)

10. **School districts have affirmative duty:** At present, where unlawful segregation exists, school districts have an affirmative duty to take steps to get rid of it. (§ II.C.4.b.)

11. **"De facto" defined:** Segregation that results "naturally," *i.e.*, not by reason of official action, is termed *de facto* segregation. (§ III.A.1.)

12. **No obligation to correct:** A school district has no obligation to correct common forms of de facto segregation, such as that brought on by the uniform application of local zoning ordinances. (§ III.B.2.)

13. **Power to correct:** In most cases, school officials are empowered to eradicate de facto segregation if they so choose. (§ III.B.3.)

14. **Race-based teacher assignments unconstitutional:** The assignment of teachers based on race violates the equal educational opportunities of students and is therefore unconstitutional. (§ IV.A.1.)

15. **Goal of teacher desegregation:** The U.S. Supreme Court has affirmed desegregation plans which seek to achieve the same ratio of black and white teachers within a particular school as exists in the district as a whole. (§ IV.A.2.)

16. **Multidistrict remedies inappropriate:** Multidistrict remedies, which occur when more than one school district is involved in remediating a constitutional violation, are not proper where *de jure* segregation is found in only one district, and where there is no finding that the other districts failed to operate unitary school systems. (§ III.C.)

NOTES:

Introduction: There is perhaps no other area of education law in which the federal courts, and particularly the United States Supreme Court, have been as active in dictating policy and prompting change as that of desegregation. The law of desegregation concerns itself with rectifying discriminatory practices or results that have violated the equal educational opportunity rights of minority students. The legal basis for desegregation lies in the U.S. Constitution's Equal Protection Clause.

CONSTITUTIONAL AND STATUTORY UNDERPINNINGS

I. CONSTITUTIONAL AND STATUTORY UNDERPINNINGS

A. U.S. Constitutional Right Implicated by Segregation

1. *Equal Protection Clause:* The primary constitutional safeguard against state-sponsored group discrimination lies in the Equal Protection Clause of the Fourteenth Amendment to the United States Constitution.

2. *Limitation on the equal protection guarantee:* The Equal Protection Clause does not guarantee absolute equality of treatment. Rather, it protects individuals from adverse treatment that cannot be justified by a sound governmental purpose.

3. *Three constitutional standards:* The U.S. Supreme Court has enunciated three different standards for determining which group classifications are justified and which are not.

   a. *"Rationality" test:* Under this standard, laws promoting classifications which do not infringe *fundamental rights* or adversely affect *protected minorities* will be upheld if they serve *reasonable governmental purposes* and use reasonable means to achieve those purposes. If such is the case, incidental adverse effects on groups of individuals are permissible.

   b. *"Intermediate scrutiny" test:* Under this standard, laws promoting classifications that discriminate based on *gender* will be upheld so long as they serve *important governmental objectives* and are substantially related to those objectives.

   c. *"Strict scrutiny" test:* Under this standard, laws promoting classifications based on *race* or infringing *fundamental rights* are deemed *suspect classifications*. Such classifications are presumed to be unconstitutional and will be invalidated unless the government is able to prove that the classifications serve *compelling governmental interests* and employ the least offensive means of carrying out those interests. The government rarely meets its burden under this test.

B. Statutory Remedies for Discrimination

1. *The need for statutory protections:* The Fourteenth Amendment implicates official, *i.e.,* state-sponsored, discrimination only. Only state and federal legislation can outlaw private discrimination. Furthermore, there is no right to sue for monetary damages under the U.S. Constitution. The right to sue for damages based on unconstitutional discrimination must therefore be provided by statute.

2. *Civil rights statutes:* Federal and state civil rights statutes have been enacted to provide stronger legal remedies to discrimination.

II. CHALLENGES TO STATE-FOSTERED (DE JURE) SCHOOL SEGREGATION

CHALLENGES TO STATE-FOSTERED (DE JURE) SCHOOL SEGREGATION

A. De Jure Segregation

1. *De jure defined:* Segregation that results from classifications instituted or permitted by state law is termed *de jure* segregation and is unconstitutional. However, this was not always the case. *See* II.B., below.

2. *Elements of de jure segregation:* De jure segregation exists only if the following elements are present:

   a. *Government action:* The segregation in question must have been instituted or supported by the state;

   b. *Intent to discriminate:* The segregation must have been instituted with an actual intent or motive to discriminate; and

   c. *Net increase in segregation:* The net effect must be the creation of segregation or an increase in segregation that already exists.

B. "Separate but Equal" — The Law prior to the U.S. Supreme Court's Landmark *Brown v. Board of Education* Decision

1. *Racial integration not constitutionally mandated:* In *Plessy v. Ferguson,* 163 U.S. 537, 16 S. Ct. 1138 (1896), the U.S. Supreme Court interpreted the Equal Protection Clause as permitting state-sponsored racial segregation by holding that the U.S. Constitution did not require racial integration so long as blacks and whites were treated equally.

2. **"Separate but equal" in the public schools:** The Court subsequently extended the "separate but equal" doctrine to the public schools in *Gong Lum v. Rice,* 275 U.S. 78, 48 S. Ct. 91 (1927).

C. **Brown v. Board of Education and the End of the "Separate but Equal" Doctrine.**

1. *Inherent inequality:* In *Brown v. Board of Educ. of Topeka (Brown I), supra,* the U.S. Supreme Court held that racially segregated schools were "inherently unequal," thereby repudiating its "separate but equal" interpretation of the Equal Protection Clause.

2. *Implementation of* **Brown I** *holding:* A year later, the Supreme Court decided *Brown v. Board of Educ. of Topeka (Brown II),* 349 U.S. 294, 75 S. Ct. 753 (1955), in which it declared that segregated, dual school districts must be converted to integrated, unitary districts with "all deliberate speed."

3. *Implications of* **Brown I** *and* **Brown II:** In attempting to adhere to the mandates of *Brown I and Brown II,* lower federal courts have faced a dual task — that of determining whether official action or inaction has created or perpetuated unlawful segregation in violation of the Equal Protection Clause and, if a violation is established, that of fashioning an appropriate remedy.

4. *Aftermath of* **Brown I** *and* **Brown II:** Because the *Brown* decisions neglected to set forth its view as to the specific conditions that contributed to the unconstitutional segregation of students, lower courts were at a loss when it came to fashioning segregation remedies. Some courts held that their constitutional obligations were satisfied so long as remedies were provided which removed all barriers to integration, i.e., so long as the state remained "neutral" to integration.

a. *Slow pace of desegregation:* Because *Brown II* had not set a specific deadline for the implementation of the *Brown I* mandate, the pace of desegregation dragged on in the decade that followed. In 1964, the Court declared that the time for "deliberate speed" had run out — a clear indication that vindication of the constitutional rights of schoolchildren was long overdue. *Griffin v. County School Bd. of Prince Edward County,* 377 U.S. 218, 84 S. Ct. 1226 (1964).

b. *"Deliberate speed" not speedy enough:* Finally, in 1969, the Court completely discarded its "all deliberate speed" criterion for evaluating school desegregation, deciding instead that "the obligation of every school district is to terminate dual school systems at once and to operate now and hereafter only unitary schools." *Alexander v. Holmes County Bd. of Educ.*, 396 U.S. 19, 90 S. Ct. 29 (1969). Mere state neutrality toward integration was no longer acceptable. After the *Alexander* decision, many lower courts issued orders requiring that school districts take *affirmative action* with regard to the slow pace of school desegregation.

c. *Characteristics and remedial actions to be taken:* In the landmark case of *Swann v. Charlotte-Mecklenburg Bd. of Educ.*, 402 U.S. 1, 91 S. Ct. 1267 (1971), the U.S. Supreme Court for the first time identified the characteristics of a segregated school system and some of the steps that may be required to bring about a unitary system.

(1) The existence of state-imposed segregation can be determined by looking to the quality of buildings and equipment, construction or abandonment of buildings, the racial composition of teachers and staff, the quality and extent of activities offered, and the like.

(2) Acceptable remedies for state-imposed segregation include the redrawing of attendance zones, the reassignment of teachers, use of racial quotas (even though it is not a requirement that every school in a district reflect the racial composition of the district as a whole), and, in some circumstances, busing.

d. *Continuation of constitutional oversight:* In *Swann*, the Court also discussed the continuing role of the federal courts in correcting de jure violations. It concluded that "[n]o fixed . . . guidelines can be established as to how far a court can go, but it must be recognized there are limits." A host of considerations must be taken into account in identifying and remedying unconstitutional segregation, including demographics, financial resources, geographical considerations, and student welfare.

III. CHALLENGES TO NONPURPOSEFUL (DE FACTO) SCHOOL SEGREGATION

CHALLENGES TO NONPURPOSEFUL (DE FACTO) SCHOOL SEGREGATION

A. De Facto Segregation

1. *De facto defined:* Segregation that results "naturally," *i.e.,* not as a result of official action intended to bring it about, is de facto segregation. True de facto segregation is not unconstitutional.

13

2. ***Characteristics of de facto segregation:*** De facto segregation looks similar to de jure segregation; in a common example, it is characterized by a school that is populated by a large majority of students who are of a racial minority.

B. **Case Law pertaining to De Facto Segregation**

1. ***Discriminatory motive signals de jure, not de facto, segregation:*** In 1973, the Supreme Court considered for the first time allegations of unconstitutional desegregation within a school district outside of the South. Because the City of Denver had no statutory dual system to begin with, the Court concluded that to prevail, the plaintiffs would have to prove both the existence of segregation and that the segregation was a product of "intentional state action," *i.e.*, was maintained with a discriminatory motive. *See Keyes v. School District No. 1*, 413 U.S. 189, 93 S. Ct. 2686 (1973). Without an underlying discriminatory motive, what might appear to be unconstitutional, de jure segregation is actually permissible de facto segregation.

2. ***No obligation to correct de facto segregation:*** Most federal courts which have passed on the issue of a school district's obligation to correct common forms of de facto segregation, such as that brought on by a uniform application of local zoning ordinances, have concluded that no such obligation exists.

3. ***Eradication of de facto segregation permissible:*** While no obligation to correct de facto segregation exists, school officials are empowered to make corrections if they so choose. Legal challenges may arise from those who consider such remedial measures inappropriate under the notion of a "color-blind" Constitution (insofar as they are clearly based on race yet are not constitutionally required). Such challenges rarely prevail.

4. ***Attempts to prevent the eradication of de facto segregation:*** In the past, some state legislatures have attempted to thwart the voluntary efforts of local boards to prevent de facto segregation. Federal courts will generally not permit such actions if they interfere with lawful plans designed to protect the constitutional rights of students.

C. **Multidistrict Remedies:**

1. ***Multidistrict remedy needed:*** Multidistrict remedies are often proposed where a single-district remedy is inadequate to accomplish desegregation.

2. ***Landmark Opinion:*** *Milliken v. Bradley*, 418 U.S. 717 (1974), established case law regarding multidistrict remedies. In the

lower courts, the federal district court had held that Detroit was segregated on the basis of de jure racial policies and practices. The district court concluded that a multidistrict plan for remedying racial violations was proper.

a. *The issue considered:* The question which the Supreme Court sought to answer was whether a multidistrict remedy was proper where de jure segregation was found in only one district, and where there was no finding that the other districts failed to operate unitary school systems.

b. *Present court position:* Based on the *Milliken* decision, a multidistrict remedy is only possible where de jure segregation is found in each and every school district involved in the remedy. Clearly, there is a nexus between intentional acts of segregation and the existence of segregation. Further, the extent of the remedy should be limited by the extent of the de jure violations proven, i.e., the more violations, the greater the potential scope of the remedy. *See Milliken v. Bradley, supra; see also Dayton Board of Education v. Brinkman,* 433 U.S. 406 (1977).

IV. DESEGREGATION OF TEACHERS

A. **Faculty Integration Designed to Protect Students' Constitutional Rights**

1. *Purpose behind desegregation of teachers:* Because the assignment of teachers based on race violates the *equal educational opportunities* of students, it is an appropriate subject for court-ordered desegregation plans.

2. *History of teacher desegregation:* In *Bradley v. School Bd. of the City of Richmond,* 382 U.S. 103, 86 S. Ct. 224 (1965), the U.S. Supreme Court first passed on the issue of teacher desegregation, noting that race-based faculty assignments affected students' rights. In *United States v. Montgomery County Bd. of Educ.,* 395 U.S. 225, 89 S. Ct. 1670 (1969), and later in *Swann, supra (see* I.C.4.c., above), the Court affirmed desegregation plans which sought to achieve the same ratio of black and white teachers within a particular school as existed in the district as a whole.

3. *Reduction in teaching force brought on by district-wide school desegregation plans:* In some school districts, the consolidation of dual systems into unitary systems pursuant to court-imposed desegregation plans has resulted in a reduction of teaching personnel. In the leading case of *Singleton v. Jackson Municipal Separate School Dist.,* 419 F.2d 1211 (5th Cir. 1970),

cert. den. 396 U.S. 1032, 90 S. Ct. 612 (1970), the U.S. Court of Appeals for the Fifth Circuit set forth staff reduction criteria in order to prevent black teachers from bearing a greater burden under these consolidation efforts than their white counterparts:

a. *Elimination of the race factor:* Hirings, firings, promotions, demotions, and assignments may not be made on the basis of race; and

b. *Development of objective standards:* Reductions in teaching staff must be based on objective criteria that were developed by the local school board prior to the institution of any reductions.

Note: The *Singleton* criteria apply only to those districts that have not attained unitary status. Since most districts are no longer segregated, the *Singleton* criteria are rarely relied on in connection with staff reduction lawsuits.

c. *Impairment of seniority rights:* Lower courts have held that even teacher seniority rights may be impaired. Of course, when a district court limits statutory or contractual rights of teachers, it must do so narrowly. *See Arthur v. Nyquist,* 712 F.2d 816 (2nd Cir. 1983).

B. The Effect of Faculty Integration on Teachers' Rights

1. *Conflict with efforts to vindicate students' rights:* In some cases, efforts to achieve racially balanced teaching staffs (pursuant to desegregation order aimed at vindicating students' rights) have violated the rights of teachers.

2. *Minority hiring and promotional preferences aimed at achieving desegregation goals:* Recent lawsuits have focused on the rights of teachers who have suffered in the wake of hiring and promotional preferences aimed at achieving racially balanced teaching staffs. Such preferences have been upheld when their use has contributed to the elimination of unconstitutional school segregation.

3. *Minority protection from layoffs in connection with consolidations:* Still other recent lawsuits have focused on the seniority rights of nonminority teachers who have been laid off in order to protect minority teachers (and thereby achieve racial balance).

a. *Permissible in most cases so long as segregation still in place:* Some courts have upheld race-based preferences in the laying off of teachers where the districts in question had not attained unitary status.

b. *Not permissible where no desegregation plan in effect:* In *Wygant v. Jackson Bd. of Educ.*, 476 U.S. 267, 106 S. Ct. 1842 (1986), the U.S. Supreme Court struck down a school board's attempt to protect its minority teachers from layoffs under these circumstances insofar as the district in question was not operating under a court-ordered desegregation plan.

V. RECENT COURT ACTIVITY

A. Cost of Desegregation Remedy

1. *Educational programs:* A federal district court may require a state to bear the cost of educating students who have been subject to past acts of de jure segregation. *See Milliken v. Bradley,* 433 U.S. 267 (1977) (Milliken II).

2. *Ordering a tax increase to fund desegregation costs:* In the Kansas City (Missouri) School District, tax levies aimed at supporting the court-imposed desegregation plan were consistently voted down. The federal district court ordered a property tax increase. The Supreme Court held that a federal district court may not order a tax levy to fund (in part) a desegregation plan. This was an abuse of discretion and violative of principles of federal-state comity. Nevertheless, the district court may require that the levy be increased to an amount adequate to fund the school district's portion of the plan—but it may not itself increase the levy. *See Missouri v. Jenkins,* 495 U.S. 33 (1990).

3. *Continuing duty to eradicate effects of segregation:* A school board has a continuing duty to eradicate the effects of segregation brought about by its former operation of dual systems. Thus, a school board must do more than abandon past discriminatory acts; it must actively insure that the negative effects of its past policies are not perpetuated. *See Dayton Board of Education v. Brinkman,* 443 U.S. 526 (1979) *(Brinkman II). Also see Columbus Board of Education v. Penick,* 443 U.S. 449 (1979).

4. *State removal of decision-making power over racial issue:* A state may not abrogate a local district's decision-making power in connection with an issue that is racial in nature. Thus, a local district that wishes to provide more extensive equal protection guarantees may do so without fear of a state initiative removing that guarantee. *See Washington v. Seattle School District No. 1,* 458 U.S. 457 (1982).

5. *District Court relinquishing control incrementally:* In the course of supervising a desegregation plan, a district court has the authority to relinquish supervision and control of a school

district in incremental stages, before full compliance has been achieved. *See Freeman v. Pitts,* 503 U.S. ____ (1992).

13

NOTES:

BROWN v. BOARD OF EDUCATION OF TOPEKA (BROWN I)
347 U.S. 483, 74 S. Ct. 686 (1954).

NATURE OF CASE: Review of decision denying black students admission to public schools on a nonsegregated basis.

GENERAL RULE OF LAW: Segregated public school systems are a violation of the Equal Protection Clause of the Fourteenth Amendment.

PROCEDURE SUMMARY:
Plaintiff: Brown (P), a black student.
Defendant: Board of Education of Topeka (D) (Board).
U.S. District Court Decision: Held for Board (D), finding separate but equal school systems permissible.
U.S. Court of Appeals Decision: Reversed.
U.S. Supreme Court Decision: Affirmed.

FACTS: The Board (D) operated 22 elementary schools, 18 for white students and 4 for black students. The schools were operated under the separate but equal doctrine, announced by the Supreme Court in *Plessy v. Ferguson*, 163 U.S. 537, 16 S. Ct. 1138 (1896). Brown (P), a black student, filed suit, claiming that the schools were not equal but that the minority schools were inferior to the white schools in physical facilities, curricula, teaching resources, and student personal services, among other items. Brown (P) argued that this segregation, along with its accompanying inequalities, violated the Equal Protection Clause of the Fourteenth Amendment. The district court, relying on *Plessy*, where the Supreme Court declared separate but equal school systems permissible, found the facilities comparable and not in violation of the Constitution. The court of appeals reversed, and the U.S. Supreme Court granted review.

ISSUE: Does the operation of segregated schools by a school system violate the Equal Protection Clause of the Fourteenth Amendment of the Constitution?

HOLDING AND DECISION: (Warren, C.J.) Yes. Segregated school systems are a violation of the Equal Protection Clause of the Fourteenth Amendment. Even where all-minority and all-white schools are equal with respect to tangible factors such as facilities and curricula, there are intangible factors which prevent children in all-minority schools from truly receiving an equal education. Separating them from others of similar age and qualifications solely because of their race generates a feeling of inferiority in minority students. Thus, separate facilities are inherently unequal. Affirmed.

COMMENT: *Brown* unanimously overruled the separate but equal doctrine announced in *Plessy* by alluding to the intangibles which minority students are denied by attending all-segregated schools. However, the Court did little to define what these intangibles are and based its finding of inherent inequality principally upon social science and empirical evidence, for which it has been criticized. But despite the criticism, *Brown* is important in that it set forth the mandate for integrated public education by adopting the argument put forth by the first Justice Harlan in his eloquent dissent in *Plessy*. *Brown* was actually a consolidation decision involving four other cases, three from different states challenging the separate but equal doctrine and the other from the District of Columbia, where the Fourteenth Amendment argument did not apply (D.C. is not a state), and a Fifth Amendment due process challenge was posited. The reason for accepting five cases was so that the Supreme Court's decision could not be questioned on technical grounds — all types of separate but equal school applications were analyzed. In addition to being the most important court case in education law, *Brown* also had another impact, in that it opened the door to public scrutiny and challenge of public education. Since 1954, legal challenges have been raised in almost every conceivable educational area, including discipline, gender equity, finance, teacher rights, etc. This public scrutiny has been persistent and will continue.

NOTES:

BROWN v. BOARD OF EDUCATION
OF TOPEKA (BROWN II)
349 U.S. 294, 75 S. Ct. 753 (1955).

NATURE OF CASE: Reargument to determine proper relief after Court held segregated public schools unconstitutional.

GENERAL RULE OF LAW: The district courts are to enter such orders as are necessary and proper to admit black students to public schools on a racially nondiscriminatory basis with all deliberate speed.

PROCEDURE SUMMARY:
Plaintiff: Brown (P), a black student.
Defendant: Board of Education of Topeka (D) (Board).
U.S. Supreme Court Decision: Ordered admittance of blacks to public schools on racially nondiscriminatory basis with all deliberate speed.

FACTS: In 1954, the Court held in *Brown I* that maintaining segregated schools was inherently unequal and violated the Equal Protection Clause of the Fourteenth Amendment. After its decision in *Brown I*, the Court requested further argument on the question of relief, *viz.*, to correct the constitutional violations found in *Brown I*.

ISSUE: Is the proper relief for the desegregation of public schools the decree of such orders as are necessary and proper to admit black students to public schools on a racially nondiscriminatory basis with all deliberate speed?

HOLDING AND DECISION: (Warren, C.J.) Yes. The district courts are ordered to enter such decrees as are necessary and proper to admit black students to public schools on a racially nondiscriminatory basis with all deliberate speed. In fashioning such decrees, the courts are to be guided by equitable principles, which will allow them flexibility and the ability to fully consider both public and private needs. Nevertheless, the school authorities have the primary responsibility for solving these problems and implementing the desegregation mandate of *Brown I*. So ordered.

COMMENT: The ordering of the desegregation of public schools with all deliberate speed was a break from the usual rule that individuals whose rights are violated by state action are entitled to immediate relief. In departing from this rule, it seems the Court not only was concerned with the threat that mandatory immediate desegregation would lead to violence but was cognizant of the difficulty of fashioning a single decree or plan to deal with the multitude of complexities and issues to be faced by local school districts in their efforts to desegregate. In some respects this was an accurate prediction, as there was initial opposition and even some violence, associated with the implementation of remedial orders. Nevertheless, the common pattern was that local districts tended to avoid attempts to implement desegregation plans. The definition of "with all deliberate speed" was simply unworkable from the perspective of correcting constitutional violations in the volatile environment of public school systems. It was not until *Alexander v. Holmes County Board of Education*, 396 U.S. 19, 90 S. Ct. 29 (1969), that the Court finally ordered immediate action, stating that after 15 years since the *Brown I* decision, further delays would not be tolerated.

NOTES:

13

SWANN v. CHARLOTTE-MECKLENBURG BOARD OF EDUCATION
402 U.S. 1, 91 S. Ct. 1267 (1971).

NATURE OF CASE: Review of order vacating a desegregation plan requiring the pairing and grouping of elementary schools, which was challenged as placing an unreasonable burden on the school board and students.

GENERAL RULE OF LAW: The district courts have power to fashion remedies eliminating public school segregation where school authorities fail to fashion such remedies themselves.

PROCEDURE SUMMARY:
Plaintiff: Swann (P), a black student.
Defendant: Charlotte-Mecklenburg Board of Education (D) (Board).
U.S. District Court Decision: Ordered the adoption of a plan which paired and grouped elementary schools.
U.S. Court of Appeals Decision: Vacated.
U.S. Supreme Court Decision: Reinstated district court order.

FACTS: The Board (D) operated a school system with over 84,000 students. Approximately 24,000 of these students were black, of whom 14,000 attended schools which were 99% black. Swann (P), a black student, brought suit for relief requiring the Board (D) to produce a plan to take further steps to eliminate state-imposed segregation from its public school system. The district court ordered the Board (D) to provide a desegregation plan for elementary schools. The court found the plan submitted by the Board (D) unsatisfactory and appointed an expert to provide such a plan. The court ordered adoption of the expert's plan, but the court of appeals vacated the order, fearing that the plan's pairing and grouping of elementary schools unreasonably burdened the Board (D) and pupils. The U.S. Supreme Court granted review.

ISSUE: May district courts fashion remedies eliminating public school segregation, where the school authorities fail to fashion such remedies themselves?

HOLDING AND DECISION: (Burger, C.J.) Yes. District courts may fashion remedies eliminating public school segregation, where the school authorities fail to fashion such remedies themselves. Such power is fully consistent with this Court's mandate in *Brown v. Board of Education,* 347 U.S.

483, 74 S. Ct. 686 (1954), where state-imposed segregation in the public schools was found constitutionally impermissible, and district courts were ordered to use their equitable powers in decreeing its elimination. Furthermore, Title IV of the Civil Rights Act of 1964 does not restrict or abridge these powers but was merely designed to ensure that it was not interpreted as expanding these equitable powers. The district court order was correct. Order of the district court reinstated.

COMMENT: Apart from instructing district courts on the extent of their powers to fashion remedies, *Swann* also set forth the test for when remedial action is warranted: school boards may not be ordered to adjust the racial composition of any school unless there has been a finding that there was intentional, or de jure, segregation, as opposed to de facto segregation. *Swann* further indicated what were permissible means of implementing a desegregation plan, including busing, rezoning of attendance zones, and limited use of racial quotas. However, it should be noted that *Swann* does not require that each and every school meet a specific racial balance. In fact, a school of one race can be accepted as part of a comprehensive desegregation plan, but the court will carefully scrutinize the rationale for including a single-race school.

NOTES:

KEYES v. SCHOOL DISTRICT NO. 1, DENVER, COLORADO
413 U.S. 189, 93 S. Ct. 2686 (1973).

13

NATURE OF CASE: Review of reversal of decision holding that a district need not desegregate certain segregated schools because it was not shown to be the result of intentional segregation by the district.

GENERAL RULE OF LAW: Where a policy of intentional segregation has been proved with respect to a significant portion of the school system, the burden is on school authorities to prove that segregation in other portions of the system is not also the result of such an intent.

PROCEDURE SUMMARY:
Plaintiff: Keyes (P), parent of a student.
Defendant: School District No. 1, Denver, Colorado (D) (District).
U.S. District Court Decision: Held for District (D), that it need not desegregate certain segregated schools but merely provide equal facilities.
U.S. Court of Appeals Decision: Affirmed in part; reversed in part.
U.S. Supreme Court Decision: Reversed and remanded.

FACTS: Keyes (P), parent of a student, filed suit, seeking the desegregation of Park Hill area schools in Denver. After the district court granted Keyes (P) relief as to those schools, Keyes (P) expanded the suit to include the remaining schools within the District (D). The district court denied relief as to the remaining District (D) schools, holding that proof of segregation policy as to the Park Hill schools did not constitute proof of such a policy as to other schools within the District (D) and that Keyes (P) would have to prove de jure segregation for each additional Denver school area. The court then held that since there was no proof of such an intentional segregative policy, the District (D) need not desegregate the schools but merely provide equal facilities. The court of appeals reversed the portion of the order mandating the provision of equal facilities but affirmed that the proof offered of intentional segregation as to the Park Hill schools was insufficient to grant relief as to the remaining schools. The U.S. Supreme Court granted review.

ISSUE: Where a policy of intentional segregation has been proved with respect to a significant portion of a school system, do school authorities have the burden of proving that segregation in other portions of the system is not also the result of such a policy?

HOLDING AND DECISION: (Brennan, J.) Yes. Where a policy of intentional segregation has been proved with respect to a significant portion of a school system, school authorities have the burden of proving that segregation in other portions of the system is not also the result of such a policy. Proof that school authorities have pursued an intentional policy of segregation in a substantial portion of the school district will, without more, support a trial court's finding of a dual system. The lower court's rulings were incorrect because Keyes (P) did not have to prove that de jure segregation occurred in every school, merely that it occurred in a substantial portion of the schools. Remanded to determine sufficiency of proof.

COMMENT: *Keyes* reaffirms that relief may only be granted for de jure, or intentional, segregation. However, it amends this rule by adding that a finding of de jure action in one part of a school district can create a prima facie case of such action in the entire district. This shifted an important burden of proof to the school boards, forcing them to show that the part of the district found to be intentionally segregated should be viewed as separate and unrelated to the other parts of the district to rebut this prima facie case. Also, *Keyes* held that Hispanics should be considered with blacks in such desegregation actions because both suffered from the same educational inequalities relative to white students. The proper handling of Hispanic children as part of a comprehensive desegregation plan has caused some concern. Each U.S. District Court has adopted its own policy regarding the legal status of Hispanics and other minority children. Classification of Hispanics as either black or white can have a tremendous impact on their involvement in the student transportation plan.

NOTES:

MILLIKEN v. BRADLEY (MILLIKEN I)
418 U.S. 717, 94 S. Ct. 3112 (1974).

NATURE OF CASE: Review of decision requiring multiple school districts to provide desegregation relief, though only one of the districts was found to have practiced de jure segregation.

GENERAL RULE OF LAW: A multidistrict remedy is improper where de jure segregation is found as to only one district, and there is no finding that the other districts have failed to operate unitary systems.

PROCEDURE SUMMARY:
Plaintiff: Bradley (P), a class of parents and students.
Defendant: Milliken (D), Governor of Michigan, and the Detroit Board of Education (D) (Board).
U.S. District Court Decision: Held for Bradley (P), ordering the Board (D) to submit a multidistrict desegregation plan.
U.S. Court of Appeals Decision: Affirmed.
U.S. Supreme Court Decision: Reversed and remanded.

FACTS: In 1970, Bradley (P), representing a class of parents and students, filed suit, alleging that the Detroit public school system was segregated on the basis of race as a result of official policies of Milliken (D), the Governor of Michigan, and the Board of Education (D). Bradley (P) sought the implementation of a plan desegregating the system. The district court found that various actions and policies of the Board (D) did, in fact, constitute de jure segregation of the Detroit schools and ordered it to submit Detroit-only desegregation plans. The Board (D) was also ordered to submit plans covering multiple districts that were not parties to the action. The district court thereafter ruled that consideration of the multidistrict plans was proper because the Detroit-only plans were inadequate to accomplish desegregation. The court of appeals affirmed. The Board (D) sought review, alleging the implementation of a multidistrict plan was improper because there was no finding that the other districts had also practiced de jure segregation or failed to maintain unitary school systems.

ISSUE: Is a multidistrict remedy proper where de jure segregation is found as to only one district, and there is no finding that the other districts failed to operate unitary school systems?

HOLDING AND DECISION: (Burger, C.J.) No. A multidistrict remedy is not proper where de jure

segregation is found as to only one district, and there is no finding that the other districts failed to operate unitary school systems. In fashioning a desegregation remedy, the court may not casually ignore school district lines. The multidistrict remedy at issue could extensively disrupt and alter the structure of the Michigan school system by requiring, in effect, the consolidation of 54 independent school districts. Before a court may properly require such a monumental effort, it must be shown that there has been a constitutional violation within one district that produces a significant segregative effect in another district. Or, in other words, it must be shown that racially discriminatory acts of the state or local district have been a substantial cause of interdistrict segregation. The district court erred in fashioning the multidistrict remedy because there was no showing of significant violation by any district other than the Detroit district and no evidence the segregation in the Detroit district had any segregative effect on the other districts. Reversed and remanded.

COMMENT: On remand, the district court limited the order requiring that only the Detroit school district take desegregation measures. *Milliken* illustrates how narrowly the Court intended to interpret its finding of de jure segregation requirement. The Court clearly sees the rule as requiring some clear nexus between particular intentional acts of segregation and the existence of segregation. For the Court, the obligation of the state is clearly different where segregation is intentional and where merely the result of personal living choices. In the former, the state's obligation is mandatory; in the latter, action is discretionary. Based on *Milliken*, the Court perspective is that the extent of a desegregation remedy is limited by the extent of the de jure violations proven. Although a mid-1970s case, *Milliken* is the last major position taken by the Court regarding school desegregation. While there have been Court decisions regarding staff development programs, funding, unitary status, and release from district court supervision, the 250-plus school districts still under court monitoring and supervision are still bound by the positions established by those cases up to and preceding *Milliken*.

MILLIKEN v. BRADLEY (MILLIKEN II)
433 U.S. 267, 97 S. Ct. 2749 (1977).

NATURE OF CASE: Review of decision finding the implementation of certain educational programs necessary to the desegregation of a school system and ordering the school board to bear the cost.

GENERAL RULE OF LAW: A district court may order a state to bear the cost of compensatory or remedial educational programs for schoolchildren who have been subjected to past acts of de jure segregation.

PROCEDURE SUMMARY:
Plaintiff: Bradley (P), a class of parents and students.
Defendant: Milliken (D), the Governor of Michigan (State).
U.S. District Court Decision: Ordered the State (D) to bear the cost of certain compensatory and remedial education programs.
U.S. Court of Appeals Decision: Affirmed.
U.S. Supreme Court Decision: Affirmed.

FACTS: In *Milliken I,* the Court reversed a district court's order calling for the implementation of a multidistrict desegregation plan where de jure segregation had only been shown in one district. On remand, the district court limited the order requiring that only the Detroit school district take desegregation measures. The order required the implementation of certain compensatory and remedial educational programs for schoolchildren who had suffered from the district's past acts of de jure segregation. The order also required the State (D) and local district to bear the cost of the programs. The court of appeals affirmed the order. The State (D) thereafter challenged, as a violation of the Eleventh Amendment, the order's requirement that it bear a portion of the cost. The U.S. Supreme Court granted review.

ISSUE: Does a district court order requiring a state to bear the cost of certain education programs for students who have been subject to past acts of de jure segregation violate the Eleventh Amendment?

HOLDING AND DECISION: (Burger, C.J.) No. A district court order requiring a state to bear the cost of certain education programs for students who have been subject to past acts of de jure segregation does not violate the Eleventh Amendment. The district court was authorized to provide prospective equitable relief, even though such relief

requires the expenditure of money by the State (D). This is not a violation of the Eleventh Amendment's prohibition of the award of money damages against the state based upon the prior conduct of state officials. This case fits squarely within *Edelman v. Jordan,* 415 U.S. 651, 94 S. Ct. 1347 (1974), a suit alleging that the state had improperly withheld disability benefits from a class of plaintiffs, where the Court held that the payment of state funds to ensure future compliance with federal law was a proper remedy and not in violation of the Eleventh Amendment. The remedy at issue in this case does no more than ensure future compliance with federal law, which in this case is the Constitution's mandate that the state eliminate all vestiges of state-maintained school segregation. Affirmed.

COMMENT: As a result of *Milliken II,* states have more closely monitored the activities of local school districts in an effort to save the state from having to share financial responsibility for the effect of activities found to be intentionally segregative. It should be noted that the costs for educational programs can be extensive. These costs which the state must pay usually come from the general fund or from funds that would support education programs throughout the state. This reduced funding has generated significant complaint. The costs, for example, in the *Kansas City* case quickly passed $100 million.

NOTES:

DAYTON BOARD OF EDUCATION v. BRINKMAN (BRINKMAN I)

433 U.S. 406, 97 S. Ct. 2766 (1977).

NATURE OF CASE: Review of order requiring school district-wide desegregation within a set percentage of the racial composition of the city's black-white ratio.

GENERAL RULE OF LAW: A system-wide desegregation remedy is improper where there is no showing that the homogenous character of a school is the result of intentionally segregative actions.

PROCEDURE SUMMARY:

Plaintiff: Brinkman (P), a class of parents of black schoolchildren.

Defendant: Dayton Board of Education (D) (Board).

U.S. District Court Decision: Held for Brinkman (P), ordering the Board (D) to implement a system-wide remedy to correct the racial imbalances within its schools.

U.S. Court of Appeals Decision: Affirmed.

U.S. Supreme Court Decision: Vacated and remanded.

FACTS: In 1972, Brinkman (P), and the class of parents of black students, filed suit against the Board (D), alleging that certain policies and actions, primarily the use of optional attendance zones in three high schools implemented by the Board (D), resulted in a cumulative violation of the Equal Protection Clause of the Fourteenth Amendment. Brinkman (P) sought the formulation of a desegregation plan, and the district court so ordered. Subsequently, the court ordered implementation of a plan requiring the elimination of optional attendance zones and the tailoring of faculty assignment and hiring practices to achieve in all Board (D) schools representative racial distribution. The court of appeals affirmed the district court's findings of fact but remanded for redetermination of the proper remedy, finding that the remedy ordered was inadequate given the scope of the violations. The district court thereafter ordered implementation of a broader, system-wide plan, which the court of appeal affirmed. The Board (D) appealed, and the U.S. Supreme Court granted review.

ISSUE: Is a system-wide desegregation remedy proper where there is no showing that the homogenous character of a school is the result of a board's intentionally segregative actions?

HOLDING AND DECISION: (Rehnquist, J.) No. A system-wide desegregation remedy is not proper where there is no showing that the homogenous character of a school is the result of a board's intentionally segregative actions. The district court's findings as to the optional attendance zones were limited to three offending high schools, thus only raising the potential for remedial action in system-wide high school districting. Thus, the sweeping system-wide remedy ordered was by no means justified by the violation found by the district court. And the district court's use of the ambiguous phrase "cumulative violation" in no way cured this disparity. More findings of fact must be made, and since mandatory racial segregation has long since ceased, it must be determined whether the Board (D) intended to, and did in fact, discriminate, resulting in system-wide segregation, before a system-wide remedy may be imposed. Vacated and remanded.

COMMENT: *Brinkman I* reconfirms that the Court is going to require a showing of system-wide discrimination before a system-wide remedy may be granted. Further, it confirms the Supreme Court's position in *Milliken I*, that the extent of the remedy is limited to the extensiveness of the constitutional violations established. It is but another demonstration of the Court's concern for tailoring the remedy to match the proven harm. Such a concern exists throughout the Court's equal protection cases, including more recent cases such as *City of Richmond v. J.A. Croson*, 488 U.S. 469, 109 S. Ct. 706 (1989), where the Court invalidated a city program which required at least 30% of the city's construction contracts to go to minority contractors. The Court held that there was no compelling reason for the ordinance to discriminate based on race, even beneficially. Although there was evidence of discrimination in the construction industry in other parts of the country, there was no evidence of past discrimination in Richmond's construction industry.

DAYTON BOARD OF EDUCATION v. BRINKMAN (BRINKMAN II)
443 U.S. 526, 538, 99 S. Ct. 2971, 2979 (1979).

13

NATURE OF CASE: Review of reversal of dismissal of action for order to desegregate a school district.

GENERAL RULE OF LAW: A school board has a continuing duty to eradicate the effects of segregation where it is found that the board operated dual systems in 1954.

PROCEDURE SUMMARY:
Plaintiff: Brinkman (P), a class of parents of black students.
Defendant: Dayton Board of Education (D) (Board).
U.S. District Court Decision: Held for the Board (D), dismissing Brinkman's (P) action.
U.S. Court of Appeals Decision: Reversed, holding for Brinkman (P) and finding that the Board (D) had operated a dual school system in 1954.
U.S. Supreme Court Decision: Affirmed.

FACTS: In *Brinkman I*, the Supreme Court reversed and remanded a lower court order that a systemwide desegregation plan be implemented, finding that there was insufficient evidence to support a finding of system-wide segregation. On remand, the district court found that the Board (D) had taken intentional segregative actions in the past but dismissed Brinkman's (P) complaint because there was insufficient evidence to prove that the Board's (D) past acts of intentional segregation had any current incremental segregative effects. The court of appeals reversed, finding that the Board (D) had maintained dual systems in 1954 (when *Brown v. Board of Education of Topeka,* 347 U.S. 483, 74 S. Ct. 686 (1954) was decided) and holding that the evidence demonstrated that the Board (D) failed to eliminate the continuing system-wide effects of its prior discrimination. It further found that the Board (D) had, in fact, exacerbated the racial separation. The U.S. Supreme Court granted review.

ISSUE: Does a school board have a continuing duty to eradicate the effects of segregation where it is found that the board operated dual systems in 1954?

HOLDING AND DECISION: (White, J.) Yes. A school board has a continuing duty to eradicate the effects of segregation where it is found that the board operated dual systems in 1954. There is no basis to disturb the court of appeals' finding that

dual school systems existed in 1954. And this finding furnishes prima facie proof that current segregation in the school system was at least in part caused by that past segregative policy. In fulfilling its obligation to cure the wrongs of its past acts, the Board (D) must do more than abandon its past discriminatory activities. It has the affirmative duty of ensuring that the effects of this past policy are not perpetuated. The issue is not the purpose of the Board's (D) actions since 1954 but the effectiveness of its actions to eliminate segregation. Affirmed.

COMMENT: *Brinkman II* creates a presumption that pre-1954 official segregation is causally related to present racial imbalance. Nineteen fifty-four is the critical date because that is the year the Supreme Court found the maintenance of segregated school systems unconstitutional and mandated that they be eliminated. It was the first case in which the Court announced that the state not only had to cease discriminatory activity but had to take affirmative steps to eliminate the effects of its past discriminatory acts. The dissent strongly disagreed with the notion that discrimination which occurred in the school systems in 1954 could place a greater burden on those districts' boards to satisfy a greater affirmative duty to eliminate current discrimination, even where the boards are no longer engaging in discriminatory activities.

NOTES:

ARTHUR v. NYQUIST

712 F.2d 816 (2nd Cir. 1983).

NATURE OF CASE: Appeal of a court-ordered desegregation plan designed to achieve a goal of 21% minority teachers in all teaching areas through a race-conscious system for hiring and laying off teachers.

GENERAL RULE OF LAW: A desegregation plan's requirement that laid off teachers be rehired without regard to seniority rights is constitutionally impermissible.

PROCEDURE SUMMARY:

Plaintiff: Arthur (P), a student in the Buffalo City School District, et al.

Defendant: Nyquist (D), Commissioner of Education of the State of New York, and Buffalo Teachers Federation (D) (Federation).

U.S. District Court Decision: Ordered the implementation of a desegregation plan to achieve 21% minority teachers that required that seniority be ignored with respect to rehiring laid-off teachers.

U.S. Court of Appeals Decision: Reversed in part.

FACTS: In 1976, the Arthurs (P) and other white and black parents whose children attended school in the Buffalo Metropolitan School District brought a class action to force desegregation of their school system. The district court found in favor of plaintiffs and ordered the schools desegregated. Among the discriminatory policies enjoined was the intentional segregation of the teaching and administrative staffs. Buffalo had intentionally assigned all minority teachers and staff to schools with a predominately minority student body, while assigning white teachers and staff to schools with mostly white students. The court ordered implementation of a desegregation plan designed to achieve 21% minority teachers in all teaching areas through a race-conscious system for hiring and laying off teachers. The plan required that a minority teacher be hired for every majority teacher hired, even with respect to the rehiring of laid-off teachers. The Federation (D) appealed the plan, contending that imposition of the one-for-one hiring requirement, without regard to seniority with respect to rehiring laid-off teachers, was constitutionally impermissible.

ISSUE: Is the imposition of the one-for-one requirement with respect to rehiring decisions an impermissible infringement of the teachers' seniority rights?

HOLDING AND DECISION: (Newman, J.) Yes. The imposition of the one-for-one requirement with respect to rehiring decisions is an impermissible infringement of the teachers' seniority rights. A remedial plan that infringes statutory and contractual rights of majority teachers is not per se invalid. The district court clearly has power to override any practice that perpetuates unconstitutional practices. However, the court may not exercise that power excessively or too harshly. That portion of this plan which impairs the seniority rights of laid-off teachers is an abuse of that power. According to their contract with the state, although teachers may be laid off when the number of positions shrinks, those teachers have a right to first consideration should a position become available. The court's order required Buffalo to hire minority teachers instead of laid-off personnel. This would have the same effect as if the court had ordered Buffalo to fire teachers and hire minority staff. This would have been beyond the court's power and, therefore, so is that part of the court's order affecting laid-off teachers. Reversed in part and remanded.

COMMENT: The *Nyquist* court clearly indicated that some impairment of teachers' seniority rights can be imposed in efforts to desegregate school faculty. The limitation is that the impairment cannot be too harsh. The court gave no definition of what makes a particular action too harsh. However, this qualification evidences the court's recognition of a necessary balancing of interest: to allow the seniority system to continue unaffected would only serve to perpetuate the segregation, but to allow substantial impairment of the system could create a new injustice in the effort to alleviate the effects of another.

NOTES:

MISSOURI v. JENKINS
495 U.S. 33 (1990).

13

NATURE OF CASE: Review of denial of order to enjoin enforcement of a district court-ordered increase of a property tax levy to fund a portion of the cost of a desegregation plan.

GENERAL RULE OF LAW: A federal district court may not order a tax levy increase of a specific percentage to fund in part a desegregation plan.

PROCEDURE SUMMARY:
Plaintiff: Jenkins (P), a taxpayer.
Defendant: The State of Missouri (D) (State).
U.S. District Court Decision: Held for the State (D), declining to enjoin enforcement of a court-ordered local property tax levy increase.
U.S. Court of Appeals Decision: Affirmed.
U.S. Supreme Court Decision: Reversed.

FACTS: In a separate action, the Kansas City, Missouri School District was found to have been operating a segregated school system. As a result, the district court ordered the creation of a desegregation plan detailing the financing necessary to implement the plan. The court ordered the school district to pay a portion of the cost of the plan, but it was found to have exhausted all available means of raising additional revenue to pay its portion of the cost. The court, therefore, ordered that the school district's tax levy be increased by a certain percentage to pay the cost, despite the fact that state law limitations prevented such an increase. Jenkins (P), a taxpayer, sought to enjoin the court-ordered tax increase, contending the district court abused its discretion in fashioning this remedy. The court of appeals disagreed and affirmed the tax increase but with the caveat that the district court in the future not set a percentage itself. The U.S. Supreme Court granted review.

ISSUE: May a district court order a tax levy increase of a specific percentage to partially fund the cost of a desegregation plan?

HOLDING AND DECISION: (White, J.) No. A federal district court may not order a tax levy increase of a specific percentage to fund in part a desegregation plan. Such an order is an abuse of discretion and violative of principles of federal-state comity. Local authorities have primary responsibility for assessing and solving problems of desegregation, including the financing of desegregation. Though the district court may require that the levy be increased to an amount adequate to fund the school district's portion of the plan, it may not itself increase the levy, especially where the court has failed to consider permissible alternatives. The local officials should have been given the opportunity to come up and present such alternatives. Reversed.

COMMENT: Justice White says that a federal court may set aside state laws prohibiting any further tax increase and order a school district to increase its levy, but the court may not increase the levy itself. Some commentators argue that this is a distinction without any true difference. Nevertheless, the case demonstrates just how expansive the Court views district courts' power to effectuate their desegregation decrees. The recurring cry heard by Kansas City residents was "taxation without representation." This was, and remains, an extremely sensitive situation. Nevertheless, it is a clear indication of the remedial power of a federal district court.

NOTES:

COLUMBUS BOARD OF EDUCATION v. PENICK

443 U.S. 449, 99 S. Ct. 2941 (1979).

NATURE OF CASE: Review of grant of injunction against continuing racial discrimination and ordering that a system-wide desegregation plan be formulated.

GENERAL RULE OF LAW: A school board has an affirmative and continuing duty to eliminate the effects of its past discriminatory policies and actions.

PROCEDURE SUMMARY:
Plaintiff: Penick (P), a student.
Defendant: Columbus Board of Education (D) (Board).
U.S. District Court Decision: Held for Penick (P).
U.S. Court of Appeals Decision: Affirmed.
U.S. Supreme Court Decision: Affirmed.

FACTS: Penick (P), a student, brought an action alleging that the Board's (D) policies and actions had the purpose and effect of causing and perpetuating racial segregation in public schools in violation of the Equal Protection Clause. At trial, the district court found that the Board (D) maintained dual school systems in 1954 and had since failed to discharge its duty to eliminate this segregation. It further found that current segregation in the schools was the effect of the Board's (D) past discriminatory actions and policies. The district court thereafter enjoined the Board (D) from continuing to discriminate and ordered it to submit a system-wide desegregation plan. The Board (D) appealed, contending the system-wide remedy was improper. The court of appeals disagreed and affirmed the district court decision. The U.S. Supreme Court granted review.

ISSUE: Does a school board have an affirmative and continuing duty to eliminate the effects of its past discriminatory policies and actions?

HOLDING AND DECISION: (White, J.) Yes. A school board has an affirmative and continuing duty to eliminate the effects of its past discriminatory policies and actions. There was sufficient basis for the lower courts to conclude that the Board's (D) conduct at the time of and before trial sufficiently perpetuated the effects of past intentional segregative acts to justify imposition of a system-wide remedy. The Board (D) failed to present evidence sufficient to demonstrate that its past acts were not causally related to current discrimination in its schools. It also failed to prove that it was now taking affirmative action to eliminate any such discriminatory effects. In fact, the record supports the lower court's finding that the Board's (D) current actions were merely perpetuating current system-wide discrimination, which is a proper basis for a system-wide remedy. Affirmed.

COMMENT: *Penick* reaffirms the notion that school boards must not only cease intentionally discriminatory actions and policies but must take affirmative steps to eliminate the effects of past discriminatory action. Distinct in *Penick*, however, is the Court's approval of the lower courts' use of disparate impact evidence to find that the Board's (D) current actions had the effect of perpetuating past discrimination. Disparate impact evidence is simply a showing that services and facilities provided minority students are less than those provided white students.

NOTES:

WASHINGTON v. SEATTLE SCHOOL DISTRICT NO. 1.
458 U.S. 457, 102 S. Ct. 3187 (1982).

13

NATURE OF CASE: Appeal from injunction against enforcement of a state initiative which required students to attend the school closest to their home.

GENERAL RULE OF LAW: A state initiative which removes decision-making power over a particular issue from the local school board merely because of the racial nature of the issue, thereby placing a substantial and unique burden on racial minorities, is unconstitutional.

PROCEDURE SUMMARY:
Plaintiff: Seattle School District No. 1 (P) (District).
Defendant: State of Washington (D) (State).
U.S. District Court Decision: Held for the District (P), enjoining enforcement of the initiative.
U.S. Court of Appeals Decision: Affirmed.
U.S. Supreme Court Decision: Affirmed.

FACTS: In 1978, the District (P) enacted a voluntary desegregation plan for its schools that made extensive use of mandatory busing. Subsequently, a statewide initiative was drafted to terminate the use of mandatory busing to correct racial imbalances. With only a few exceptions, the initiative would prohibit school districts such as Seattle (P) from requiring a student to attend any school other than one nearest or next nearest to his home. After the initiative was passed, the District (P) filed suit against the State (D) to enjoin enforcement of the initiative, alleging that it violated the Equal Protection Clause of the Fourteenth Amendment. The district court agreed and permanently enjoined enforcement of the initiative, which the court of appeals affirmed. The State (D) appealed to the U.S. Supreme Court.

ISSUE: May a state, by initiative, remove the decision-making power over a particular issue from the local school board merely because of the racial nature of the issue?

HOLDING AND DECISION: (Blackmun, J.) No. A state may not, by initiative, remove the decision- making power over a particular issue from the local school board merely because of the racial nature of the issue. Such action imposes substantial and unique burdens on racial minorities in violation of the Equal Protection Clause of the Fourteenth Amendment. A government may allo- cate power among its parts by any general principle but not by use of impermissible criteria. The very act of placing power over desegregative busing at the state level allocates this power solely by reason of the racial nature of the subject matter is such an impermissible criteria. Under the initiative, nonintegrative busing is still permissible, but integrative busing is not. This is an irrational and unjustifiable racial distinction, and the law is clear that unjustified distinctions based on race are impermissible. Affirmed.

COMMENT: The scope of this decision is limited. The state could have changed the busing scheme if control over the issue had previously been handled at the state level. Additionally, even if the matter was previously handled by local officials, the state could have asserted control over the entire matter. All that is prohibited is the state's seizing control of one issue in a particular matter because of that issue's racial implications. However, the dissent thought this result bizarre given that the district could have canceled the busing plan anytime. In the same session, the Supreme Court, in *Crawford v. Bd. of Education of Los Angeles,* 458 U.S. 527, 102 S. Ct. 3211 (1982), upheld California's Proposition I, which limited the more extensive California state constitutional Equal Protection Clause (which barred de facto as well as de jure segregation) so that California's Equal Protection Clause provisions mirrored those of the Fourteenth Amendment of the U.S. Constitution. Looking at both *Crawford* and *Washington v. Seattle,* the Supreme Court seemed to send out the message that the minimum guarantee for all Americans was that found in the Fourteenth Amendment. A state could withdraw some additional protections provided in a state constitution but could not adopt a state law that inhibited a guaranteed Fourteenth Amendment right.

NOTES:

FREEMAN v. PITTS
503 U.S. _____, 112 S. Ct. 1430 (1992).

NATURE OF CASE: Appeal by a school district from the reversal of a federal district court decision that the court could relinquish its remedial control of a school system in incremental stages of desegregation compliance when each stage reached compliance, rather than having to retain control until full compliance was achieved.

GENERAL RULE OF LAW: A district court that has supervision and jurisdiction over a school district under a desegregation decree can relinquish its remedial control in areas of compliance while maintaining remedial control over areas of noncompliance.

PROCEDURE SUMMARY:
Plaintiff: Freeman (P) and other officials of De Kalb County, Georgia School District (DCSS).
Defendant: Pitts (D), representative of a class of black school children and parents.
District Court: Held for defendant, in part.
U.S. Court of Appeals: Reversed.
U.S. Supreme Court: Reversed, for DCSS, permitting the court to relinquish partial control.

FACTS: In De Kalb County, Georgia, an Atlanta suburb, a 1969 court-ordered school desegregation decree placed the De Kalb County School System (DCSS), represented by Freeman (P), under the supervision and jurisdiction of the U.S. District Court for Northern Georgia. In 1986, Freeman (P) filed a motion for final dismissal. At the time, DCSS served approximately 73,000 students, ranging from kindergarten to high school. Finding that DCSS had achieved desegregation in four of six categories delineated by Green v. New Kent County School Board, 391 U.S. 430, the district court relinquished remedial control in regard to those categories where unitary status (i.e., compliance) had been achieved. At the same time, the court retained its supervisory control over those areas not yet in full compliance. The Eleventh Circuit Court of Appeals reversed the district court's ruling, holding that the district court had to "retain full remedial authority over a school system until it achieves unitary status in six categories at the same time for several years." The U.S. Supreme Court granted review.

ISSUE: Can a district court relinquish its supervision and jurisdiction over areas of a school system in which desegregation compliance exists,

even though other areas in the system remain in noncompliance?

HOLDING AND DECISION: (Kennedy, J.) Yes. In the course of supervising a desegregation plan, a district court has the authority to relinquish supervision and control of a school district in incremental stages, before full compliance has been achieved in every aspect of school operations. The duty and responsibility of a school district once segregated by law is to eliminate all traces of the unconstitutional de jure system. The court's goal, on the other hand, is to remedy the violation and to return a school district that is operating in compliance with the Constitution to the control of local authorities. Local autonomy of school districts is a vital national tradition, because only those school districts that are making decisions on their own, without judicial supervision, can be held accountable to citizens, courts, and the political process. Partial relinquishment of judicial control, where justified by the facts of the case, is within the court's discretion, and can be a significant step in fulfilling the court's duty to return control to local authorities. Furthermore, by partially withdrawing control, a court can better concentrate its resources, and the resources of the school district, on the areas where discrimination has not been eliminated. In ordering partial withdrawal, the court should consider whether (1) there has been full compliance in those aspects of the system where supervision is to be withdrawn; (2) retention of judicial control is necessary to achieve compliance in other facets of the system and (3) the school district has demonstrated a good faith commitment to the equal protection guarantees of the Constitution. DCSS "has traveled the often long road to unitary, status almost to its end." DCSS is a unitary — i.e., desegregated — system with regard to student assignments, transportation, physical facilities, and extracurricular activities. But in those areas where compliance has not been achieved — namely, teacher and principal assignments, resource allocation, and quality of education — DCSS has neither acted in bad faith nor engaged in further acts of discrimination. Therefore, the court of appeals erred in holding, as a matter of law, that the district court could not permit DCSS to regain control over areas in compliance with the desegregation decree. Reversed and remanded.

COMMENT: This decision does not break new

13

NOTES:

ground in the area of school desegregation litigation, but it does provide federal district courts
with greater latitude when working with a school
district. The Court has avoided any major decisions in this area in recent years. Nevertheless,
the holding in this case should provide greater
flexibility in the more than 250 desegregation
cases where federal courts still retain authority
over school districts.

13

STATUTES

Selected Provisions of the
CONSTITUTION
of the United States of America

We the People of the United States, in Order to form a more perfect Union, establish Justice, insure domestic Tranquility, provide for the common defence, promote the general Welfare, and secure the Blessings of Liberty to ourselves and our Posterity, do ordain and establish this Constitution for the United States of America.

Article I
* * *

Section 8. [1] The Congress shall have Power to lay and collect Taxes, Duties, Imposts and Excises, to pay the Debts and provide for the common Defence and general Welfare of the United States; . . .

[3] To Regulate Commerce with foreign Nations, and among the several States, and within the Indian Tribes; . . .

[18] To make all Laws which shall be necessary and proper for carrying into Execution the foregoing Powers, and all other Powers vested by this Constitution in the Government of the United States, or in any Department or Officer thereof . . .

Section 10. [1] No State shall . . . pass any . . . Law impairing the Obligation of Contracts . . . .

Article III

Section 1. The judicial Power of the United States, shall be vested in one supreme Court, and in such inferior Courts as the Congress may from time to time ordain and establish. The Judges, both of the supreme and inferior Courts, shall hold their Offices during good Behaviour, and shall, at stated Times, receive for their Services, a Compensation, which shall not be diminished during their Continuance in Office.

Section 2. [1] The Judicial Power shall extend to all Cases, in Law and Equity, arising under this Constitution, the Laws of the United States and Treaties made, or which shall be made, under their Authority; . . . to Controversies to which the United States shall be a Party; — to Controversies between two or more States; — between a State and Citizens of another State; — between Citizens of different States; — between Citizens of the same State claiming Lands under Grants of different States, and between a State, or the Citizens thereof, and foreign States, Citizens or Subjects . . . .

Article VI

[2] This Constitution, and the Laws of the United States which shall be made in Pursuance thereof; and all Treaties made, or which shall be made, under the Authority of the United States, shall be the supreme Law of the Land; and the Judges in every State shall be bound thereby, any Thing in the Constitution or Laws of any State to the Contrary notwithstanding.

* * *

Amendment I [1791]

Congress shall make no law respecting an establishment of religion, or prohibiting the free exercise thereof; or abridging the freedom of speech, or of the press; or the right of the people peaceably to assemble, and to petition the Government for a redress of grievances.

* * *

Amendment IV [1791]

The right of the people to be secure in their persons, houses, papers, and effects, against unreasonable searches and seizures, shall not be violated, and no Warrants shall issue, but upon probable cause, supported by Oath or affirmation, and particularly describing the place to be searched, and the persons or things to be seized.

Amendment V [1791]

No person shall be . . . compelled in any criminal case to be a witness against himself, nor be deprived of life, liberty, or property, without due process of law; nor shall private property be taken for public use, without just compensation.

* * *

Amendment IX [1791]

The enumeration in the Constitution, of certain rights, shall not be construed to deny or disparage others retained by the people.

Amendment X [1791]

The powers not delegated to the United States by the Constitution, nor prohibited by it to the States, are reserved to the States respectively, or to the people.

* * *

Amendment XIII [1865]

Section 1. Neither slavery nor involuntary servitude, except as a punishment for crime whereof the party shall have been duly convicted, shall exist within the United States, or any place subject to their jurisdiction.

Section 2. Congress shall have power to enforce this article by appropriate legislation.

Amendment XIV [1868]

Section 1. All persons born or naturalized in the United States, and subject to the jurisdiction thereof, are citizens of the United States and of the State wherein they reside. No State shall make or enforce any law which shall abridge the privileges or immunities of citizens of the United States; nor shall any State deprive any person of life, liberty, or property, without due process of law; nor deny to any person within its jurisdiction the equal protection of the laws.

* * *

Amendment XXVII [proposed]*

Section 1. Equality of rights under the law shall not be denied or abridged by the United States or by any State on account of sex.

Section 2. The Congress shall have the power to enforce, by appropriate legislation, the provisions of this article.

Section 3. This amendment shall take effect two years after the date of ratification.

*Submitted by Congress for ratification on March 22, 1972. The amendment was neither ratified nor adopted.

PRINCIPAL FEDERAL LAWS AFFECTING
EQUAL OPPORTUNITY IN SCHOOLS

Early (Civil War) Statutes

Civil Rights Acts of 1866, 1870   (race) 42 U.S.C. §§ 1981, 1988
Civil Rights Act of 1871   (injury under color of law)
        42 U.S.C. § 1983
Civil Rights Act of 1871   (conspiracy) 42 U.S.C. § 1985, § 1986

Modern Statutes and Executive Orders

Civil Rights Act of 1964, 42 U.S.C. § 2000
    Title VI   (general prohibition—§ 2000 (d))
    Title VII   (employment discrimination — § 2000 (e))

Education Amendments of 1972
    Title IX, 20 U.S.C. § 1681 (sex discrimination in education programs)
    Title IX Regulations, 34 C.F.R. § 106-1 et seq.

Equal Pay Act of 1963, 29 U.S.C. 206(d) (sex discrimination in pay)

Age Discrimination in Employment Act of 1967, as amended, 29 U.S.C.
    § 621

Equal Educational Opportunities Act of 1974, 20 U.S.C. § 1703

Rehabilitation Act of 1973, 29 U.S.C. § 794 (discrimination against people
    with disabilities)

Individuals with Disabilities Education Act (formerly Education of the
    Handicapped Act), 20 U.S.C. § 1401

Americans with Disabilities Act of 1990 — 42 U.S.C. § 12101

Civil Rights Restoration Act of 1991 (various titles)

SUMMARY OF FEDERAL CIVIL RIGHTS STATUTES

A. Civil Rights Acts of 1866, 1870 — 42 U.S.C. § 1981

Section 1981 provides: *"All persons* within the jurisdiction of the United States shall have the same right . . . *to make and enforce contracts,* to sue, be parties, give evidence, and to the full and equal benefit of all laws and proceedings for the security of persons and property as is enjoyed by white citizens, and shall be subject to like punishments, pains, penalties, taxes, licenses, and exactions of every kind, and to no other."

B. Civil Rights Act of 1871 — 42 U.S.C. § 1983

Section 1983 provides: "Every person who, under color of any statute, ordinance, regulation, custom or usage, of any State or Territory, subjects, or causes to be subjected, any citizen of the United States or other person within the jurisdiction thereof to the *deprivation of any rights,* privileges or immunities *secured by the Constitution and laws,* shall be liable to the party injured in an action at law, suit in equity, or other proper proceeding for redress."

C. Civil Rights Act of 1871 — 42 U.S.C. §§ 1985 and 1986

Section 1985(3) provides in part: "If two or more persons in any State or Territory conspire . . . for the purpose of depriving . . . any person or class of persons of the *equal protection of the laws,* or of equal privileges and immunities under the laws: or . . . of preventing or hindering the constituted authorities of any State . . . from . . . securing to all persons within such State...the equal protection of the laws . . . the party so injured . . . may have an action for the recovery of damages . . . against any one or more of the conspirators."

Section 1986 provides in part: "Every person who, having knowledge that any of the wrongs conspired to be done . . . [under Section 1985]. . . and having the power to prevent . . . the . . . same, neglects or refuses so to do . . . shall be liable to the party injured . . . for all damages caused by such wrongful act . . ."

D. Civil Rights Acts of 1866, 1870 — 42 U.S.C. § 1988

As amended 1980, § 1988 provides in part:

Proceedings in Vindication of Civil Rights . . . In any . . . proceeding to enforce a provision of sections 1981, 1982, 1983, 1985, and 1986 of this title, title IX of Public Law 92-318, or Title VI of the Civil Rights Act of 1964, the court, in its discretion, may allow the prevailing party . . . *a reasonable attorney's fee as part of the costs.* As amended Pub. L. 94-559, § 2, Oct. 19, 1976, 90 Stat. 2641.

E. Civil Rights Act of 1964, Title VI — 42 U.S.C. § 2000(d)

Section 601 of Title VI provides in part: *"No person . . .*shall, on the ground of *race, color, or national origin,* be excluded from participation in, be denied the benefits of, or be subjected to discrimination *under any program or activity receiving Federal financial assistance."*

F. Civil Rights Act of 1964, Title VII — 42 U.S.C. § 2000(e)

Section 702 of Title VII provides in part: *"This subchapter shall not apply to a . . . religious corporation, association, educational institution, or society with respect to the employment of individuals of a particular religion* to perform work connected with the carrying on by such corporation, association, educational institution, or society of its activities."

    Section 703(a) provides in part that: "It shall be an unlawful employment practice for an *employer —* (1) . . . to discriminate against any individual with respect to his compensation, terms, conditions, or privileges of employment, because of such individual's *race, color, religion, sex, or national origin;* or (2) to limit, segregate, or classify his employees . . . in any way which would deprive any individual of employment opportunities or otherwise adversely affect his status as an employee, because of such individual's race, color, religion, sex, or national origin."

    Section 703(e) provides: "Notwithstanding any other provision of this [title], (1) *it shall not be an unlawful employment practice* for an employer to hire and employ employees . . . for a labor organization to classify its membership or to classify . . . any individual . . . on the basis of his religion, sex, or national origin *in those certain instances* **where religion, sex, or national origin is a bona fide occupational qualification reasonably necessary to the normal operation of that particular business or enterprise** . . ." (emphasis added).

    Section 703(h) reads in relevant part: ". . . it shall not be an unlawful employment practice for an employer to apply different standards of compensation, or different terms . . . of employment *pursuant to a* **bona fide seniority or merit system** . . . provided that such differences are not the result of an intention to discriminate because of race, color, religion, sex, or national origin . . ." (emphasis added).

G. Education Amendments of 1972, Title IX — 20 U.S.C. § 1681

Section 901 of Title IX provides in part:
(A) *No person* . . . shall, on the basis of *sex,* be excluded from participation in, be denied the benefits of, or be subjected to discrimination under any *education program* or activity *receiving Federal financial assistance,* except that:
    (1) in regard to admissions . . .
    (3) this section *shall not apply* to an educational institution which is controlled by a religious organization if the application . . . would not *be consistent with the religious tenets* of such organization . . .

Title IX regulations provide in part:

"Nondiscrimination on the Basis of Sex in Education Programs and Activities; Receiving or Benefiting from Federal Financial Assistance" 34 C.F.R. § 106.1-106.71

Title IX Regulations, 34 C.F.R. § 106-1 et seq.

Subpart C — Discrimination on the Basis of Sex in Admission and Recruitment Prohibited

§ 106.21 Admission

(a) *General.* No person shall, on the basis of sex, be denied admission, or be subjected to discrimination in admission . . .

(b) *Specific prohibitions.*
   (1) [a] recipient . . . shall not:
      (i) Give preference to one person over another on the basis of sex, by ranking applicants separately on such basis . . .
      (ii) Apply numerical limitations upon the number or proportion of persons of either sex who may be admitted . . .
   (2) A recipient shall not administer . . . any test . . . for admission which has a disproportionately adverse effect on persons on the basis of sex unless the use of such test . . . is shown to predict validly success in the education program or activity in question and alternative tests . . . which do not have such a disproportionately adverse effect are shown to be unavailable.

(c) *Prohibitions relating to marital or parental status* . . . a recipient . . . :
   (1) Shall not apply any rule concerning . . . parental, family, or marital status . . . which treats persons differently on the basis of sex . . .

* * *

   (3) Shall treat disabilities related to pregnancy, childbirth, termination of pregnancy, or recovery therefrom in the same manner . . . as any other temporary disability . . . and
   (4) Shall not make pre-admission inquiry as to the marital status of an applicant for admission, . . .

Subpart D — Discrimination on the Basis of Sex in Education Programs and Activities Prohibited

§ 106.31 Education Programs and Activities

(a) *General.* Except as provided elsewhere in this part, no person shall, on the basis of sex, be excluded from participation in, be denied the benefits of, or be subjected to discrimination under any academic, extracurricular, research, occupational training, or other education program or activity operated by a recipient which receives or benefits from Federal financial assistance . . .

(b) *Specific prohibitions.* Except as provided in this subpart, in providing any aid, benefit, or service to a student, a recipient shall not on the basis of sex . . .

* * *

(2) Provide different aid, benefits, or services or provide aid, benefits, or services in a different manner . . .

* * *

(4) Subject any person to separate or different rules of behavior, sanctions, or other treatment . . .

§ 106.34 Access to Course Offerings

A recipient shall not provide any course or otherwise carry out any of its education program or activity separately on the basis of sex . . .

(b) This section does not prohibit grouping of students in physical education classes and activities by ability as assessed by objective standards of individual performance developed and applied without regard to sex.

(c) This section does not prohibit separation of students by sex within physical education classes or activities during participation in wrestling, boxing, rugby, ice hockey, football, basketball and other sports the purpose or major activity of which involves bodily contact.

(d) Where use of a single standard of measuring skill or progress in a physical education class has an adverse effect on members of one sex, the recipient shall use appropriate standards which do not have such effect.

(e) Portions of classes in elementary and secondary schools which deal exclusively with human sexuality may be conducted in separate sessions for boys and girls.

(f) Recipients may make requirements based on vocal range or quality which may result in a chorus or choruses of one or predominantly one sex.

* * *

§ 106.36 Counseling and Use of Appraisal and Counseling Materials

(a) *Counseling.* A recipient shall not discriminate against any person on the basis of sex in the counseling or guidance of students or applicants for admission.

(b) *Use of appraisal and counseling materials.* A recipient which uses testing or other materials for appraising or counseling students shall not use different materials for students on the basis of their sex or use materials which permit or require different treatment of students on such basis unless such different materials cover the same occupations and interest areas and the use of such different materials is shown to be essential to eliminate sex bias . . . Where the use of a counseling test or other instrument results in a substantially disproportionate number of members of one sex in any particular course of study or classification, the recipient shall take such action as is necessary to assure itself that such disproportion is not the result of discrimination in the instrument or its application.

(c) *Disproportion in classes.* Where a recipient finds that a particular class contains a substantially disproportionate number of individuals of one sex, the recipient shall take such action as is necessary to assure itself that such disproportion is not the result of discrimination on the basis of sex in counseling or appraisal materials or by counselors.

§ 106.40 Marital or Parental Status

(a) *Status generally.* A recipient shall not apply any rule concerning a student's actual or potential parental, family, or marital status which treats students differently on the basis of sex.

(b) *Pregnancy and related conditions.* (1) A recipient shall not discriminate against any student, or exclude any student from its education program or activity, including any class or extracurricular activity, on the basis of such student's pregnancy, childbirth, false pregnancy, termination of pregnancy or recovery therefrom, unless the student requests voluntarily to participate in a separate portion of the program or activity of the recipient.

(2) A recipient may require such a student to obtain the certification of a physician that the student is physically and emotionally able to continue participation in the normal education program or activity . . .

(3) A recipient which operates a portion of its education program or activity separately for pregnant students, admittance to which is completely voluntary on the part of the student . . . shall ensure that the instructional program in the separate program is comparable to that offered to non-pregnant students.

(4) A recipient shall treat pregnancy, childbirth, false pregnancy, termination of pregnancy and recovery therefrom in the same manner and under the same policies as any other temporary disability with respect to any medical or hospital benefit, service, plan or policy which such recipient administers, operates . . . with respect to students . . .

§ 106.41 Athletics

(a) *General.* No person shall, on the basis of sex, be excluded from participation in, be denied the benefits of, be treated differently from another person or otherwise be discriminated against in any interscholastic . . . club or intramural athletics offered by a recipient . . .

(b) *Separate teams.* Notwithstanding the requirements of paragraph (a) of this section, a recipient may operate or sponsor separate teams for members of each sex where selection for such teams is based upon competitive skill or the activity involved is a contact sport. However, where a recipient operates or sponsors a team in a particular sport for members of one sex but operates or sponsors no such team for members of the other sex, and athletic opportunities for members of that sex have previously been limited, members of the excluded sex must be allowed to try out for the team offered unless the sport involved is a contact sport. For the purposes of this part, contact sports include boxing, wrestling, rugby, ice hockey, football, basketball and other sports the purpose or major activity of which involves bodily contact.

(c) *Equal opportunity.* A recipient which operates or sponsors . . . athletics shall provide equal athletic opportunity for members of both sexes. In determining whether equal opportunities are available the Director will consider, among other factors:

   (1)   Whether the selection of sports and levels of competition effectively accommodate the interests and abilities of members of both sexes;

   (2)   The provision of equipment and supplies;

   (3)   Scheduling of games and practice time;

   (4)   Travel and per diem allowance;

   (5)   Opportunity to receive coaching and academic tutoring;

   (6)   Assignment and compensation of coaches and tutors;

   (7)   Provision of locker rooms, practice and competitive facilities;

   (8)   Provision of medical and training facilities and services . . .

* * *

(10) Publicity.

Unequal aggregate expenditures for members of each sex or unequal expenditures for male and female teams if a recipient operates or sponsors separate teams will not constitute noncompliance with this section, but the Assistant Secretary may consider the failure to provide necessary funds for team for one sex in assessing equality of opportunity for members of each sex.

H. Equal Pay Act of 1964 — 29 U.S.C. § 206(d)

Section 206 provides in part: *"No employer* having employees subject to [the minimum wage provisions] shall discriminate . . . between employees on the basis of *sex* by paying wages . . . at a rate less than the rate at which he pays wages to employees of the opposite sex . . . for equal work on jobs the performance of which requires *equal skill, effort, and responsibility* . . . under similar working conditions."...

The Act nevertheless permits differences in wages if paid pursuant to "(i) a *seniority system*; (ii) a *merit system* . . . ; or (iv) a differential based on any factor other than sex."

I. Age Discrimination in Employment Act of 1967 (§ 623) — 29 U.S.C. § 621

"(a) It shall be unlawful for an *employer* —

(1) to fail or refuse to hire or to discharge any individual or otherwise discriminate against any individual *with respect to* his . . . *employment, because of such individual's age;*

* * *

(f) It *shall not be unlawful* for an employer, employment agency, or labor organization —

(1) to take any action otherwise prohibited . . . *where age is a bona fide occupational qualification* reasonably necessary to the normal operation of the particular business . . .

* * *

(3) to discharge or otherwise discipline an individual for good cause."

J. Equal Educational Opportunities Act of 1974 — 20 U.S.C. § 1703

Section 1703 provides: *"No State shall* deny equal educational opportunity to an individual on account of his or her *race, color, sex, or national origin,* by —
(a)   . . . deliberate segregation by an educational agency . . . within schools . . .
(c)   the assignment . . . of a student to a school, other than the one closest to his or her place of residence . . . if the assignment results in a greater degree of segregation . . .
(d)   discrimination . . . in the employment . . . or assignment . . . of its faculty or staff, except to fulfill the purposes of subsection (f) below;
(e)   the transfer . . . of a student . . . if the purpose and effect . . . is to increase segregation . . .
(f)   the failure . . . to take appropriate action to overcome *language barriers* that impede equal participation by its students in its instructional programs."

K. Rehabilitation Act of 1973 (§ 504) — 29 U.S.C. § 794

The Act provides in part: "No *otherwise qualified handicapped individual* . . . shall, solely by reason of his handicap, be excluded from the participation in, be denied the benefits of, or be subjected to discrimination under any program or activity *receiving Federal financial assistance."*

L. Individuals with Disabilities Education Act (formerly Education of the Handicapped Act) — 20 U.S.C. § 1401

§ 1412 of the Act provides in part: "In order to qualify for [federal] assistance under this subchapter . . . a State shall demonstrate . . . that the following conditions are met:

(1)   The State has in effect a policy that assures all handicapped children the right to a *free appropriate public education.*

(2)   The State has developed a plan pursuant to . . . this title . . . so as to comply with the provisions of this paragraph."

M. Americans with Disabilities Act of 1990 — 42 U.S.C. § 12112

Section 102(A) provides: "No covered entity shall discriminate against a qualified individual with a disability [as defined in the Act] because of the disability of such individual in regard to job application, procedures, the hiring, advancement, or discharge of employees, employee compensation, job training, and other terms, conditions, and privileges of employment."

N. Civil Rights Restoration Act of 1991

The meaning of this new law was, and at this writing still is, hotly debated even by the Senators who introduced it. In order to obtain necessary bipartisan votes for passage, some critical provisions were left purposely ambiguous. Resolving contested interpretations of those provisions will probably require years of litigation. Generally speaking, the Act sought to achieve the following principal changes:

(a)   To undo the Supreme Court decision in *Wards Packing Co. v. Atonio,* 490 U.S. 642 (1989), which effectively overruled *Griggs V. Duke Power Co.,* 401 U.S. 424(1971), and to restore the "disparate impact" standard of establishing a prima facie case of Title VII employment discrimination, and thus casting on defending employers the burden of producing evidence that the challenged practices are job related and dictated by business necessity. (See §§ 105 of the Act, amending 42 U.S.C. §§ 2000-e-2)

(b)   To provide that court-approved consent decrees in employment discrimination cases may not be challenged by persons not party to the consent decree, *if* either the challenger had notice of and opportunity to object to the decree or the court finds that the interests of the challenger were fairly represented by one of the parties to the consent decree (and thus to undo the contrary Supreme Court decision in *Marlin v. Wilks,* 490 U.S. 754 [1989]). (§§ 108 of the Act, amending 42 U.S.C. §§ 2000-e-2)

(c)   To provide that employment discrimination occurs where race, gender, or national origin was a motivating factor in making that decision, even though other valid motives existed for the employment practice (and thus undercut the Supreme Court decision in *Price-Waterhouse v. Hopkins,* 490 U.S. 228 [1989]). (§ 107 of Act, amending 42 U.S.C. § 2000-e-2)

(d)   To amend 42 U.S.C. § 1981, to forbid racial or ethnic discrimination in employment practices beyond initial hiring decisions, and to cover all employment practices affecting employment opportunities, conditions and benefits (thus undercutting the Supreme Court decision in *Patterson v. McLean Credit Union,* 491 U.S. 164 [1989], which limited § 1981 to conduct in making the original contract). (§ 101 of Act, amending 42 U.S.C. § 1981)

(e) To permit recovery of compensatory and punitive damages including nonmonetary losses (emotional pain and suffering) for *intentional* workplace discrimination and unlawful harassment against women, persons with disabilities, and religious minorities, subject, however, to dollar caps specified in the Act. This provision does not affect the right of *racial* minorities under Section 1981 to seek such damages, without dollar limitation. (§ 1977A(b) of the Act, adding 42 U.S.C. § 1981a)

(f) To provide a right to jury trial in cases seeking compensatory and punitive damages for alleged intentional discrimination under Title VII, the Americans with Disability Act, and the Rehabilitation Act. (§ 1977A (c) of the Act, adding 42 U.S.C. § 1981a)

(g) To prohibit alteration or adjustment of employment tests, of test scores or of use of different cutoff scores on the basis of race, color, religion, sex or national origin (viz. "norming" of employment tests scores for racial or other groups). (§ 106 of the Act, amending 42 U.S.C. § 2000-e-2)

(h) To permit court discretion to award a civil rights litigant's costs of "expert fees" (assessed against the losing party), which were not allowed under prior law. (§ 113 of the Act, amending 42 U.S.C. §§ 1988, and 2000-e-5)

GLOSSARY

Glossary of Legal Terms
and Phrases   G-2

GLOSSARY OF LEGAL TERMS AND PHRASES

The following definitions have been quoted or abridged from *Black's Law Dictionary*, with kind permission from West Publishing Company.

A

ABATEMENT: A reduction, a decrease, or a diminution.

ABSOLUTE: Unconditional; complete and perfect in itself; without relation to or dependence on other things or persons.

ACT: A law passed by the Congress or a state legislature; a statute.

ACTION: A court/judicial proceeding, in which one party prosecutes another for the enforcement or protection of a right, for the redress or prevention of a wrong, or for punishment of a public offense. Rough synonyms: suit, case, trial, litigation.

ADDUCE: To present as evidence.

ADMISSION: A voluntary acknowledgement made by a party of the existence of the truth of certain facts which are inconsistent with his claims in an action.

ADVOCATE: To speak in favor of.

AFFIRM: In the practice of appellate courts, to *affirm* a judgment, decree, or order, is to declare that it is valid and right and must stand as rendered below.

A FORTIORI: With stronger reason. A term used in logic to denote an argument to the effect that because one ascertained fact exists, therefore another, which is included in it, or analogous to it, and which is less improbable, unusual, or surprising, must also exist.

AFFIDAVIT: A written or printed declaration of statement of facts, made voluntarily, and confirmed by the oath or affirmation of the party making it, taken before an officer having authority to administer such an oath.

AMICUS CURIAE: Means, literally, friend of the court. A person with strong interest in or views on the subject matter of an action, but not a party to the action, may petition the court for permission to file a brief, ostensibly on behalf of a party but actually to suggest a rationale consistent with its own views.

APPEAL: The complaint to a superior court of an injustice done or error committed by an inferior court, whose judgment or decision the court above is called upon to correct or reverse (civil practice).

APPELLANT: The party who takes an appeal from one court or jurisdiction to another.

APPELLATE COURT, COURT OF APPEALS: A state or federal court that may review the judgment of a lower court. In a trial de novo, the appeals court may also hear new or redetermine the facts that appear in the record of the original trial. The U.S. Supreme Court is the final court of appeals. Most cases reach the Supreme Court by appeal of the losing side in a lower court (usually a federal court or a state supreme court), provided that the Supreme Court agrees to accept the case and issues a writ of certiorari.

APPELLEE: Party against whom an appeal is taken.

ARRAIGNMENT: Procedure whereby the accused is brought before the court to plead to the criminal charge against him in the indictment or information.

ASSAULT: Any intentional display of force or a movement that could reasonably give the victim reason to fear or expect immediate bodily harm.

B

BATTERY: Intentional and wrongful physical contact of a person without his or her consent that entails some injury or offensive touching.

BILL: The draft of a proposed law.

BILL OF RIGHTS: The first ten amendments to the U.S. Constitution.

BRIEF: A written statement prepared by the counsel arguing a case in court. It contains a summary of the facts of the case, the pertinent laws, and an argument of how the law applies to the facts supporting counsel's position.

C

CASE: An action, cause, suit or controversy; a question contested before a court of justice.

CERTIORARI: Writ issued by a superior to an inferior court requiring the latter to produce a certified record of a particular case tried therein. The Supreme Court of the United States uses the writ of certiorari as a discretionary device to choose the cases it wishes to hear.

CHALLENGE: To object or take exception to.

CITE: To read or refer to legal authorities in support of propositions of law.

CLASS ACTION: Provides a means by which, where a large group of persons are interested in a matter, one or more may sue or be sued as representatives of the class without needing to join every member of the class.

CLAUSE: A subdivision of a legal document, such as a contract, deed, will, constitution, or statute.

COMMON LAW: A body of law derived from usages and customs of antiquity, or from court judgments affirming and enforcing such usages and customs, as distinguished from legislative enactments.

COMPLAINT: The original or initial pleading by which an action is commenced under codes or Rules of Civil Procedure.

CONCURRING OPINION: see opinion.

CONSTITUTIONAL: Consistent with or authorized by the constitution; or not conflicting with any part of it — in which case the law or practice is "not unconstitutional."

CONSTRUE: To ascertain the meaning of language by arranging and interpreting the words of an instrument, statute, regulation, court decision, or other legal authority.

COUNT: A charge, one of the offenses in the plaintiff's stated causes for an action.

D

DECIDE: To arrive at a determination. To "decide" includes the power and right to deliberate, to weigh the reasons for and against, to see which preponderate, and to be governed by that preponderance.

DECLARATORY JUDGMENT: Statutory remedy for the determination of a justiciable controversy where the plaintiff is in doubt as to his legal rights.

DE FACTO: In fact, actually, a reality.

DE JURE: Of right, legitimate; lawful.

DE MINIMIS: Under this doctrine, the law does not care for, or take notice of, very small or trifling matters.

DEMURRER: An objection made by one party to his opponent pleading, alleging that he ought not to answer it for some defect in law. It admits the facts but this does not warrant legal action.

DE NOVO TRIAL: Anew; afresh, a second time. New trial. New evidence.

DEPOSITION: The testimony of a witness taken upon interrogatories, not in open court, but in (presence) of a commission to take testimony issued by a court, or under a general law on the subject, and reduced to writing and duly authenticated, and intended to be used upon the trial of an action in court.

DICTUM: ABBREVIATED FORM OF OBITER DICTUM: ("a remark by the way"):

Statements and comments in an opinion concerning some rule of law or legal proposition not necessarily involved nor essential to determination of the case in hand. Dicta are opinions of a judge which do not embody the resolution or determination of the court.

DIRECTORY: A provision in a statute, rule or procedure, or the like, which is mere direction of no obligatory force, and involving no invalidating consequence for its disregard. As opposed to "mandatory" (see definition).

DISSENTING OPINION: see opinion.

DISTINGUISH: To point out an essential difference; to prove a case cited as applicable, inapplicable.

DOCTRINE: A rule, principle, theory, or tenet of the law.

DUE PROCESS: A course of legal proceeding according to those rules and principles which have been established in our systems of jurisprudence for the enforcement and protection of private rights.

E

EN BANC: Full bench. Refers to a session where the entire membership of the court will participate in the decision rather than the regular quorum. Only occurs when the issues involved are unusually novel or of wide impact.

EQUAL PROTECTION OF THE LAW: The equal access to courts; to life, liberty, property, and pursuit of happiness; and subject to no special restrictions or burdens.

ERROR: A mistake of law, or false or irregular application of it, such as vitiates the proceedings and warrants the reversal of judgment.

EX CURIA: Out of court.

EX PARTE: ("in behalf of"): Judicial proceeding or order taken or granted at the instance and for the benefit of one party only, and without notice to, or contestation by, any person adversely interested.

EX POST FACTO LAW: Every law that creates and punishes a criminal offense which, when done before the passing of the law, was innocent, and every law that aggravates a crime or makes it greater than it was when committed, and every law that inflicts greater punishment than was attached to the crime when committed.

EX REL: (Abbreviated form of Ex Relatione) ("on the relation"): Legal proceedings which are instituted by the attorney general (or other proper person) in the name and behalf of the state, but on the information and at the instigation of an individual who has a private interest in the matter.

EXPRESS AUTHORITY: Authority delegated to agent by words which expressly authorize him to do a delegable act. That which confers power to do a particular identical thing set forth and declared exactly, plainly, and directly within well-defined limits.

F

FEDERAL COURTS: (principal ones) **District Court:** a trial court of general federal jurisdiction. **U.S. Courts of Appeal:** intermediate appellate courts sitting in eleven numbered circuits, the District of Columbia, and the Court of Appeals for the Federal Circuit, having jurisdiction over most cases decided by District Courts. The decisions of the Courts of Appeals are reviewable on appeal only by the **U.S. Supreme Court.**

FELONY: Generally a crime punishable by death or imprisonment for a term exceeding one year.

FINDING: A court's decision—as to the facts in a case, an interpretation of the facts, or the case as a whole.

FRIVOLOUS APPEAL: One in which no justiciable question has been presented and appeal is easily recognizable as devoid of merit in that there is little prospect it can ever succeed.

G

GUEST: A guest in an automobile is one who takes a ride in an automobile driven by another person, merely for his own pleasure or on his own business, and without making any return or conferring any benefit on automobile driver.

H

HABEAS CORPUS AD SUBJICIENDUM: A writ directed to the person detaining another and commanding him to produce the body of the prisoner with the day and cause of his caption and detention (Art. I, Sec. 9 U.S. Constitution, "The privilege of the write of habeas corpus shall not be suspended unless when in cases of rebellion or invasion the public safety may require it").

I

ILLICIT: Not permitted or allowed; prohibited; unlawful.

IMPLIED: This word is used in law in contrast to "express"; i.e., where the intention in regard to the subject-matter is not manifested by explicit and direct words, but is gathered by implication or necessary deduction from the circumstances, the general language, or the conduct of the parties.

IN DELICTO: In fault.

INDICTMENT: An accusation in writing found and presented by a Grand Jury, legally convoked and sworn, to the court in which it is impaneled, charging that a person therein named has done some act, or been guilty of some omission which by law is a public offense.

INJUNCTION: A court order prohibiting someone from doing some specified act or commanding someone to undo some wrong or injury.

IN LOCO PARENTIS: In the place of a parent.

IN RE: ("in the matter of"): In the title of a case, usually indicates that it is not an adversary proceeding, but merely asking for a judgment about some matter.

INTER ALIA: Among other things. A term used in pleading, especially in reciting statements where the whole statute was not set forth at length.

INTERVENOR: Person, not originally a party to the suit, who, claiming an interest in the subject matter, voluntarily interposes in an action or other proceeding with the leave of the court.

INTRA VIRES: ("within the power") An act within the scope of a person's or corporation's powers or authority. It is the opposite of ultra vires.

INVITEE: A person who is on land of another by invitation.

IPSO FACTO: By the fact itself; by the mere fact.

J

JURISDICTION: The power of the court to decide a matter in controversy. Presupposes the existence of a duly constituted court with control over the subject matter and the parties.

JUSTICE: Title given to judges, particularly to judges of U.S. and state supreme courts, and as well to judges of appellate courts.

L

LIABLE: Bound or obliged in law or equity, responsible, chargeable; answerable; compellable to make satisfaction, compensation, or restitution.

LICENSEE: A person who has a privilege to enter upon land arising from the permission or consent, express or implied, of the possessor of land, but who goes on the land for his own purpose rather than for any purpose or interest of the possessor.

M

MALFEASANCE: The doing of an act which a person ought not to do at all.

MAJORITY: see opinion.

MANDATORY: Containing a command; preceptive; imperative; peremptory; obligatory. A "mandatory" provision in a statute is one the omission to follow which renders the proceedings to which it relates void, while a "directory" provision is one the observance of which is not necessary to validity of the proceeding.

MINISTERIAL DUTY: One regarding which nothing is left to discretion. A simple and definite duty imposed by law.

MISFEASANCE: The improper performance of some act which a person may lawfully do (a misdeed).

MOOT CASE: A case is "moot" when a determination is sought on a matter which, when rendered, cannot have any practical effect on the existing controversy.

N

NEGLIGENCE: The omission to do something which a reasonable man, guided by those ordinary considerations which ordinarily regulate human affairs; would do, or the doing of something which a reasonable and prudent man would not do. The failure to use ordinary care.

NISI PRIUS: *Nisi prius* courts are such as are held for the trial of issues of fact before a jury and one presiding judge. In America the phrase was formerly used to denote the forum (whatever may be its statutory name) in which the cause was tried to a jury, as distinguished from the appellate court.

NOLENS VOLENS: Whether willing or unwilling; consenting or not.

NONFEASANCE: Nonperformance of some act which person is obligated or has responsibility to perform; omission to perform a required duty at all; or, total neglect of duty.

NUGATORY: Futile; ineffectual; invalid. A legislative act may be "nugatory" because it is unconstitutional.

O

OBITER DICTUM/A: see dictum.

OPINION: The statement by a judge or court of the decision reached in regard to a cause tried or argued before them, expounding the law as applied to the case, and detailing the reasons upon which the judgment is based.

 Majority Opinion: is usually written by one judge and represents the principles of law which a majority of his colleagues on the court deem operative in a given decision; it has more precedential value than any of the following.

 Concurring Opinion: agrees with the result reached by the majority, but disagrees with the precise reasoning leading to that result.

 Dissenting Opinion: disagrees with the result reached by the majority and thus disagrees with the reasoning and/or the principles of law used by the majority in deciding the case.

 Plurality Opinion: is agreed to by less than a majority as to the reasoning of the decision, but is agreed to by a majority as to the result.

 Per Curiam Opinion: an opinion "by the court" which expresses its decision in the case but whose author is not identified.

ORDINANCE: A municipal law.

P

PARENS PATRIAE: ("parent of the country") Refers traditionally to role of state as sovereign and guardian of persons under legal disability, such as juveniles or the insane.

PARI MATERIA: Of the same matter, on the same subject.

PASSENGER: A person whom a common carrier has contracted to carry from one place to another. One carried for hire or reward as distinguished from a "guest" who is carried gratuitously.

PASSIVE: As used in law, this term means inactive; permissive; consisting in endurance or submission, rather than action; and in some connections it carries the implication of being subjected to a burden or charge.

PER CURIAM: By the court to distinguish an opinion of the whole court from written opinions of one judge.

PEREMPTORY: Self-determined; arbitrary; not requiring any cause to be shown. A "peremptory ruling" is one made by a trial judge "on the spot" without taking the matter under advisement. (See **Summarily**).

PLAINTIFF: A person who brings an action; the party who complains or sues in a civil action and is so named on the record.

PLENARY POWERS: Authority and power as broad as is required in a given case.

POLICE POWER: A state's power to make and enforce laws for the general welfare of the public—including regulation of education, both public and nonpublic.

PROCEDURAL LAW: That which prescribes method of enforcing rights or obtaining redress for their invasion.

PROCEEDING: Any action, hearing, investigation, inquest, or inquiry in which, pursuant to law, testimony can be compelled to be given; also called judicial proceeding/s.

PRO TANTO: For so much; for as much as may be; as far as it goes.

PROXIMATE CAUSE: That which, in a natural and continuous sequence, unbroken by an efficient intervening cause, produces the injury and without which the result would not have occurred.

Q

QUID PRO QUO: Giving one valuable thing for another.

QUO WARRANTO: A common law writ designed to test whether a person exercising power is legally entitled to do so. An extraordinary proceeding, prerogative in nature, addressed to preventing a continued exercise of authority unlawfully asserted.

R

REHEARING: Second consideration of cause for purpose of calling to court's or administrative board's attention any error, omission, or oversight in first consideration.

RELATOR: An informer; the person upon whose complaint, or at whose instance certain writes are issued.

REMAND: To send back. The act of an appellate court when it sends a case back to the trial court and orders the trial court to conduct limited new hearings or an entirely new trial, or to take some further action.

REPORTS: Published volumes of case decisions by a particular court or group of courts; e.g: Supreme Court Reporter.

RESPONDENT: The party who makes an answer to a bill or other proceeding in an equity. In appellate practice, the party who contends against an appeal; appellee.

REVERSE: To overthrow, vacate, set aside, make void, annul, repeal, or revoke; as, to reverse a judgment, sentence, or decree of a lower court by an appellate court, or to change to the contrary or to a former condition.

S

SECT: As applied to religious bodies, a party or body of persons who unite in holding certain special doctrines or opinions concerning religion, which distinguish them from others holding the same general religious belief.

SERIATIM: Separately; individually, one by one.

SINE DIE: Without assigning a day for a further meeting or hearing.

SOVEREIGN IMMUNITY: A judicial doctrine which precludes bringing suit against the government without its consent.

STANDING TO SUE DOCTRINE: The right to take the initial step that frames legal issues for ultimate adjudication by court or jury.

STARE DECISIS: ("stand by what has been decided"): Adhering to precedent, applying a previous decision to the present case; the previous decision has become the rule.

STIPULATION: A material condition, requirement, or article in an agreement. Voluntary agreement between opposing counsel concerning disposition of some relevant point so as to obviate need for proof or to narrow range of litigable issues.

STRICT CONSTRUCTION: A close or rigid reading and interpretation of a law. It is said that criminal statutes must be strictly construed. Rule of "strict construction" has no definite or precise meaning, has only relative application, is not opposite of liberal construction, and does not require such strained or narrow interpretation of language as to defeat object of statute.

SUBPOENA: A command to appear at a certain time and place to give testimony upon a certain matter.

SUBSTANTIVE LAW: That part of law which creates, defines, and regulates rights.

SUI GENERAS: Of its own kind of class; i.e., the only one of its own kind, peculiar.

SUMMARILY: Without ceremony or delay. A "summary" proceeding is a short, concise, and immediate proceeding.

SUMMONS: Instrument used to commence a civil action or special proceeding and a means of acquiring jurisdiction over a party.

SUMMARY JUDGMENT: Procedural device available for prompt and expeditious disposition of controversy without trial when there is no dispute as to either material fact or inferences to be drawn from undisputed facts, or if only question of law is involved.

SUPRA: Above; upon. This word occurring by itself in a book refers the reader to a previous part of the book.

T

TERM: When used with reference to a court, signifies the space of time during which the court holds session. A session signifies the time during the term when the court sits for the transaction of business, and the session commences when the court convenes for the term and continues until final adjournment, either before or at the expiration of the term.

THEORY: see doctrine.

TORT: A private or civil wrong or injury for which the court will provide a remedy in the form of an action for damages.

U

ULTRA VIRES: An act performed without any authority to act on subject. Acts beyond the scope of the powers of a corporation, as defined by its charter or laws of state of incorporation.

UNANIMOUS: To say that a proposition was adopted by a "unanimous" vote does not always mean that every one present voted for the proposition, but it may, and generally does, mean, when a *viva voce* vote is taken, that no one voted in the negative.

V

VENIRE: To come, to appear in court.

VENUE: A neighborhood, place or county in which an injury is declared to have been done or fact declared to have happened. Venue does not refer to jurisdiction.

W

WARRANT: (arrest warrant) A written order of the court which is made on behalf of the state, or United States, and is based upon a complaint issued pursuant to statute and/or court rule and which commands law enforcement officer to arrest a person and bring him before a magistrate.

WRIT OF MANDAMUS: ("we command") Writ which issues from a court of superior jurisdiction, directed to a private or municipal corporation, or any of its officers, or to an executive, administrative or judicial officer, or to an inferior court, commanding the performance of a particular act therein specified.

G

TABLES OF AUTHORITIES

TABLES OF AUTHORITIES

Cases Cited in the Main Outline

TA

TA

TABLE OF CONSTITUTIONAL PROVISIONS, STATUTES AND RULES

Code of Federal Regulations

Federal Rules of Civil Procedure

State Statutes and Rules of Court

TA

CROSS-REFERENCE CHART

Casebook Cross-Reference
Chart   CR-2

CR ▶

EDUCATION LAW *Casenote Course Outline* Cross-Reference Chart	Law of Public Ed. 3d ed. Reuter	American Public School Law, 3d ed. Alexander & Alexander	Law in the Schools 3d ed. Valente	Public School Law 3d ed. McCarthy & Cambron-McCabe	School Law 4th ed. La Morte
CHAPTER 1: Introduction to the Legal System and Legal Research					
I. Case Law		1-11	5-9		10-11
II. Descriptions of Publications					
III. The Components of Our Case Briefs					
CHAPTER 2: The Church-State Distinction					
I. The Overriding Principle-Government Must Remain Neutral toward Religion	3-4, 16, 44-48, 61-70, 903	113-121	85-94, 97-99, 553-554	25-28	75-78
II. Government Support and Regulation of Parochial Education	17-29, 44-48, 58-85	121-163, 177-185	95-96	43-53	
III. Religious Influences in Public Schools	29-44, 48-58	163-177	89-94	28-40	28-56, 63-65
IV. Religious Objections to Public School Practices	38-40, 160-162	185-188	91-94	40-43	56-63
CHAPTER 3: Education of the Disabled					
I. Overview of Federal Disabilities Statutes		359-405, 673, 853-856	351-358, 545-546	164-180	154-171
II. Individuals with Disabilities Education Act of 1990 (IDEA)		366-367	352-357	165-180	155
III. Americans with Disabilities Act (ADA)		673, 853-854	351-352		276
IV. Section 504 of the Rehabilitation Act of 1973	155-158, 906	706, 856	351-352, 356-358	165-166	155, 181-185, 276-277, 442
V. Due Process Issues and Concerns				170-171	
CHAPTER 4: Local School Boards					
I. Authority of the Local School Board	140-214, 883-884	71-94, 229-277	16-30, 57-64	1-7, 79-88	171-181
II. School Board Officers and Elections	139-140, 871-883, 889-902	94-101	29-30, 31-32	5	
III. School Board Meetings	856-871, 884-889	101-111	30-31, 32-34	6	
CHAPTER 5: Financing of Public Schools					
I. Public School Revenues	215-222, 228-235, 243-249	767-772	476-484, 492-493	77-79	356-359

EDUCATION LAW Casenote Course Outline Cross-Reference Chart	Law of Public Ed. 3d ed. Reutter	American Public School Law, 3d ed. Alexander & Alexander	Law in the Schools 3d ed. Valente	Public School Law 3d ed. McCarthy & Cambron-McCabe	School Law 4th ed. La Morte
II. Allocation of State Funds	222-228, 250-255	772-801	472-474		359-388
III. Local School District Budgets and Expenditures	235-243, 255-273	801-811	474-475, 484-485		
CHAPTER 6: School Property and Fund Uses					
I. School Property	292-302, 314-328	813-817, 820-837	96-97		65-75
II. Use of School Funds for Particular Purposes	274-286, 287-291, 302-314	817-819			
CHAPTER 7: Tort Liability of School Districts, Officers, and Employees					
I. Elements of the Tort of Negligence	343-350	463-471	432-434	451-456	406-408
II. Tort Liability and Defenses against Liability in the School Setting	329-343, 359-363, 374-386	459-463, 471-484, 501-554	434-435, 437-443, 444-448	456-472	393-406, 408-413, 415
III. Federal Tort Liability	337-338, 341-342, 363-374, 386-388, 620, 907	484-498	443-444	89-92	395-405, 413-415
CHAPTER 8: Contractual Liability of Local School Boards					
I. General Principles of Statutory Contract Liability	389-393, 415-417		485-486		
II. The Competitive Bidding Process	393-404, 417-426		487-492		
III. Recovery under the Various Forms of Contract	404-413, 426-436				
IV. Conflicts of Interest	413-415		486-487		
CHAPTER 9: Teachers—Certification and Contracts for Employment					
I. Teacher Certification	437-446, 470-487	557-570	136-139	242-245	
II. Employment of Teachers	446-454, 487-496	623-638	139-148	245-250, 254-263	
III. Teachers' Contracts	454-470, 496-516	570-589, 591-602	148-150	250-254	
CHAPTER 10: Teacher Employment Issues					
I. The Collective-Bargaining Process	533-551, 571-580	729-765	189-200	419-441	277-291

CR

EDUCATION LAW *Casenote Course Outline* Cross-Reference Chart	Law of Public Ed. 3d ed. Reutter	American Public School Law, 3d ed. Alexander & Alexander	Law in the Schools 3d ed. Valente	Public School Law 3d ed. McCarthy & Cambron-McCabe	School Law 4th ed. La Morte
II. Other Terms and Conditions of Teacher Employment	517-533, 552-570	673-725	229-241	243, 275-309	196-251
CHAPTER 11: Teacher Dismissal and Retirement					
I. Termination of Employment through Dismissal	499-512, 581-620, 627-663	589-591, 603-623, 641-671	150-161, 222-228	373-404	189-196
II. Termination of Employment through Retirement	620-627, 664-667				
CHAPTER 12: Student Rights and Regulations					
I. School Attendance	668-677, 703-721	191-226	52-56	69-79	20-28
II. Student Conduct	677-693, 721-729	316-338	276-284	109-133	87-112, 145-154, 171-185
III. Student Discipline	693-703, 729-779	279-316, 338-354	285-294	199-230	113-145, 185-188
CHAPTER 13: School Desegregation					
I. Constitutional and Statutory Underpinnings	780-783, 788-794	409-412	334-336	483-486	293-303
II. Challenges to State-Fostered (De Jure) School Segregation	783-788, 805-822	412-424, 430-455	337-348	486	303-311
III. Challenges to Nonpurposeful (De Facto) School Segregation	794-805, 822-839, 844-855	424-430	337-347	486-497	311-355
IV. Desegregation of Teachers	790-794, 839-844		348-351	497-499	
V. Recent Court Activity	827-855	435-455	362-385	487-491	327-354

INDEX

INDEX

IN

V

VACCINATION

(*See* **PUBLIC HEALTH REGULATION**)

NOTES